Improving Quality in Education

This book explores an approach to school improvement that merges the traditions of educational effectiveness research and school improvement efforts. It displays how the dynamic model, which is theoretical and empirically validated, can be used in both traditions. Each chapter integrates evidence from international and national studies, showing how the knowledge-base of educational effectiveness research can be used for improvement purposes. In a clear and practicable manner it outlines:

- foundations of the improvement approach
- research projects investigating the impact of the dynamic approach
- guidelines and practical solutions to translating the approach into action
- further developments for school improvement.

Exploring the crucial factors in the establishment of this environment, the authors outline a dynamic framework that helps schools collect data, through self-evaluation mechanisms, taking decisions about priorities for improvement, and developing appropriate policies and action plans. This approach emphasises educational targets and provides means to achieve them that are flexible enough to fit in with the circumstances of the individual school. The book draws upon research across the world, conducted especially in the United States, Europe, and Australasia, expertly showcasing how the dynamic approach can be used in a wide variety of educational settings.

A key book for all professionals working in education; academics, researchers, policy-makers, school advisors and practitioners will find it invaluable. Not only it is a must for graduate students, university libraries, and individual academics but also for school management teams, school support agencies and officials in educational policy.

Bert P.M. Creemers is Professor in Educational Sciences at the University of Groningen, the Netherlands. He is the founding editor of the journals *School Effectiveness and School Improvement* and *Educational Research and Evaluation*.

Leonidas Kyriakides is Associate Professor of Educational Research and Evaluation at the University of Cyprus. He is a member of the editorial board and book review editor of *School Effectiveness and School Improvement*.

Improving Quality in Education

Dynamic approaches to school improvement

Bert P.M. Creemers and
Leonidas Kyriakides

Routledge
Taylor & Francis Group

LONDON AND NEW YORK

First published 2012
by Routledge
2 Park Square, Milton Park, Abingdon, Oxon OX14 4RN

Simultaneously published in the USA and Canada
by Routledge
711 Third Avenue, New York, NY 10017

*Routledge is an imprint of the Taylor & Francis Group, an informa
business*

© 2011 Bert P.M. Creemers and Leonidas Kryriakides

British Library Cataloguing in Publication Data
A catalogue record for this book is available from the British
Library

Library of Congress Cataloging in Publication Data
Creemers, Bert P.M.
Improving quality in education : dynamic approaches to school
improvement / Bert Creemers and Leonidas Kyriakides.
p. cm.
Includes bibliographical references and index.
1. School improvement programs. I. Kyriakides, Leonidas. II. Title.
LB2822.8.C75 2012
371.2'07--dc23
2011029423

ISBN 978-0-415-54873-1 (hbk)
ISBN 978-0-415-54874-8 (pbk)
ISBN 978-0-203-81753-7 (ebk)

Typeset in Galliard
by Saxon Graphics Ltd, Derby

MIX
Paper from
responsible sources
FSC
www.fsc.org   FSC® C004839

Printed and bound in Great Britain by
TJ International Ltd, Padstow, Cornwall

Contents

PART A
Foundations of the improvement approach   1

PART B
Research projects on the dynamic approach to
school improvement   67

PART C
Translating the approach into action:
guidelines and instruments   157

PART D
Further developments of the dynamic approach
to school improvement   201

List of figures

List of tables

List of appendices

Preface

More than five years ago, we published the first results of our joint efforts in the development of a dynamic perspective of educational effectiveness. In the last section of that book, it was claimed that our dynamic model cannot only be used for research and theory purposes, but can also contribute to the promotion of improvement of education. In that book, we also reported the results of our first studies that tested the validity of the dynamic model. Since then we not only conducted studies that demonstrated the dynamic nature of effectiveness, but we also looked for possibilities of using these findings for improvement purposes, at both the teacher and school levels. Experimental studies testing the impact of the approach that we gradually developed provided support to our effort and presented the conditions under which the dynamic model can be used for improvement purposes.

In this book we present the journey and the results of our efforts, in order to make a contribution to knowledge and theory building in the field of school improvement and in relation to educational effectiveness research. We believe that we have kept that promise given five years ago and are now in a position to share with policy makers, educators, school managers and researchers our suggestions for how quality of education can be improved. This book refers to an approach to school improvement that attempts to contribute to the establishment of the merging of traditions of educational effectiveness research and school improvement efforts. This is achieved by presenting how the dynamic model, which is theoretical and empirically validated, can be used in both traditions. Each chapter therefore integrates evidence from international and national studies, showing how the knowledge-base of educational effectiveness research can be used for improvement purposes. Evidence is also provided to support the importance of our dynamic approach to school improvement.

In order to demonstrate the development and use of this approach in educational practice, we also present results of school based projects which show how, and under which conditions, this approach can be used. The use of this approach is shown to have assisted participating schools in developing their own strategies and actions for improvement, in relation to the specific challenges that they are facing, as well as aiding the improvement of their effectiveness status.

These projects were conducted in differing educational systems and contexts. Therefore, readers can easily see that our approach to improvement can be applied in various situations and by different stakeholders of education, such as teachers, school advisors, policy-makers and researchers.

The third part of the book draws on implications of the results of these projects for practice and research on school improvement. It also facilitates further use of the dynamic approach to school improvement by providing guidelines to schools on how they can use this approach in order to promote learning and learning outcomes. In this way, the book offers a basis for establishing networks of professionals, researchers and policy makers of schools in different countries, to make use of this approach and of the practical tools for establishing their school improvement projects.

The book concludes with a chapter which discusses the viability of the dynamic approach to school improvement and provides suggestion for the further development of our proposed approach.

In the writing of this book we received support from many colleagues, policy makers, professionals in schools, and our families. We would like to make a special mention for some of them. Two chapters presenting experimental studies that were conducted in order to test the impact of the dynamic approach to school improvement were written together with our colleagues Demetris Demetriou and Panayiotis Antoniou. A chapter presenting the results of two case studies which investigated the use of the dynamic approach in establishing school self evaluation mechanisms in Slovenia was written by our colleagues Matevž Bren, Alenka Hauptman, Gašper Cankar and Darko Zupanc. Our friend Christos Parpounas who used to be a teacher for many years and is currently the director of the Curriculum Development Unit at the Ministry of Education in Cyprus helped us identify the extent to which our work could contribute in the improvement of policy and practice. We would also like to thank him for helping us to draft a figure illustrating the steps of the proposed dynamic approach to school improvement. The research assistants of our team, and especially our PhD students, provided us with comments from the perspective of young researchers in the field of educational effectiveness and improvement. Evi Charalambous helped us in the production of the manuscript and Katherine Walker, Lauren Cross, Laura Jenks, and Emma Watson supported us in the process of linguistic editing. They did this not only from a strictly linguistic perspective, but were also critical in helping us to clarify the meaning of the book. Finally, our Universities were supportive in facilitating our academic efforts to write the book. We like to thank them all for their help and we hope that they will be pleased with the final product. Of course, any mistakes that remain are ours.

As mentioned previously, the book is a report of our journey of studying the improvement of educational effectiveness from different perspectives and of proposing a dynamic model. We welcome comments, criticisms and contributions for further development and research from our readers with different perspectives in education. We hope that you will join us on our journey to the establishment of an evidence-based and theory-driven approach to school improvement.

Foundations of the improvement approach

Chapter I

Developments in school improvement

The value of a theory-driven approach

Introduction

Educational Effectiveness Research (EER) can be seen as a conglomerate of research in different areas: research on teacher behaviour, curriculum, grouping procedures, school organisation, and educational policy. The main aim of EER is to investigate which factors, within teaching, curriculum, and learning environment at different levels such as the classroom, the school, and the above-school levels can directly or indirectly explain the differences in the outcomes of students, taking into account background characteristics, such as ability, Socio Economic Status (SES), and prior attainment (Raudenbush & Bryk, 1986). During the last three decades, EER has been improved considerably by working on criticisms of research design, improvements in sampling techniques, and improvements in statistical techniques. Methodological advances, particularly the availability of software for the analysis of multilevel data, have enabled more efficient estimates of teacher and school effects on student achievement (Goldstein, 2003). There is also substantial agreement on appropriate methods of estimating school differences/effects and the kinds of data required for valid comparisons (Creemers, Kyriakides & Sammons, 2010). In regard to the theoretical component of the field, progress was made creating more precise definitions of the concepts used and outlining clearer relations between them (e.g., Mortimore et al., 1988; Scheerens, 1992; Levin & Lezotte, 1990; Teddlie & Reynolds, 2000). However, there is a shortage of well-developed theoretical models from which researchers in the area of educational effectiveness can build theories and the problem is aggravated by infrequent use of existing models (Scheerens & Bosker, 1997).

There are several reasons to argue for the need to develop and test theoretical models of effectiveness that help us explain differences in student learning by specifying the relationships between the components in the models and student outcomes (Kyriakides, 2005a). First, a model serves to explain previous empirical research parsimoniously. Second, the establishment and testing of models of educational effectiveness may generate a guide to the field to prevent new entrants from re-inventing the wheel by repeating existing research. It also maps a series of avenues for future research, which may help us expand our knowledge base of educational effectiveness. Finally, a model may provide a useful guidebook for practitioners, and indeed there are hints that it has been partially the absence of educational effectiveness theory that has hindered the uptake of effectiveness knowledge by practitioners in schools (Creemers & Kyriakides, 2006).

In this context, the dynamic model of educational effectiveness (Creemers & Kyriakides, 2008a) has recently been developed. The dynamic model attempts to define the dynamic relations between the multiple factors found to be associated with educational effectiveness (Sammons, 2009). It is also important to note that a series of studies provide some empirical support to the validity of the model (Creemers & Kyriakides, 2009, 2010a, 2010b; Kyriakides & Creemers, 2008, 2009; Kyriakides, Creemers & Antoniou, 2009). The dynamic model is established in a way that helps policy makers and practitioners improve educational practice by encouraging rational decision-making concerning the optimal fit of the factors within the model and the present situation of the factors in the schools or educational systems (Campbell, 2010). Therefore, this book claims that the dynamic model can be treated as the theoretical framework for establishing a theory-driven and evidence-based approach to school improvement. More specifically, in this chapter, a background of research on school improvement is provided and the relationship between school improvement and EER is explored. It is argued that there have been examples of productive co-operation between research on educational effectiveness and school improvement.

However, three decades of research on educational effectiveness and school improvement suggest that the link between EER and school improvement is still problematic (Hallinger & Heck, 2011a). The reasons for this disappointing situation are analysed in hope of creating a more productive cooperation between research and improvement. Specifically, after a careful analysis of the failure to link EER and school improvement effectively, we propose the establishment of strategies for school improvement which give emphasis on the evidence stemming from theory and research. Thus, the value of a theory-driven approach to school improvement is stressed. The need to collect multiple data about student achievement and the classroom and school processes is also emphasised. In this way, a theory-driven and evidence-based approach to school improvement is promoted.

Historical links between research on educational effectiveness and school improvement

Formal education, as it takes place in classrooms, schools and other learning environments, is the responsibility of practitioners like teachers, principals and other professionals. Policy makers are also responsible for improving learning outcomes, especially since they are expected to contribute in setting appropriate aims of education and creating the conditions for teachers and other practitioners to meet. Thus, professionals in education are expected to develop education and improve its quality. On the other hand, researchers in the area of educational effectiveness are expected to develop and test theories about quality in education. The intention is to establish a theory that can explain variation in outcomes between students (Creemers, 1994; Scheerens & Bosker, 1997; Teddlie & Reynolds, 2000). Moreover, the generated knowledge is expected to be used by practitioners and policy makers in their attempt to face challenges in education and to improve the practice in classes and schools. Although the responsibility for educational practice and the improvement of practice is not the responsibility of educational theory and research, it is a major objective of educational science to contribute to the effectiveness and the improvement of education by providing a knowledge base for practice and helping schools develop effective intervention programmes (Creemers & Kyriakides, 2006).

However, the relationship between science and practice in education in general and in educational effectiveness specifically has not been always successful (Creemers & Reezigt, 2005; Reynolds, Hopkins, & Stoll, 1993). There are many publications which spell out the problems between theory and practice in education. These publications point at the differences in approach, the implementation problems and the differences between teachers and schools which should make it almost impossible to use existing 'knowledge' in school improvement (e.g., Creemers & Reezigt, 1997; Scheerens & Bosker, 1997; Teddlie & Reynolds, 2000).

One could also argue that in many areas the relationship between theory and practice is almost always troublesome. A beautiful combination seldom exists and hardly ever succeeds. Why then should it be expected to establish links between EER and school improvement? One important reason could be that from the start, educational effectiveness had its roots not only in theory and research (e.g., Brookover, Beady, Flood, Schweitzer, & Wisenbaker, 1979; Rutter, Maughan, Mortimore, Ouston, & Smith, 1979) but in educational practice as well, especially since improvement projects introducing effective factors in schools were undertaken at the very early stage of EER (Edmonds, 1979). Moreover, at least in the early stages, it was expected that a more or less 'simple' application of educational effectiveness knowledge about 'what works' in education would result in school improvement (Creemers, Stoll, & Reezigt, 2007). Furthermore, at this early stage, doubts about the importance of education for student outcomes (Coleman et al., 1966; Jencks et al., 1972; Jensen, 1969) had caused a coalition of practitioners (teachers, principals, school improvers) and researchers. This coalition continued through the development of theories about education and the testing of these theories.

It is, therefore, reasonable to expect that there would be a strong relationship between EER, which aims to develop the knowledge basis about what works in education and why, and the school improvement, which aims to improve and develop education in classrooms and schools. The explicit purpose of the researchers who initiated the research on the effectiveness of classrooms, schools and educational systems was to use the results of the research in practice. For example, it has been one of the major aims of the Congress of School Effectiveness and Improvement (ICSEI), a research establishment set up in 1988, to bring together researchers, practitioners, and policy makers in a productive cooperation for the benefit of education and for the development of the participating 'disciplines'.

In recent years, there have been examples of productive co-operation between EER and school improvement, in which new ways of merging the two traditions/ orientations have been attempted (see Creemers & Reezigt, 2005; Gray et al., 1999; MacBeath & Mortimore, 2001; Reynolds & Stoll, 1996; Stoll, Reynolds, Creemers, & Hopkins, 1996; Reynolds, Teddlie, Hopkins, & Stringfield, 2000). Research results are being used in educational practice, sometimes with good results (Antoniou, 2009; Creemers & Kyriakides, 2010c; Demetriou, 2009; Hallinger & Heck, 2011a). In addition, school improvement findings are sometimes being used as an input for new research. Some authors therefore hold very favourable views on linking research on educational effectiveness and school improvement. For example, Renihan and Renihan (1989) state that 'the effective schools research has paid off, if for no other reason than that it has been the catalyst for school improvement efforts' (p.365). Most authors, however, are more sceptical (Reynolds, Hopkins, & Stoll, 1993). For example, Stoll and Fink (1992) think that school effectiveness should have done more to explain how schools can become effective. On the other hand, Mortimore (1991) argues that a lot of improvement efforts have failed because research results were not translated adequately into guidelines for educational practice. Changes were sometimes forced into schools, and when the results were disappointing the principals and teachers were blamed. Teddlie and Roberts (1993) argue that effectiveness and improvement representatives do not cooperate automatically, but tend to see each other as competitors.

Links between EER and school improvement were stronger in some countries than in others (Datnow, Borman, Stringfield, Overman, & Castellano, 2003; Reynolds, 1996; Townsend, 2007). In the early years of EER, links were rather strong in the United States and never quite disappeared there (Reynolds, Hopkins, & Stoll, 1993). During the 1980s, over half of all American school districts attempted to run improvement programmes based upon, or related to, the effective schools knowledge base. It must be noted, however, that the knowledge base within these improvement programmes was likely to be of the earlier simplistic variety of 'five factor' theories developed by Edmonds (1979) and popularised by Lezotte (1989), rather than the more recently developed theories which are from a considerably more advanced research base which enforces the importance of using integrated multilevel models to explain the nature of effectiveness (Kyriakides, 2008; Scheerens & Bosker, 1997). It is also important to note that it is the well known demonstration projects which involved the direct, controlled transfer of research knowledge into school improvement programmes with built-in evaluation of outcomes, which have demonstrated enhanced educational effectiveness (e.g. McCormack-Larkin, 1985). In Canada likewise there have been programmes which involve the utilisation of educational effectiveness knowledge within school improvement programmes (Stoll & Fink, 1989, 1992), and the educational effectiveness knowledge base has also penetrated many other ongoing improvement projects (Sackney, 1989).

In spite of the evident relationship between the two bodies of knowledge (educational effectiveness and school improvement) at the level of practice, and at the intellectual level there is less of a relationship or communality of perspective between the scholars who contribute to their respective knowledge bases. Recently, many districts have implemented effective schools programs, but research in the field has gone down at the same time and because of this. School improvement is sometimes considered 'a remarkable example of ... over-use of a limited research base' (Stringfield, 1995, p.70).

The situation of two separate, discrete bodies of knowledge and two separate research communities that exist in North America is also apparent in most other parts of the world; indeed in certain parts of the world the separation is even more evident. The Netherlands and the United Kingdom are examples of such countries (Mortimore, 1991; Reynolds et al., 1993), although the recent situation in the United Kingdom seems to be changing (Reynolds, Stringfield & Schaffer, 2006). More specifically, in the United Kingdom, there has, until recently, been little collaboration between those working within the EER and school improvement paradigms, little practitioner take up of the knowledge base of educational effectiveness (Mortimore, 1991; Reynolds, 1991), little use of the research in school improvement or school development programmes (Reid et al., 1987), and little appreciation or referencing of educational effectiveness material in the works of 'school improvers' (and vice versa) (Reynolds, 1996).

Similarly, New Zealand was the site of pioneering EER (Ramsay et al., 1982), but there are no current signs of engagement in this knowledge base by those working within the school improvement field through the 'decentralisation paradigm' that has existed since the Picot Report in the late 1980s. In Australia, links have always existed and continue to exist. Some of the knowledge base of EER has been linked to school improvement especially through the school self-management approach of Caldwell and Spinks (1988). But again, more developmentally-orientated material from Australia shows only limited uptake of, or reliance on, educational effectiveness literature. Indeed, the Australian school improvement tradition relates primarily to the literature on educational management and administration. Educational management and administration is responsible for the absence of relationships between the body of knowledge of school improvement and educational effectiveness and also for the lack of theoretical models of both school improvement and effectiveness which refer to factors situated at different levels (Creemers, 2006).

After three decades of research on educational effectiveness and improvement, one might conclude that the relationship between EER and school improvement is still problematic (Townsend, 2007). Research on educational effectiveness has strongly focused on student outcomes and the characteristics (factors) of classrooms, schools and systems associated with these outcomes without looking at the processes that are needed to change the situation in classes, schools and systems. School improvement, by contrast, is mainly concerned with the process of change in classes and to a larger extent in schools without looking too much at the consequences for student outcomes. In several publications, the reasons for this disappointing situation, mentioned above, are taken into account and ways for a more productive cooperation between research and improvement are provided (Creemers & Reezigt, 1997, Reynolds et al., 2000). After a careful analysis of the failure to associate research and improvement effectively, some proposed strategies for school improvement which have been developed attempt to combine the strong elements of research and improvement (Creemers & Kyriakides, 2008a; Townsend, 2007). Major elements of this combination are an emphasis on the evidence stemming from theory and research, a need to collect multiple data about the achievement of students, classroom and school processes on one hand and an emphasis on the context of individual schools and thereby the development and implementation of programmes for classes and schools by schools themselves on the other.

In practice, however, there is not much evidence in terms of contribution to student achievement outcomes. One problem might be that concentrating on processes at the level of individual schools in many cases almost necessarily implies loosing a clear focus on the research evidence. For example, in the ESI (Effective School Improvement) project, which attempted to combine the knowledge base of EER with the knowledge about school improvement, the final framework still reflects the different orientations (Creemers, 2006). One can easily observe that achievement outcomes do not belong to the core of the improvement process which encompasses the improvement of school culture and school process. It is also important to note that Meijs, Houtveen, Wubells and Creemers (2005) conducted a meta-analysis of successful programmes for school improvement and provided support for using a systematic approach to change directed at internal conditions with respect to teaching and learning and to support the school level aiming to improve the quality of teaching and learning. No evidence supporting the idea that the content of the improvement programme has to be developed by the school itself has been generated. Therefore, we argue here that there are still serious problems in the relation between effectiveness and improvement. The question of how to apply the effectiveness knowledge base in practice still persists. In other words, how is valid and useful information about school improvement out of educational effectiveness achieved? (Creemers & Kyriakides, 2006).

Nevertheless, it should be acknowledged that the tensions between the two fields have also led to further clarification about what is at stake. The educational effectiveness knowledge base certainly needs to be expanded. In addition, it has to be acknowledged that school improvement is more than just application of the available knowledge base. It needs intermediate goals and careful research and evaluation about how the ultimate goals, such as student performance and the characteristics at the school and classroom levels (the so-called effective characteristics) are related to the objectives of the improvement policies. Thus, in the next section of this chapter, a background of research on school improvement is provided which helps us to identify strategies for a more productive cooperation between research and improvement. Specifically, we claim for the establishment of strategies for school improvement which give emphasis on the evidence stemming from theory and research.

School improvement: major outcomes and theories

This section attempts to provide a review of the major outcomes and theories that emerged from research on school improvement. The term 'school improvement' is taken as 'a strategy for educational change which enhances student outcomes as well as strengthening the school's capacity for managing change' (Hopkins et al., 1994, p.3). This definition emphasises the importance of *strategies* on the one hand, and the school's *internal conditions* on the other, as key variables in educational reform (Chapman & Hadfield, 2010). In the literature on educational effectiveness and school improvement, a distinction is often made between theory and research on the one hand, mirrored by effectiveness: and practice and policymaking on the other hand, mirrored by improvement (Teddlie & Reynolds, 2000; Townsend, 2007). Even though improvement is rooted in educational practice, there is also a need for theories on how to improve schools (Hopkins, 1995; Creemers, 2002). However, there are no empirically validated improvement theories that map what can and should be done to improve the effectiveness status of schools. Although in educational practice schools and classrooms can be found to succeed much better than others (in terms of their contribution to the achievement of specific learning outcomes in children), theories cannot be based on exemplary practice only (Creemers, Kyriakides, & Sammons, 2010). If theories are derived from a unique practice of a teacher/school/country, they will be filled with concrete, exact, unique, specific concepts which may not necessarily be applicable to other contexts. Moreover, the school improvement literature pays more attention to the description of projects and to the formulation of practical advice than to the development and systematic testing of theories on what to improve and how to do this. Also, there are no clear notions about the range of educational levels that improvement should deal with and the range of people/ stakeholders that should be involved.

Although different theoretical notions of effective school improvement processes have been developed from school improvement practice, they have not yet been empirically and systematically tested. For example, the types of school cultures (see Hargreaves, 1995) have not yet been systematically studied and thereby there is no information about their effects on the success of school improvement. Moreover, their relationship with the first criterion for school improvement (i.e., enhancing student outcomes) is not clear yet. The same holds for the factors that are supposed to be important in different stages of educational change outlined by Fullan (2001), and his ideas about the essential elements in educational change at the classroom level (beliefs, curriculum materials and teaching approaches). Even though these ideas are derived from school improvement practice, their importance, and their potential effects are not accounted for in detail, and have not yet been studied in research.

A useful contribution to theory development is the generic framework for school improvement delivered by Hopkins (1996). In this framework three major components are depicted: educational givens, a strategic dimension, and a capacity-building dimension. Educational givens cannot be changed easily. Givens can be external to the school (such as an external impetus for change) and internal (such as the school's background, organization and values). The strategic dimension refers to the competency of a school to set its priorities for further development, to define student learning goals and teacher development, and to choose a strategy to achieve these goals successfully. The capacity-building dimension refers to the need to focus on conditions for classroom practice and for school development during the various stages of improvement. In addition, the school culture has a central place in the framework. Changes in the school culture are expected to support the teaching-learning processes which will in their turn improve student outcomes (Hopkins, 1996).

Looking at the literature on school improvement, one can claim that research on school improvement is not about how to implement centralized reforms in an effective way. It has more to do with how schools in an era of change can use the impetus of external reform in order to improve themselves. This implies that the decision to engage in school improvement should be based on clear evidence of effective practices that promote learning in children. There is some evidence that when schools recognise *consonance* (i.e. the extent to which internally identified priorities coincide or overlap with external pressures for reform), this provides them with opportunities as well as problems and they are better able to respond to external demands (Hopkins, 1995; Townsend, 2007).

Development or growth planning is another important preliminary factor and contributor to school improvement. Schools often get confused between a *strategy* which provides the framework for solving problems in development planning, and *tactics* which are the detailed operational activities required to put the strategy into effect. A strategy can be implemented by a variety of tactics, the choice being constrained by the aspects of time and location. Keeping in mind the distinction between strategy and tactics can help effective development planning. It is important for example not to get bogged down in tactical details until the strategy is clear, or to abandon a strategy just because a particular tactic did not work. The distinction between development and maintenance, introduced in the *Empowered School* (Hargreaves & Hopkins, 1991), may also contribute to more effective strategic planning. Maintenance structures established to organise teaching, learning and assessments cannot also cope with developmental activities which inevitably cut across established hierarchies, curriculum areas, meeting patterns, and timetables. The innovative responses required for *sustained* development are inimical to successful maintenance. Maintenance structures, however well developed, often do not cope well with development. There is some empirical evidence supporting that structures that attempt to do both, usually do neither satisfactorily. What is required is to develop complementary structures, each with its own purpose, budget, and ways of working. Obviously the majority of a school's time and resources will go on maintenance; but unless there is also an element dedicated to development then the school is unlikely to progress in times of change (see Stoll, Wikeley, & Reezigt, 2002; Gray et al., 1999).

It is also important to note here that many studies revealed that available resources define the successful implementation of an improvement strategy (Reezigt & Creemers, 2005). For example, the ESI project revealed that in order to make school improvement effective, the resources made available by the educational context are very important. Without these, schools are likely to experience difficulties in their improvement efforts (Creemers et al., 2007). At the school level, the ESI project also identified three key concepts of school improvement:

a)   improvement culture
b)   improvement processes
c)   improvement outcomes.

Although these concepts appear to be considered by school improvement research as the key elements of the improving school, there is almost no evidence indicating the importance of these three concepts and there is no research investigating their effects on improving educational effectiveness. Nevertheless, the culture is viewed as the background against which processes are taking place and the outcomes are the goals of those processes. All three concepts are seen as inter-related and they are expected to constantly influence each other. The culture is expected to influence not only the choice of processes, but also the choice of outcomes. The chosen outcomes are expected to influence the choice of processes but their success or failure can also change the culture of the school. The outcomes may also depend on the successful implementation of the processes (Kyriakides et al., 2006).

In regard to the improvement processes, it is stressed that some schools perceive improvement as a discrete event (Reezigt & Creemers, 2005). Whenever a problem arises, it is addressed, but after that, business goes on as usual. These schools hold a static view of improvement. More dynamic schools will consider improvement as an ongoing process and as a part of everyday life. Improvement efforts are continuous, cyclical by nature, and embedded in a wider process of overall school development. Although improvement processes will rarely move neatly from one stage to the next, some stages within successful improvement processes have been identified (Chapman & Harris, 2004). These stages may overlap or return repeatedly before the full cycle of improvement is completed. Improvement processes for planning, for example, will often not be a one-stage activity that takes place relatively early in the improvement process, but plans will be constantly returned to and adapted on a continuous basis. This is especially so for complex improvement efforts that involve many staff members. More specifically, the following five factors/stages of the improvement process have been proposed:

1   Assessment of improvement needs
2   Diagnosis of improvement needs and setting of detailed goals
3   Planning of improvement activities
4   Implementation
5   Evaluation and reflection.

Assessment of improvement needs   The cycle of an improvement process starts with a phase of assessing improvement needs. Before a school can start improving, it must be clear why improvement is required in the first place and what the starting point for the school is. Such an assessment can be made by school stakeholders and/or by external agents in the form of an audit. The assessment phase ends when a diagnosis of the problems that need to be solved is delivered. Improvement processes that are mandated by the system level (e.g., national reform policies) also need this phase in order to assess how the specific needs of the school can be best met (Creemers & Kyriakides, 2008a; Fitz-Gibbon, 1996; Kyriakides et al., 2006).

Diagnosis of improvement needs and setting of detailed goals   The next phase involves agreeing on the detailed goals that the school wants to achieve. General goals must be broken down into more detailed targets. These more detailed goals can function as support for the persons involved in the improvement efforts by giving indicators of success that will promote the desired outcomes (Scheerens, Glass, & Thomas, 2003).

Planning of improvement activities   The third phase is the planning of the improvement activities. In this phase, decisions need to be made about several issues such as the amount of time needed for each activity, priorities (e.g., tackling visible issues first, especially when the improvement being undertaken is very complex), involvement of different stakeholders, use of incentives, and dissemination of results.

Implementation   The implementation phase follows and may influence the further planning of activities, when developments differ from initial expectations. The precise focus of the implementation depends on the goals that the school wants to achieve. The implementation phase is the most substantial phase in the cycle of improvement and when it is not successful, all preceding efforts have been in vain and the pursued goals are not being achieved. Teachers are central to implementation and regular feedback is necessary if it is to be successful.

Evaluation and reflection   The final phases of the cyclical improvement process are evaluation and reflection, which may create a new cycle of improvement. In this phase, the school needs to assess, by means of self-evaluating procedures whether the goals of improvement have been achieved (Miles, 1993; Creemers, Kyriakides, & Sammons, 2010). For researchers, the effective use of the previous stages and their effects on improving educational effectiveness should be investigated (Hofman, Dijkstra, & Hofman, 2009). This analysis of the improvement process should be investigated and further operationalised. Research is also needed to search for inter-relationships among these five stages and to highlight the cyclical nature of effective school improvement that has been achieved.

Despite the gaps in theory development and testing in the field of school improvement, there are already some elements of a knowledge-base that can be useful for understanding the dynamic nature of improving educational effectiveness. By trying to improve schools, knowledge became available about the implementation of classroom and school effectiveness factors in educational practice. This implies that there is a need to study the influence of factors and variables on educational outcomes (Stoll & Fink, 1994). Even more important is the fact that school improvement, by its specific nature, can point at shortcomings in educational effectiveness theory and research which do not systematically take into account the dynamic nature of educational effectiveness. The emphasis in improvement is on schools in transition, mostly from an ineffective situation to a more effective situation. This has illuminated that there is a need for more sensitive theoretical explanations than the integrated models of educational effectiveness developed during the 1990s (e.g., Creemers, 1994; Scheerens, 1994; Stringfield & Slavin, 1992). Therefore, EER should pay more attention to schools in progress (i.e., schools trying to become effective or schools trying to stay effective) and further studies investigating school effectiveness over a long period of time are needed (Thomas, Peng, & Gray, 2007). It is also important to note that the limited number of studies focusing on longer-term changes in schools seems also to reveal that improvement is not an impossible task (e.g., Gray, Goldstein, & Jesson, 1996; Gray, Goldstein, & Thomas, 2001; Thomas, 2001). It is also shown that effective school improvement has to deal with the problem of influences of the context on effective school improvement (Creemers & Kyriakides, 2010a).

Theories of educational change and school improvement are sensitive to contextual differences (Chapman & Harris, 2004). Contextual differences are linked to innovative strategies, but not to educational effectiveness (Creemers & Reezigt, 2005). Educational effectiveness research has coined a concept of differential educational effectiveness (Campbell et al., 2003), and has the methodology to search for generic and differential factors in schools (Kyriakides & Campbell, 2004). The Contingency Theory, central in the study of organisations, assumes that there is no best way to make an organisation effective; and that which one of several ways to be effective is contingent upon situational and contextual factors (Mintzberg, 1979). A comprehensive theoretical framework of educational effectiveness and improvement may combine these elements to develop hypotheses about contextual differences, innovation strategies, and differential educational effectiveness (Levin, 2010). In this context, the dynamic model of educational effectiveness (Creemers & Kyriakides, 2008a) was developed. This model attempts to define the dynamic relations between the multiple factors found to be associated with effectiveness. The establishment of the dynamic model and its empirical testing is expected to help EER to establish stronger links with school improvement (Creemers & Kyriakides, 2006). It is also important to note that studies testing the validity of the dynamic model provided some support to the assumption that different improvement strategies are necessary to help teachers and schools become more effective (e.g., Antoniou, 2009; Creemers & Kyriakides, 2010c). For example, it was found that a strategy for moving a school from being 'among the least effective' to being average is different from a strategy that enables a school which is among the most effective to remain a most effective school (see Creemers & Kyriakides, 2010a). For this reason, in the next chapter we will discuss the possibility to effectively use the knowledge base of educational effectiveness and specifically the conceptual framework provided by the dynamic model for improvement purposes. Specifically, we propose for the establishment of strategies for school improvement which give emphasis on the evidence stemming from theory and research. Thus, the value of a theory-driven approach to school improvement is stressed. The need to collect multiple data about student achievement, and the classroom and school processes is also emphasised. In this way, a theory-driven and evidence-based approach to school improvement is promoted.

Additional insights of school improvement from other theoretical traditions

To avoid a restricted scope on improving effectiveness, we provide below a brief review of the literature on improvement which is concerned with other theoretical orientations within education that examine the process of change such as theories on curriculum change and disciplines in psychology and sociology which are concerned with the process of change.

Organisational theories   In organisational theories, three other effectiveness criteria or perspectives are used rather than the criterion of improvement of student outcomes:

1   Adaptability or responsiveness to external circumstances or changes;
2   Continuity of the organisation in terms of stability of the internal structure and acquisition of resources;
3   Commitment and satisfaction of the members of the organisation (Fairman & Quinn, 1985).

These three criteria of effectiveness are also embedded in theories as supportive conditions of educational change and improvement (Fullan, 2001). In addition, in theoretical models of educational effectiveness the three criteria of effectiveness are interpreted as supportive conditions and brought into means-goal relationships with the primary criterion of output effectiveness (Scheerens, 1992, 1993). Adaptability and continuity of the school organisation and the commitment and satisfaction of its members are treated as conditions that indirectly support educational effectiveness by stimulating the school organisation and its members to work towards effective school improvement (Cheng, 1993). Therefore, adaptability of the school organisation to change may be seen as a necessary condition of effective school improvement (Scheerens, Glas, & Thomas, 2003).

Curriculum theories   Curriculum theories provide other models that link the school as an organisation to the work of teachers (Shipman, 1985; Campbell, 1985). Curriculum theories deal with the characteristics of curricula in relation to the implementation of curricula and the outcomes in student achievement. Examples of curriculum theories are curriculum implementation strategies, such as the fidelity perspective, the mutual adaptation perspective or strategies of curriculum enactment; other examples are models of control, varying from the centre-periphery model (Schon, 1971) to the school based curriculum development model which gives professional power to teachers and schools (Simons, 1990; Snyder, Bolin, & Zumwalt, 1992). In some cases, the curriculum theory was also integrated with a theoretical framework of educational effectiveness (Hoeben, 1994; Datnow, Borman, & Stringfield, 2000). In these theories, EER is also taken into account, especially by studies evaluating the impact of curriculum reform policies upon student achievement (Kyriakides, 1999).

Behavioural theories   Behavioural theories in (social) psychology attempt to explain work towards changes in behaviour by stressing the mechanisms of evaluation, feedback, and reinforcement (Carver & Sergiovanni, 1969; Debus & Schroiff, 1986). These mechanisms work by explaining and improving effective instruction in classrooms (Creemers, 1994) and by explaining and improving the impact of curricula on achievement (Hoeben, 1994). Rational control of organisations that depend on monitoring, evaluation, and appraisal of the functioning of the (people within) organisations, also comes close to the findings of EER which consistently demonstrates that school evaluation and student assessment are associated with student achievement (Scheerens, 1994).

Organisational learning theories   Organisational learning involves all processes of adaptation to a changing environment and aims to improve a school's effectiveness in processes of purposeful change (Louis, 1994). Learning of educational organisations may be conceptualised by information richness, organisational procedures of processing and interpreting information, procedures for evaluation and monitoring, interpersonal networks of sharing and discussing information, and organisations as makers of meaning by incremental adaptation, intellectual learning style, and assumption sharing (Lundberg, 1989; Senge, 1990). Organisational learning may be studied by analysing human resources management, in-company training strategies, and by studying the claims of companies that call themselves 'learning organisations'. An important realisation that is consistent with the view that organisational learning requires considerable decentralisation is that the productive work in educational organisations is being done by highly trained professionals with a high degree of autonomy (Fullan, Bennett, & Rolheiser-Bennett, 1990). Learning by educational organisations may be studied specifically by analysing their evaluation and monitoring processes and their staff development: that is, the ways they determine their training needs and the ways they organise the training of their personnel (in-service training, apprenticeships, embedded learning). An analysis of strategies related to 'learning to learn' in 'rich learning environments' with a focus on 'learning from experience' may also provide insight by analogy into the learning of organisations. Teachers are trained to know about these learning strategies.

The analysis of the above theoretical traditions reveals that they had significant effects upon the design and development of studies on educational effectiveness and school improvement. Therefore, these theoretical traditions are taken into account in our attempt to propose and promote the dynamic approach to school improvement which will not only contribute in establishing strong links between EER, and improvement of practice but will also enable us to develop the knowledge base of effective school improvement.

Aims and outline of the book

A) The aims of the book

The principal objective of this book is to make a major contribution to knowledge and theory building in the field of school improvement in relation to educational effectiveness research. It refers to a dynamic perspective of educational effectiveness and improvement stressing the importance of using an evidence-based and a theory-driven approach. It develops an approach to school improvement based on the work done in relation to the dynamic model of educational effectiveness and elaborates on possibilities of using the model for improvement purposes in educational practice. This approach puts emphasis on the quality of teaching and on the conditions created at different levels for improving the quality of teaching. Moreover, it stresses the importance of the school as a learning environment and provides the factors that are important for improving the School Learning Environment (SLE). For improvement purposes, the dynamic model points at the importance of a whole school approach using a conceptual framework which specifies the factors related to the quality of teaching and the school as a learning environment. Furthermore, the improvement approach promoted in this book emphasises the use of the available knowledge base in relation to the main aims of schools to deal with different challenges/problems they are facing. This framework is expected to help schools collect data through school self-evaluation mechanisms, to make decisions about priorities for improvement and to develop appropriate policies and action plans. Thus, an evidence-based and theory-driven approach to school improvement is promoted which emphasises the targets of education and provides a means to achieve these targets, but these means can be used in a flexible way and adapted to the specific settings of schools and systems.

B) The nature and structure of the book

The book is organised in three parts. A summary of the main points of each part is provided at the end of it. Part One provides the background of the proposed improvement approach and outlines the approach itself. A background of research on improvement is provided in the first chapter. It is also argued in Chapter One that we should take a broader perspective in understanding the dynamic process of effective school improvement and consider several theoretical traditions investigating the process of change beyond the traditional fields of educational effectiveness and school improvement. In the second chapter, it is argued that a theory-driven approach to school improvement should be established. The dynamic model is treated as a theoretical framework for establishing this approach. Finally, in Chapter 3 we provide specific strategies that can be used by different stakeholders who are planning to make use of the dynamic model to improve educational practice at different levels.

In the second part of the book we present projects based on the dynamic approach to improvement outlined in the first part. In order to illustrate the general applicability of this dynamic approach, the projects presented in this part are addressing improvement at different levels and deal with various challenges/ problems contemporary schools are facing. Moreover, the design of these projects is based on a variety of research methods ranging from experimental studies to case studies. Furthermore, the projects took place at different educational systems and contexts. Thus, the readers can see how the dynamic approach can be used for improvement in a wide variety of educational settings. Results concerned with the impact of these improvement efforts on the functioning of different factors and on learning outcomes are also presented in order to show how and under what conditions the dynamic approach to improvement can contribute to the quality of education.

Finally, Part Three draws implications for practice and research on school improvement and facilitate further use of the dynamic approach. Specifically, we provide guidelines to schools on how they can use the proposed improvement approach and build school self-evaluation mechanisms which will help them take decisions on their priorities for improvement and on how to design relevant action plans. We also provide a collection of instruments and guidelines for measuring quality of teaching and the functioning of school factors which can be used for establishing school self-evaluation mechanisms and for developing strategies and actions to address their improvement priorities.

Thus, in the first two parts of the book, we explain the proposed approach and its assumptions, provide examples on how school stakeholders can apply this approach to specific areas of improvement, and generate empirical evidence for the impact of this approach on educational effectiveness. In Part Three, we move a step forward and provide practical support to school stakeholders who may like to follow this approach. The book concludes with a chapter discussing the viability of the proposed improvement approach and also provides suggestions for further development of the dynamic approach to school improvement.

Chapter 2

Establishing links between effectiveness research and school improvement

The contribution of the dynamic model

Introduction

There are many stands of educational and social scientific theory that can be used to explain the process of school improvement which emphasise incentives and consumer-controlled accountability (Scheerens & Demeuse, 2005). These arise from:

–   Curriculum theories (e.g., Campbell, 1985; Fullan, 2001; Simons, 1990; Snyder, Bolin, & Zumwalt, 1992)
–   Organisational theories (e.g., Fairman & Quinn, 1985; Mintzberg, 1979)
–   Organisation learning theories (Morgan, 1986)
–   Micro-economic theory and public choice theory (Scheerens & Demeuse, 2005).

These theories point out the importance of using specific strategies and taking into account specific factors for establishing improvement culture at the school level (such as shared vision, autonomy used by schools, staff stability, and ownership). The creation of a climate conducive to improved performance is seen as essential for schools attempting to introduce interventions that will help them become more effective. For school improvement to occur, characteristics of the school culture must be favourable (Harris, 2001; Leithwood & Jantzi, 2006). Schools, for example, must have shared goals and feel responsible for success (Cheng, 1993, 1996; Townsend, 2007). Other requirements are collegiality, risk taking, mutual respect and support, openness, and a positive attitude towards lifelong learning (Cook, Murphy, & Hunt, 2000; Datnow, Borman, Stringfield, Overman, & Castellano, 2003). However, research suggests it is schools which manage to establish a climate of trust, openness, and collaboration which are among the most effective (Freiberg, 1999; Reynolds et al., 2002). It can be claimed that there is something highly tautological in the argument. Further, it may be suggested that it offers no help in getting from the former state to the latter (Kyriakides & Campbell, 2004).

The dynamic model acknowledges the importance of the school climate. For this reason actions taken to improve teaching are treated as factors of effectiveness. Actions to improve the School Learning Environment (SLE) are also suggested to be important. Combined, the above components are seen as essential characteristics of effective schools (Creemers & Kyriakides, 2008a). It also is assumed that teachers should be considered an essential lever of change, because change is explicit in their classrooms and daily practices (Cheng & Mok, 2008). However, for effective school improvement, individual teacher initiatives are not enough. Teachers can succeed in achieving major changes in their classrooms with strong effects on student outcomes, but these intervention programmes are not expected to have a lasting impact on the school as an organisation. Improvement efforts initiated by one teacher will generally disappear (e.g., when the teacher changes schools), unless the school as an organisation sustains the efforts. This important notion is problematic for educational systems that do not have strong traditions of school-level improvement, even when teacher improvement activities may occur (Kyriakides, 2005b). However, one explanation may be that all improvement activities necessarily concern all members of the staff. In practice, this will not happen very often. At the same time, it is argued in this book the culture of a school should not be used as a starting point for an improvement effort but we should try to use the knowledge base of Educational Effectiveness Research (EER) in order to identify needs/priorities for improvement (Creemers & Kyriakides, 2010c).

The improvement of school culture might be a welcome consequence of an effective improvement effort, but at the same time the determined outcomes (in this case the improvement of the factors in the dynamic model should be achieved.

Specifically, the dynamic model gives emphasis to the development of school-based programmes that are aiming to improve:

a)   The quality of teaching at classroom and school level
b)   Aspects of the school learning environment.

These may contribute directly and/or indirectly to the improvement of teaching practice. In this chapter, it is therefore argued that the dynamic model of educational effectiveness could contribute in establishing a theory-driven and evidence-based approach to school improvement. This is due to the essential characteristics of the model which differentiate this model from the integrated models of educational effectiveness developed during 1990s (e.g., Creemers, 1994; Scheerens, 1992).

The dynamic model is established in a way that helps policy makers and practitioners to improve educational practice by taking rational decisions concerning the optimal fit of the factors within the model and the present situation in the schools or educational systems (Sammons, 2009). As a consequence, the essential characteristics of the dynamic model are outlined and the effectiveness factors are presented at the classroom, school and system level.

It also is stressed that the validity of the model has been systematically tested and thereby we refer to available evidence supporting the value of the model for improvement purposes.

The dynamic model of educational effectiveness: An overview

The development of the dynamic model is based on the results of a critical review of the main findings of EER and of a critical analysis of theoretical models of educational effectiveness which were developed during 1990s (e.g., Creemers, 1994; Scheerens, 1992; Stringfield & Slavin, 1992). Moreover, studies testing the validity of the comprehensive model of educational effectiveness (Creemers, 1994), which is considered as the most influential theoretical construct in the field (Teddlie & Reynolds, 2000), reveal that some empirical support to the comprehensive model has been provided (e.g., de Jong, Westerhof, Kruiter, 2004; Driessen & Sleegers, 2000; Kyriakides, 2005a; Reezigt, Guldemond, & Creemers, 1999). It also is demonstrated that some characteristics of the comprehensive model can be seen as starting points for the development of the dynamic model of educational effectiveness which attempts to address weaknesses of the previous models (Kyriakides, 2008). The following section refers to the main assumptions and elements of the dynamic model. This is followed by a discussion of the main factors included in the model which are presented in the next section.

A) The rationale of the model

The dynamic model is based on the following three main assumptions. First, it is taken into account that most of the effectiveness studies are exclusively focused on language or mathematics rather than on the whole school curriculum aims (cognitive, psychomotor, metacognitive and affective). This suggests that the models of EER should take into account the new goals of education, and relate to this, their implications for teaching and learning (van der Werf, Opdenakker, & Kuyper, 2008). This means that the outcome measures should be defined in a broader way rather than being restricted to the achievement of basic skills. It also implies that new theories of teaching and learning should be used in order to specify variables associated with quality of teaching. Second, an important constraint of the existing approaches of modelling school effectiveness is the fact that the whole process does not contribute significantly to the improvement of school effectiveness.

Thus, the dynamic model is established in a way that helps both policy makers and practitioners to improve educational practice through rational decisions concerning the optimal fit of the factors within the model and the present situation in the schools or educational systems (Creemers & Kyriakides, 2010c). Finally, the dynamic model should not only be parsimonious but should also be able to describe the complex nature of educational effectiveness. This implies that the model is based on specific theory, but at the same time some of the factors included in the major constructs of the model are expected to be interrelated within and/or between levels.

B) The essential characteristics of the dynamic model

There are five main characteristics of the dynamic model. Firstly, the dynamic model takes into account the fact that effectiveness studies conducted in several countries reveal that the influences on student achievement are multi-level (Teddlie & Reynolds, 2000). Therefore, the model is multi-level in nature and refers to factors operating at the four levels shown in Figure 2.1. Figure 2.1 reveals the main structure of the dynamic model. Teaching and learning situations are emphasised and the roles of the two main actors (i.e., teacher and student) are analysed. Above these two levels, the dynamic model also refers to school-level factors. It is expected that school-level factors influence the teaching-learning situation by developing and evaluating the school policy on teaching and creating a learning environment at the school. The system level refers to the influence of the educational system through a more formal way, especially through developing and evaluating the educational policy at the national/regional level. It also takes into account that the teaching and learning situation is influenced by the wider educational context in which students, teachers, and schools are expected to operate. Factors such as the values of the society for learning and the importance attached to education play an important role both in shaping teacher and student expectations as well as in the development of the perceptions of various stakeholders about effective teaching practice.

Second, the dynamic model (Figure 2.1) does not only refer to factors situated at the four levels of the model and each level's association with student outcomes. The interrelations between the components of the model are also illustrated. In this way, the model supports the notion that factors at the school and system level have both direct and indirect effects on student achievement since they are able to influence not only student achievement but also teaching and learning situations.

Third, the dynamic model supports that the impact of the school and system level factors has to be defined and measured in a different way than the impact of classroom level factors. Policy on teaching and actions taken to improve teaching practice must be measured over time and in relation to the weaknesses that occur in a school. The assumption is that schools and educational systems which are able to identify their weaknesses and develop a policy on aspects associated with teaching and their School Learning Environment (SLE) are also able to improve the functioning of classroom level factors and their effectiveness status. Only changes in those factors for which schools face significant problems are expected to be associated with the improvement of school effectiveness. This implies that the impact of school and system level factors depends on the current

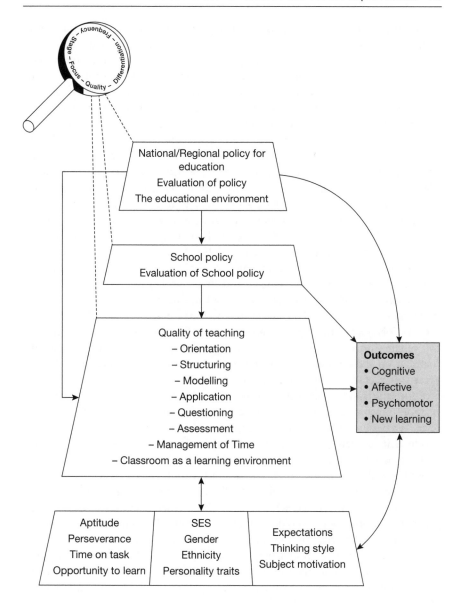

Figure 2.1 The dynamic model of educational effectiveness.

situation of the objects under investigation (Creemers & Kyriakides, 2009). This characteristic of the dynamic model does not only reveal an essential difference in the nature of this model with all the integrated models of EER but it also has some significant implications for using the dynamic model for improvement purposes.

Fourth, the dynamic model is based on the assumption that the relation of some effectiveness factors with achievement may not be linear. This assumption is supported by results of studies investigating the effect of some effectiveness factors upon student achievement (Campbell et al., 2004; Kyriakides, 2007; Scheerens & Bosker, 1997). These studies revealed that although these variables have been perceived as factors affecting teacher or school effectiveness, the research evidence is problematic. For example, teacher subject knowledge is widely perceived as a factor affecting teacher effectiveness (Scriven, 1994). However teachers' subject knowledge, regardless of how it is measured, has rarely correlated strongly with student achievement (Borich, 1992; Darling-Hammond, 2000). The explanation may be, as Monk (1994) reported, that the relationship is curvilinear: A minimal level of knowledge is necessary for teachers to be effective, but beyond a certain point, a negative or even no relation at all may occur. Similar findings have been reported for the association of self-efficacy beliefs with teacher effectiveness (Schunk 1991; Stevenson, Chen, & Lee, 1993) and for the impact of classroom emotional climate (Dowson & McInerney, 2003). A negative emotional climate usually shows negative correlations, but a neutral climate is at least as supportive as a warm climate. Beyond an optimal level of teacher direction, drill or recitation becomes dysfunctional (Soar & Soar, 1979). This implies that optimal points for the functioning of factors in relation to student outcomes have to be identified. By doing so, different strategies focusing on the improvement of specific factors for each teacher/school could emerge (Creemers & Kyriakides, 2006).

Fifth, the model assumes that there is a need to carefully examine the relationships between the various effectiveness factors which operate at the same level. Walberg's (1984) model, which is one of the most significant educational productivity models, attempts to illustrate such relationships. Aptitude, instruction and the psychological environment are seen as major direct causes of learning. They also influence one another and are in turn influenced by feedback on the amount of learning that takes place. Walberg's model was tested as a structural equation model on science achievement. The results indicated more complex, indirect relationships (Reynolds & Walberg, 1990). This implies that there is a need to refer to the relationships between the effectiveness factors which operate at the same level. Such approaches to modelling educational effectiveness reveal grouping of factors that make teachers and schools effective. Therefore, strategies for improving effectiveness which are comprehensive in nature may emerge (Creemers & Kyriakides, 2006).

Looking at qualitative characteristics of factors to provide feedback for improvement purposes

Finally, an essential difference of the dynamic model from all the previous models (Creemers, 1994; Scheerens, 1992; Stringfield & Slavin, 1992) is its attempt to look at qualitative characteristics of factors and provide more precise feedback on how the functioning of factors can be improved. The dynamic model is based on the assumption that different dimensions for measuring the functioning of effectiveness factors should be used to collect data and provide constructive feedback to teachers and schools. The integrated models of educational effectiveness (Creemers, 1994; Scheerens, 1992; Stringfield & Slavin, 1992) however do not explicitly refer to the measurement of each effectiveness factor. For example, the comprehensive model of educational effectiveness states that there should be control at school level. This means that goal attainment and the school climate should be evaluated (Creemers, 1994). In line with this assumption, studies investigating the validity of the model revealed that schools with an evaluation policy focused on the formative purposes of evaluation are more effective (e.g., Kyriakides, 2005b; Kyriakides, Campbell, & Gagatsis, 2000). The examination of evaluation policy at school level can be examined not only in terms of its focus on the formative purpose but also in terms of many other aspects of the functioning of evaluation such as the procedures used to design evaluation instruments, the forms of record keeping, and the policy on reporting results to parents and pupils.

Although there are different effectiveness factors and groupings of factors, it is assumed that each factor can be defined and measured using similar dimensions. This approach considers each factor as a multidimensional construct and at the same time is in keeping with the parsimonious nature of the model. More specifically, each factor is defined and measured using five dimensions: *frequency, focus, stage, quality,* and *differentiation.* Frequency is a quantitative way to measure the functioning of each effectiveness factor whereas the other four dimensions examine qualitative characteristics of the functioning of each factor at the system/school/classroom level. Using this measurement framework implies that each factor should not only be examined by measuring how frequently the factor is present in the system/school/class (i.e., through a quantitative perspective) but also by investigating specific aspects of the way the factor is functioning (i.e., looking at qualitative characteristics of the functioning of the factor). The use of different measurement dimensions reveals that looking at just the frequency of an effectiveness factor does not help us identify those aspects of the functioning of a factor which are associated to student achievement.

Considering effectiveness factors as multi-dimensional constructs not only provides a better picture of what makes teachers and schools effective, but also helps us develop specific strategies for improving educational practice (Kyriakides & Creemers, 2008). For example, a teacher may raise frequently questions and enough process questions but she/he may not give any feedback to students or even when she/he gives feedback, this is not helpful for students to identify the wrong parts of their answers and find the correct answer. Similarly, a teacher may provide enough structuring tasks but these are too specific and do not help students understand how the previous lesson is related with the present one and how the next lesson will cover issues not dealt by the present one. A brief description of the five dimensions is given below. Also highlighted is the importance of using these dimensions not only for measurement purposes but also for providing feedback to teachers and schools for improvement purposes.

First, the *frequency* dimension refers to the quantity that an activity associated with an effectiveness factor is present in a system, school or classroom. This is probably the easiest way to measure the effect of a factor on student achievement and almost all studies used this dimension to define effectiveness factors (see Creemers, Kyriakides, & Sammons, 2010; Teddlie & Reynolds, 2000). However, this dimension may not always be related in a linear way with student outcomes (Heck & Moriyama, 2010). For example, personal monitoring at school level can be measured by taking into account how often the head teachers use a monitoring system to supervise their teachers. EER should attempt to identify whether this dimension of measuring personal monitoring is not only related directly to student outcomes but also indirectly through teacher behaviour in the classroom. Further, it is questionable that there is a linear relation between frequency of personal monitoring and both type of outcomes. However, what can be assumed is: after an optimal value of using a monitoring system, this factor may not have an additional effect on outcomes. Moreover, it may even lead to negative effect in teacher behaviour and ultimately in student outcomes.

Second, the factors are measured by taking into account the *focus* of the activities which reveal the function of the factor at classroom, school and system level. Two aspects of focus of each factor are measured. The first refers to the specificity of the activities which can range from specific to general. For example, in the case of school policy on parental involvement, the policy could either be more specific in terms of concrete activities that are expected to take place (e.g., the policy refers to specific hours that parents can visit the school) or more general (e.g., it informs parents that they are welcome to the school but without giving them specific information about what, how and when).

The second aspect of this dimension addresses the purpose for which an activity takes place. An activity may be expected to achieve a single or multiple purposes. In the case of school policy on parental involvement, the activities might be restricted to a single purpose (e.g., parents visit schools to get information about student progress). On the other hand, the activities may be concerned with the achievement of more than one purpose (e.g., parents visit the school to exchange information about children progress and to assist teachers in and outside the classroom).

It is expected that the measurement of the focus of an activity (either in terms of its specificity or in terms of the number of purposes that is expected to achieve) may be related in a curvilinear way with student outcomes. For example, the guidelines on parental involvement which are very general may not be helpful either for parents or teachers in establishing good relations which can result in supporting student learning. On the other hand, a school policy which is very specific in defining activities may restrict the productive involvement of teachers and parents in creating their own ways for implementing the school policy. Similarly, Schoenfeld (1998) suggests that if all the activities are expected to achieve a single purpose then the chance to achieve this purpose is high. However, the effect of the factor might be small due to the fact that other purposes are not achieved and/or synergy may not exist since the activities are isolated. On the other hand, if all the activities are expected to achieve multiple purposes, there is a danger that specific purposes are not addressed in such a way that they can be implemented successfully (Pellegrino, 2004). This example also points to the possibility that an interaction between the two aspects of this dimension may exist.

Third, the stage at which tasks associated with a factor taking place is also examined. It is supported that the factors need to take place over a long period of time to ensure that they have a continuous direct or indirect effect on student learning (Creemers, 1994). This assumption is partly based on the fact that evaluations of programmes aiming to improve educational practice reveal that the extent to which these intervention programmes have any impact on educational practice is partly based on the length of time that the programmes are implemented in a school (e.g., Gray et al., 1999, Stufflebeam & Shinkfield, 1990). Moreover, the importance of using the stage dimension to measure each effectiveness factor arises from the fact that it has been shown that the impact of a factor on student achievement partly depends on the extent to which activities associated with this factor are provided throughout the school career of the student (Slater & Teddlie, 1992). For example, school policy on opportunity to learn (which refers to policy on cancellation of lessons and absenteeism) is expected to be implemented throughout the year and not only through specific regulations announced at a specific point of time (e.g., only at the beginning of the school year). Although measuring the stage dimension gives information about the continuity of the existence of a factor, activities associated with the factor may not necessarily be the same. Therefore, using the stage dimension to measure the functioning of a factor can help us identify the extent to which there is constancy at each level, and flexibility in using the factor during the period that the investigation/measurement takes place (Driessen & Sleegers, 2000).

Fourth, the *quality* dimension can be discerned in two different ways. The first one refers to the properties of the specific factor itself, as these are discussed in the literature. For instance, school policy on assessment can be measured by looking at the mechanisms which have been developed in order to establish instruments which meet psychometric standards (e.g., valid, reliable, representative to the content taught). At the same time, this policy both clarifies and guarantees that teachers are expected to make use of the information gathered from assessment. This is in order to meet their student needs and this gives more emphasis to the formative function of assessment (Black & Wiliam, 1998; Harlen & James, 1997; Kyriakides et al., 2000).

Finally, *differentiation* refers to the extent to which activities associated with a factor are implemented in the same way for all the subjects involved with it (e.g., all the students, teachers, schools). It is expected that adaptation to specific needs of each subject or group of subjects will increase the successful implementation of a factor and will ultimately maximise its effect on student learning outcomes (Sammons, 2010). It can be argued that the dynamic model takes into account the findings of research into differential educational effectiveness (Campbell et al., 2003; den Brok, van Tartwijk, Wubbels, & Veldman, 2010; Kyriakides, 2007; Nuttall, Goldstein, Prosser, & Rasbach, 1989; Strand, 2010). Specifically, it is acknowledged that the impact of effectiveness factors on different groups of students may vary. As a consequence, differentiation is treated as a measurement dimension and is concerned with the extent to which activities associated with a factor are implemented in the same way for all the subjects involved with it. Although differentiation could be considered a property of an effectiveness factor, it was decided to treat differentiation as a separate dimension of measuring each effectiveness factor rather than incorporate it into the quality dimension. In this way, the importance of taking into account the special needs of each group of students is recognised. Thus, the dynamic model is based on the notion that it is difficult to deny that persons of all ages learn, think, and process information differently.

One way to differentiate instruction is for teachers to teach according to individual student learning needs as these are defined by their background and personal characteristics such as gender, socio-economic status, ability, thinking style, and personality type (Kyriakides, 2007). However, the differentiation dimension does not imply that these groups of students are not expected to achieve the same purposes. On the contrary, adapting the functioning of each factor to the specific needs of each group of students may ensure that all of them will become able to achieve the same purposes (Kyriakides & Creemers, 2010). This argument is partly supported by research into adaptive teaching and the evaluation projects of innovations concerned with the use of adaptive teaching in classrooms (e.g., Houtveen, van der Grift, & Creemers, 2004; Noble, 2004). Moreover, it is acknowledged that the use of differentiation as a measurement dimension does not imply that all instruction has to be individualised since findings on Aptitude Treatment Interaction research reveal that in real classroom situations is neither feasible nor effective to offer only individual tasks during the whole teaching time (Salomon, 1979; Clark & Salomon, 1986).

The dynamic model: Factors operating at student, classroom, school, and system level

This section provides a description of the factors of the model situated at four different levels: student, classroom, school and system/context. The way these levels and factors are defined is in line with the main principles of the model presented in the previous section. Although the dynamic model is multi-level in nature, more emphasis is given to factors operating at the teacher and the school level since the main aim of EER is to identify factors in education that promote learning. However, it also is stressed that student background characteristics should be taken into account because they explain to a large extent the variance

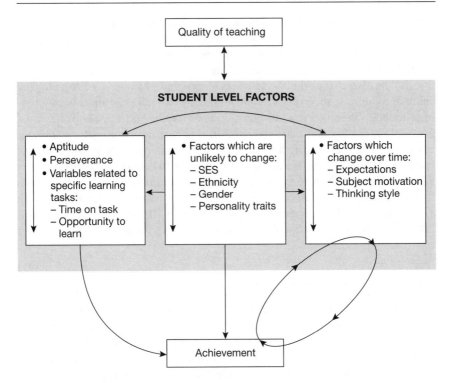

Figure 2.2 Factors of the dynamic model operating at the student level.

between students in learning and achievement. Moreover, these factors should be taken into account in promoting differentiation at different levels.

A) Student factors

The dynamic model refers to two main categories of background factors operating at the student level which can influence the effectiveness of education. The two categories are:

a) Sociocultural and economical background variables emerged from the sociological perspective of EER
b) Background variables emerged from the psychological perspective of EER.

In addition, variables related to specific learning tasks emerged from the psychological perspective. These are also treated as significant student level factors (see Figure 2.2). Some evidence showing that these variables affect learning is provided in the first part of this section. Moreover, Figure 2.2 shows that a distinction is made among the student-level factors by referring to factors which are unlikely to change (e.g., gender, SES, ethnicity, personality) and factors that may change over time (e.g., subject motivation and thinking styles). Factors that are likely to change over time are more closely related to the aims of EER. These factors could be treated both as explanatory and as outcome variables. For example, subject motivation may be related with student achievement gains, but it is also likely to change due to the teacher behaviour (Bamburg, 1994). Helping children to increase their motivation could be considered as an affective outcome of schooling (Busato, Prins, Elshout, & Hamaker, 1999; van der Werf et al., 2008). It is also argued that research into differential educational effectiveness could help teachers identify how to adapt their teaching practice to the specific learning needs of groups of students. This in turn will help teachers become more effective (Kyriakides & Creemers, 2006). In this context, relations between factors operating at the student level and factors operating at higher levels, such as the teacher level are expected to exist (Kyriakides, 2008; Teddlie & Reynolds, 2000). Therefore, these should be taken into account for promoting quality and equity in education.

Socio-cultural and economic background factors

The first group of student level factors refers to the socio-cultural and economical background characteristics of students, such as SES, ethnic background, and gender. Many studies showed that the majority of variance in student outcomes could be explained by student background characteristics like SES, ethnicity and gender (Opdenakker & van Damme, 2006; Sirin, 2005). Thus, these variables are not only treated as student level factors but also highlight the importance of investigating school effectiveness in terms of the equity dimension. For example, the evaluation of any policy promoting equal opportunities could be based on investigating its impact on promoting educational progress of socially disadvantaged students and on reducing unjustifiable gender differences at the school level (Lamb, 1996).

Beyond indicating the importance of treating background variables as student-level factors, and providing suggestions on how research into differential effectiveness could help teachers/schools/systems become more effective, the dynamic model also refers to the importance of looking at relations between these variables. For example, studies showing that there are significant interactions between social groups and sex, indicating that the gender effect is not consistent across all social classes, can help us evaluate policies on providing equal opportunities and develop them further by taking into account that gender differences are bigger in lower SES groups (Gray, Peng, Steward, & Thomas, 2004; Strand, 2010). Thereby, improvement efforts should be concerned with these groups that are facing problems at a higher level.

Finally, it is important to acknowledge that at the level of the classroom, students should be treated as individuals rather than as representing stereotypical groupings so that the promotion of learning for all students is encouraged. However, at the level of the school or the system, if groups of students are systematically being disadvantaged in their rate of learning in comparison to other groups, as some effectiveness studies in different countries have shown (Gorard, Rees, & Salisbury, 2001; Gray et al., 2004; Beaton, Mullis, Martin, Gonzalez, Kelly, & Smith, 1996; Harskamp, 1988; Kyriakides, 2004), interventions for promoting equity both at the school and the system level should be developed.

Background variables that emerged from the psychological perspective of EER

The dynamic model also refers to five background variables that emerged from the psychological perspective of EER, and which were found to be related with student achievement: aptitude, motivation, expectations, personality, and thinking style (e.g., Bamburg, 1994; Bandura, 1996, 1997; Marsh, 2008; Marsh & Parker, 1984; Pajares, 1999; Walberg, 1986). Aptitude, for example, is seen as one of the most critical background variables associated with student achievement. Aptitude embraces general intelligence and prior learning and is one of the best predictors of performance. Several studies (de Jong et al., 2004; Kyriakides, 2005a) show that the effect of aptitude on student achievement is even higher than the effect of SES. Similarly motivation and expectations were found to be related with student achievement and need to be considered in projects attempting to improve the quality and equity of education (Baumert & Demmerich, 2001; Kline & Gale, 1977; Kuyper, Dijkstra, Buunk, & van der Werf, 2011; Pajares & Schunk, 2001; Wehrens, Kuyper, Dijkstra, Buunk, & van der Werf, 2010).

Finally, personality characteristics of students (i.e., personality traits and thinking styles) have recently been a particular area of focus since recent effectiveness studies have highlighted these variables as predictors of student achievement (Kyriakides, 2005a). They have also been linked to ways of adapting teaching and assessment approaches to the needs of specific groups of students. For example, teachers may have found out that some students managed to perform better in a written test than during the normal teaching lessons and may attribute this result to cheating. However, these students may be introverted and consequently not like to express their ideas publicly and this is not because they don't have something to say but due to the fact that they tend to be shy, and inhibited. In such case, teachers may consider the possibility to address those students to answer a question or express their ideas even if they did not call for attention. As far as the importance of treating measures of thinking style as a predictor of student achievement is concerned, it is important to note that in the search for variables that contribute to school achievement, psychologists have devoted considerable attention to the so-called stylistic aspects of cognition. The idea of a style reflecting a person's typical or habitual mode of problem solving, thinking, perceiving, and remembering was initially introduced by Allport (1937). In the past few decades, the style construct has employed a great deal of research interest, and many theoretical models have been postulated. There are at least three reasons for not only treating personality traits, but also styles associated with the theory of mental self-government (Sternberg, 1988), as student level factors.

First, there are many studies which reveal that measures of thinking styles associated with this theory explain individual differences in performance not attributable to abilities (e.g. Grigorenko & Sternberg, 1997; Zhang & Sternberg, 1998; Zhang, 2001). Second, it has been shown that the thinking styles and personality overlap are limited (Messick, 1996; Sternberg, 1994; Zhang, 2002). This implies that not only intelligence and personality traits, but also thinking styles, should be taken into account in order to explain variation in student achievement. Finally, there is some evidence supporting the existence of differential effectiveness in relation to student personality traits and styles of thinking (Kyriakides, 2005a; Zhang, 2011).

Time on task (time students are really involved in learning tasks)

The impact of time on task on student achievement is also taken into account. The variable time on task refers to the time students are willing to spend on learning and on educational tasks. It is determined not only by motivation and expectations, but also by the time provided by the school/teacher and by processes at the school and classroom levels. It is also important to note that time on task refers to the time in which students are really involved in learning (provided that this time is filled with opportunities to learn). Therefore, there are several reasons for which, in the dynamic model, the variables *time on task* and *opportunity to learn* belong in the same category. An obvious reason is concerned with the fact that both variables refer to specific learning tasks that define the criteria for measuring effectiveness. In addition, these variables belong to the same category because they are not only determined by student background factors but also influence learning directly. Thus, time on task and opportunity to learn are seen as the first steps in the search for intermediary processes (for example, the cognitive processes of students and mediating teacher activities). In the dynamic model, time on task and opportunity to learn are put in an intermediary position. Elements of education at the classroom level, such as the ability of teacher to manage the classroom time, can contribute in an increase in time on task, (assuming they are effective), (Kumar, 1991).

Opportunity to learn

The variable *opportunity to learn* refers to the fact that in order to achieve educational outcomes, students should at least have some opportunity to acquire knowledge and skills (Creemers, 1994). Despite the difficulties of measuring opportunity to learn at a classroom, or even at higher level, this variable has been included in international studies conducted by the IEA which show that variations between countries in the opportunity to learn are very large (Campbell & Kyriakides, 2000). Similarly, studies investigating the validity of Creemers' model (e.g., de Jong et al., 2004; Kyriakides, 2005a; Kyriakides et al., 2000; Isac, Maslowski, & van der Werf, in press) suggest that time spent doing homework and time spent on private tuition could also be seen as measures of the 'opportunity to learn' factor. These measures of the opportunity factor were also found to be closely related with student achievement (e.g., Brookhart, 1997; Trautwein, Koller, Schmitz, & Baumert, 2002). However, it has to be acknowledged that the amount of time students spend voluntarily on specific learning tasks (e.g., mathematics, music, physical education) may not only be seen as a measure of opportunity to learn but may also be an indicator of students' interests and motivation about the subject associated with these tasks. Spending additional time on private tuition or on homework does not necessarily mean that the students make use of this extra time for learning purposes (Kyriakides & Tsangaridou, 2008). Therefore, a distinction is made between learning opportunities offered in the instructional process during and/or after the school time and the actual use of these opportunities that each student makes (see also Creemers, 1994). In this context, the students' use of opportunities to learn is treated as a student level factor whereas the findings of studies investigating the impact of opportunity to learn on student achievement are taken into account in defining factors at teacher, school, and context levels.

B) Classroom factors of the dynamic model

At the classroom level, the teacher is an important actor (Kyriakides et al., 2000; Rosenshine & Furst, 1973; Scheerens & Bosker, 1997; Teddlie & Reynolds, 2000). Teacher background characteristics such as gender, age, education, beliefs and motivation are an important topic in theory and research because these characteristics may explain differences between teachers in the way they behave in classrooms (Fraser, 1995). However, these characteristics are not included in the dynamic model as it primarily concentrates on the teaching activities teachers perform in order to initiate, promote, and evaluate student learning. Based on the main findings of teacher effectiveness research (e.g., Brophy & Good, 1986; Doyle, 1986; Emmer & Stough, 2001; Muijs & Reynolds, 2001; Rosenshine & Stevens, 1986), the dynamic model refers to factors which describe teachers' instructional role and are associated with student outcomes (see Figure 2.3).

Teacher factors refer to observable instructional behaviour of teachers in the classroom rather than on factors that may explain such behaviours (e.g., teacher beliefs and knowledge and interpersonal competences). The eight factors included in the model are as follows: *orientation, structuring, questioning, teaching-modelling, applications, time management, teacher role in making classroom a learning environment, and classroom assessment*. These eight factors, which are briefly described in Table 2.1., were found to be associated with student outcomes (e.g., Brophy & Good, 1986; Darling-Hammond, 2000; Muijs & Reynolds,

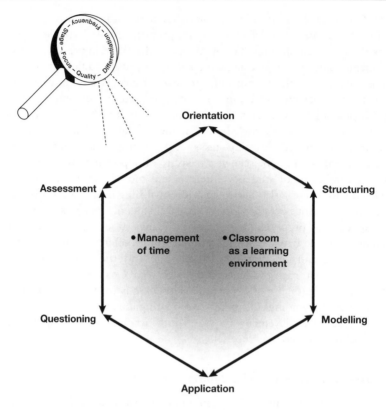

Figure 2.3 Factors of the dynamic model operating at the classroom level.

2000; Rosenshine & Stevens, 1986; Scheerens & Bosker, 1997). They do not, however, refer to only one approach of teaching such as structured or direct teaching (Joyce, Weil, & Calhoun, 2000) or to approaches associated with constructivism (Schoenfeld, 1998). An integrated approach in defining quality of teaching is adopted (Elboj & Niemela, 2010). Specifically, the dynamic model does not only refer to skills associated with direct teaching and mastery learning such as structuring and questioning, but also to orientation and teaching modelling which are in line with theories of teaching associated with constructivism. These two factors also are in keeping with the principles of teaching for understanding. Moreover, they promote the achievement of the new goals of education such as the development of metacognitive skills. Furthermore, the collaboration technique (Slavin, 1983; Slavin & Cooper, 1999) is included under the overarching factor contribution of teacher to the establishment of classroom learning environment (see Table 2.1). Studies investigating differential teacher effectiveness revealed that the previously listed eight factors may have a stronger impact on the learning of specific groups of students, but can be treated as generic in nature as research highlights a link with the achievement of each group of students (Campbell et al., 2004).

Table 2.1 The main elements of each teacher factor included in the dynamic model

Factors	Main elements
1) Orientation	a) Providing the objectives for which a specific task/lesson/ series of lessons take(s) place; and b) challenging students to identify the reason why an activity is taking place in the lesson.
2) Structuring	a) Beginning with overviews and/or review of objectives; b) outlining the content to be covered and signalling transitions between lesson parts; and c) drawing attention to and reviewing main ideas.
3) Questioning	a) Raising different types of questions (i.e., process and product) at appropriate difficulty level; b) giving time for students to respond; and c) dealing with student responses.
4) Teaching modelling	a) Encouraging students to use problem solving strategies presented by the teacher or other classmates; b) inviting students to develop strategies; and c) promoting the idea of modelling.
5) Application	a) Using seatwork or small group tasks in order to provide needed practice and application opportunities; and b) using application tasks as starting points for the next step of teaching and learning.
6) The classroom as a learning environment	a) Establishing on task behaviour through the interactions they promote (i.e., teacher-student and student-student interactions); and b) Dealing with classroom disorder and student competition through establishing rules, persuading students to respect them and using the rules.
7) Management of time	a) Organising the classroom environment; and b) Maximising engagement rates.
8) Assessment	a) Using appropriate techniques to collect data on student knowledge and skills; b) analysing data in order to identify student needs and report the results to students and parent; and c) evaluating their own practices.

Studies testing the validity of the model also revealed that these factors are interrelated and can be grouped into five types of teacher behaviour. These are discerned in a distinctive way and move gradually from skills associated with direct teaching to more advanced skills concerned with new teaching approaches, and differentiation of teaching (Kyriakides, Creemers, & Antoniou, 2009). Teachers exercising more advanced types of behaviour have better student outcomes. This result is taken into account for developing teacher professional improvement programmes. Early findings of studies evaluating these programmes provide support for the development of a dynamic integrated approach to teacher professional development (see chapter 7 for a more comprehensive review).

The dynamic model is based on the assumption that although there are eight teacher factors, each factor can be defined and measured using the five dimensions: *frequency, focus, stage, quality, and differentiation.* These dimensions are supposed to contribute to the effects that a factor is expected to have on student outcome measures. They also help to describe the functioning of a factor more effectively. The importance of taking each dimension of teacher effectiveness factors into account is illustrated below by explaining how one of the factors included in the model (*orientation*) is defined.

Orientation refers to teacher behaviour in providing the objectives for a specific task, lesson or series of lessons. It also encompasses challenging students to identify the reason for which an activity takes place within the lesson. The engagement of students with orientation tasks may encourage them to actively participate in the classroom, as the tasks that take place are meaningful for them (De Corte, 2000; Paris & Paris, 2001). As a consequence, the frequency dimension is measured by taking into account the number of orientation tasks that take place in a typical lesson as well as how long each orientation task takes place. These two indicators help us identify the importance that the teacher attaches to this factor.

The effectiveness factors are also measured by taking into account the focus of the activities which are associated with each factor. Two aspects of focus for each factor are measured. First, it is taken into account that each task associated with the functioning of an effectiveness factor may not take place by chance but for a reason. Thus, according to the dynamic model, the first aspect of the focus dimension of each factor addresses *the purpose(s)* for which an activity takes place. It is taken into account that an activity may be expected to achieve single or multiple purposes. In the case of orientation, this aspect of focus is measured by examining the extent to which an activity is restricted to finding one single reason for doing a task or finding the multiple reasons for doing a task. The second aspect of this dimension refers to the specificity of the activities. These can range from specific to general. The specificity of the orientation tasks is measured taking into account that an orientation task may refer to a part of a lesson or to the whole lesson or even to a series of lessons (e.g., a lesson unit). Effective teachers encourage students to be engaged in different types of orientations tasks (Kyriakides & Creemers, 2008).

Activities associated with a factor can be measured by taking into account the *stage* at which they take place. In the case of orientation, it is taken into account that orientation tasks may take place in different parts of a lesson or series of lessons (e.g., introduction, core, ending of the lesson). Effective teachers are expected to offer orientation tasks at different parts of lessons (Killen, 2007). Further, it is expected that effective teachers are able to take others' perspectives into account during this orientation phase. For example, students may come with suggestions for the reasons of doing a specific task. An effective teacher is expected to take this into account (Gijbels, Van de Watering, Dochy, & Van den Bossche, 2006).

The *quality* dimension refers to the properties of the specific factor itself, as these are discussed in the literature. This implies that the quality dimension deals with the process of teaching and is not concerned with the effects of teaching in terms of student outcomes. It is assumed that this dimension, in combination with others, may help us explain variation on student outcomes and for this reason it is included in the model. The importance of using this dimension also arises from the fact that looking at the quantity elements of a factor ignores the fact that the functioning of the factor may vary. The quality dimension measures the properties of the orientation task, and specifically whether it is clear for the students. It also refers to the impact that the task has on student engagement in the learning process. For example, teachers may present the reasons of doing a task simply because they have to do it, and it is part of their teaching routine without having much effect on student participation. On the other hand, others may encourage students to identify the purposes that can be achieved by doing a task. Therefore, this increases their motivation towards a specific task/lesson/ series of lessons.

Finally, *differentiation* is measured by looking at the extent to which teachers provide different types of orientation tasks to students according to their learning needs and especially by taking into account differences in the personal and background characteristics of students. Using different orientation tasks is expected to help all students to find out the reasons for which specific tasks take place in their classroom. Moreover, taking into account the different types of objectives that are supposed to be covered during the instruction, teachers are also expected to use different orientation tasks in order to introduce students to the importance of different objectives that have to be acquired. Finally, teachers may differentiate the orientation tasks in relation to the organisational and cultural context of their school or classroom in order to facilitate their understanding of the purposes of learning tasks (Kyriakides, 2007).

C) School factors of the dynamic model

The definition of the school level is based on the assumption that factors at the school level are expected to have both direct effects and indirect effects on student achievement. School factors are expected to influence classroom-level factors, particularly teaching practice. This assumption is based on the fact that EER has shown that the classroom level is more significant than the school level (e.g., Kyriakides et al., 2000; Teddlie & Reynolds, 2000). Moreover, defining factors at the classroom level is seen as a pre-requisite for defining the school level (Creemers, 1994). Therefore, the dynamic model refers to factors at the school level which are related to the same key concepts of quantity of teaching, provision of learning opportunities, and quality of teaching which are used to define the classroom level factors of the dynamic model. Meta-analyses have shown that they are related with student achievement (Kyriakides et al., 2010; Scheerens et al., 2005; Witziers, Bosker, & Kruger, 2003). Specifically, emphasis is given to the following two main aspects of the school policy. These affect learning at both the teacher and student level:

a)   School policy for teaching and
b)   School policy for creating a learning environment at school.

Guidelines are seen as one of the main indications of school policy. This is reflected in the way each school level factor is defined (see Creemers & Kyriakides, 2008a). In using the term guidelines, the dynamic model refers to a range of documents. These include: staff meeting minutes, announcements, and action plans. These make the policy of the school more concrete to the teachers and other stakeholders. However, this factor does not imply that each school should simply develop formal documents to install policy. The factors concerned with the school policy mainly refer to the actions taken by the school to help teachers and other stakeholders have a clear understanding of what is expected from them to do. Support offered to teachers and other stakeholders to implement the school policy is also an aspect of these two factors (Creemers & Kyriakides, 2010b).

Based on the assumption that the essence of a successful organisation in the modern world is the search for improvement (Hopkins, 2001), the processes and the activities which take place in the school in order to improve the teaching practice and the School Learning Environment (SLE) are also examined. For this reason, the processes which are used to evaluate the school policy for teaching and the SLE are investigated. Thus, the following four factors at the school level are included in the model (see Figure 2.4):

a)   School policy for teaching and actions taken for improving teaching practice
b)   Policy for creating the SLE and actions taken for improving the SLE
c)   Evaluation of school policy for teaching and of actions taken to improve teaching
d)   Evaluation of the SLE.

School policy for teaching and actions taken for improving teaching

The definition of the dynamic model at the classroom level refers to factors related to the key concepts of *quality*, *time on task*, and *opportunity to learn*. Therefore, the model attempts to investigate aspects of school policy for teaching associated with the quantity of teaching, provision of learning opportunities, and quality of teaching. Actions taken for improving the above three aspects of teaching practice, such as the provision of support to teachers in improving their teaching sills, are also taken into account. Specifically, the following aspects of school policy on quantity of teaching are taken into account:

–   School policy on the management of teaching time (e.g., lessons start on time and finish on time; there are no interruptions of lessons for staff meetings and/or for preparation of school festivals and other events)
–   Policy on student and teacher absenteeism
–   Policy on homework
–   Policy on lesson schedule and timetable.

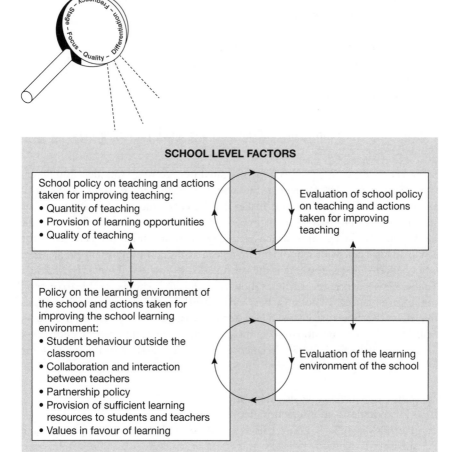

Figure 2.4 Factors of the dynamic model operating at the school level.

School policy on provision of learning opportunities is measured by looking at the extent to which the school has a mission concerning the provision of learning opportunities. This is also reflected in the school policy on curriculum. School policy on long-term and short-term planning, and school policy on providing support to students with special needs is also examined. Furthermore, the extent to which the school attempts to make good use of school trips and other extra-curricular activities for teaching/learning purposes is investigated. Finally, school policy on the quality of teaching is seen as closely related to the teacher factors of the dynamic model.

Therefore, the way school policy for teaching is examined reveals that effective schools are expected to make decisions on maximising the use of teaching time and the learning opportunities offered to their students (Anderson, 1995). In addition, effective schools are expected to support their teachers in their attempt to help students learn by using effective teaching practices (Heck & Moriyama,

2010; Hallinger & Heck, 2011b). In this context, the definition of this factor implies that schools should:

a)   Make sure that teaching time is offered to students
b)   Offer to students learning opportunities beyond those offered by the official curricula
c)   Attempt to improve the quality of teaching practice.

School Policy for creating the SLE and actions taken for improving the SLE

School climate factors have been incorporated in effectiveness models in different ways. Stringfield (1994) defines the school climate very broadly as the total environment of the school. This makes it difficult to study specific factors of the school climate and examine their impact on student achievement. The dynamic model refers to the extent to which a learning environment has been created in the school. This element of school climate is seen as the most important predictor of school effectiveness as learning is the key function of a school (Linnakyla, Malin, & Taube, 2004). Moreover, EER has shown that effective schools are able to respond to the learning needs of both teachers and students. Furthermore, research indicates that effective schools are involved in systematic changes of the internal processes in order to achieve educational goals more effectively in conditions of uncertainty (Teddlie & Stringfield, 1993; Creemers & Kyriakides, 2010a). In this context, the following five aspects which define the SLE are taken into account:

a)   Student behaviour outside the classroom
b)   Collaboration and interaction between teachers
c)   Partnership policy (i.e., relations of school with community, parents, and advisors)
d)   Provision of sufficient learning resources to students and teachers
e)   Values in favour of learning.

The first three aspects refer to the rules which the school has developed for establishing a learning environment inside and outside the classrooms. Here the term learning does not refer exclusively to student learning. For example, collaboration and interaction between teachers may contribute in their professional development (i.e., learning of teachers) but may also have an effect on teaching practice and thereby may also improve student learning. The fourth aspect refers to the policy on providing resources for learning. The availability of learning resources in schools may not only have an effect on student learning, but may also encourage the learning of teachers. For example, the availability of computers and software for teaching Geometry may contribute to teacher professional development as it encourages teachers to find ways to make good use of the software in their teaching practice. Thereby the teacher becomes more effective. The last aspect of this factor is concerned with the strategies which the school has developed in order to encourage teachers and students to develop positive attitudes towards learning.

Following a similar approach as the one concerned with school policy on teaching, the dynamic model attempts to measure the school policy for creating a SLE. Actions taken for improving the SLE beyond the establishment of policy guidelines are also taken into account. Specifically, actions taken for improving the SLE can be directed at:

a) Changing the rules in relation to the first three aspects of the above SLE factor
b) Providing educational resources (e.g., teaching aids and educational assistance)
c) Helping students/teachers develop positive attitudes towards learning.

For example, a school may have a policy for promoting teacher professional development. However, this might not be enough- especially if some teachers do not consider professional development as an important issue. In this case, actions should be taken to help teachers develop positive attitudes towards learning, which may help them become more effective.

School Evaluation

The last two overarching school factors of the dynamic model refer to the mechanisms used to evaluate the functioning of the first two overarching factors. Creemers (1994) claims that control is one of the major principles which operate in generating educational effectiveness. This implies that goal attainment and the school climate should be evaluated. In addition, studies investigating the validity of the model provided empirical support for the importance of this principle (e.g., de Jong et al., 2004; Kyriakides et al., 2000; Kyriakides, 2005a). It was thus decided to treat evaluation of policy for teaching and other actions taken to improve teaching practice, and evaluation of the SLE as two overarching factors operating at school level. The ways the five proposed dimensions are used to measure these two factors are described below. The following section aims to clarify how the five dimensions of the dynamic model are used to measure each school factor.

Frequency   First, frequency is measured by investigating how many times during the school year the school collects evaluation data concerning its own policy for teaching or its own policy for the SLE. Emphasis is also given to the sources of evaluation data. This is attributed to the fact that studies on school evaluation reveal that evaluators should employ a multi-dimensional approach in collecting data on school and teacher effectiveness (e.g., Beerens, 2000; Danielson & McGreal, 2000; Johnson, 1997; Kyriakides & Campbell, 2004; Nevo, 1995). These comparisons of various sources might increase the internal validity of the evaluation system (Campbell & Fiske, 1959; Cronbach, 1990).

Focus   The focus dimension refers to the aspects of the school policy for teaching or the aspects of the school policy of SLE which are evaluated. More specifically, evaluation of school policy may attempt to measure the properties of the school policy (e.g., clear, concrete, in line with the literature), its relevance to the problems which teachers and students have to face, and its impact on school practice and student outcomes. It also is examined whether each school evaluates not only the content of the policy for teaching and the actions taken to improve teaching practice but also the abilities of people who are expected to implement the policy. Moreover, the focus dimension is measured by looking at the extent to which information gathered from the evaluation is too specific (e.g., teacher X cannot do this) or too general (e.g., teachers are not able to teach effectively). Research on school self-evaluation reveals that data collected should not be too specific or place blame on any individual (e.g., Fitz-Gibbon, 1996; Hopkins, 2001; Patton, 1991; Visscher & Coe, 2002) because such an approach serves the summative purpose of evaluation and does not help the schools to take decisions on how to improve their policy. At the same time, information gathered from evaluation should not be too general but should be focused on how to influence decision-making. In particular, the process of allocating responsibilities to school partners in order to introduce a plan for improving the effectiveness of their school is influential (Kyriakides & Campbell, 2004; MacBeath, 1999; Meuret & Morlaix, 2003).

Stage   The stage dimension of this factor is examined by looking at the period in which evaluation data are collected. Schools could either conduct evaluation at the end of certain periods (e.g., end of semester) or establish evaluation mechanisms which operate on a continuous basis during the whole school year. Schools are also expected to review their own evaluation mechanisms and adapt them in order to collect appropriate and useful data (see also Cousins & Earl, 1992; Torres & Preskill, 2001; Preskill et al., 2003; Thomas, 2001).

Quality   Quality is measured by looking at the psychometric properties (i.e., reliability, validity and use) of the instruments used to collect data. It also is expected that evaluation data will be used for formative rather than summative reasons as school evaluation is seen as closely related to the school improvement process (Kyriakides, 2005b; Hopkins, 1989).

Differentiation   Finally, the differentiation dimension is measured by looking at the extent to which the school places a greater emphasis on conducting evaluation for specific aspects/reasons of the policy for teaching. This is especially relevant to those aspects which refer to the major weaknesses of the school. For example, if policy on homework is considered problematic the school may decide to collect data for homework more often and in greater depth instead of collecting data for any other aspect of school policy for teaching.

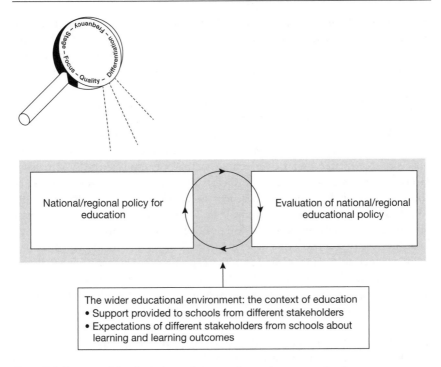

Figure 2.5 Factors of the dynamic model operating at the context level.

D) System level factors

The dynamic model does not refer to all of the characteristics of an educational system which reveal variations in the operation of the educational systems around the world. For example, the dynamic model does not refer to the structure of the system but to aspects of the national policy that affect learning inside and outside the classroom. This assumption is based on international studies and meta-analyses of comparative studies which suggest that the effectiveness of an educational system cannot be attributed to whether it is a centralised or a decentralised system (see Fullan, 2001; Kyriakides & Charalambous, 2005; Schmidt, Jakwerth, & McKnight, 1998; Schmidt & Valverde, 1995). Thus, the definition of the system level is based on the assumption that factors at the system level are expected to have not only direct effects on student achievement but also mainly indirect effects. System factors are expected to influence the school and/or classroom level factors, especially the teaching practice and the SLE (see Figure 2.5).

Thus, the first overarching system level factor refers to the national educational policy on teaching practice and the SLE. Policy is expected to not only directly affect teaching practice and the SLE but also indirectly through encouragement of schools to develop their own policies. As in the case of the school level, actions taken for improving national policy in relation to the teaching and the learning environment of the schools are also taken into account. Moreover, the term policy guidelines is used in a more broad way to indicate a variety of documents sent to schools by the context/system level. These documents highlight the meaning of the national/regional policy and what teachers and other stakeholders are expected to do.

The evaluation mechanism of the national educational policy may also contribute to the improvement of the national policy (Mintrop & Trujillo, 2007; Yeh, 2009). Therefore, through this, it may also contribute to the improvement of educational effectiveness. Thus, the evaluation of national policy is also treated as an overarching factor operating at the system level. However, an essential difference to factors operating at the school level is the consideration of the wider environment of education. Specifically, the wider educational environment of a country or a region and its ability to increase opportunities for learning and develop positive values for learning is considered as an important context/system level factor. This is due to the fact that it is acknowledged that student learning is not expected to only take place in schools but also in the wider school community. Thus, the dynamic model refers to the most important factors operating at the system level that may affect achievement. Emphasis is given to the:

a) National policy and the actions taken to improve the quality of teaching and the School Learning Environment (SLE)
b) Evaluation of the national educational policy
c) Wider educational environment of a country and especially its ability to increase opportunities for learning and develop positive values for learning.

National policy for education with consequences for actions taken for improving teaching and the learning environment of the school

The first overarching context level factor refers to the national education policy in relation to teaching and aspects associated with the learning environment of the school. As far as the national policy on teaching is concerned, the factor refers to the same three aspects which are included in the relevant school-level factors (i.e., quantity of teaching, provision of learning opportunities, and quality of teaching).

In the case of the *quantity* of teaching, national policy/regulations concerned with the timetable of the school, the long-term and short-term planning, and the policy on absenteeism and drop-out levels, are considered. In an effective educational system, these regulations will ensure that the quantity of teaching is kept to a maximum level, or even provide support to the schools to keep it to a maximum level (Levin, 2010). As far as the *quality* of teaching is concerned, educational systems may develop standards for teaching to ensure that teaching practice is in line with each of the eight classroom-level factors (van der Schaaf & Stokking, 2011). Alternatively, educational systems may build teacher evaluation policy in such a way that the criteria for teacher evaluation refer to the quality of teaching in relation to the eight classroom-level factors of the dynamic model.

Finally, national policy on provision of learning opportunities is associated with the policy on the national curriculum. This aspect of the first overarching factor is also concerned with policy-makers' attempts to support/encourage students, teachers and schools to undertake extracurricular activities which contribute to the achievement of the aims of the curriculum - for example, encouraging students and schools to participate in competitions, or encouraging participation in action research projects attempting to help students to achieve curricular aims.

As it has been mentioned above, the second aspect of this factor is concerned with the national education policy and its consequences for improving the learning environment of the schools. It also considers actions taken by the policy makers for improving the learning environment of the schools. Specifically, the second aspect of this factor may refer to the provision of guidelines/rules and the establishment of strategies that may:

a) Support collaboration of teachers within a school (e.g., by giving teachers free time to use for co-ordination
b) Help schools establish networks to support each other
c) Encourage schools to use specific partnership types in order to improve their effectiveness
d) Provide suggestions on how schools can treat student misbehaviour outside and inside the classroom (e.g., how to deal with bullying).

The educational system is also expected to provide resources to schools for improving their learning environment (Spencer, Noll, & Cassidy, 2000). These could refer to the financial support that is provided to the schools and/or to other types of support associated to learning such as the provision of:

a) In-service training to the school staff which is not only expected to help teachers to improve their teaching practice but may also refer to strategies that can be used to improve the SLE
b) School advisory systems which may provide support to schools in improving teaching practice and their SLE
c) Textbooks, teaching aids, and other learning resources.

Evaluation of national educational policy

The second overarching system/context level factor is concerned with the evaluation mechanisms that each educational system may establish in order to collect data about the appropriateness of its national policy. Evaluation data of other actions taken by policy-makers for improving teaching and the SLE could also be collected. The measurement of this factor is done in a way very similar to the two relevant school level factors concerning the evaluation of the school policy.

The wider educational environment: The context of education

The wider educational environment of a country and its ability to increase opportunities and develop positive values for learning is considered as an important system level factor (Bamburg, 1994; Lee & Smith, 1999). The dynamic model concentrates on two aspects of the wider educational environment which are expected to influence learning. First, the support provided to schools from different stakeholders (e.g., church, companies, universities, educational researchers, institutions responsible for providing support/advice/in-service training to schools) is examined. However, we are not only concerned with the financial support which different stakeholders provide to schools (Hanushek, 1986). Support provided to schools may also refer to strategies/advice offered to schools which may help them improve their teaching practice or establish better learning environments (e.g., help them establish better relations among teachers and/or between teachers and students; help them identify ways to treat student misbehaviour outside and inside the classroom; support their attempts to undertake extra curricular activities that are related to the official aims of the curriculum).

The second aspect of this overarching factor refers to the expectations of different stakeholders (e.g., employers, policy-makers, parents, and public) from schools about learning and learning outcomes. These expectations may result in achievement press and, through that, in student achievement gains (Valverde & Schmidt, 2000). The importance of the second aspect of this overarching factor is justified by the results of a secondary analysis of PISA 2000 data (from 32 countries, 4,159 schools, and 97,384 students). This analysis revealed that the PISA index of 'achievement press' aggregated at the country level is associated with student achievement (Kyriakides & Demetriou, 2006). This implies that the schools of most effective countries are driven by a quest for academic excellence. Although further empirical evidence to support the generalisability of this finding is needed, the fact that this factor, and not any other contextual factor measured by the PISA study (e.g., the average SES of students), was found to be associated with student achievement should be emphasised.

Empirical evidence supporting the dynamic model

Some supportive material for the validity of the dynamic model at the classroom and school level has been provided. Specifically, a longitudinal study measuring teacher and school effectiveness in three different subjects (i.e., mathematics, Greek language, and religious education) was conducted in order to test the main assumptions of the model (Kyriakides & Creemers, 2008). Using Structural Equation Modelling (SEM) techniques, it was possible to demonstrate that classroom and school factors can be defined by reference to the five dimensions of the dynamic model (see Kyriakides & Creemers, 2008; Creemers & Kyriakides, 2010b). The added value of using these five dimensions of the classroom and school level factors to explain variation on student achievement in both cognitive and affective outcomes of schooling was also demonstrated. Specifically, taking into account the combination of frequency dimension with other dimensions of teacher and school factors increases the explained variance on student achievement.

Some factors were found to have no statistically significant effect on student achievement by measuring the impact of their frequency dimension but had a significant impact on student achievement when other dimensions were taken into account. Finally, it was possible to generate evidence supporting the assumption that the impact of school factors depends on the current situation of the school and on the type of problems/difficulties that the school is facing. Specifically, school factors were found to have situational effects. The development of a school policy for teaching and the evaluation of school policy for teaching were found to have stronger effects in schools where the quality of teaching at classroom level was low (Creemers & Kyriakides, 2009).

Second, a study investigating the impact of teacher factors on achievement of Cypriot students at the end of pre-primary school was conducted (Kyriakides & Creemers, 2009). By comparing the results of this study with the findings of the first study testing the validity of the model, similarities and differences in effective teaching of two different subjects (mathematics and Greek language) and at two different phases of schooling (pre-primary and primary education) were identified. This comparison revealed that almost all teacher factors were associated with achievement in language and mathematics at both phases of schooling (see Kyriakides & Creemers, 2009). Some factors were also found to be more important for one age of schooling. This indicates the possibility of different factors having differential effects. For the purpose of testing the generic nature of the model, this difference does not question the importance of teacher factors within the model. These differences in effect sizes might be attributed to differences in the developmental stages of the two groups of students and related that to the functioning and the curriculum of each phase of schooling. Therefore, the assumption that factors included in the dynamic model are generic was mainly supported.

The validity of the dynamic model at the school level was supported by the results of a quantitative synthesis of 67 studies exploring the impact of school factors on student achievement (Kyriakides, Creemers, Antoniou, & Demetriou, 2010). This meta-analysis revealed that effective schools are able to develop policies and take actions in order to improve their teaching practice and their learning environment. Moreover, factors excluded from the dynamic model were found to be weakly associated with student achievement.

A follow-up study testing the validity of the dynamic model was conducted during the school year 2008-2009 (Creemers & Kyriakides, 2010a). The methods used were identical to those followed by the original study testing the validity of the model. This study provided support to the generalisability of the original study. Very similar results on the impact of teacher and school factors upon student achievement emerged from both the original and the follow-up study. Since the follow-up study took place in the same schools where the original study took place, changes in the effectiveness status of schools and in the functioning of effectiveness factors were also identified.

Discriminant function analysis reveals that changes in the functioning of some school factors, and in the quality of teaching practice, can help classify the schools into those which managed to improve their effectiveness status or remained equally effective or even reduced their effectiveness status (see Creemers & Kyriakides, 2010a). Thus, this study was able to test one of the essential differences of the dynamic model. This is an attempt to relate changes in the effectiveness status of schools to the changes in the functioning of school factors.

A re-analysis of the original and the follow-up study testing the validity of the model was conducted. This identified whether school factors included in the dynamic model were associated with student progress in different learning outcomes (i.e., the quality dimension of educational effectiveness). It also explored the extent to which teachers and schools manage to reduce unjustifiable differences in student outcomes (i.e., the equity dimension of effectiveness). Separate multi-level analyses for each subject were conducted and it was found that the effectiveness status of schools does not change significantly when the two dimensions (equity and quality) are used to measure their effectiveness status in each subject. Changes in their effectiveness status in terms of each dimension of measuring effectiveness were also examined. In each subject, schools which were found to improve their effectiveness status in terms of the equity dimension were also found to improve their effectiveness status in terms of the quality dimension. Moreover, schools which were found to improve their effectiveness status in terms of one dimension were also found to decline their effectiveness in terms of the other dimension of effectiveness. It is important to note that some factors were not only associated with student achievement gains, but were also found to explain variation of the school impact on the reduction of the initial achievement gap. Specifically, two dimensions of the school policy for teaching factors (i.e., stage and differentiation), the quality dimension of the two school evaluation factors (evaluation of school policy for teaching and evaluation of SLE), and two dimensions (quality and differentiation) of the two aspects of the SLE factor (i.e., collaboration among teachers and use of resources) could be considered generic. Both studies reveal that they can explain variation of school effectiveness in each subject. By taking into account specific dimensions of all school level factors are associated with both student achievement gains and reduction of initial achievement gaps, it could be claimed that schools can make use of the model for promoting both quality and equity in education.

A longitudinal study was conducted to explore whether the dynamic model could be expanded at the school level by introducing the concept of school policy in action (Kyriakides & Demetriou, 2010). In this way, not only the policy at the school level is examined but also the actions of teachers in regard to their school policy are taken into account. This study revealed the need to investigate not only the content of the school policy but also the extent to which the stakeholders of a school act in accordance with the guidelines of the school policy. Cluster analysis revealed that there were schools which managed to develop appropriate policy on teaching and their SLE, but their teachers did not implement their school policy.

There were also two cluster groups which had completely opposite results meaning that they did not develop any policy on teaching and SLE but their teachers took initiatives and actions in order to improve their teaching practice and their SLE. However, neither of the two cluster groups consisted of schools which can be considered as among the most effective schools. On the other hand, almost all schools which managed to get high scores both in the policy and in the action scales were among the most effective schools. These results provide support for the importance of investigating the *school policy in action* factor rather than looking at either the school policy only or the actions that teachers take. In addition, it was demonstrated that the school policy in action factor has a larger effect size on student achievement than the school policy factor. For this reason, in this book we do not only refer to the school policy factors but also provide suggestions to schools on how to take actions to ensure that teachers implement the policy and evaluate more systematically the functioning of the school factors for improvement purposes (see Part C).

The above studies provide support for the main characteristics and assumptions of the dynamic model. However, comparative studies are needed to find out whether the factors of the model are associated with student achievement in different countries. International studies may also provide evidence about the effects of the system level factors. This may help develop a better understanding of the characteristics of effective educational systems.

A comparative study was conducted investigating the importance of grouping teacher factors into stages of teaching (Janosz, Archambault, & Kyriakides, 2011). Seven primary schools in the suburb area of Montreal (Canada) participated in the study and its results were compared with the previously mentioned studies'. The study in Canada provided further support to the assumption of the dynamic model that teacher level factors are interrelated and should not be treated as isolated. Moreover, it was demonstrated that the use of specific ways to describe not only quantitative but also qualitative characteristics of these factors help us to classify teaching skills into types of teacher behaviour. The four types of behaviour emerged from this study are similar to the five levels identified by the study conducted in Cyprus. However, skills associated with the differentiation of teaching were not found to belong to a separate level. It is finally important to note that this study can be seen as a step towards the development of a comparative research programme searching for stages of teaching skills by using the dynamic model as a theoretical framework (see also Chapters 7 and 8).

In this chapter, the theoretical background of the proposed improvement approach and the factors included in the dynamic model was presented. Further, evidence collected on the importance of the factors of the model and its essential characteristics have been provided. These bring us into to question whether the dynamic approach can also be used for improvement purposes. Thus, in the next chapter, we show which strategies for school improvement are promoted by the dynamic model and how the model can be used for improvement purposes.

Chapter 3

The dynamic approach to school improvement

Introduction

In the previous chapter, the dynamic model was presented and evidence supporting its validity was provided. One of the studies testing its validity revealed that schools which are among the most effective cannot remain so over a long period of time, unless effort is made to further improve the functioning of school factors (Creemers & Kyriakides, 2010a). It was also shown that improvement in the functioning of school factors is associated with improvement of the effectiveness status of schools. These findings are in line with the attempt of the dynamic model to demonstrate the dynamic nature of effectiveness. Given that the dynamic model was developed in order to establish stronger links between EER and improvement of practice, in this chapter we show how the dynamic model can be used in policy and practice for improvement purposes. Thus, the Dynamic Approach to School Improvement (DASI) is presented. Specifically, we refer to strategies that can be used by different stakeholders who are planning to make use of DASI to improve practice at different levels.

Before we move on to presenting DASI, it is stressed that the improvement efforts should be based at the school level and that these can be undertaken from stakeholders who support the idea that schools should always search for improvement, irrespective of how effective they are. School stakeholders are expected to look at the relations between the school factors and the aims of their specific improvement project. This implies that school stakeholders should make use of the literature associated with the aims of the specific improvement project and merge the findings of this research area with the value assumptions and essential characteristics of the dynamic model. This is feasible as the model is flexible enough and able to incorporate evidence stemming from different research areas (knowledge and discipline). Yet equally it has its own assumptions which deal with quality of teaching and the school learning environment, that are supported by evidence (see Chapter 2) and should be taken into account when establishing improvement strategies and action plans.

In this chapter, the main steps of the dynamic approach to school improvement are presented. It is shown that these steps can be followed by stakeholders operating at different levels of the educational system such as the classroom, the school and the context level. This is due to the fact that in the dynamic model, the factors operating at different levels are able to influence the quality of the school learning environment, the quality of teaching, and the learning and its outcomes. Before we introduce these steps, the conditions under which this approach can be applied are discussed. First, it is important to stress that schools in most countries are under pressure for improvement. External evaluation through school inspection or through the announcement of student results is expected to impose change. The various accountability systems which have been developed are based on the assumption that the announcement of the results of a summative evaluation will induce improvement efforts by schools, especially for those with relatively low performance (Reynolds, 1996; Murphy, 2009). However, the proposed approach is not based on this assumption for several reasons. First, studies testing the validity of the model reveal that improvement efforts should take place in all schools irrespective of how effective they are (see Chapter 2). For example, it has been shown that schools which were among the most effective and did not take any action to improve the functioning of their school factors dropped to average effectiveness. Second, the dynamic model focuses not only on the school policy, but also on the actions taken to improve this policy, as factors associated with student achievement and recent studies reveal that actions taken to improve teaching and the school learning environment are strongly associated with the outcomes of schooling. Third, the assumption that having an accountability system will make schools more effective has already been contradicted by evaluation studies showing that schools which were found to be among the least effective did not manage to improve their status simply because of the pressure placed upon them (Murphy, 2009; Good et al., 2010).

On the contrary, the dynamic approach to school improvement proposed in this book is based on the assumption that not all schools are equally effective, and therefore that the same improvement strategy should not be used for all in order to help them improve their effectiveness. For example, schools which are among the most effective and have in place their own mechanisms for improving the functioning of their school factors may not necessarily need external support to develop their School Self Evaluation mechanisms, design their strategies and action plans for improvement. On the other hand, those schools which are among the least effective may need external support and more systematic guidance to establish strategies and action plans to improve their effectiveness status. At the same time, it should be acknowledged that for each of these groups of schools, different priorities for improvement can be identified. Even for schools which are amongst the most effective, there is still space for improvement of some factors associated with effectiveness and there remains a need to identify priorities, develop strategies and actions plans. In order to achieve this aim, external support may be required. The proposed approach takes into account the dynamic nature of educational effectiveness and supports that different improvement strategies should be used from schools, depending on the knowledge, experiences and aims that are addressed, but also that improvement strategies must be based on evidence.

Each school is expected to develop its own strategies and action plans for improvement, but it is acknowledged that support to schools should also be offered by an Advisory and Research Team (A&R Team), which is able to provide technical expertise and the available knowledge-base on improvement of factors addressed by the school. Although a school is treated as a professional community responsible for designing and implementing its own improvement strategies and action plans, school stakeholders are not left alone to design and implement their strategies and actions, but are encouraged to make use not only of the A&R Team, but also of other available resources within and outside of the school. For example, schools who may develop strategies and action plans to deal with bullying could ask for support from not only the A&R Team, who will help identify improvement priorities and develop such strategies, but also from researchers and clinical psychologists with experience of bullying incidents, who may also help them to deal with specific students that need special treatment. Therefore, a systematic research based approach to design, implement, and evaluate improvement efforts is promoted by DASI. Finally, it is important to note that school stakeholders should be encouraged to treat the challenges and/or problems that their school is facing as a chance for them to define new goals of schooling and to develop strategies to improve the functioning of those factors included in the dynamic model that will help them achieve these new goals. In this way, if a problem occurs school stakeholders can deal with it by identifying the aims associated with the problem. For example, if a dramatic increase in bullying incidents is identified, stakeholders may need to develop their school policy on teaching to promote the achievement of aims, which may not be directly promoted by the official curriculum (e.g. understanding of social values, emotional recognition, developing positive attitudes towards the school). In order to meet these new aims and deal with the new challenge they are facing, it may therefore be important for stakeholders to improve their school policy on teaching, especially the aspect concerned with the provision of learning opportunities and adopt their improvement strategies and action plans (see Chapter 5).

Major steps for effective school improvement

In the introductory part of this chapter, we discuss the main conditions upon which the dynamic approach to school improvement is based. In this section, the major steps expected to be followed by schools are presented. These are further explored in the second and third part of the book, where we refer to concrete examples of improvement projects that made use of this approach. In these parts, we also provide evidence which show that DASI had a significant impact on the improvement of school effectiveness.

A) Establishing clarity and consensus about the general aims of school improvement by considering student learning as the main function of the school

The first step of any school improvement effort is based on the assumption that it is important to start with a clear understanding of the destination and how improvement of quality in education will be achieved. This could be considered as 'a purposeful task analysis' (Wiggins & McTighe, 1998, p.8), which suggests a planning sequence. Moreover, commitment to collaborative work needs to be established, however as Fullan (2001) emphasises, people have different perceptions of change. Thus, it is difficult to reach consensus among the participants in school reform efforts, albeit a crucial agreement. Therefore, it is important to establish procedures to ensure clear understanding among stakeholders as to the aims of school improvement. At this very first stage of the dynamic approach to school improvement, two major issues are discussed with the school stakeholders. First, this approach is based on the assumption that student learning should be considered as the ultimate aim of any school improvement effort. Unless learning and learning outcomes are improved, any school improvement effort should not be considered successful no mater how much it may manage to improve any aspect of the climate of the school or any other factor which is not related with student learning. This is due to the fact that learning is the mission of the school and emphasis should be placed on improving learning outcomes.

At this point, presenting the DASI to school stakeholders can assist with the realisation that the ultimate aim of any school reform effort should be to improve student achievement across the school and thereby improve the effectiveness status of their school, in terms of both quality and equity dimensions. Presenting the dynamic approach may also help school stakeholders design improvement programmes for a single school, building relevant School Self Evaluation (SSE) mechanisms, or even to design an improvement project for a network of schools which is supported by a central agency (e.g. a Local Education Authority or a professional association, such as the association of teachers of mathematics). Specifically, the model may assist school stakeholders to define not only the ultimate aim of the school improvement effort, which should be concerned with the improvement of learning outcomes, but also its intermediate objectives which may contribute in the achievement of aims associated with the challenges that they are facing (e.g. reduction of bullying incidents, reduction of school drop-outs). Since the dynamic approach is based on the dynamic model which refers to factors that are changeable and associated with student learning outcomes, the intermediate objectives should also address the needs of schools to improve the functioning of specific factors included in the dynamic model (see step B).

In presenting the dynamic approach to school improvement, it is likely that not every school teacher will agree or commit himself/herself to the school improvement project. Although the approach promoted in this book gives emphasis to the involvement of the whole-school community, it is not feasible to expect that all individual members of the school community will participate in the improvement project. However, it is critical at this point that a sufficient number of teachers (key persons) agree with the main aim and the intermediate objectives of the improvement project and are willing to participate by offering their time and energy for the successful implementation of the project. Commitment to the implementation of the project by both the school community and the research advisory team must be established before moving on to the second step of this approach, which is concerned with the identification of school priorities for improvement.

B) Establishing clarity and consensus about the aims of school improvement by addressing school factors that are able to influence learning and teaching

Adopting the dynamic model extends beyond providing support to school stakeholders in the design of improvement programmes, by establishing a theory driven approach to school improvement. This implies that school stakeholders should attempt to build whole school reform efforts with the potential to improve functioning of the school level factors included in the model. Despite inclusion of factors which operate at different levels within the dynamic model, school level factors are expected to have both direct and indirect effects on student learning outcomes. As mentioned in Chapter 2, school level factors are expected to influence not only student achievement, but also the functioning of classroom level factors (see Figure 2.1). Therefore, designing improvement efforts focusing on the classroom level factors may improve the teaching practice of individuals, yet may not necessarily improve the school learning environment. In such cases, teachers who improve aspects of their teaching practice addressed by a specific improvement effort will require, at some stage, another type of support to improve other teaching skills. However, if the reform does not aim to improve the school learning environment, such support may be unavailable when required and the lasting effect of a programme that aims to improve teaching practice could be questioned. Equally, the dynamic model is based on the assumption that school stakeholders should develop interventions or improvement efforts, which will not only improve the functioning of the school level factors, but ultimately will promote quality of teaching and raise student achievement. Therefore the dynamic model supports the use of a theory driven approach to school improvement, which gives emphasis to improving teaching practice and attempts to do so not through directly influencing teaching practice, but rather indirectly by improving the functioning of school level factors. In this way, it is not only learning opportunities that are offered to teachers, but also conditions that enable continuous improvement of teaching practice. Therefore, a school improvement effort is focused on how to improve the functioning of factors operating at the school level and through this notion to improve teaching practice and promote student learning and learning outcomes.

In order to elaborate further on this point, readers are reminded that the two main overarching school factors are concerned with the school policy for teaching and the school learning environment yet, the model does not only refer to these. Actions taken to improve these two aspects of school policy are viewed as characteristics of effective schools. This implies that schools cannot remain effective unless actions are taken to improve the teaching practice and their learning environment. This is an essential characteristic of the model which highlights its dynamic nature. Thus, the school effect is considered a set of ongoing processes in which both schools and teachers fall along a set continuum of development (e.g. Creemers & Kyriakides, 2008b; Slater & Teddlie, 1992; Teddlie & Reynolds, 2000). Since schools and their effectiveness status do not remain stable, research on improvement efforts and evaluation mechanisms, as well as research on school effectiveness, should be developed in such a way that relevant changes in activities can take place continuously. But in order to study change over time, it is also necessary to study teachers and schools longitudinally (i.e. over the course of multiple years). The dynamic model reflects this, not only in the use of 'stage' as a measurement of effectiveness factors (see Chapter 2), but also in its conceptualisation of effectiveness factors at the school and education levels. More specifically, the capacity of schools/educational systems to improve their policy of teaching and of the school learning environment is considered to be an essential characteristic for effectiveness. Therefore, the assumption that effectiveness is a stable characteristic of a school over time is not promoted by the dynamic model. On the contrary, fluctuations in results over time may reflect 'real' improvement or decline in school/teacher performance, as well as any random variations. Changes in results may be explained by planned or naturally occurring school/teacher improvement, or by stable school policies and teacher practices in a changing context, or by both.

Effective schooling is seen as a dynamic, ongoing process. Therefore, to be considered effective, schools/educational systems are expected to adapt with the changing contexts. Similarly, ineffective schools may be encouraged by the community and local school boards to improve. This notion is consistent with the contingency theory (Donaldson, 2001; Mintzberg, 1979) and can be viewed as one of the main assumptions upon which the dynamic model is based (see Chapter 2). Therefore, the dynamic model presents the process of improving effectiveness as one that should take place in all schools, irrespective of how effective they are. Moreover, it implies that schools which are among the most effective should take action to remain so and that such actions should have a direct effect on improving teaching and the SLE (Creemers & Kyriakides, 2010a).

Therefore presenting the dynamic model, particularly its school level factors, can assist school stakeholders' understanding of the necessity of developing a SSE mechanism, which will attempt to collect data about each factor and its dimensions. In this way, school stakeholders are not only aware of the factors that need to be addressed, they further understand that addressing them can help achieve better learning outcomes. By following this approach, the authors take into account that schools should not only make use of evidence emerging from EER, but also understand the processes through which learning can be achieved in classrooms, schools and externally. For example, factors concerned with school policy on teaching expect all stakeholders (teachers, parents and students) to ensure that the use of teaching time is maximised, that extra-curricular learning opportunities are offered to students and that teaching quality is improved. Although specific aspects of these factors may be more relevant for some stakeholders than others, it is necessary to involve each of them in an improvement strategy and for this reason partnership policy has a central role in the dynamic model (see Chapter 2). Resultantly, the teachers and other school stakeholders involved in the project should be persuaded that the factors included in the model are associated with learning and learning outcomes, and need to be addressed in order to improve the effectiveness of their schools, which was stated as the main aim of school improvement (see step A). It is also important to stress that not all factors can be addressed at once and that specific improvement priorities should be identified instead, to aid the development of a more systematic and focused intervention. Thus, at this point data should be collected with a view to identifying priorities for improvement, which will concern factor(s) that are not functioning at a satisfactory level. The next step therefore is concerned with the collection of evaluation data and the identification of improvement priorities.

C) Collecting evaluation data and identifying priorities for improvement

The use of a valid theory to design an improvement effort cannot in itself ensure that its aims will be achieved, even if the proposed reform is implemented in the way it was designed (Kyriakides, Charalambous, Philippou, & Campbell, 2006). In this chapter, the authors do not only argue for following a theory-driven approach for improving school quality, as emphasis is also placed on collecting data in order to identify the strengths and weaknesses of a school and design relevant improvement efforts. The importance of using an evidence-based approach for school improvement reflects the nature of the dynamic model by treating school policy, teaching and the SLE as important overarching school level factors to be evaluated. Therefore, the definition of factors at the school and classroom level, especially their five measurement dimensions, can be used first for designing instruments that will help schools collect data about the functioning of these factors. Research instruments of studies investigating the validity of the dynamic model (Kyriakides & Creemers, 2008) can be found in part C of this book. The strengths and weaknesses of schools will be identified based on the results that emerge from measuring the functioning of the school and classroom level factors. Moreover stakeholders may identify priorities for improving the functioning of specific factors and/or grouping of factors. At this point readers are reminded that, according to the dynamic model, each factor is defined in relation to five dimensions. This implies that evaluation data may reveal more than one improvement priority for each school. For example, using these five dimensions to measure the quality of teaching at teacher or school level could produce different teaching profiles which are associated with student achievement, as at least one empirical study has demonstrated (Antoniou, Creemers, & Kyriakides, 2009).

Therefore, using the dynamic model to collect data on teacher behaviour in the classroom will reveal the extent to which their teaching practices fit these profiles and whether specific changes to their practices are needed to develop a more effective profile. For example, teachers may discover that the effectiveness of a group of teachers is limited due to the fact that:

a) they do not use enough teaching modelling activities that could assist students in using or developing strategies for solving problems
b) the great majority of the orientation tasks they offer are at the introduction of the lesson.

The identification of more than one weakness may not be helpful for ascertaining how one can develop professionally, however due to the dynamic nature of the model, different professional development priorities for each teacher may be identified. This is due to the effects of an improved factor on student outcomes, depending on the stage at which each individual teacher is when measurement occurs (Creemers & Kyriakides, 2009). Thus a teacher who attempts to improve her/his own orientation skills may result in improving student outcomes more than improving her/his own skills in teaching modelling. Yet a completely different interpretation could be drawn for another teacher, by focusing on the situation at which she/he is at that time. Following this approach, actions taken to improve teaching may prove more flexible, as the support provided to individual teachers may differ in order to meet the professional needs of each, or for each group of teachers in a school, or a network of schools.

School stakeholders may draw similar conclusions when using the dynamic model to collect data on the functioning of the overarching school factors concerned with the SLE. Thus, the priorities of school improvement efforts concerned with either teaching or the SLE must be considered in relation to the current situation of the specific schools and teachers involved. The authors could even provide similar suggestions to policy makers and other external school advisors who are planning to use the dynamic model, in order to develop a theory-driven and evidence-based approach in their attempt to improve the quality of education. Specifically, policy makers and other stakeholders are expected to conduct large-scale evaluation studies to collect data concerned with the five dimensions of the dynamic model, since emergent data will assist them in designing a reform effort likely to improve the quality of education. Moreover, since some of the effectiveness factors are expected to have a curvilinear relationship with student achievement, the impact of an intervention programme that attempts to improve a specific aspect of teaching practice will depend on the current situation of the objects under consideration (i.e. students, classrooms, schools, system). Therefore, data collected through these studies may facilitate policy-makers' identification of the dimensions constituting the major weaknesses of the system, and subsequently assist the design of relevant intervention programmes which aim to improve the quality of education (see Chapter 4).

By the end of this step, data on the functioning of school factors will be available and analysis of data will reveal which factors or grouping of factors need to be addressed. By presenting the results of the evaluation to the various stakeholders the improvement priorities of the school are made clear, and all stakeholders should be in a position to acknowledge that improvement of learning will be achieved by commitment to the improvement of relevant factor(s). In the next step, strategies and action plans to address these priorities should be developed. In order to achieve this aim, school stakeholders should make use of available evidence, providing guidelines and suggestions on how the functioning of these factors can be improved.

D) Designing school improvement strategies and action plans by considering the available knowledge-base about the factor(s) addressed

The dynamic model refers to school factors which were found to be associated with student achievement. For each of these factors a number of studies and meta-analyses have been conducted, which do not only look at the impact of the factor, but also refer to the conditions under which these factors have stronger effects. Consequently, the dynamic model refers to qualitative characteristics of the functioning of factors which increase their impact on learning. For example, the factor concerned with the school partnership policy takes into account the varying types of parental involvement that occur in different schools, and shows under which conditions each type of involvement is effective (see Chapter 2). Similarly, policy on homework is treated as an important aspect of the overarching factor concerned with policy on teaching. When developing school policy, issues arising from the literature need to be taken into account, for example the type of homework that should be assigned to students and the need to correct homework. Schools should therefore draw lessons from the literature on the factors that are addressed, and develop their strategies and action plans accordingly.

At this point, the role of the research advisory team is considered to be essential. Members of this team should be able to share their expertise and knowledge with school stakeholders, providing additional input to existing ideas, experiences and knowledge in order to develop their strategies and action plans. Although the action plans were initially developed by school stakeholders, members of the research advisory team should provide schools with guidelines of how to improve the functioning of the factors. Whilst the research advisory team is expected to provide suggestions based on the research evidence, it is the schools themselves that decide on the content of their action plans, having considered the available research evidence and evaluation data (step C). The authors stress that effective policies are not only those which are clear to the stakeholders and address their needs, but also take into account the ability of the stakeholders to implement the policy (see Chapter 2). For this reason the final decision is taken by the school, as development of action plans does not only require putting into practice what is available in the literature, but also adapting the guidelines to the needs and abilities of the stakeholders of each school. In developing action plans it is important to specify which tasks need to be undertaken, who is going to be responsible for implementing each task, when each task is expected to be implemented and which resources should be provided to the stakeholders to implement these tasks (see part C). In several cases, some parts of the action plans cannot be implemented and unless evaluation data is collected, the school stakeholders will not take decisions on how to improve their action plans and resultantly the aims of the school improvement project will not be achieved. Therefore school stakeholders should not only develop strategies and action plans which they are ready to implement, but should also attempt to establish evaluation mechanisms which will enable them to improve their action plans.

E) Monitoring the implementation of the improvement project through establishing formative evaluation mechanisms

At this step, school stakeholders are expected to develop internal evaluation mechanisms to monitor the progress of their improvement efforts. A developmental evaluation strategy should be produced and the formative aim of school evaluation should be achieved for schools to identify how their action plans can be improved. The role of the research advisory team is important, as their expertise in conducting evaluation is shared with school stakeholders. However, the DASI is based on the assumption that school stakeholders should be directly involved in conducting formative evaluation. Thereby, an internal school evaluation mechanism is developed and teachers are encouraged to reflect on their abilities, not just to implement, but also to improve the functioning of school factors. Thus, the results emerging from this evaluation mechanism can be used to improve action plans, and simultaneously to create an environment which supports the gathering of evidence for improvement purposes. Such a setting is necessary for building self-evaluation mechanisms, both at the individual (i.e. teacher self-evaluation) and school level.

The dynamic model is based on the assumption that stakeholders should be able to establish a developmental evaluation strategy, in their attempt to improve the effectiveness status of their schools. According to the dynamic model, school evaluation is treated as an overarching school factor comprised of stages, which implies that a continuous model of school evaluation will allow schools to adapt their own policy decisions based on the needs of different groups of school stakeholders (see Creemers & Kyriakides, 2010a). Thus, the dynamic model supports the notion that a developmental evaluation strategy may contribute to the improvement of the effectiveness status of schools, which has been supported through substantial research evidence (Kyriakides, 2008; Gray et al. 1999; Shaw & Replogle, 1996).

For example, a developmental evaluation strategy of school policy and of the actions taken to improve the relations of school with parents can be used. In such cases, the evaluation process is expected to follow a linear sequence that starts with the development of a plan for school policy on partnership, from which priorities and targets will emerge with associated performance indicators. At the next stage, evaluation questions arising from the targets and performance indicators will be established, which will provide the criteria for data collection. Subsequently, the data will be analysed and fed back into the formative process of evaluation. In this way, stakeholders will be informed of what is happening during the implementation of the school policy on partnership.

This strategy for improving effectiveness has a number of significant features. The evaluation process is expected to assist the implementation and development of a school policy, as the establishment of targets and performance indicators may specify the developmental process of the partnership policy. Moreover evaluation data may be related, through the evaluation questions, to the aims of the policy. Consequently, a logical chain of action can be established that relates aims to targets, evaluation questions, and particular information sources. However, the evaluation process is likely to be more complex in practice than its linear presentation here. Once the evaluation process is underway, different working groups of stakeholders (e.g. co-ordinators of partnership policy, teachers of different subjects) may implement areas of the policy at differing rates (Kyriakides, 2005b). The extent to which there is a difference between the implementation of a reform policy and the design of an intervention will be identified. Thus, the results of formative evaluation may assist stakeholders' decisions for improving the quality of their strategies and action plans for improvement, and eventually the functioning of school factors. The school-level factors included in the dynamic model are based on evidence supporting the use of this strategy to improve effectiveness. Beyond this assumption, the model may also help stakeholders to establish targets and performance indicators and thereby specify the developmental process of designing and implementing their school improvement strategies and action plans.

As a result of establishing formative evaluation mechanisms and collecting data, school stakeholders can identify weaknesses in their action plans. Thus, decisions can be made on how these action plans can be improved. Exchange of ideas and experiences between stakeholders and the A&R Team is likely to help school stakeholders agree on how to improve their action plans, by taking into account the needs of those involved in each task and their ability to implement it. If extra support needs to be offered to those who are expected to implement some tasks of the school action plans, the A&R Team can give suggestions on the kind of support that could be provided. Again the authors stress that the final decision should be the responsibility of the school stakeholders, who are also expected to evaluate the implementation of the modified action plans for formative reasons, especially since it is likely that further weaknesses to the modified action plans may emerge. The establishment of formative evaluation mechanisms is considered important, as the use of the available knowledge-base to develop strategies and action plans does not necessarily result in a school's development of the perfect solution for improving the functioning of school factors. On the contrary, it is often taken for granted that the school stakeholders and the A&R Team are not in a position to predict all the possible obstacles that may arise during the implementation of the school action plans. Thus by building a continuous evaluation mechanism, schools can identify problems with their action plans and improve them further. Although school stakeholders may be able to effectively solve all problems that arise and not have to further develop their action plans resultantly, it is important to consider that the undertaken tasks will not necessarily remain the same throughout the project. According to the stage dimension of the dynamic model, actions associated with a factor need to be implemented over time, but these actions may not necessarily be the same (see Creemers & Kyriakides, 2010b).

F) Conduct a summative evaluation to measure the impact of DASI

At some stage, school stakeholders (with the support of the research advisory team) should measure the impact of their improvement efforts upon the improvement of the functioning of school factors and upon the learning outcomes (i.e. the intermediate and ultimate aims of improvement). The results of a summative evaluation will assist school stakeholders to determine whether it is worthwhile to implement the improvement project, at the expense of their effort. Positive findings of summative evaluations are expected to increase the commitment of a school to this approach. Announcement of the results may even serve to change the attitudes of stakeholders not actively involved in the project and encourage participation in a project that appears promising. Moreover, through summative evaluation the theory which provides the basis for the intervention can be tested, for example some schools may develop strategies and action plans concerned with specific school factors which aim to reduce drop out level. Summative evaluation does not only allow us to ascertain if the drop out level has reduced, it also tests the assumption that improvement of school factors has an impact on reducing drop out. Finally, those involved in a project using DASI are expected to consider the evidence and collection of data as essential issues in decision making. Therefore, summative evaluation is required in order to help school stakeholders make decisions on whether their project is worthwhile, or whether they should reconsider their strategies and action plans.

In order to conduct a summative evaluation of their improvement project, school stakeholders (with the support of the research advisory team) need to collect comparable data with those that emerge from step C, and evaluate their interventions by following a value-added assessment approach. At this point the research advisory team has an important role to play, as their members have relevant expertise and can design the summative evaluation, as well as analyse quantitative data using appropriate advanced techniques (Creemers, Kyriakides, & Sammons, 2010). First of all, the quality of the instruments used to collect data should be examined. This is because the construct validity of the instruments must be demonstrated for the impact of DASI to be evaluated. Evidence supporting the validity of the instruments and the reliability of the measures could be produced by the A&R Team, and the impact of DASI on different dependent variables should be examined. Although the figures that emerge from data analysis should be made available, not all of the statistical figures that emerge from using advanced quantitative techniques should be reported back to the schools by the A&R Team. This is due to the likelihood that school stakeholders will not have extensive expertise on the use of advanced quantitative research methods, and therefore only the main figures should be presented to a meeting of school stakeholders. For example, when a group randomisation study is conducted, evaluating the impact of DASI (see Chapters 4, 5 and 6) is important, not only for academic reasons, but also for aiding school stakeholders' understanding of the study. Such evaluation can assist the stakeholders' realisation that whilst the beginning of the intervention presented no statistically significant differences between the control and experimental groups, differences (in favour of the DASI group) were identified at the end of the intervention. Similarly, the A&R Team should present a SEM model that is likely to be used to test the theory upon which an intervention is based, without providing too much technical information. What is essential for the A&R Team is to find simple methods of explaining the interrelations between the variables associated with the intervention and the achievement of the intervention aims (direct and intermediate). For example in Chapter 5, the research team was required to develop and test a SEM model which was presented to school stakeholders to show that the DASI intervention influenced all final measures of the project (i.e. the two scales measuring bullying and the functioning of school factors). DASI was also shown to have both direct and indirect effects on the reduction of bullying. These results support the importance of using DASI to improve the quality of education.

Summative evaluation will not only help stakeholders measure the impact of their intervention, it will also test the theory upon which the intervention is based. Summative evaluation may also help school stakeholders to decide whether the factor(s) addressed have been substantially improved, and resultantly if a new priority for improvement and new action plans need to be developed. If a new priority is identified, school stakeholders (with the support of the A&R Team) should:

a) develop new action plans
b) give responsibilities to individual stakeholders for implementing them
c) establish monitoring mechanisms.

In some cases, the collection of further data may be required for the development of action plans, especially if factors other than those included in the dynamic model are associated with the achievement of the aims of the intervention.

Overview of the major steps of DASI

Figure 3.1 illustrates the steps of DASI. It is shown that school stakeholders and the A&R Team are expected to be actively involved in each step of DASI. Their ability to work together and exchange skills, expertise and experiences is critical to the success of the school improvement project. Readers can also see that the first two steps are concerned with the establishment of clarity and consensus about the aims of the school improvement project. Initially, the importance of promoting student learning is stressed (step A). Thus, school stakeholders and the A&R Team are expected to develop the general aim of their intervention by taking into account that promotion of student learning should be the ultimate aim of any intervention that takes place in schools. At the second step, the dynamic model and its factors are presented to the school stakeholders. This presentation will help them understand how and why addressing the school factors promotes student learning. Thus, the specific aims of their improvement project could be developed and the agenda of their school self evaluation can be defined. Specifically, Figure 3.1 shows that at the third step schools should develop their own school self evaluation mechanisms in order to collect and analyse data about the functioning of school factors and identify their priority area(s) for improvement. The fourth step is one of the most important steps of DASI. The A&R Team should work closely with the school stakeholders in order to help them define their strategies and action plans for improvement. School stakeholders are expected to take into account the available knowledge base of EER and adopt the guidelines emerged from the literature on their school context (with the help of the A&R Team) in order to improve the functioning of school factors addressed by their project. Then school stakeholders and the A&R Team should develop mechanisms for monitoring the implementation of the intervention (see step E). At this point, we stress the role of formative evaluation and the importance of using evaluation data to further develop their strategies and action plans. Finally, the A&R Team and the school stakeholders should develop summative evaluation mechanisms in order to measure the impact of DASI on promoting student learning. This step will not only help school stakeholders test the theory upon which their intervention is based but may also reveal the importance of identifying a new priority area for improvement. If summative evaluation reveals that a school has managed to substantially improve the functioning of the factor addressed, school stakeholders and the A&R Team may decide to collect new evaluation data and identify a new priority improvement area. By conducting school self evaluation (moving back to step C) the new priority area will be identified and a new improvement project will be developed and implemented. It can therefore

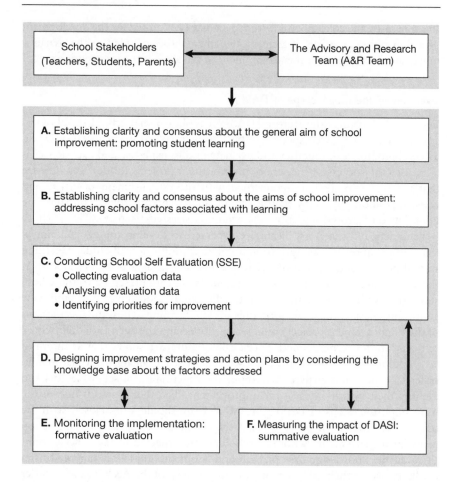

Figure 3.1 The major steps of the Dynamic Approach to School Improvement (DASI).

be claimed that the Figure 3.1 shows that schools should always search for improving their effectiveness status irrespective of how effective they are and this element of DASI is in line with the dynamic character of the nature of educational effectiveness.

Main conclusions emerging from the first part of the book

The main arguments emerging from the first part of the book are presented in the final section of this chapter. In the first chapter, a background of research on school improvement is provided and the relationship between school improvement and Educational Effectiveness Research (EER) is explored. It is argued that there have been examples of productive co-operation between school effectiveness and school improvement. However, after two decades of research on these areas, one might conclude that the association between EER and school improvement is still problematic. After the analysis of previous ineffective attempts to link EER to school improvement, the authors aim to establish strategies for school improvement that place emphasis on the evidence stemming from theory and research. The need for a theory-driven approach to school improvement, as well as the collection of multiple data about student achievement, the classroom and school processes are also emphasised. In this way, a theory-driven and evidence-based approach to school improvement is promoted.

In the second chapter, the dynamic model of educational effectiveness is argued to contribute to establishing the theory-driven and evidence-based approach to school improvement promoted in the first chapter. For this reason, the main assumption and essential characteristics of the dynamic model are presented. The chapter further presents that the dynamic model has been established to help policy makers and practitioners improve educational practice, through encouraging rational decisions concerning the optimal fit of the factors within the model and the present situation in the schools or educational system. In this chapter, we also refer to the factors of the model which are situated in four levels: student, classroom, school and context/system. Furthermore, the factors and the dimensions used to measure their functioning are described, as well as the reasoning for using this model as a theoretical framework of the proposed school improvement approach. Finally, the authors stress that the validity of the dynamic model has been systematically tested, by referring to studies demonstrating the validity of the model and presenting how the findings of these studies aid its further development. A dynamic approach to school improvement is also established, which is based on theory (i.e. the dynamic model) that has been systematically tested.

In the third chapter, the authors stress that improvement efforts should be based at the school level, which can be achieved by focusing on the relations between the school factors and the aims of the specific improvement project. This implies that school stakeholders should make use of the literature associated with the aims of the specific improvement project. They should also merge the findings of this research area with the value assumptions and essential characteristics of the dynamic model. This chapter further supports the implementation of this approach, as the dynamic model is flexible enough to incorporate evidence stemming from different research areas (knowledge and discipline). The assumptions of the dynamic approach to school improvement are also referred to here, as well as explanation of which conditions this approach requires for improvement purposes. Furthermore, the main steps of the dynamic approach to school improvement are presented, with discussion of the interrelating roles of the school stakeholders and research advisory team. When identifying priorities for improvement, the importance of school self evaluation is stressed. Support is also provided for the systematic use of the knowledge-base and expertise of the research advisory team in developing strategies and action plans, as well as the development of formative internal evaluation mechanisms for monitoring the implementation of school improvement efforts.

It can therefore be claimed that the first part of this book provides the background of the proposed dynamic approach to school improvement and outlines the approach itself. It is also argued that a theory-driven approach to school improvement should be established, whilst the importance of treating the dynamic model as a theoretical framework for establishing this approach is shown. Moreover, specific strategies are presented that could be used by different stakeholders who are planning to use the dynamic model for improving educational practice at different levels. In the next part of the book, we present projects based on the dynamic approach to school improvement, which address improvement at different levels and deal with the various challenges/problems that contemporary schools are facing. Results concerned with the impact of these improvement efforts on the functioning of different factors and on learning outcomes are also presented. These show how, and under which conditions, the dynamic approach to school improvement can contribute to the quality and equity of education.

Part B

Research projects on the dynamic approach to school improvement

Establishing school self-evaluation mechanisms to improve the quality of education

*Demetriou Demetris, Kyriakides Leonidas,
& Creemers Bert P.M.*

Introduction

This chapter presents a research project based on the Dynamic Approach to School Improvement (DASI) that aimed to establish effective school self-evaluation (SSE) mechanisms. In Chapter 3, it was stressed that the improvement efforts in education should be based at the school level. This can be done by looking at the relations between the school factors and the aims of the specific improvement project. This implies that school stakeholders should make use of the literature associated with the aims of the specific improvement project and merge the findings of this research area with the value assumptions and the essential characteristics of the dynamic model. Moreover, in Chapter Three, the main steps of the DASI were presented and the roles of school stakeholders and the research advisory team and their interrelations were discussed. Finally, the role of SSE for identifying priorities for improvement was stressed, and it was argued that DASI could be used as the means of developing and sustaining such effective SSE mechanisms.

In this context, the study reported in this chapter investigates the effect of three main approaches to establishing SSE mechanisms upon student achievement and provides evidence for the added value of using DASI to establish SSE mechanisms. In the first part of the chapter a brief description of the theoretical background of three main approaches to SSE is provided. Then, we refer to the multi treatment experimental design that was used to compare the impact of these approaches upon student achievement. It is shown that the first approach is related to the assumption that stems from the grounded theory that the school stakeholders are able to develop SSE mechanisms and define their own improvement strategies. In this way, ownership is established and is seen as a stimulus for taking responsibility for school improvement. Thus, for the purpose of this study, the first group of schools were encouraged to establish SSE mechanisms and design their improvement strategies by themselves. The second approach is related to the school improvement movement which emphasises the importance of establishing a positive climate in the school which will support change. Thus, school stakeholders of the second group were offered support to create first a climate of openness and trust and then establish their own SSE mechanisms and through that design their own improvement strategies. Finally, the DASI was used with the third group of schools. Specifically, this group was encouraged not only to establish SSE mechanisms but also to make decisions for their improvement strategies which were in line with the assumptions and steps of the dynamic model (see Chapter 3). After discussing the three approaches to SSE, we refer to the multi treatment experimental design that was used to compare the impact of these approaches upon student achievement. In addition, in this chapter, readers who are interested in using the DASI may find examples of how DASI was used in order to develop effective SSE mechanisms.

Since multilevel analysis was used to identify the impact of the three approaches, the chapter also refers to the results of this analysis and some technical information are provided for readers who may like to conduct an experimental study and measure the impact of DASI on student outcomes for research purposes. However, a brief summary of the main results of the study is also provided to show how the research advisory team could present them in a simple way to school stakeholders and students. Finally, we discuss the implications of the findings of this study regarding using DASI to improve school effectiveness by establishing SSE mechanisms.

Using SSE to improve the quality of education

In this section, three main approaches for developing SSE mechanisms are presented. The first approach (Treatment 1) is related to the assumption that the school stakeholders are able to develop SSE mechanisms and define their own improvement strategies. The involvement of students, parents, and the wider community is seen as a crucial factor determining the success of participatory models of evaluation (Coleman, 1998; Hopkins, 2001; McTaggert, 1997). Specifically, the involvement of school stakeholders in defining the criteria of SSE may eventually encourage their active participation in using SSE for improvement purposes since teachers may adopt a more positive attitude towards evaluation results when they are involved in the evaluation procedure (Fullan, 2001).

Teacher participation in school-level decision making has been advanced for a wide variety of reasons (Smylie, Lazarus & Brownlee-Conyers, 1996). Most often, participation is thought to enhance communication among teachers and administrators and improve the quality of educational decision making (Conway, 1984). Participation may also contribute to the quality of teachers' work life (Conley, Schmidle, & Shedd, 1988). In addition, participation has been promoted on the basis of ethical arguments such as 'professionalizing' teaching and 'democratizing' school workplaces (Duke, Showers, & Imber, 1981; Murphy & Beck, 1995). However, Mijs, Houtveen, Wubells and Creemers (2005) conducted a meta-analysis of successful programmes for school improvement and provided support for using a systematic approach to change directed at internal conditions with respect to teaching and learning and to support at the school level aiming to improve the quality of teaching and learning. Nevertheless, no evidence for the need of school-generated programmes was found.

The second approach to SSE (Treatment 2) is based on the view of schools as mini political systems with diverse constituencies. Micropolitics of education has emerged in clearly articulated form in the research literature within the past 30 years (Hoyle & Skrla, 1999). Micropolitics recognises the diversity of interests, multiple sources of power, and the potential for - if not constant presence of - conflict (Ball, 1987). This allows for the possibility that coalitions and conflict may occur both across and within organizations such as schools (Firestone & Fisler, 2002). Therefore, the development and the adoption of a SSE system is not just a technocratic affair because it is also determined by political influences (Stronge & Tucker, 2000).

Berman (1978) argues that the implementation success of a policy is a function of two important variables: the content of the policy and the institutional context in which the policy is being implemented in. Constituency groups nowadays have the ability not only to resist to governments policy will, but also to induce that will. Therefore, the feasibility studying policy resistance groups when a SSE system is proposed is a heated area. Research findings during the last two decades have underlined that teachers can play a decisive role in the implementation and future success of an innovation (e.g., Kyriakides, 1997; Polettini, 2000; Ponte, Matos, Guimaraes, Leal, & Canavarro, 1994; Sztajn, 2003; van den Berg, Sleegers, Geijsels, & Vandenberghe, 2000).

Teachers are increasingly considered by most policy-makers and school change experts to be the centrepiece of educational change (Datnow, Hubbard, & Mehan, 2002). Therefore, examining teachers' attitudes, thoughts, and criticism regarding a reform is judged imperative. When introducing SSE, the various constituency groups within education which have the ability to influence educational arrangements may try to promote their own interests in order to increase their professional power. Therefore, the success of SSE may be determined by the ways used to design and introduce the use of SSE for improvement purposes (Kyriakides & Demetriou, 2007). This is because beyond, and of course before, setting the layout of a SSE mechanism, it is important to estimate, recognise and take into account those factors that might influence the constituency proposals, with regard to the framework (content) of the SSE system. As a consequence, this approach to SSE encourages stakeholders to examine and resolve their concerns regarding their SSE before establishing their own SSE mechanisms.

The third approach to SSE (Treatment 3) is based on the assumption that the knowledge-base of Educational Effectiveness Research (EER) should be taken into account in developing SSE mechanisms (Teddlie & Reynolds, 2000). The DASI approach that was promoted in Chapter 3 is also based on the above assumption. The first part of the book provides a dynamic perspective of educational effectiveness and improvement, stressing the importance of using an evidence-based and theory-driven approach. In addition, the third approach also emphasises the role of SSE in improving the effectiveness status of schools. The dynamic model, which is the theoretical framework of DASI, is based on the assumption that effective schools develop their own SSE mechanisms and use evaluation for improvement purposes.

Empirical support to the validity of the model has also been provided through longitudinal studies and meta-analyses (see Chapter 2). By using the DASI, teachers and other school stakeholders involved in improvement efforts are expected to become aware of both the empirical support for the factors involved in their project and the way these factors operate within a conceptual framework (see step B of DASI). Through this approach, teachers and the other school stakeholders are offered the opportunity to use this knowledge-base in a flexible way, to adapt it to their specific needs, and to develop their own strategies for school improvement (Creemers & Kyriakides, 2010c). By using DASI as the basis for SSE, each school is expected to develop its own strategies and action plans for improvement but it is acknowledged that support to schools should also be offered by a research advisory team which is able to provide technical expertise. Support should also be offered by providing an available knowledge-base of how the factors addressed by the school can be improved. Although school is treated as a professional community which is responsible for designing and implementing its own improvement strategies and action plans, school stakeholders are not solely responsible for designing and implementing their strategies and actions but are encouraged to make use of not only the research advisory team but also of other available resources within and outside the school.

It was in this context that an experimental study was conducted. This study is presented in the next part of the chapter and helps the readers see how each approach of SSE can be carried out for educational improvement purposes. This chapter also provides evidence about the impact of each of the three approaches of establishing SSE mechanisms on student achievement in mathematics. The choice of mathematics as an outcome measure of the impact of SSE is based on practical considerations. Moreover, the research team had a battery of valid tests, each test for a different age group of students (see Kyriakides & Creemers, 2008). In this way, the impact of SSE on achievement of students of different age groups was measured. The SSE initiatives were not designed in order to address mathematics teaching exclusively but the functioning of school factors and it is, therefore, assumed that we may get similar findings about the impact of different approaches to SSE on student achievement if different learning outcomes were taken into account. Finally, it is important to stress that this study does not concern stakeholders' views about the appropriateness of each of these three approaches, but the impact of each approach upon student learning outcomes.

Methods

A) Designing a multi-treatment experimental study in Cyprus

Since the study reported in this chapter was undertaken in Cyprus, a brief description of the educational system is provided below to provide better understanding for the international reader. One of the main characteristics of the educational system in Cyprus is that its administration is centralized and both primary and secondary schools are under the authority of the Ministry of Education which is responsible for the educational policy making, the administration of education and the enforcement of educational laws. In addition, teachers' appointments, transfers, and promotions are the responsibility of the Educational Service Commission, an independent five-member body, which is appointed by the President of the Republic. There are local school committees which are responsible for the construction, maintenance and equipment of school buildings but they are not responsible to contribute to educational matters such as policy-making. The maintenance of the centralised system is due to historical and political reasons as well as the fact that in a small country like Cyprus, the centralised system is more effective in that it is less demanding on manpower than a more decentralised system would be. With 380 primary schools and 120 secondary schools, it has roughly the same administrative range as a large local educational authority in England. It is, also, much smaller than an administrative region for education in France.

In Cyprus, the Ministry of Education attempts to control the system through the curriculum and related regulations concerning external teacher and school evaluation. Inspectors, who are responsible for the supervision and inspection of schools, are appointed by the Ministry of Education and have a twofold responsibility. They are required to give guidance to the teachers and at the same time, to evaluate their work by giving marks, which play a decisive role in teachers' career development. Their role as assessors creates a climate of mistrust, which tends to undermine their principal role in curriculum and school improvement. Policy makers and representatives of the Teachers' Trade Union identified a number of limitations of the current teacher and school evaluation system and reported that neither the formative nor the summative purpose of evaluation was being achieved. In this context, policy makers and representatives of the Teachers' Trade Union attempt to develop an evaluation reform which encouraged schools to develop their own SSE mechanisms for improvement purposes. Although there is consensus about the need to use SSE for designing improvement strategies and actions, there is a debate about the approaches to be used for developing and sustaining SSE mechanisms (Kyriakides & Demetriou, 2007). Therefore, SSE is not compulsory and is very rarely used by schools in order to develop their strategies and actions for school improvement purposes (Kyriakides, 2005b). As a consequence, participation in this study was on a volunteer basis and it was possible to establish a control group where no SSE mechanisms were developed.

More specifically, at the beginning of the school year of 2007–2008, a sample of 60 primary schools in Cyprus was selected and a group randomization study (Brooks, Burton, Cole, Miles, Torgerson & Torgerson, 2008) was undertaken. The school sample was randomly split into four groups of 15 schools. Information on the background characteristics of students of each group is provided in Appendix 4.1. It is shown that there is no statistically significant difference among the four groups in regard to their background characteristics and their prior achievement in mathematics. Different types of support were provided to the first three groups of schools to establish different SSE mechanisms for improvement purposes, whereas no SSE mechanism was established in the schools of the fourth group, the control group. In regard to the different treatments offered to the other three groups of schools, each of them was in line with one of the main approaches to SSE mentioned above. School stakeholders were informed about the process that they had to follow in order to develop specific SSE mechanisms and about the fact that there was a control group in order to measure the impact of SSE. However, they were not informed about the other treatments offered to the other experimental groups. Support was provided by the project team and the same amount of time and effort was allocated to each treatment group (see Demetriou, 2009).

Table 4.1 provides information about the steps followed by each experimental group for developing their strategies and action plans for improvement. The only difference between schools following treatment 2 with those following treatment 1, had to do with the first stage of the intervention. Before designing their SSE mechanisms, stakeholders of treatment 2 were asked to express their concerns about SSE and exchange them with each other. Moreover, decisions were taken on how to deal with their concerns and a SSE protocol was developed and signed by all stakeholders (see step 1 of treatment 2). The presence of the protocol ensured that all stakeholders' concerns against the development of a SSE system were taken into account before employing a SSE mechanism and that the development and the application of the SSE system would respect every single concern that was raised (for instance, concerns for the self, the amount of the job, the relations between stakeholders etc).

In regard to the process used to develop SSE mechanisms, three group interviews, one with each group of stakeholders (i.e., teachers, parents and students) were conducted in each school of the first two experimental groups and a questionnaire on the appropriateness of different criteria of SSE emerged from each interview. The three questionnaires were administered, one to each group of school stakeholders. In addition, an analysis of data was conducted in order to identify which criteria of SSE were considered equally important by all groups of stakeholders (steps 3 and 4 of treatment 1). Then, at each school, a group interview with representatives of teachers, parents, and students was conducted (see step 5). During this interview, the results concerned with the perceptions of stakeholders about the criteria of evaluation were presented and each school managed to generate its evaluation criteria and then develop relevant SSE mechanisms. By taking into account the results emerged from conducting SSE, school stakeholders made a decision about their priorities for improvement and managed to develop their own strategies and action plans for improving the effectiveness of their schools.

Table 4.1 Steps followed by each treatment group to develop their strategies and action plans for improvement

Treatment 1	Treatment 2	Treatment 3 – Using DASI
1) Training about SSE and the process that they had to follow in order to develop their strategies and action plans for improvement.	Group interviews with school stakeholders to present the aims of SSE and explain the process that their school had to follow. Stakeholders were encouraged to express their concerns about SSE. Decisions on how to deal with their concerns were taken and a SSE protocol was developed and signed by all stakeholders.	1) Presentation of the dynamic model to stakeholders and discussion about its value assumptions. Establishing consensus that the final aim of SSE should be the improvement of student learning (see step A of DASI).
2) Three group interviews with each group of stakeholders (i.e., parents, students, and teachers) were conducted in order to generate criteria of school evaluation. Development of three questionnaires concerned with the criteria of evaluation emerged from each interview.	Step 2 of treatment 1	2) School factors included in the dynamic model were presented to school stakeholders and a discussion about the importance of each factor took place. It was agreed that SSE had to be concerned with the functioning of school factors (step B of DASI).
3) Administration of the questionnaires to all teachers, parents and students.	Step 3 of treatment 1	3) Administration of instruments used to measure the factors of the dynamic model (step C of DASI: collection of data).
4) Analysis of data emerged from the administration of the questionnaires in order to classify criteria into areas that need to be evaluated.	Step 4 of treatment 1	4) Analysis of data to identify the first three priorities of improvement which need to be addressed by the school (step C of DASI: analysis of data).
5) Presentation of results to a focus group interview with representatives of stakeholders to define the content of SSE and develop relevant evaluation instruments.	Step 5 of treatment 1	5) Evaluation results were presented to the teachers. Teachers took a decision about the area(s) that could be addressed by their improvement strategies (step C of DASI: identifying priorities).

Treatment 1	Treatment 2	Treatment 3 – Using DASI
6) Analysis of data emerged from each instrument and presentation of results to a group interview with representatives of school stakeholders to identify their area(s) for improvement.	Step 6 of treatment 1	6) School stakeholders were invited to express their views about the area(s) that need to be addressed. Analysis of the responses of stakeholders helped schools to clarify their improvement area(s). (step C: clarifying the improvement area).
7) Group interview with representatives of stakeholders to develop their strategies and action plans for improvement. (The research team acted as the critical friend of the school.)	Step 7 of treatment 1	7) Group interviews to develop strategies and action plans. (In order to develop their action plans, the research team provided suggestions about the effective functioning of each factor of the dynamic model.) (see step D of DASI).
8) Establishing formative evaluation mechanisms to monitor the progress of their action plans for school improvement.	Step 8 of treatment 1	Step 8 of treatment 1 (see step E of DASI).

On the other hand, schools receiving Treatment 3 were asked to establish SSE mechanisms by following the steps of DASI (see Table 4.1). Thus, the dynamic model, its assumptions, and especially its school level factors were presented to the school stakeholders and the criteria for school evaluation were not emerged through interviewing school stakeholders but by taking into account the school factors of the dynamic model (see step 2 of treatment 3). The presentation of the dynamic model served to help school stakeholders not only to be aware of the factors that need to be addressed but also to understand why addressing these factors could help them achieve better learning outcomes for students. By following this approach, it was clear to school stakeholders that in order to promote learning, it is imperative to both understand the processes under which learning can be achieved in classrooms, schools and outside the school and make use of research evidence on the school level for the above.

In step 3, schools had to collect evaluation data and then the research team helped schools to analyse the data and identify priority areas of improvement (step 4). Instead of developing their own evaluation instruments, these schools had to use the instruments already developed in order to test the validity of the model (see Part C of the book). The aim of this evaluation was to help stakeholders identify their main priority area for improvement which was concerned with factor(s) that were not functioning at a satisfactory level. The dynamic approach to school improvement is based on the assumption that we cannot develop strategies and action plans which address all school factors; instead a more focused approach is needed. Due to this, only the most important factors operating at the school level were treated as possible priority areas for improvement. In each school using this experimental procedure, the evaluation results were presented to the school stakeholders and they were encouraged to design their own school improvement initiatives (step 5). At step 6, school stakeholders were invited to express their views about the results of SSE and to select among the three priorities, the one that was seen as the most important to deal with. In this way, not only the interpretive validity of the school evaluation was examined but also stakeholders were given the opportunity to develop an improvement strategy that was not only a priority for improvement of their schools but was also in line with their interests. At step 7, guidelines on actions and strategies that could be considered in designing their improvement strategies to address school factors were also offered to the school stakeholders. The research team was responsible only to provide suggestions, leaving the decisions about the content of the action plans ultimately to the stakeholders. Thus, the strategies and action plans to address the priority for school improvement were developed by the school stakeholders but the aims of these action plans were defined by taking into account the research evidence and the data from SSE. This is an essential difference between treatment 3 and treatments 1 and 2, where school stakeholders had the chance to define the content of SSE and address any factor they may consider important.

Finally, all three groups of schools were asked to develop mechanisms in order to monitor the progress of their school improvement plans (see step 8). In developing the action plans, all schools had to specify which tasks needed to be undertaken, who was going to be responsible for implementing each task, when each task was expected to be implemented, and what resources should be provided to the stakeholders in order to implement these tasks. The research team was available to provide support when needed.

B) Data analysis

Multilevel modelling techniques were used to measure the impact of these three approaches on Grade 4 and 5 students in the mathematics achievements each experimental school. Since our assumption was that not all schools of each treatment group would achieve the same results, we also attempted to find out whether variation in student achievement gains could be explained by variables associated with the implementation of each intervention. Our interest to identify factors other than the use of a specific SSE approach arises from the fact that evaluation studies of reform efforts reveal that irrespective of the nature/content of the reform that is implemented in schools, there is variation in the ability of teachers and schools to implement the reform (Worthen et al., 1997). As a consequence, in our effort to compare the impact of the three approaches to student achievement, we collected data on factors situated at student, teacher, and school levels which were expected to have an effect on schools using SSE for improvement purposes. Details of the data collected are presented below (sections D and E).

C) Dependent Variable: Student achievement in mathematics

Curriculum-based written tests in Mathematics were administered to all grade 4 and grade 5 students of our school sample (n=4212) at the beginning and at the end of the school year of 2007–2008. The written tests were subject to control for reliability and validity. None of the respondents gave full scores. Moreover, less than 5% of the students gave over 80% of the maximum score and less than 12% of the students gave over 70% of the maximum score. Therefore, the ceiling effect was less probable (see Demetriou, 2009). The floor effect was also not apparent in the data, because no student showed full zero performance. For each student, two different scores for his/her mathematics achievement at the beginning and at the end of the intervention were generated.

D) Explanatory variables at student level

Student Background Factors

Information was collected on two student background factors: sex (0=boys, 1=girl) and socio-economic status (SES). Five SES variables were available: father's and mother's education level (i.e., graduate of a primary school, graduate of secondary school or graduate of a college/university), the social status of father's job, the social status of mother's job and the economical situation of the family. Following the classification of occupations used by the Ministry of Finance, it was possible to classify parents' occupation into three groups which have relatively similar sizes: occupations held by working class (33%), occupations held by middle class (37%) and occupations held by upper-middle class (30%). In addition, relevant information for each child was taken from the school records. Then standardized values of the above five variables were calculated, resulting in the SES indicator.

E) Explanatory variables at school level

Teachers' perceptions towards the value assumptions and the procedural dilemmas of SSE

A questionnaire investigating teachers' perceptions towards the value assumptions and the procedural dilemmas of SSE was administered to all teachers of the school sample (n=1316) both at the beginning and at the end of the school year in order to measure whether teachers' attitudes towards SSE had any effect on the effective use of each approach to SSE. The value assumptions reflect an ideology of self-evaluation particularly related to the fact that schools as organisations are predicated upon a moral order which typically involves commitment to fairness, consistency, an ethic of care and inclusion, as well as learning. This is because schools are primarily organisations in which the process of learning embodies value judgments about how people, especially young people, should be treated (Kyriakides & Campbell, 2004). More specifically, the following value assumptions are seen as particularly related to SSE:

a)   commitment to treating human beings as natural learners
b)   commitment to change from within the organization
c)   commitment to developing ownership
d)   commitment to gathering evidence.

At the same time, several procedural dilemmas have to be faced during the implementation of SSE.

Thus, the second frame concerns procedures that, according to research, are most likely to help realise the value assumptions of SSE (e.g., MacBeath, Schratz, Meuret,, & Lakobsen, 2000; Meuret & Morlaix, 2003; Saunders, 1999). These procedural dilemmas arise from:

a)   establishing clarity and consensus about the aims of SSE
b)   creating an appropriate school climate
c)   establishing rules for the use of data
d)   generating criteria (see Kyriakides & Campbell, 2004).

Our decision to measure this variable is due to the fact that SSE cannot easily be implemented in a school unless teachers share the value assumptions of SSE (Kyriakides & Campbell, 2004). The importance of this variable is also pointed out by research on the political dimension of evaluation which draws attention to teacher concerns over evaluation whenever an evaluation reform is introduced (Bridges & Groves, 1999; Stronge & Tucker, 2000).

By employing exploratory factor analysis on teachers' responses to these items, it was found that the 28 items of this part of the questionnaire could be classified into the following four broader categories which refer to the value assumptions and the procedural dilemmas of SSE (MacBeath, 1999). The first factor consists of items which support that human beings should be treated as natural learners. The second factor refers to the establishment of a commitment to gathering evidence and implies that schools which are able to use SSE mechanisms to improve practice are those where a culture in favour of research is in place. The third factor refers to items associated with two value assumptions of SSE which are seen as closely related to each other. The first value assumption supports that authentic change must come primarily from within the organization and the second supports that ownership is a prerequisite for establishing successful school improvement strategies. Finally, the fourth factor refers to the various procedural dilemmas that schools have to face in their attempt to use SSE mechanisms for improvement purposes. These procedural dilemmas arise from: establishing clarity and consensus about the aims of SSE, creating an appropriate school climate, establishing rules for the use of data, and generating criteria for the SSE.

The score for each school in each factor was the mean factor scores of the teachers. Since teachers were asked to answer anonymously the questionnaire, the aggregated factor scores at the level of school were treated as explanatory variables, instead of individual teacher factor scores.

School climate

Teachers' responses to the questionnaire helped us also to measure the school climate and especially the extent to which the school puts emphasis on achievement, and a climate of openness and trust can be observed in the school. After demonstrating the validity of the questionnaire (see Demetriou, 2009), two different scores measuring climate, were generated for each school.

The priority area for which school improvement efforts took place

The content of the priority area for which school improvement efforts took place in each school was classified as follows. First, it was examined whether each priority area was in line with the school factors included in the dynamic model. Schools of the first and the second experimental group were not aware of the dynamic model and were given the opportunity to select any priority area of improvement they considered important. However, some of the schools of these two groups identified priority areas which were in line with the factors included in the dynamic model. By investigating the effect of this dummy variable upon student achievement, one can identify whether the impact of the treatments offered to the first two groups of schools depended on the extent to which their chosen priority area was in line with the dynamic model. We also classified the priority areas that were in line with the dynamic model further by taking the two overarching school factors of the model into account. Specifically, two broader categories were established by investigating whether their priority area was concerned either with the school policy on teaching or with the policy on the broader learning environment of the school. This explanatory variable was taken into account in order to find out whether school improvement efforts should be concerned with specific factors of the dynamic model in order to be effective.

Implementation effort

Since one of the main threats to the internal validity of experimental studies has to do with the extent to which all the groups put the same amount of effort in achieving the schooling outcomes (this threat is known in the literature as the threat of 'experimental mortality'), different sources of data were used to measure the extent to which each participating school had put effort to implement their improvement strategies. Specifically, we conducted content analysis of the reflective diaries that school coordinators kept in order to identify the extent to which each school put in effort to use SSE for improvement purposes. Moreover, the constant comparative method was used to analyse data from interviews with head teachers, school coordinators, and teachers from each school. These interviews were concerned with the experiences and attitudes of school stakeholders towards the implementation of the interventions that took place in their schools. The analysis of the qualitative data from each source of data helped us establish a scale measuring the effort that each school put in implementing the intervention (see Demetriou, 2009).

Results

Since multilevel analysis was used in order to identify the impact of the three approaches, the next section provides some information on the analysis that was conducted. This section may be useful to readers who would like to conduct a similar study. In addition, a brief summary of the main results is provided before the discussion section.

The first step of our analysis was to determine how much of the variance of student achievement was situated at each of the three levels (students, classrooms and schools). Table 4.2 shows that 67.3% of the total variance was situated at the student level, 18.5% of the variance was at the classroom level and 14.2% at the school level (see column 2). In model 1 the context variables (SES, gender and prior achievement) at each level were added to the empty model. The following observations arose from the figures of the third column of Table 4.2. First, model 1 explained 22.7% of the total variance and most of the explained variance was at the student level. Second, the effects of all contextual factors (i.e., SES, prior knowledge, gender) were significant.

In model 2, the school explanatory variables which were concerned with the school climate and the perceptions of teachers towards SSE were added to model 1. None of the variables associated with teacher perceptions towards SSE were found to be associated with student achievement. In regard to the impact of school climate, only the factor which refers to the extent to which pressure for success was put on teachers and students was associated with student achievement.

In model 3 the impact of the three school improvement approaches was tested. By considering the first treatment as a reference group, it was found out that the first and the second group managed to receive similar results. In addition, the results of the first two groups were better than the control group. We can also see that the third treatment group had better results than any other group.

At the next step, we attempted to identify any variable that may explain the fact that the third approach to school improvement had stronger impact upon achievement in mathematics than any other approach to SSE. For this reason, we

Table 4.2 Parameter estimates and (standard errors) for the analysis of student
achievement in mathematics (students within classes, within schools)

Factors	Model 0	Model 1	Model 2	Model 3
Fixed part (Intercept)	0.90 (.13)	0.72 (.12)	0.64 (.13)	0.41 (.13)
Student level				
Context				
Prior achievement in maths		0.31 (.08)	0.30 (.07)	0.31 (.07)
Sex (0=Girls, 1=Boys)		0.06 (.02)	0.06 (.02)	0.06 (.02)
SES		0.15 (.06)	0.15 (.05)	0.14 (.05)
Classroom level				
Context				
Average prior achievement		0.12 (.05)	0.11 (.04)	0.12 (.04)
Average SES		N.S.S.	N.S.S.	N.S.S.
Percentage of boys		N.S.S.	N.S.S.	N.S.S.
School level				
Context				
Average prior achievement		0.09 (.04)	0.09 (.03)	0.09 (.03)
Average SES		N.S.S.	N.S.S.	N.S.S.
Percentage of boys		N.S.S.	N.S.S.	N.S.S.
Teachers' perceptions towards:				
Value assumptions of SSE*			N.S.S.	N.S.S.
Procedural dilemmas of SSE			N.S.S.	N.S.S.
School climate				
A) Openness and trust			N.S.S.	N.S.S.
B) Achievement press			0.08 (.03)	0.08 (.03)
SSE approach				
Control group				-.12 (.03)
Dealing with the concerns of stakeholders (2nd Treatment)				N.S.S.
Using the dynamic model (3rd Treatment - DASI)				.14 (.04)
Variance components				
School	14.2%	11.0%	9.5%	6.2%
Class	18.5%	15.2%	14.8%	13.0%
Student	67.3%	51.1%	51.0%	49.4%
Explained		22.7%	24.7%	31.4%
Significance test				
X^2	1113.4	797.3	762.1	702.1
Reduction		316.1	35.2	60.0
Degrees of freedom		5	1	2
p-value		.001	.001	.001

* We entered separately the following three factor scores which were concerned with the value
assumptions of SSE: a) human beings should be treated as natural learners, b) commitment to
gathering data, and c) authentic change must come primarily from within the organization and by
following this approach ownership can be established.

conducted a multilevel analysis of mathematics achievement of all students but those participating in the control group. The results of this analysis are presented in Table 4.3. By comparing the figures of this table with those of Table 4.2, it can be observed that the same variables which were found to be associated with achievement of the whole sample are also associated with achievement of students in the three experimental groups. In addition, model 2 revealed that the third approach had a stronger effect than the other two approaches on SSE. Furthermore, model 3 revealed that the effect of the approach based on DASI was still stronger than the other two approaches even when other explanatory variables concerned with the implementation of the school improvement approaches to these 45 schools were taken into account.

Table 4.3 also shows that experimental mortality was associated with the effective implementation of each approach to SSE. Schools which put more effort to use SSE for improvement purposes were more effective than others. By taking this variable into account, one can see that the added value of the third approach was not influenced since the effect sizes reported in models 2 and 3 were very similar. It is finally important to note that the schools which had the smallest effect sizes were those schools of the first and second experimental group which designed an improvement strategy which was not in line with any of the factors included in the dynamic model. On the other hand, schools which attempted to develop an improvement strategy concerned with aspects of their policy on teaching had the same effect as those which were interested to improve their learning environment in a broader way.

Based on the results of the multilevel modeling analysis illustrated in the previous section, the added value of the use of DASI in designing a successful SSE mechanism has been identified. More specifically, all three experimental groups had better results than the control group, implying that SSE can contribute to establishing effective school improvement strategies. By comparing the impact of the use of DASI on student achievement with the impact of the other two approaches to SSE, it was found that DASI approach had the strongest effect. Moreover there weren't statistically significant differences between the effects of the treatment 1 and the effects of treatment 2.

The results of this study also helped us to find the minimum requirements for developing effective SSE mechanisms: First, it has been shown that each overarching school factor illustrated by the dynamic model is equally important for designing a school improvement approach. The fact that some schools took some initiatives concerned with the school policy for teaching, and others with their learning environment, had nothing to do with the impact of their school improvement approach on student achievement. Second, the fact that the factor concerned with the extent to which a climate of openness and trust exists in schools was not found to be associated with student achievement raises doubts about the importance of establishing such a climate before establishing any SSE mechanism aiming to improve school effectiveness. This argument is also supported by the fact that the impact of treatment 2 was as big as that of treatment 1.

Table 4.3 Parameter estimates and (standard errors) for the analysis of mathematics achievement of students in the three experimental groups only

Factors	Model 0	Model 1	Model 2	Model 3
Fixed part (Intercept)	0.87 (.13)	0.72 (.12)	0.64 (.13)	0.35 (.13)
Student level				
Context				
Prior achievement in maths		0.30 (.08)	0.31 (.07)	0.31 (.07)
Sex (0=Girls, 1=Boys)		0.06 (.03)	0.06 (.02)	0.06 (.02)
SES		0.16 (.06)	0.15 (.04)	0.15 (.04)
Classroom level				
Context				
Average prior achievement		0.11 (.05)	0.12 (.04)	0.12 (.04)
Average SES		N.S.S.	N.S.S.	N.S.S.
Percentage of boys		N.S.S.	N.S.S.	N.S.S.
School level				
Context				
Average prior achievement		0.09 (.04)	0.10 (.03)	0.10 (.03)
Average SES		N.S.S.	N.S.S.	N.S.S.
Percentage of boys		N.S.S.	N.S.S.	N.S.S.
Teachers' perceptions towards:				
Value assumptions of SSE*			N.S.S.	N.S.S.
Procedural dilemmas of SSE			N.S.S.	N.S.S.
School climate				
A) Openness and trust			N.S.S.	N.S.S.
B) Achievement press			0.09 (.04)	0.09 (.03)
SSE approach				
Dealing with the concerns of stakeholders (2nd Treatment)			N.S.S.	N.S.S.
Using the dynamic model (3rd Treatment - DASI)			.15 (.05)	.13 (.04)
Priority Area				
Policy on SLE				N.S.S.
Nothing to do with the factors included in the dynamic model				-0.08 (.03)
Amount of effort put to SSE				0.12 (.03)
Variance components				
School	14.0%	11.1%	9.5%	5.5%
Class	17.5%	16.0%	14.5%	13.3%
Student	68.5%	51.1%	50.1%	49.0%
Explained		21.8%	25.9%	32.2%
Significance test				
X^2	1023.4	797.3	768.1	704.8
Reduction		226.1	29.2	63.3
Degrees of freedom		5	2	2
p-value		.001	.001	.001

* Note: Abbreviations as in Table 4.2

Discussion

By comparing the impact of the DASI on student achievement with the impact of the other two approaches to SSE, we can see that the DASI approach had the strongest effect on student achievement. The essential difference of the third approach to the other two approaches is that it is a systematic research based approach that evaluates improvement efforts. Through this approach, school stakeholders were encouraged to treat the challenges and/or problems that their school was facing as a chance for them to define new goals of schooling and to develop strategies and actions to improve the functioning of those factors included in the dynamic model that would help them achieve the new goals that emerged from this challenge. In this way, school stakeholders viewed a school problem as a benchmark that had to be surpassed by identifying aims associated with this problem and adopting strategies and action plans in order to meet these new aims and solve the problem.

The impact of the DASI could be most probably attributed to the procedure that was followed in order to achieve school improvement. School stakeholders were able to make use of the literature associated with the aims of the specific improvement project and merge the findings of this research area with the value assumptions and the essential characteristics of the dynamic model. The procedure that was followed may have made them feel more confident in their decisions. For example, on several occasions, school stakeholders saw that their interventions had obvious effects in facing their problems. This probably made them not only to feel confident in their actions but also boosted their willingness to engage in the school improvement procedure.

The schools of this experimental group were asked to develop their improvement strategies and action plans by taking into account not only the priorities for improvement which SSE revealed that they had but also by taking the evidence of EER (as it is reflected in the dynamic model) into account. This finding seems to be in line with the results of studies investigating the impact of the Comprehensive School Reform program (CSR) on student achievement (Rowan et al, 2009). The results of third group have some common characteristics with the CSR program which attempts to use a 'school improvement by design' approach to encourage schools to work with outside agencies and implement new designs for educational practice. A meta-analysis investigating the achievement effects of CSR reveals that the schools which implemented CSR models for five years or more had particularly strong effects on achievement and the benefits were consistent across schools of varying poverty levels (Borman et al., 2003). Given that this study took place for only one school year, the results about the effect of the third approach to SSE on student achievement appear to be promising. Thus, this study provides further support for the argument that a long-term commitment to research-proven educational reform is needed in order to improve the quality of education (Stringfield, 2000).

The claim that the third approach (DASI) had stronger effect than the other two approaches is further supported by the fact that those schools of the first two groups which developed action plans to address factors included in the dynamic model (without being aware of the dynamic model) had better results than the other schools of these two experimental groups (see Table 4.3). This finding seems to provide further support to the internal validity of the study. In addition, this study shows that school variation in the impact of the third approach (DASI) cannot be attributed to the content of the priority area for improvement that each school had to address and especially whether the area was concerned with school policy for teaching or with the learning environment of the school. This finding seems to reveal that the two overarching school factors of the dynamic model are equally important for designing school improvement projects.

Another reason supporting the effectiveness of the third approach over the other two is presented in Table 4.3. Table 4.3 reveals that the effect size of the treatment is much higher in those schools of group 3 which put more effort in using SSE for improvement purposes. This suggests that the systematic use of the dynamic model by the schools may have a relatively large effect on student outcomes. It also shows how critical the role of school stakeholders is in achieving the aims of an improvement strategy. This finding is taken into account in developing DASI and the role of both the research advisory team and school stakeholders is stressed (see Figure 3.1).

Finally, this study investigates the impact of SSE upon only one cognitive outcome (mathematics); however SSE is expected to contribute to the achievement of cognitive as well as affective outcomes of schooling. Further research is needed to identify the impact of SSE upon multiple outcomes of schooling (cognitive and affective). It should also be acknowledged that the effect size of each approach to SSE is relatively small. However, these results are in line with the results of evaluation studies measuring the impact of interventions in education which show that during the early phases of effective interventions their impact on achievement is relatively small (Slavin, Lake, & Groff, 2009). Thus, we need longitudinal studies involving both quantitative and qualitative research methods, which could provide answers to questions dealing with the short and the long-term effect of each approach to SSE upon different outcomes of schooling. Moreover, different types of studies, both experimental and case studies, are needed not only to identify the extent to which schools can make use of the DASI to develop SSE mechanisms on their own; but also to identify the difficulties which schools face in their attempt to make use of the DASI framework in order to improve their practice.

Chapter 5

Facing and preventing bullying through improving the school learning environment

Introduction

This chapter deals with the use of the dynamic approach to school improvement in establishing strategies to face and reduce bullying. The project was conducted in five European countries (i.e. Belgium/Flanders, Cyprus, England, Greece, the Netherlands) and was financially supported by the European Union under the European Commission's Daphne III Programme (Daphne project JLS/DAP/2007-1/226). The overall objective of this project was to develop an evidence-based and theory-driven approach to deal with bullying in schools, by integrating research on bullying with the knowledge-base of Educational Effectiveness Research, as outlined by the dynamic model. In this chapter, the theoretical background of the project is presented and the methodology of the project is shown to be in line with the Dynamic Approach to School Improvement (DASI). Moreover, examples of strategies and action plans developed by schools in different countries are presented. Evidence is provided for the results of the summative evaluation of this approach, concerned with the impact of the project on:

a)   the reduction of bullying
b)   the improvement of quality of school life (as perceived by students).

Finally, implications of the evaluation findings for the development of DASI are shown and the extent to which research on bullying can be integrated with research on educational effectiveness is examined.

The theoretical background of the project: using the dynamic model to design strategies and actions to face bullying

Bullying is not a contemporary phenomenon in the educational setting. A quick glance at the old records of schools would reveal the longitudinal character of the problem. However, in many countries it is only since the early 1970s that the topic has been receiving substantial research attention (e.g. Alsaker & Brunner,

1999; Besag, 1989; Charach et al., 1995; Smith et al., 1999; Mellor, 1990; Olweus, 1978). A possible reason for this delay could be the multidimensional character of the problem that raises a variety of constraints in its definition and measurement.

Definition: What is bullying?

In an incident of bullying behaviour there are many persons involved, either as bystanders or as participants. Each one experiences and regards bullying in a different way and consequently, defines it according to his/her perceptions. In addition bullying behaviour can take different forms in different environments, according to the factors that determine the bully's relationships with others. Nonetheless, a definition of bullying behaviour based on common characteristics that are acknowledged by both the participants and the bystanders is provided below. Specifically, for the purposes of the project presented in this chapter, the following definition of bullying is taken into account in order to identify the special characteristics of bullying behaviour and distinguish this from other types of student misbehaviour.

> 'A student is being bullied or victimized when he or she is exposed, repeatedly and over time to negative actions on the part of one or more other students. It is a negative action when someone intentionally inflicts, or attempts to inflict, injury or discomfort upon another. There should also be an imbalance in strength: the student who is exposed to negative actions has difficulty in defending him/herself and is somewhat helpless against the student or students who harass.'
>
> (Olweus, 1994, p. 9)

Based on the above definition, one can see that bullying is a form of aggressive behaviour intentionally carried out by the bully over lengthy periods of time (sometimes continuing for weeks, months, or even years). Moreover, victims of bullying have difficulty in defending themselves and as such, bullying behaviour is seen as an abuse of power and a desire to intimidate (Sharp & Smith, 1994).

Bullying is not simply an isolated, aggressive action between the 'bully' and 'victim'. It is rather a dynamic social relationship problem (Swearer et al., 2009) which is often due to hectic human relations involving more participants. As such, it is influenced by peers, families, schools, and communities, and consequently the phenomenon of bullying should concern the entire school population, inclusive of all factors responsible for the quality of education (Espelage & Swearer, 2004). Bullying affects the quality of the school learning environment and is therefore an issue that concerns all of the school stakeholders. Research has shown that victims of aggressive behaviour feel useless and/or experience depression, which is likely to have a negative effect on their learning and academic achievement (e.g. Kochenderfer & Ladd, 1996; Slee, 1994).

Using whole-school approaches to face bullying

Bullying is often viewed as irrelevant to teaching and the learning process. However, teaching and learning take place within a social context which bullying comprises a part of. Moreover, bullying is very likely to negatively affect the learning opportunities of students, as well as increasing teachers' levels of stress (Byrne, 1992; Charlot & Emin, 1997; Nakou, 2000). Since bullying has negative implications on the functioning and role of various school stakeholders, whole-school approaches should be used to face it. Programmes preventing school bullying should have multiple components that operate simultaneously at different levels in the school community, such as the student, teacher and school level. During the last five years, various research syntheses of the effectiveness of this approach have been conducted (e.g. Smith et al., 2004; Wilson et al., 2003). These syntheses did not simply provide empirical support to whole-school approaches, but further recommended theoretically grounded interventions which are able to disentangle the effectiveness of different programme components, in order to increase the effects of comprehensive school based programmes (Baldry & Farrington, 2007; Rigby et al., 2005).

Integrating research on bullying with EER to develop strategies and actions to reduce bullying

The project presented in this chapter is based on the assumption that the theoretical foundation for developing whole-school approaches to face bullying, may emerge through integrating research on bullying with Educational Effectiveness Research (EER). This refers to factors that operate at different levels that need to be considered in order to improve practice. As previous research has shown, programmes aiming to reduce bullying are most successful when establishing a positive and safe school learning environment (Rigby et al., 2005). This finding provides support to the assumption that a framework based both on research on bullying and on the dynamic model of educational effectiveness, should be offered to schools for them to identify what can be achieved and how, to deal with and prevent bullying. This framework emphasises the use of a whole-school approach to face bullying which is concerned with factors that contribute in the improvement of the quality of the school and the classroom environment, inclusive of student behaviour outside the classroom, the partnership policy, and collaboration between teachers. Research has shown that these factors have both direct and indirect effects on student achievement in different outcomes of schooling (Creemers & Kyriakides, 2010b; Kyriakides, Creemers, Antoniou, & Demetriou, 2010). School policy for opportunities to learn is also taken into account. The authors stress that school policy for teaching should refer to aims associated with bullying (e.g. understanding of social values, emotional recognition, developing positive attitudes towards the school) and should also include rules for handling and sanctioning bullying when it occurs. In this approach, emphasis is given to the development of school self-evaluation mechanisms, which help schools to identify priorities for improvement and develop strategies and action plans to face and reduce bullying.

Some empirical support to this approach has been provided through a longitudinal study, which has been conducted in one of the participating countries to test the validity of the dynamic model of educational effectiveness. The study provided empirical support to the model and revealed that the dynamic model can be used to describe and explain why some teachers and schools are more effective in dealing with bullying than others (Kyriakides, Creemers, & Charalambous, 2008). Thus, one of the main theoretical assumptions of the project is that support should be provided to schools, in order to help them identify factors of the dynamic model which contribute to explaining and/or facing bullying. Furthermore, schools should be encouraged to treat bullying as a challenge which needs to be dealt with, by introducing and achieving relevant affective and cognitive aims (i.e. social cognition, understanding of social values, emotional recognition, and positive attitudes towards peers) beyond those included in the formal curriculum. Finally, School Self-Evaluation (SSE) is treated as a starting point for developing strategies and actions which aim to face bullying (see Kyriakides, Charalambous, Kaloyirou, & Creemers, 2011).

Another major element of this project, which is line with the Dynamic Approach to School Improvement is the emphasis placed on evidence stemming from *theory and research*. Consequently, this project is based on the assumption that the knowledge-base of EER should be taken into account when developing SSE mechanisms. More specifically, the dynamic model of educational effectiveness is used as a framework for establishing SSE mechanisms. This framework is expected to assist schools in collecting data, using school self-evaluation mechanisms and deciding of priorities for improvement, as well as developing appropriate policies and action plans. In addition the dynamic model can help schools establish school improvement strategies, not only by establishing clarity and consensus about the aims of school improvement (see step A of DASI), but also by collecting evaluation data and identifying priorities for improvement (see step B of DASI in Chapter 3). In this way, a developmental evaluation strategy is established and schools are expected to collect data to monitor the implementation of their strategies and action plans for reducing bullying (see steps C and D of DASI). Finally, it was assumed that teachers may become aware of both the empirical support for the factors involved in their project and the way in which these factors operate within a conceptual framework. This assumption is based on the fact that the dynamic model not only refers to factors that are important for explaining variation in educational effectiveness, it also attempts to explain *why* these factors are important by integrating various theoretical orientations of effectiveness (see Chapter 2). Thus, school stakeholders are offered the opportunity to use this knowledge-base in a flexible way, adapting it to their specific needs and developing their own strategies for school improvement.

The aims of the project

The general aim of the project is to help schools in the five participating countries use an *evidence-based and theory-driven approach* to deal with bullying among students of diverse socio-ethnic backgrounds. Furthermore, the impact of the implementation of these strategies and actions (i.e. intervention programmes) will be evaluated. In this way, the authors will be able to determine whether schools in different countries effectively use DASI to face and reduce bullying.

The methodology of the project: using the dynamic approach to school improvement to reduce bullying

This section is mainly concerned with the second phase of the Daphne project, mentioned previously, in which a network of schools for each of the countries involved (i.e. Belgium, Cyprus, England, Greece, the Netherlands) was encouraged to use the DASI in order to reduce bullying. A brief description of the first phase is provided below to assist readers' understanding of the context of this school improvement project. Initially, a sample of approximately 40 primary schools was drawn from each country and a pre-measure was conducted with respect to:

a)   the extent to which bullying incidents occurred in each school
b)   the functioning of factors included in the framework of DASI.

For this reason, the Revised Olweus Bully/Victim Questionnaire (OBVQ) (Olweus, 1996) and a teacher questionnaire measuring the functioning of school level factors were administered to the school sample in each country. Analysis of the data collected during this phase revealed the existing anti-bullying techniques in different schools and the functioning of the schools in relation to school and classroom learning environment factors, included in the dynamic model. Analysis further demonstrated the range of variation among schools concerning the functioning of school factors and resultantly the identification of different priorities for improvement in each school. Using the Rasch model, it was also possible to provide empirical support to the construct validity of the OBVQ and thereby the Rasch person estimates were used to investigate whether there is variation among schools in the extent to which bullying incidents can be identified. Specifically, one way analysis of variance was initially conducted which revealed that students' Rasch scores are similar for each scale when compared within a school, but different in comparison to students in other schools (Scale A was concerned with the extent to which students are victims of bullying: $F=3.4$, $p=.001$; Scale B was concerned with the extent to which students bully others: $F=4.6$, $p=.001$). This implies that scores can be generated at the school level and for this reason the authors calculated the aggregated scores of Rasch person estimates of each scale at the school level. By exploring descriptive figures of the school scores of each scale, a substantial amount of variance was discovered in levels of bullying between schools, with relatively high standard deviations for each scale (i.e. scale A: 1.45 logits and scale B: 1.52 logits) and the school scores ranging higher than 5 for each scale (scale A: from -4.00 to 1.61 and scale B: from -4.00 to 1.74). These values aid identification of schools where bullying incidents were reported often, as compared to schools in which there almost none of the students reported bullying incidents, thereby zero scores from each scale were obtained. More information about the results of the first phase of the project can be found in the final report of the project, which is available from the web page of the project (http://www.ucy.ac.cy/goto/jls/en-US/WelcomeMessage.aspx).

During the second phase of the project, we initially established a network of at least 15 schools within each country which were willing to establish strategies and actions to face and reduce bullying by using DASI. Training and provision of guidelines were offered to the participating schools within each country, taking into consideration the differing national contexts. A handbook was also produced which presents the theoretical framework and provides suggestions to schools on how to build school self-evaluation mechanisms that aim to prevent bullying and improve the educational practices at school and classroom level. The handbook also includes the rationale of the project and clarifies the role of the Advisory and Research Team (A&R Team). This team provides support to school stakeholders in order to assist them in carefully setting up their own strategy and action plans for facing and reducing bullying. The handbook also placed emphasis on the strategies and action plans, which should aim to:

- Raise the awareness of pupils, teachers, parents and supervisors about bullying and how to deal with it.
- Encourage the students, parents and teachers to report any bullying incident, as well as take appropriate actions for all students when bullying happens.
- Take actions to improve the school learning environment and the School Policy.

Moreover, the handbook stated that the A&R Team was responsible to help schools identify what can be achieved with ease, as well as when and how this can be done to deal with and prevent bullying. As a consequence, the aim of the handbook (produced by our research team) was mainly to help schools develop and implement their strategies and action plans, by providing concrete and specific guidelines to the teachers (the practitioners), management team (principal and deputy heads) and school team. Specifically, the A&R Team provided the aims, content, target groups and, most importantly, the activities and actions that schools could carry out in order to face school bullying effectively. These guidelines were expected to enable the development of specific strategies and actions to face bullying among students and thereby to work towards the prevention and reduction of the problem. Thus, the handbook included specific suggestions for handling and sanctioning bullying when it occurs. In addition, it provided clear suggestions on how to build school self-evaluation mechanisms, including the collection of relevant data, and the use of this information to prevent bullying and improve the educational practices, both at the school and classroom levels. To assist readers' understanding of the type of suggestions provided to schools on actions that can be taken to address each school factor, Appendix 5.1 consists of the section of the handbook which was concerned with school policy on student behaviour outside the classroom. This factor is seen as an important aspect of the school learning environment which is the overarching school factor included in the dynamic model (see Creemers & Kyriakides, 2008a). The handbook can be accessed from the web page of the project (http://www. ucy.ac.cy/goto/jls/en-US/WelcomeMessage.aspx).

At the next step of this phase, the A&R Team provided support to the schools to help them establish school self-evaluation mechanisms. In addition, the research team conducted analysis of the data that emerged from the pre-measure and provided feedback to each school indicating its priorities for improvement. School stakeholders had the chance to discuss the findings of SSE and decide whether their action plans would address one, or a combination of priorities concerning the factors included in the dynamic model. It was strongly recommended that decisions of their priorities for improvement should be taken not only by the teachers and the school management team, but also students and parents who should also be actively involved in the decision making process itself. For this reason, schools were encouraged to establish a committee with representatives of parents, students and teachers to discuss the results and gradually reach a consensus about the priorities of the school and how to deal with them. *The final decision was expected to be announced to the whole school community and feedback was to be provided which would assist with a clear definition of the priority for improvement.*

Subsequently, school stakeholders (in co-operation with the A&R Team) developed their strategies and action plans addressing specific aspects of the domains that they were focusing on. It was explicitly stated in the action plan that it is important not only to *specify the activities* that can be taken, but also to indicate *who is supposed to do it*, what the *time-schedule* is and what resources are needed. At this point, the schools were also reminded to make use of the suggestions and additional reading sources provided in the handbook, in order to specify the activities which had to take place. For this reason, school stakeholders had to divide the work for developing their action plans by appointing different groups or committees for specific areas. At all stages, and especially in developing action plans, members of the A&R Team were invited to support schools. Readers who may like to view some examples of action plans developed by schools participating in this project can visit the web page of the project (http://www. ucy.ac.cy/goto/jls/en-US/WelcomeMessage.aspx).

Beyond designing action plans, school stakeholders were further asked to make decisions regarding the monitoring of the implementation (see Chapter 3, step

E). For example, some schools decided that a log book should be kept by the coordinator of the improvement effort, as well as of the stakeholders' implementation of the action plans, who also had to share their experiences / views with the management team and other stakeholders. If a problem arose in implementing aspects of the action plans, school stakeholders (in cooperation with the A&R Team) had to improve their action plans and/or provide support to those stakeholders not in a position to implement particular tasks of the action plans.

The implementation phase lasted for approximately eight months and the A&R Team provided support to the school stakeholders by helping them overcome difficulties and problems that emerged during the implementation of their action plans. In some cases, the A&R Team provided school based in-service training to staff to help them face difficulties in implementing their action plans. Moreover, schools established continuous formative evaluation mechanisms which helped them modify their strategies and plans, according to the circumstances and specific needs of different groups of the school population. In some cases, schools had to modify their plans up to four times during a school year. This does not necessarily imply that the original action plans were insufficient, but rather suggests that they did not remain relevant for a length of time, due to the fact that bullying is a dynamic phenomenon. On the contrary, one is likely to expect that a specific action plan developed at a certain period of time will be subject to change over a length of time. If this is the case, it might indicate that the school monitoring system did not provide valid data (e.g. everyone attempts to please one another by indicating that all the actions are implemented sufficiently and major progress has been made). The apt modification of action plans was found to contribute to achieving the ultimate aims of this intervention and reduce the chance of a school discovering only too late that no progress was made through the school year, due to the poor implementation of its action plans which could not contribute to the reduction of bullying.

The above procedure stresses the importance of a shared responsibility of the whole school community in developing and implementing strategies and actions to combat bullying. However, it should also be acknowledged that the role of the teachers and their active involvement is crucial for the success of this intervention. Therefore the successful implementation of this project depends on the active involvement of teachers and their contribution to designing the action plans which will be benefited by their knowledge and experiences in dealing with bullying.

Summative evaluation of the impact of the project

In order to evaluate the impact of the project, a summative evaluation was conducted. For the purposes of the summative evaluation, in each country, the A&R Team provided feedback to a second group of schools about the results that emerged from the pre-measure and these schools were supported to develop their own strategies and actions to face bullying, without using the DASI. Thus, this group of schools was treated as a control group and data were collected in order to compare the impact of the two approaches on:

a)   reduction of bullying
b)   improving the quality of school life (as perceived by students).

In order to achieve this aim, the Revised OBVQ and a questionnaire measuring the quality of school life as perceived by students (Kyriakides, 2005a) were administered both at the beginning and at the end of intervention. In the Netherlands, a third group of schools was also established, which was encouraged to develop strategies and actions to face bullying by making use of data on the type of networks that existed in schools. The data that emerged from this study assisted us in identifying whether use of the DASI or the network approach had greater impact on the two dependent variables. Moreover, in Cyprus and Greece, data on the functioning of school factors were collected both at the beginning and end of the intervention. This allowed the authors to investigate the impact of DASI, not only on reduction of bullying, but also on improving the functioning of school factors. Furthermore, it was possible to test the main assumption of this project: schools were encouraged to develop strategies and action plans to improve the functioning of school factors, as these factors were assumed to predict the school's effectiveness of reducing bullying. Thus, analysing the data collected in these two countries will determine whether schools using DASI reduced bullying through improving the functioning of school factors (i.e. searching for the mediating effects of DASI on the reduction of bullying).

Below the main results of the summative evaluation are presented, yet it is important to note that some of the statistical figures presented in this chapter may be found useful for readers, but less so for school stakeholders. For interpretation of the findings, only the main figures can be presented to the school stakeholders, yet the A&R Team is expected to take time to discuss the implications of these findings with the school stakeholders. For example, it is important for school stakeholders to know that there were no statistically significant differences in bullying incidents between the control and experimental group at the beginning of the intervention, whereas differences (in favour of the DASI group) are reported at the end of the intervention. Similarly, the A&R Team can present the results that emerged from the SEM analysis (see section B), without providing excessive technical information (e.g. the fit indices of the different models), yet still explain the interrelations between variables that are associated with the intervention and its impact. Specifically, the A&R Team can show stakeholders that the DASI intervention had an effect on all final measures (i.e. the two scales measuring bullying and the functioning of school factors) and that the improvement of school level factors had an impact on the reduction of bullying. These results support the importance of using DASI to face and reduce bullying, whilst providing some empirical support to the theory upon which the intervention is based.

A) The impact of DASI approach on reduction of bullying and on improving the quality of school life: a cross country analysis

This section provides the main results of the summative evaluation of the project which attempts to identify the impact of using DASI upon the reduction of bullying, and upon the development of positive attitudes towards the quality of school life. In order to measure the impact of DASI on the reduction of bullying, we conducted two separate multilevel analyses of student estimates which emerged from use of the Rasch model to analyse data of each of the two scales of the OBVQ. The OBVQ was administered to the student sample at the beginning and end of the intervention and thereby the prior measure was also taken into account (see the previous part of this chapter).

Since the number of countries involved in this project is relatively small, it was decided to model the country effects by adding relevant dummy variables into the empty model and not to consider the country as an extra level of the data. Thus, the first step in the analysis was to determine which levels to include in order to reflect the hierarchical structure of the data. Empty models with all possible combinations of the levels of analysis (i.e. student, class, and school) were established and the likelihood statistics of each model were compared (Snijders & Bosker, 1999). An empty model consisting of student and school level represented the best solution, which was a common finding that emerged from analysing the final Rasch scores of students in each of the two scales of the OBVQ. This implies that the school effect is more important than that of the classroom effect in bullying. This finding can be attributed to the greater likelihood that bullying incidents will occur outside of the classroom, therefore the school rather than the classroom level can be viewed as more important in dealing with bullying. These findings are also in line with the results of a recent longitudinal study investigating teacher and school effectiveness in reduction of bullying (Kyriakides et al., 2008).

Table 5.1 illustrates the parameter estimates and the standard errors derived from the multi-level analysis of student scores in each scale of the OBVQ. The first model presents the variance at individual and school level without explanatory variables (empty model or model 0). The variance at each level reached statistical significance ($p<.05$), which revealed that multilevel analysis should be conducted in order to identify the explanatory variables which are associated with student scores in each scale. It can be observed that more than 20% of the variance is explained by the extent to which students are either being bullied (scale A) or are bullying others (scale B) at the school level. In model 1 the three dummy variables measuring the impact of the country (with England as a reference group) and two background factors (prior score and gender) were added to the empty model measuring achievement in each scale of the OBVQ. The likelihood statistic (X^2) shows a significant change between the empty model and model 1 ($p<.001$) for both scales. Moreover, over 50% of the

Table 5.1 Parameter Estimates and (Standard Errors) for the analysis of Scales A and B (Students within schools)

Factors	Model 0	Scale A Model 1	Model 2	Model 0	Scale B Model 1	Model 2
Fixed part (Intercept)	-2.77 (.07)	-1.21 (.09)	-1.01 (.09)	-3.31 (.05)	-1.21 (.09)	-1.01 (.09)
Student level *Context* Prior Measure		0.65 (.01)*	0.65 (.02)*		0.56 (.01)*	0.65 (.02)*
Sex (0=boys, 1=girls)		0.02 (.04)	0.02 (.04)		-0.01 (.03)	-0.01 (.03)
School level *Type of intervention* Daphne			-0.41 (.07)*			-0.18(.05)*
Network			-0.13 (0.13)			-0.12(0.09)
Country The Netherlands		0.05 (.10)	0.01 (.10)		0.25(.07)*	0.25(.08)*
Cyprus		0.36 (.11)*	0.36 (.10)*		0.34 (.07)*	0.34(.07)*
Greece		-0.73 (.10)*	-0.71 (.10)*		-0.45(.08)*	-0.45(.08)*
Variance components School	24%	4.9%	3.2%	21.9%	5.5%	4.4%
Student	76%	41.2%	41.2%	78.1%	43.0%	42.9%
Explained		53.9%	55.6%		51.5%	52.7%
Significance test X^2	9559.6	7534.8	7503.4	8031.4	6120.2	6107.1
Reduction		2024.8	31.4		1911.2	13.1
Degrees of freedom		3	1		3	1
p-value		.001	.001		.001	.001

* Statistically significant effect at level .05.

variance of student achievement in each scale was explained. It can also be observed that the effect of prior measure was statistically significant and relatively high, whereas gender did not have any effect on the extent to which students are either being bullied or bully others. Country effects were also reported, yet the authors recommend interpreting these with caution, as none of the samples were nationally representative. For example, the highest scores were reported in Cyprus, although this might be attributable to the sampling procedure used in Cyprus for the school sample (see Chapter 2 section C.1 of the final report which describes the methodology of the project). In model 2, the impacts of the two different types of interventions (the dynamic integrated approach and the network approach) were measured by inclusion of the two relevant dummy variables into the first model, whilst treating the control group as a reference group. The figures of Table 5.1 reveal that both the extent to which students are being bullied and the extent to which students bully others were reduced significantly more at schools in which the dynamic integrated approach was implemented, than those that did not. These findings provide support to the use of the dynamic integrated approach to face and reduce bullying.

Table 5.2 Parameter Estimates and (Standard Errors) for the analysis of student attitudes towards the quality of school life (Students within schools)

Factors	Model 0	Model 1	Model 2
Fixed part (Intercept)	1.26 (0.05)	0.75 (0.07)	-1.01 (0.09)
Student level			
Context			
Prior Measure		0.43 (0.02)*	0.43 (0.02)*
Sex (0=boys, 1=girls)		0.01 (0.04)	-0.01 (0.03)
School level			
Type of intervention			
Daphne			0.26 (0.08)*
Network			0.02 (0.18)
Country			
The Netherlands		0.08 (0.07)	0.07 (0.08)
Cyprus		-0.12 (0.10)	-0.17 (0.11)
Greece		-0.02 (0.10)	-0.10 (0.10)
Variance components			
School	15.2%	14.5%	8.4%
Student	84.8%	48.9%	48.6%
Explained		36.6%	43.0%
Significance test			
X^2	6328.2	5816.3	5776.1
Reduction		511.9	40.2
Degrees of freedom		1	1
p-value		.001	.001

* Statistically significant effect at level .05.

Table 5.2 illustrates the parameter estimates and the standard errors derived from the multi-level analysis of student attitudes towards the quality of their school life. The first model presents the variance at individual and school levels without any explanatory variable (empty model). Readers can observe that 15.2% of the variance was at the school level, a finding that is in line with results of studies measuring school effectiveness in relation to the achievement of affective outcomes (e.g. Kyriakides, 2005a; Knuver & Brandsma, 1993; Opdenakker & Van Damme, 2000). In model 1, the three dummy variables measuring the impact of the country (with England as a reference group) and the two student background factors (prior attitude and gender) were added to the empty model. The following observations arise from Table 5.2. Firstly, model 1 explained 36.6% of the total variance and the likelihood statistic (X^2) revealed a significant change between the empty model and model 1 (p<.001). Secondly, the variable measuring prior attitudes towards the quality of school life was the only variable found to be associated with the final attitudes of students towards the quality of school life. This implies that there is no country effect or gender effect on student attitudes towards the quality of school life. Model 2 is concerned with the impact of the two different types of interventions to face and reduce bullying (the DASI and the network approach) upon student attitudes towards the quality of the school life. The figures of the last column of Table 5.2 reveal that students of schools which made use of DASI improved their attitudes towards school life at a higher level than students of all the other schools. This implies that the proposed approach did not have only an effect on reducing bullying but also on the achievement of a relevant affective outcome of schooling.

At this point, it is important to note that the above findings were also supported by conducting separate within-country analysis. In each country, schools which made use of DASI managed to reduce bullying at a higher level than the schools of the control group. However, in some countries (e.g. Cyprus and Greece) the reported effect sizes were much bigger than in others. Nevertheless, in each country the effect sizes were bigger for the impact of DASI upon the reduction of bullying than upon the development of positive attitudes towards the quality of school life. This finding appears to be in line with results of other effectiveness studies, which show the impact of the school in the achievement of affective outcomes to be very small (e.g. Kyriakides, 2005a; Knuver & Brandsma, 1993; Opdenakker & Van Damme, 2000). Therefore, the findings of this project suggest that it is easier for schools to manage to reduce bullying rather than help their students develop positive attitudes towards school life.

B) Testing the theoretical assumption of the project: To what extent does improving school factors have any effect on reduction of bullying?

In this section, the main theoretical assumption of the project is tested and the success of the project in reducing bullying is explained. As explained previously, the project is based on the assumption that improving the functioning of school factors can aid schools to become more effective and reduce bullying incidents. Due to the data of school factor functioning being collected for two participating countries both at the beginning and end of the intervention, we explored whether this intervention had not only direct effects on the reduction of bullying, but also indirect effects on improving the functioning of school factors.

The following three conceptual models were used to test the effect of the intervention on the reduction of bullying, as measured by comparing the scores of students on each scale of the OBVQ, both before and after the intervention was put into practice:

1   the direct effect model
2   the indirect effect model
3   the direct and indirect effect model.

Table 5.3 Summary of fit results for the three alternative models concerned with the effect of intervention upon the reduction of bullying

Alternative models	X^2	Df	p	CFI	TLI	RMSEA	SRMR(B)	SRMR (W)
Cyprus								
1) The direct effect model	155.8	65	.001	.94	.93	.09	.162	.009
2) The indirect effect model	149.2	60	.001	.95	.94	.10	.173	.011
3) The direct and indirect effect model	64.9	59	.279	.98	.98	.05	.124	.006
Greece								
1) The direct effect model	155.8	65	.001	.94	.93	.09	.162	.009
2) The indirect effect model	149.2	60	.001	.95	.94	.10	.173	.011
3) The direct and indirect effect model	64.9	59	.279	.98	.98	.05	.124	.006

Note: CFI = Comparative Fit Index; TLI = Tucker-Lewis Fit Index; RMSEA = Root Mean Square Error of Approximation; SRMR(W) = Square root mean error for the student level; SRMR(B) = Square root mean error for the school level.

In the first model, we assume that the intervention has only direct effects upon each of the two indicators that measure reduction of bullying and upon improvement of the functioning of school factors. It is also assumed that for each scale of the OBVQ, student factors (i.e. gender, SES, ethnicity) and prior Rasch measures have direct effects on student final score. In the second model, we did not expect any direct effect of the intervention on either of the two indicators measuring the reduction of bullying. It was only the indirect effects for improving the functioning of school factors that were assumed in the second model. Finally, the third model is based on the assumption that the intervention has both direct and indirect effects on student final score in each scale of the OBVQ. For the purposes of this analysis, MPlus was used to test the three conceptual models and identify which of the three models fits our data most accurately. The main results that emerged from this analysis are presented below.

Model fit statistics for each of the three models are reported in Table 5.3. For each country, it is clear that model 3 fits the data best. Specifically, in each subject the p value for the chi-square test of model 3 was found to be higher than 0.05. Moreover, both the Comparative Fit Index (CFI) and the Tucker-Lewis Index (TLI) were higher than 0.95. As far as the value of the RMSEA is concerned, in each country it was lower than 0.06. These results reveal that model 3 is well fit to the data (see Hu & Bentler, 1999). Figures 5.1 and 5.2 illustrate the best

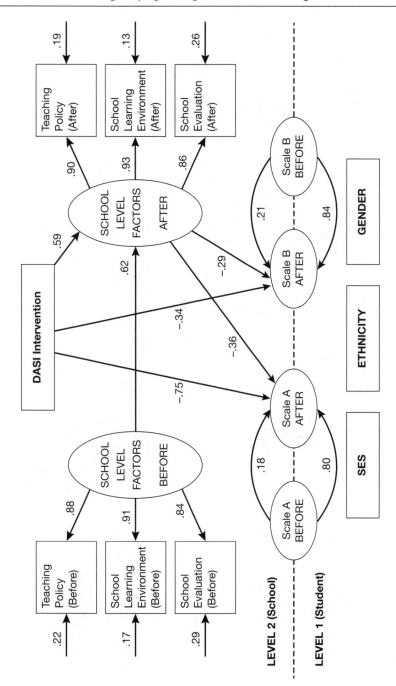

Figure 5.1 A multilevel model illustrating the direct and indirect effect of DASI upon reduction of bullying in Cypriot primary schools.

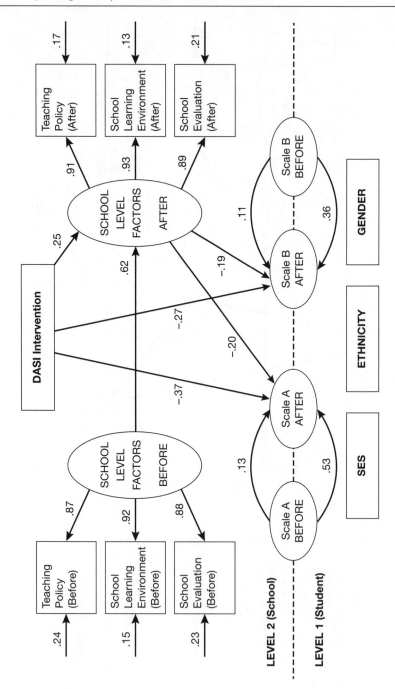

Figure 5.2 A multilevel model illustrating the direct and indirect effect of DASI upon reduction of bullying in Greek primary schools.

fitting models that emerged from the data collected in Cyprus and Greece respectively and the estimated standardised parameters are presented. At the lowest level, none of the background variables (i.e. SES, ethnicity, and gender) were found to be associated with either of the two indicators measuring bullying at the end of the intervention. On the other hand, the pre-measures were found to be relatively good predictors of the final measure of bullying, which provides support to the predictive validity of the OBVQ. At the school level, both figures reveal that the use of the DASI approach had a positive direct impact on the reduction of bullying. However, the reported effect sizes reveal that the impact of DASI was stronger for reducing the extent to which students are being bullied, rather than the extent to which students bully others. An indirect effect upon the reduction of bullying can also be identified, due to school use of the DASI approach which improved the functioning of school level factors which were associated with the reduction of bullying. It is important to take into consideration that the measures of the three school level factors were found to belong to a latent variable, implying that the school level factors of the dynamic model are related to each other. This finding provides further support to the assumption of the dynamic model that factors operating at the same level are related to each other (see Chapter 2). It can therefore be claimed that the results of the SEM analysis provide support to the main assumption upon which this intervention was based.

Schools which made use of DASI improved the functioning of their school factors. Their efforts to do so had an indirect effect on the reduction of bullying, as these factors were associated with the extent to which bullying incidents are observed in the school. Therefore, the assumption of DASI that school improvement efforts should address school factors (see step B of DASI) is justified. In addition, the intervention has been shown to have a direct impact on the reduction of bullying. This might be attributed to the intervention not only improving the functioning of school factors, but also providing support to different stakeholders for dealing with bullying, through making use of the relevant literature. Our attempt to integrate research on bullying with EER and thus develop this project, has resulted in both direct and indirect effects of the DASI treatment on the reduction of bullying.

Conclusions

In this section, we provide a brief summary of the main findings of summative evaluation and draw implications for the use of DASI to face and reduce bullying. The main results of this project are as follows: first, during the initial phase of the study, significant variation was discovered among schools (within and across countries), as to the extent to which students are being bullied or bully others, and on the functioning of school factors included in the theoretical framework of DASI. Secondly, the data that emerged from this phase provided support to the validity of the OBVQ and of the questionnaire measuring the functioning of school factors. During this second phase, we were also in a position to demonstrate the validity of the student questionnaire, which measures the quality of school life. These instruments can be used for research and improvement efforts by schools in the participating countries. Thirdly, qualitative data collected during the second phase of the project revealed that schools did not face significant difficulties in developing their own school self evaluation mechanisms, and generally supported the proposed dynamic approach to face and reduce bullying. In the next stage, multilevel modelling techniques were used and significant differences were discovered amongst schools in their effectiveness status for reducing bullying. The importance of school effectiveness is demonstrated by using either data that emerged from scale A of the OBVQ (which refers to the extent to which students are being bullied) or scale B (which refers to the extent to which students bully others). The following stage consisted of multilevel analysis once again, which revealed that schools making use of DASI were able to reduce bullying at a significantly higher level than the schools of the control or network groups. The use of DASI to face bullying also had a significant effect in the development of positive attitudes towards schooling, but this was smaller than the effect of the dynamic approach on the reduction of bullying. Finally, it was possible to collect data on the functioning of school factors, both at the beginning and end of the intervention, for two of the participating countries. Using a SEM approach, schools which made use of DASI were demonstrated to improve the functioning of their school factors at a higher level than the schools of the control group. Moreover, those schools which improved their school factors were also found to be more effective in terms of reducing bullying. This implies that DASI had both a direct and an indirect effect on the reduction of bullying (through improving the functioning of school factors).

Implications can be drawn from the findings of this project for the development of effective policies and practices in reducing bullying. Firstly, the majority of evidence in this project suggests that there is scope to be given to school self evaluation, in order to develop effective strategies and actions to face and reduce bullying. School self-evaluation promotes the importance of collecting and analysing data at different stages of a school improvement project and thereby a continuous evaluation model is used. Moreover, schools are expected to reflect on their own strategies and actions, adapting and improving them and thereby achieving the formative purpose of evaluation. This argument was also supported by the results of the study presented in Chapter 4, concerned with the use of DASI to establish SSE mechanisms for improvement purposes. Secondly, by offering a theoretical framework to schools, it was also possible to assist stakeholders to identify their priorities for improvement (through SSE) and understand the effect that dealing with a school factor can have on reducing bullying. The use of an evidence-based and theory-driven approach can help schools to develop effective strategies and action plans, which address important school factors. These can contribute to the improvement of the school and classroom learning environments, and ultimately to the reduction of bullying.

This assumption was systematically tested and the summative evaluation revealed that this approach can have a positive impact not only upon improving the quality of school life, but also on reducing bullying (both direct and indirect effects).

In this chapter, it can further be claimed that the support provided by the A&R Team to schools in implementing their strategies and actions is also critical in reducing bullying. This is due to the A&R Team not only providing schools with the knowledge-base for dealing with the problems they face during the implementation, but also assisting them with their technical expertise to continuously evaluate their strategies and actions for facing bullying.

We would like to finally emphasise the way in which the DASI approach was used in schools in five different countries, with positive associations found with the functioning of school factors and effectiveness over different countries. Moreover, this project shows that DASI can aid schools in different countries to deal with challenges, improve their school learning environments, achieve relevant affective aims and above all, reduce bullying. Given that the other projects presented in this part of the book are concerned with the impact of DASI on the achievement of cognitive learning outcomes (see Chapters 4 and 7), one could claim that this project shows that DASI can have an impact on achieving, not only cognitive, but also affective learning outcomes.

Chapter 6

Schools establishing school self-evaluation mechanisms for improvement purposes

Case studies of two primary schools in Slovenia

Bren Matevž , Hauptman Alenka, Cankar Gašper, & Zupanc Darko

Introduction

The previous chapters reported on projects which followed an experimental approach, including a large number of schools in their samples. These projects demonstrated the impact of DASI on the improvement of the effectiveness status of schools. Chapter 4 was concerned with the impact of using DASI to develop SSE mechanisms for improvement, and their effect upon student achievement gains in mathematics. Chapter 5, on the other hand, refers to the impact of DASI on the reduction of bullying. These projects were conducted in different educational settings, and it was shown that schools in different countries were generally able to implement DASI and achieve their improvement aims. However, there was also variation in the impact of DASI upon the improvement in effectiveness status of schools participating in these two projects. This implies that different study designs, not only experimental but also case studies and mixed methods studies (Kington, Sammons, Day, & Regan, 2011), are required to identify the extent to which schools can use DASI to establish their school improvement strategies and action plans. This chapter refers to two case studies conducted in Slovenia, investigating the difficulties which schools face when attempting to use the DASI framework to establish SSE mechanisms for improvement. The methodology of these two case studies and their main results are presented in the proceeding section. Although schools in Slovenia are expected to develop SSE mechanisms, the relationship between this national policy and school improvement is not evident. Therefore the extent to which these two schools can make use of a theoretical framework to establish SSE for improvement purposes is examined. This helps to ascertain whether individual schools, largely independent of the system, can improve their effectiveness status when they use the proposed approach to design their improvement strategies and action plans. Readers can also see how DASI can be implemented in small scale projects, and adapted to the context of individual schools in order to develop strategies and action plans for improvement purposes.

Using the dynamic model as a theoretical framework to establish SSE mechanisms

Given that these two case studies were conducted in Slovenia, information about the educational system in Slovenia and its national policy on quality assessment and assurance is provided in Appendix 6.1. In Slovenia all schools are expected to establish their own SSE mechanisms, and recent legislation in the organisation and financing of education act (ZOFVI, 2008, 17. article) determines principal responsibility for assessing and ensuring the quality of education through SSE mechanisms and annual reports on SSE. Although SSE is becoming mandatory in Slovenian schools, no study has appeared to systematically investigate its impact on the effectiveness status of schools. It is also important to note that schools are not offered any conceptual framework which could assist in establishing SSE and collecting data to help improve the functioning of their school factors, teaching and learning practices. In this context, an experimental study is currently being undertaken to investigate the impact of using DASI to establish SSE mechanisms for improvement purposes (Hauptman, Zupanc, Bren, & Cankar, 2011). Following a similar methodology as described in Chapter 4, 60 primary schools were randomly selected and split into two groups. The first group is expected to use DASI and establish SSE mechanisms for improvement purposes, whereas the second group is not utilising a specific theoretical framework to develop SSE. Instead, the evaluation agenda is defined by the school stakeholders. The second group is following a similar approach as the treatment 1 described in Chapter 4, which is also in line with Slovenian national policy and is based on the assumptions that school stakeholders should define by themselves the criteria of SSE and establish their own improvement strategies for improvement. On the other hand, the first group is expected to make use of the dynamic model and establish their own SSE mechanisms. The advisory and research team provides support to school stakeholders in their attempts to establish SSE mechanisms, identify their priorities for improvement and develop both strategies and action plans.

The first step of SSE is based on the assumption that a clear understanding of the outcome and the path towards it is vital (MacBeath & McGlynn, 2003). However, individuals have different perceptions of change; it is difficult to reach consensus among participants in SSE, albeit crucial in its success (Kyriakides & Campbell, 2004). Therefore it is important to establish procedures to ensure clear understanding amongst teachers, head teachers and other stakeholders regarding the aims of SSE. Two case studies were conducted to further investigate progress in two of the schools that participated in the experimental study mentioned above, which made use of DASI to develop SSE mechanisms. The results of the case studies, presented in this chapter, may help to ascertain whether the dynamic model can be a useful tool for helping the stakeholders of each school to establish clarity and consensus about the aims of SSE.

The dynamic model of educational effectiveness was established to help policy makers and practitioners improve educational practice, by making rational decisions concerning both the optimal fit of effectiveness factors and the present situation in the school or educational system (Creemers & Kyriakides, 2008a). It is therefore expected that using this model as a framework for conducting SSE will help school stakeholders to collect empirical data. This will reveal the strengths and weaknesses of their schools and identify priority areas for improvement. In addition, providing knowledge on 'what works in education and why' to stakeholders will allow the advisory and research team to help schools to design their own strategies and action plans, to improve relevant school and classroom factors. Furthermore, by using the DASI approach and available research instruments for conducting SSE, the functioning of factors operating at different levels in education can be measured by both their quantitative and qualitative characteristics (especially by looking at the five measurement dimensions of the dynamic model, presented in Chapter 2). This should result in more comprehensive strategies and action plans for school improvement. However, a critical question is whether school stakeholders are able to follow external strategies incorporated by the A&R Team and adopt the DASI approach, which focuses on specific factors for improvement, rather than favouring their own judgements on issues which may not actually be related to student learning.

Aims of the study

The main aim of these two case studies is to identify the extent to which DASI can be used for school improvement in a country where SSE is mandatory, and school stakeholders are given the power to develop their own SSE mechanisms. Thus these case studies may help to establish if school stakeholders are willing to collaborate with the A&R Team and make use of the knowledge base available, to develop their SSE mechanisms and implement strategies and action plans for school improvement. For example, step C of DASI is concerned with the use of specific instruments to identify priorities for improvement. Yet if results showed that a school should treat a specific factor as a priority area for improvement, it is important to establish whether stakeholders will agree with this if their expect-ations followed a different direction. It is also important to identify any other obstacles in implementing DASI in these two schools. This might involve understanding how context-specific factors should be taken into account, when introducing DASI into schools already implementing other improvement projects. The aim of our study is therefore to identify challenges and gauge the best possible implementation process for the DASI approach, as well as reflect on ways in which it can be introduced into schools in different educational settings.

METHODS

A case study is an empirical inquiry that investigates a contemporary phenomenon within its real-life context. When the boundaries between phenomenon and context are not clearly evident, a case study can be conducted in order to give the opportunity to the research team to study the phenomenon in depth within a specific context. Conducting a case study also gives the opportunity to researchers to use multiple sources of evidence. For the purposes of this project, the two case studies can identify whether the contexts of the two schools have any impact upon the way that the DASI approach is used for improvement purposes. In addition, the researchers may identify obstacles which schools might face by using DASI, using different techniques and sources of data. At this point it is argued that a case study is not the study of uniqueness but of particularity. That is to say, case study is concerned with intelligibility, which in turn is a matter of connecting the case with others of its kind. It can therefore be claimed that these findings may help to identify similar schools to those examined in these case studies. These may show the same outcomes when the DASI is used for establishing SSE, rather than when schools develop their own SSE without using a theoretical framework (as occurs now in Slovenia). In this section, information about the two schools and the design of the study is provided, and it is demonstrated how small scale studies on the use of DASI can be conducted in different educational settings.

Sample

To identify the extent to which DASI can be used for school improvement purposes, case studies in two primary schools in Slovenia were conducted during the school year 2010-2011. These two schools were randomly selected from the group of 60 schools which participated in the experimental study mentioned above. They were required to use the DASI in order to establish SSE mechanisms and develop both their strategies and action plans for school improvement. The two primary schools included in the case studies differed in their features, size and context. The first case-study school was a small, rural school with approximately 200 students in Years one to nine; each year group was comprised of one class of students. It should be emphasised that Slovenian primary schools include Years one to nine (ages 6 to 15 years), which is in the International Standard Classification of Education comparable with ISCED 1 and ISCED 2 (ISCED, 1997). The first case-study school employs 23 teachers, and is situated in the centre of a small town; due to the rural location people tend to move away from the area. The school building is small, but suitable for the number of students. The majority of teachers are female (88%), with an average of 16.47 years of teaching experience (range from 2-32 years). The SES of students and their parents in the school area is below average for Slovenia.

The second case-study school is one of the biggest primary schools in Slovenia. There are approximately 800 students in 32 classes, where each Year consists of three to four classes of students. Approximately 80 teachers are employed. The school faces challenges of over-subscription, with a shortage of room to accommodate ever increasing numbers of students moving to the school's area near a large town. This occurs because primary education in Slovenia is generally public, and thus students often attend the school nearest in proximity to their homes. The school building is large, situated away from the centre of town with many facilities for students. The proportion of female teachers is even higher in this school (95 %), with an average of 14.74 years of teaching experience (range from 1–35 years). The SES of students and their parents in the school area is below average for Slovenia.

Design of the Study

At the beginning of the school year, members of the research team presented the dynamic model to the teachers in both schools. Specifically, the value assumptions of the model and its essential characteristics were discussed. Moreover, classroom and school level factors were presented, and the importance of improving the functioning of school factors was explained to teachers (see steps A and B of DASI). In order to collect data on the reactions and comments of school stakeholders towards the dynamic model, one member of the research team used a high inference observation instrument. The research team then met again with the stakeholders of each school, and presented the DASI. School stakeholders were given consent to collect data on the functioning of school factors. Then, the research team had to conduct the analyses and identify priorities for improvement (see steps C and D of DASI). Following this, the instruments developed to test the validity of the dynamic model were administered and the functioning of the school factors in each school was measured. Based on the results of the analyses, three priority areas for school improvement were identified. These results were then disseminated at a school staff meeting, and the research team attempted to assist school stakeholders in selecting the area that they needed to develop an improvement strategy for (see step D of DASI). Due to the critical nature of this stage, one member of the research team conducted a structured observation instead of participating in the discussion.

Finally, the research team arranged a meeting with the teachers of each school to help them develop their own strategies and action plans for improvement. During this meeting, suggestions on how to construct an action plan were provided to the stakeholders, as well as guidelines on how to improve the functioning of the factor(s) addressed. Subsequently, the school stakeholders agreed to implement the action plans and collect data evaluating this implementation process (see step E of DASI). The research team stressed the importance of establishing formative evaluation mechanisms, which could help them to monitor the implementation of the improvement strategy and also decide how to adapt action plans to fit the schools' needs. Members of the research team conducted observations to identify how the action plans were implemented, and if schools were faced with any obstacles in improving the functioning of school factors.

During the first four months of the implementation phase (from December to March), the research team collected data concerned with the implementation of each school's improvement strategy. For this reason, observations were conducted and both the head teacher and other teaching staff were interviewed by the research team. This gave an indication of the conditions under which schools can make effective use of DASI.

Instruments

A teacher questionnaire and observation instruments were used for the case studies. Teacher questionnaires were administered to measure the functioning of school factors in each school (see step C of DASI). All teachers in both of the schools were asked to complete the questionnaire, with response rates of approximately 78% (18 out of 23) in the first school and 50% (37 out of 80) in the second school. The teacher questionnaire examined the policy developed by each school regarding different aspects of teaching. Specifically, school policy on the quantity of teaching, provision of learning opportunities and quality of teaching was examined. Views of policy on the broader *learning environment of schools* were also examined. There were four aspects of the School Learning Environment which were taken into account:

i.   policy on student behaviour outside the classroom
ii.   teacher collaboration
iii. relations with parents and the wider school community
iv.   use of educational resources.

The analysis of the teacher questionnaire helped to measure the functioning of the nine factors of the dynamic model in each school. Using the Kendall coefficient of concordance test, it was possible to rank these nine factors and identify a list of the three factors for which each school obtained lower results than others. In this way, school stakeholders were assisted in identifying factors which required more attention, and selecting the area on which to focus their improvement efforts. The reactions of the school staff were recorded using observation. Observations were conducted by one of the researchers and were held during specific activities. Information was gathered using a digital voice recorder, to take notes on participants' activities and communication. Data were recorded with the assistance of four high-inference observation instruments. All instruments had a similar format and included a range of reactions which might have occurred during the case study. These included date, school and the case in which the observation took place. They also included specific aspects; the observer recorded whether these occurred and, if so, whether they were positive or negative towards the theoretical framework of DASI. In addition, the instrument recorded the types of interactions among school stakeholders which followed any reaction. Each observation instrument also addressed a range of non-verbal reactions possible during the meeting, which were expected to be reported.

The first observation instrument (OI1) was used to record any reactions during the meeting when the dynamic model was presented to the school staff members (see step B of DASI). OI1 includes reactions regarding the multilevel nature of the model, the factors included in the model and factors not included but might be considered important to stakeholders. Moreover, OI1 includes reactions regarding the five measurement dimensions of the model and its value assumptions (see Chapter 2). Other reactions regarding the presentation itself or the staff members' interest in participating in the project were also recorded.

The second observation instrument (OI2) includes reactions about the data collection tools, the research team and expectations from the project. The OI2 was used after the teachers completed the questionnaire.

The third observation instrument (OI3) recorded any reactions during the meeting which presented the results of the data analysis to staff. Emphasis was given to reactions concerning consensus about the results and the identification of the school's priority area (see step D of DASI). Finally, the fourth observation instrument (OI4) includes reactions to the action plan itself; the research team used this instrument during the first four months of the implementation period for practical reasons. After each observation phase the qualitative data were analysed using the constant comparative method (Denzin & Lincoln, 1998).

Implementation of DASI in the two case study schools

This section is divided into four parts reflecting the four phases of the case study:

a) presenting the Dynamic Model (DM) to the schools
b) administering questionnaires and analysing school factors
c) developing action plans
d) collecting data concerning the implementation of improvement strategies for each school.

Presenting the Dynamic Model to Schools

At the beginning of November the dynamic model was presented to teachers in the two case-study schools. The value assumptions of the dynamic model were presented and the importance of the factors included in the model was examined. The meeting ended with an open discussion, in which the whole group participated. Questions concerned the application of the dynamic model to school feedback or research design. Some teachers expressed their doubts about participating in another project, since they did not have positive experiences from similar projects they had participated in. The research team offered consistent support throughout the whole project, as well as providing feedback at the end. During breaks, the research team joined the participants' discussion of their personal views on the dynamic model and school factors, to try to ascertain whether expectations were met. One limitation of this session was time management, due to long presentations, and thus participants did not have the opportunity to carry out workshops on topics in smaller groups. However, this was resolved with good structure of the session; a whole-group discussion on partnership policy was held instead of a workshop. Therefore for future planning of dynamic model presentations and workshops, one-day seminars would be more appropriate.

Administering Questionnaires and Analysing School Factors

A fortnight after the meeting, school stakeholders returned the questionnaires which measured the functioning of school factors. The results of the analysis were later reported to each school, indicating the three school factors found to be the weakest in that particular school. This enabled a member of the research team to write separate reports for each school, containing brief descriptions of all the factors tested in the teacher questionnaire. At the end of the report, the three weakest school factors were listed.

In the smaller school the 'school policy on student behaviour outside the classroom' was found to be one of the weakest factors. Teachers of 'higher' (Years 5–9) and 'lower' (Years 1–4) classes had different opinions about the need for developing a school policy on this aspect. Teachers of lower year groups argued that their students' behaviour was not as problematic, and thus there was no need to develop a policy on this aspect of the school learning environment. However, they did subsequently agree that there was room for the improvement of this factor, and could recommend many strategies possible to improve it.

In the larger school, teachers were acquainted with the dynamic model and with the weakest school factors. Some teachers expressed their doubts about specific items of the questionnaire. For example, they reported on the short length of school breaks; this provided a challenge in giving support to students with special needs, due to activities occurring simultaneously. There were 60 teachers present at the meeting and thus it was not possible to reach consensus about their school priority area. For this reason, a decision was made to learn more about the dynamic model and the school level factors before reaching a decision. It was later established that the majority of teachers agreed on the importance of targeting the three factors identified in the evaluation results. However, it was agreed to rank these three factors and identify the one considered most important by the majority. The final results of this revealed that their priority area for improvement was the policy on the quality of teaching.

Developing Action Plans

In the next time period (December 2010–January 2011) one member of the research team organised school visits. The schools' overall engagement with improvement, based on the DASI, was reasonably different. In the small school a meeting was held prior to the visit, in which teachers reviewed the results of teacher questionnaires. They then discussed possible factors to be included in their action plan for improving school effectiveness. At the larger school, teachers were more sceptical about the dynamic model and the evaluation results. Both the teachers and the school co-ordinator who had attended the first seminar on the dynamic model did not share their experiences with other teachers prior to the visit.

The visit to the smaller school was co-ordinated by the research team member and the head teacher. They agreed that the presentation would consist of solely the school factors and measurement dimensions of the dynamic model, since the dynamic model had already been presented at a previous school meeting. The visit occurred on an afternoon during which other activities were also being held (e.g. teachers' meeting and a parents' afternoon at the school). Two members of the research team visited the school; one gave a presentation and the other observed participants' reactions with the aforementioned observation instruments. The meeting lasted 90 minutes and consisted of the presentation of the dynamic model, followed by a discussion with teaching staff on the elements of DASI and the school factors to be included in the action plan. The member of the research team also presented the discussion held at the previous school meeting, as well as their decision to consider the 'behaviour outside the classroom' factor for school improvement in the action plan. This school factor was also found to be the weakest, according to the results of the teacher questionnaire.

Reactions observed by the second research team member, using the instruments OI1 and OI3, were generally positive. These included non-verbal communication signs such as participants 'looking in approval/nodding their heads' and 'taking notes, whispering'. There were no participants 'texting or using mobile phones', 'looking in disapproval', 'drawing', nor signs that 'reveal the participants' desire to leave'. There were many suggestions on topics that should be included in the action plan; these included tidy classrooms and corridors, 'corners of well-being' and classroom panels describing the weekly activities. They also expressed that a well-regulated school and pleasant surroundings encouraged less misbehaviour and vandalism. Furthermore, support from the research team was requested, for including proposals of real actions into the school action plan and providing answers to open questions. Teachers appeared to be encouraged that the entire school was involved in the project and could benefit. They stressed that the participation of all stakeholders was vital, and that agreed actions must be implemented by all teachers. They also reported that many parents were overly critical of teachers and it was not easy to gain their co-operation. An additional view they expressed was that implementing this project might increase their workload. At the end of the formal meeting, the discussion continued between the head teacher, other teaching staff and the research team members. During the entire visit, the members of the research team felt that they received the head teacher's full support. The action plan of the small school was delivered on time.

The visit to the larger school was co-ordinated by a member of the research team and the school coordinator, and occurred on the same day as a teachers' meeting. Once again, two members of the research team visited the school; one delivered the presentation of DASI and the other observed participants' reactions. First, a short meeting was held with the head teacher and the school co-ordinator; the principles of the dynamic model and the research project were presented and the outline of the teachers' meeting was agreed. After the head teacher's introductions, the dynamic model was presented along with the results of the teacher questionnaire. Teachers actively participated; questions concerned measuring the dimensions of the dynamic model, on activities found to be effective and additional sources on DASI. In the second part there was discussion of the school factors and activities, in order to select the appropriate one to target for improvement. The reactions noted by the second research team member, using the observation instruments OI1 and OI3, were mostly positive for the non-verbal communication signs. Participants were not 'texting or using mobile phones', 'looking in disapproval', 'drawing', or showing signs that 'reveal the participants' desire to leave'. A decision was made to vote on the most appropriate area and accept the majority's consensus. There was no conflict over the final decision, yet there were reservations from some teachers when constructing the action plan. These concerned excessive paper work, or doubts that the procedure would lead to improvements. However, all teachers did co-operate with the planned activities.

The factor selected for the action plan of the larger school was the 'quality of teaching'. The action plan was well-prepared and included dates, activities, executants and holders. Alongside the action plan, instructions for the working group leaders were prepared by the school team and approved by the head teacher. The instructions specified the topics to be discussed at group meetings (e.g. the eight teacher level factors of the dynamic model and its five dimensions), the deadlines for the activities and evaluation and team co-ordination. Instructions also included questions to be elaborated upon in the discussion, and the five dimensions of the dynamic model to be used at the evaluation stage.

Collecting Data Concerning the Implementation of Improvement Strategies

During the first four months of implementation, the research team encouraged school co-ordinators to report on activities and evaluations performed for school improvement, based on the DASI. The research team remained supportive and kept regular contact every fortnight, in order for schools to continue with their action plan activities. Numerous activities were included in the action plan of the small school, but were all linked to the 'behaviour outside the classroom' factor. During implementation it was recognised that too many activities were listed and not all could be implemented. All school stakeholders (i.e. management team, teachers, students and parents) were involved in the implementation of action plans; they were creative and motivated to implement their improvement strategies. Some parents were willing to participate, and were present during school breaks and lunches. The general consensus was that more attention to problematic students, talking, persuasion and solving problems would improve students' behaviour. Consequently, most of the goals listed in the action plan were achieved during the first months of the project, and all the action plans were partly implemented. The head teacher and the co-ordinator provided regular reports to the research team, who offered their support in return.

At the larger school, the factor chosen for improvement was the quality of teaching. Activities to be held by subject working groups were divided into three one-month periods. Each group selected three teaching skills which they found most appropriate for improvement. One teacher from the group was appointed to be a moderator of the particular teaching skill; they presented the theoretical basis for it, and both good and bad practices. At regular weekly group meetings, they discussed these practices and prepared their own strategies. Teachers were then encouraged to carry out these tasks in at least four lessons each week, assess their impact on pupils' learning and evaluate their own progress. At the subject working group meeting one month later, each teacher presented their observations and evaluation, and wrote a short report. They then focused on the next teaching skill. The teachers' and group reports were delivered to the research team for further analysis. The first observation was that there was a large difference in individual reports reflecting the amount of effort teachers exerted. The teaching skills selected for improvement were numerous; they included structuring of classes, time management, posting questions, orientation, modelling and assessment. The attitudes towards these group and individual activities were mixed. Some teachers were enthusiastic reporting activities that they had practiced and then adapted; these included activities to improve their teaching skills and help to improve learning outcomes, collecting feedback on their work and learning about new techniques to implement in the class. Yet some teachers were more sceptical, with less effort exerted in their reports. There were suggestions that more time would be needed for implementing one teaching skill than the four weeks suggested in the action plan.

Discussion

Investigating how the DASI can be used in individual schools for improvement purposes is a reasonably ambitious task. Incorporating the theoretical framework of DASI into school practice demands co-operation and communication between the A&R Team, the school management team and individual teachers. The roles of students and their parents should also be clarified. Stakeholders in these two case study schools considered DASI to be a useful tool for improvement purposes, yet this judgement arose at the end of the process. The process itself is not only dependent on characteristics of the model, but equally on the characteristics of the implementation process used. The extent to which good or bad implementation can support or hinder the observed effects might overwhelm the 'true' effects of using DASI for improvement purposes. This is the main reason why case studies can be beneficial in this context. They provide examples of realistic and authentic settings from which new experiences can be drawn. Furthermore, they allow reflection on the best way to combine sound theoretical premises of the dynamic model with the supporting approach for implementation. It is the best way to capture the essence of communication and context between the research team, school improvement teams, individual teachers and other stakeholders. Case studies provide a basis to discern unimportant idiosyncrasies from valuable findings that influence and steer the underlying process.

The need for synergy between EER and school improvement is pertinent. It is the combination which ensures an increase in knowledge and progress in both research on effective school improvement and practice at the classroom and school levels. Using DASI in improvement settings is no longer questioned. It is evident that constant and stable improvement is possible only through clear and comprehensive theoretical frameworks; however, improvement activities are seldom judged in the long-term. Long-term effects are difficult to measure and discern from other influences, because they demand constant and sustained attention by schools and research teams to collect data over the years. Projects often lack long-term funding to achieve this. In cross-sectional research we are compelled to measure short-term effects and then move on to new projects. Evaluating the effects of DASI in the context of school improvement might take a considerable length of time. It is possible, however, to reflect on the current findings from case studies and re-evaluate these as projects continue to collect new data.

Overall, the two schools involved in this case study found the dynamic model a useful tool to support SSE processes. The structure, levels, factors and measurement dimensions of the factors included in the dynamic model seem reasonably complicated at first, leading to teachers in the larger school requiring more time to study the model. This reinforces the need for the value assumptions and essential characteristics of the model to be presented in a simple way, so that case studies and good practice reports may encourage the use of DASI for improvement purposes. It is inevitable that some teachers might still hold reservations about the potential impact of their improvement project, or the increased workload it may cause. In the second case-study school, it was easier to identify this group of teachers. The school management team (with the support of the A&R Team) made the decision to ask them to be involved in the project. An aspect often found to be effective in other educational settings is to work solely with individuals enthusiastic about the project, as they are more likely to acknowledge the benefits of being involved. Taking this into account, the results of these two case studies suggest that both the school management team and the A&R Team should be aware that some teachers may be more sceptical about the improvement project than others. Consequently, they may judge that their involvement may cause an increased workload. In this case, extra effort should be taken to dispel this idea, including in the design of the action plans.

The role of A&R Team is also critical; they should be actively involved at all stages. It is essential to visit schools regularly and ensure that the steps of DASI are being incorporated to maintain the positive effects on student learning. For example, teachers of the larger case-study school did not originally reach consensus on the aims of their school improvement. The A&R Team should provide further support here, and explain the importance of reaching agreement on these issues. In both examples mentioned, readers may notice that the DASI was not fully implemented; this suggests that agreement between stakeholders and the A&R Team to follow the DASI is vital before implementation. In spite of this, the main results from the two case studies were positive. In the first case-study school, the main aims for school improvement were achieved and all action plans were at least partially implemented. Most school stakeholders also expressed positive comments. Similarly, the second case-study school not only developed a policy on teaching quality, but also took action to improve teaching practice. Some teachers recognised that the action plans assisted in the improvement of their teaching skills. These results suggest that there is room for further improvement in using DASI to improve the quality of education, at both the teacher and school levels.

Chapter 7

Using DASI to improve teacher effectiveness

A group randomisation study

*Antoniou Panayiotis, Kyriakides Leonidas, &
Creemers Bert P.M.*

Introduction

This chapter is concerned with the use of the dynamic model for improvement at the teacher level. The previous chapters were concerned with studies investigating the use of DASI for improvement purposes at the school level. In the first part of the book, the importance of designing school improvement efforts was discussed. It was supported that designing improvement efforts which focus on the classroom level factors may improve the teaching practices of individuals but may not necessarily improve the school learning environment. In this case, teachers who improve some aspects of their teaching practices by one method will need, at some stage, an additional type of support to improve other teaching skills. Consequently, the dynamic approach to school improvement consists of steps which schools can follow in order to develop an evidence-based and theory-driven approach to their school improvement efforts. However, it is acknowledged that effectiveness research shows the teacher effect to be more important than the school effect (e.g. Teddlie & Reynolds, 2000; Scheerens & Bosker, 1997). For this reason, improvement of teaching practices is an important target of various efforts undertaken either within or outside the school, in order to improve the quality of education. Given that efforts to improve teacher effectiveness may originate from outside the school, through the provision of relevant in-service training courses, the last two chapters of this part of the book describe projects on teachers' professional development. These two chapters make use of the main assumptions of the DASI approach to develop a dynamic and integrated approach to teacher professional development. Specifically, the projects presented in these chapters can be seen as an attempt to integrate findings of research on teacher education with the dynamic model. The dynamic model is used as a theoretical framework to deal with policy and practice in teacher education because it emphasises the quality of teaching, and uses an integrated approach in defining effective teaching by focusing on factors found to be associated with student outcomes (see Chapter 2). In this chapter, we present the results of an experimental study investigating the impact of this approach on teacher professional development and also on student achievement gains in mathematics.

This chapter is also in line with current approaches which merge the findings of EER with initiatives to improve education, particularly teacher effectiveness, by proposing an approach that is based on the main assumptions and elements of DASI. In the first section of this chapter, it is acknowledged that the notion of effective schools draws a lot of attention in educational policy. This is to be expected, because it offers the possibility of improving schools to gain better results. This is especially relevant for policy makers, since the results of international comparative studies (e.g. Third International Mathematics and Science Study –TIMSS, Programme for International Student Assessment – PISA and Progress in International Reading Literacy Study – PIRLS) have created an accountability movement in most countries which strive for improvements in schools, and also in education in general. However as Creemers and Reezigt (2005) argue, schools do not change if the people within the schools, particularly the teaching staff, do not change. This is why it is suggested that school improvement initiatives should be mainly concerned with improving teaching skills, which were found to be associated with student achievement (Antoniou & Kyriakides, in press).

The focus on the improvement of education and schools at the teacher level is further justified by the results of effectiveness studies over the recent years. In particular, studies conducted in different countries over the last two decades revealed that the teacher effect is the most important in explaining variation in student achievement in both cognitive and affective outcomes (Teddlie & Reynolds, 2000). According to Scheerens and Bosker (1997), research on school effectiveness reveals that the teacher is an important component of the school's effect on students' progress. Furthermore, a number of studies on effective schools revealed that the classroom level is more influential than the school level, when examining students' performance (Hextall & Mahony, 1998; Kyriakides, Campbell, & Gagatsis, 2000; Muijs & Reynolds, 2000; Wright, Horn, & Sanders, 1997; Yair, 1997). Creemers (1994) suggests that students' academic outcomes are more heavily dependent on the procedures and activities carried out in the classroom than those carried out at the school level. In fact, without effective teacher guidance and instruction in the classroom, learning and progress cannot be achieved (Creemers, 1997; Munro, 1999; Scheerens & Bosker, 1997). The underlying rationale is that while organizational aspects of schools provide the necessary preconditions for effective teaching, it is the quality of teacher – student interactions that principally determines student progress.

Using the dynamic model for teacher improvement

The research findings on the importance of the teacher effect (e.g., Scheerens & Bosker, 1997; Kyriakides et al., 2000; Muijs & Reynolds, 2000; Wright, Horn, & Sanders, 1997; Yair, 1997; Opdenakker & Van Damme, 2000) were accounted for in the development of the dynamic model (Kyriakides, 2008). Teaching is emphasized in the model (see Chapter 2), and teacher behaviour in the classroom and its impact on student learning is taken into account in defining the classroom level factors. Thus, the dynamic model refers to eight teacher factors which were found to be associated with student achievement: structuring, orientation, questioning, application, management of time, assessment, teaching modelling, and classroom learning environment (see Chapter 2). These factors do not refer to only one approach of teaching, such as the direct and active teaching approach (e.g. structuring, application) or the constructivist approach (e.g. orientation, modelling). An integrated approach to effective teaching is adopted and both longitudinal studies and a relevant meta-analysis (Kyriakides & Creemers, 2008, 2009; Kyriakides & Christoforou, 2011) support the importance of these factors. In addition, these eight factors are measured using the five dimensions which describe both quantitative and qualitative characteristics of these factors.

The use of the dynamic model for improvement purposes at the teacher level assumes that teacher factors refer to knowledge and skills which can be developed. The model is also based on the assumption that teacher factors and their dimensions may be inter-related, and thus the importance of grouping specific factors to explain achievement gains is emphasised. In this way, not only the complex nature of effective teaching is illustrated but also specific strategies for teacher improvement can emerge (see also Chapter 2). In order to investigate the significance of the teacher level of the dynamic model, especially its potential to improve teaching practices and student attainment, the concept of 'groupings' of factors which operate at the same level and are inter-related were further explored in a recent longitudinal study (Kyriakides, Creemers, & Antoniou, 2009). This study is briefly presented below, because it provides empirical evidence supporting the importance of grouping factors.

A study searching for stages – levels of effective teaching

All the grade 5 students (n=2503) from each class (n=108) of 50 primary schools in Cyprus participated in this study. Student achievement in mathematics, Greek language, and religious education were measured, when the students were both at the beginning and end of grade 5. In order to collect data on teacher factors of the dynamic model, 972 observations of the 108 teachers of the student sample were conducted. Two low-inference and one high-inference observational instruments were used. These instruments were designed to collect data concerned with all the eight factors of the teacher level, in relation with the five measurement dimensions which are included in the dynamic model of EER.

By utilizing the Rasch and Saltus models, the teaching skills included in the dynamic model of educational effectiveness were grouped into five stages. These were situated in a developmental order and linked with student outcomes. Taking student outcomes as criteria, teachers who demonstrated competencies in the higher stages were found to be more effective than those situated at the lower stages, and thus students of teachers situated at higher stages showed better

Table 7.1 The five stages of teaching skills included in the Dynamic Model

Stages	Teaching Skills
1. Basic elements of direct teaching	Frequency management time Stage management of time Frequency structuring Frequency application Frequency assessment Frequency questioning Frequency teacher-student relation
2. Putting aspects of quality in direct teaching and touching on active teaching	Stage structuring Quality application Stage questioning Frequency student relations Focus application Stage application Quality of questions
3. Acquiring quality in active / direct teaching	Stage student relations Stage teacher-student relation Stage assessment Frequency teaching modelling Frequency orientation Focus student relations Quality: feedback Focus questioning Focus teacher-student relation Quality structuring Quality assessment
4. Differentiation of teaching	Differentiation structuring Differentiation time management Differentiation questioning Differentiation application Focus assessment Differentiation assessment Stage teaching modelling Stage orientation
5. Achieving quality and differentiation in teaching using different approaches	Quality teacher-student relation Quality student relations Differentiation teacher-student relation Differentiation student relations Focus orientation Quality orientation Differentiation orientation Quality of teaching modelling Focus teaching modelling

outcomes. This association is found for achievement in different subjects and for both cognitive and affective outcomes.

The five levels of the model are presented in Table 7.1. The first three levels are largely related to the direct and active teaching approach, by moving from the basic requirements concerning quantitative characteristics of teaching routines to the more advanced requirements concerning the appropriate use of these skills as these are measured by the qualitative characteristics of these factors. These skills also gradually move from the use of teacher-centred approaches to the active involvement of students in teaching and learning. The last two levels are more demanding since teachers are expected to differentiate their instruction (level 4) and demonstrate their ability to use the new teaching approach (level 5). Considering these five stages and the properties of the Rasch scale which were developed, one can conclude that some stages are more difficult to accomplish than others. This supports the conclusion that the five stages are not just a grouping of effectiveness factors, but represent equivalent developmental stages of teaching proficiency.

The findings of this study are also in line with theories related to the stage models of professional development (e.g., Dreyfus & Dreyfus, 1986; Berliner, 1988, 1992, 1994; Feiman-Nemser & Remillard, 1996; Sternberg et al., 2000). The five stages proposed by Kyriakides, Creemers and Antoniou (2009) advance on previous stage models by specifically determining the content of each stage (in terms of teaching skills), whereas previous stage models often lacked clarity on what might constitute each developmental stage.

Implications of these findings for the development of teacher professional development programmes, or specific strategies for improving teacher effectiveness, may emerge by looking at the grouping of teacher factors in the dynamic model. A question raised is the extent to which teachers can move from one stage of teaching competence to the next, by improving their teaching skills and ultimately their student achievement gains. This question is included within the scope of this book, as well as the potential of the dynamic model to improve teaching practices and ultimately student attainment.

In order to provide answers to this question, a group randomization study was conducted and will be presented in this chapter. The aim of the study was to develop and implement a teacher professional development approach based on both the DASI and the results from the study regarding the grouping of factors of the dynamic model into five stages. The effectiveness of this approach will be compared with the Holistic (or reflective) approach in improving teacher perceptions about teaching, teaching skills and student outcomes in mathematics. This comparison will be made because the Holistic approach is largely considered to be the current dominant orthodoxy in teachers' training and professional development (Golby & Viant, 2007).

A dynamic integrated approach to teacher professional development

This section demonstrates the basic steps, based on DASI, which have been utilised for developing a dynamic integrated approach to teacher professional development. This approach takes into account research findings on the grouping of factors in the dynamic model (see also Chapter 8) and their relation with student outcomes (Kyriakides et al., 2009).

A) Identify needs and priorities for improvement through empirical investigation

The first step of the proposed approach (equivalent with step B of DASI) is based on the assumption that teacher improvement efforts should consist of the development of teaching skills which relate to positive student outcomes. Research on teacher effectiveness (Brophy & Good, 1986; Creemers & Kyriakides, 2008a; Darling-Hammond, 2000; Kyriakides, 2008; Muijs & Reynolds, 2000; Rosenshine & Stevens, 1986; Scheerens & Bosker, 1997) refers to specific factors concerned with teacher behaviour in the classroom that are found to be associated with student outcomes, and thus the proposed approach refers to the development of INSET courses addressing teacher factors in the dynamic model. This implies that the proposed approach is in line with the main assumption of DASI that the ultimate aim of any improvement effort should be to promote student learning and its outcomes (see step A of DASI). To achieve this, INSET courses are expected to help teachers improve their teaching skills and therefore become more effective. This is also in line with step B of DASI, which emphasises the importance of addressing school factors to establish a school improvement project. In this case, however, the emphasis is not on the school level factors but rather on the teacher factors. Moreover, under step B of DASI a consensus among all school stakeholders about the aims of school improvement efforts should be developed, whereas students and parents are not usually involved in decisions about the aims of teacher improvement projects.

The dynamic integrated approach goes further to suggest that evaluation data are needed in order to identify the needs of each teacher participating in the improvement project. This is in line with step C of DASI, which implies that schools should develop their own School Self Evaluation (SSE) mechanisms to identify their priorities for improvement. Similarly, for the development of INSET courses an initial evaluation of staff teaching skills is important. In any effort to train teachers, an initial evaluation of their teaching skills should be conducted to investigate the extent to which they possess certain teaching skills whilst identifying their needs and priorities for improvement. The results of the initial evaluation provided suggestions for the content of training that different groups of teachers required. The teaching skills of the participants were evaluated by external observers (i.e. Kyriakides et al., 2009). The observation data of the initial evaluation were analysed in order to group teachers into corresponding developmental stages, according to their teaching skills. Using the Rasch and Saltus models, it was found that teachers could be classified into the same five developmental stages as those from the study mentioned in the previous section (Antoniou, 2009; Antoniou, Creemers, & Kyriakides, 2009). This is important, because the content and development of educational material for the training programmes corresponded to the professional needs and *proximal development* of each group of teachers, as denoted by their own stage of teaching skills. According to Berliner (1988), it may not be possible to shorten the pathway because extensive experience is fundamental to development, but it would be beneficial to assist those willing to progress by providing training and feedback appropriate to their stage of development. For example, teachers must master simple but necessary routines such as teaching skills related to the 'direct teaching approach' in order to move to higher stages involving the use of 'new teaching approaches' and differentiation. As Combs et al. (1974, p.4) argue, 'in the first place, it is a fallacy to assume that the methods of the experts either can or should be taught directly to beginners'.

Furthermore, the effort to identify teachers' needs and priorities for improvement has been guided by the teacher level of the dynamic model for educational effectiveness. This is important, since the dynamic model refers to teaching skills which were found to be related to student achievement. On the other hand, the Holistic approach to teacher professional development supports that teachers are able to identify a problem in relation to the improvement of student outcomes which they consider important, without the need to justify their selection; this is irrespective of their initial competencies or developmental stage. Therefore, a decision was taken to compare the effectiveness of these two approaches, through the experimental study which is described in the next section of this chapter.

B) Provide Guidelines for improvement: The role of the A&R Team

Having identified teachers' needs and priorities for improvement, the second step of this approach relates to the provision of appropriate material and specific guidelines for improvement. This step is equivalent to step D of DASI. In this case, the teacher professional development programme coordinators acted as the A&R Team, described in Chapter 3 of this book. For the purposes of the project described here, the A&R Team provided the teachers of each group with supporting literature and research findings related to the teaching skills in their developmental stage, with clear instructions on which area each group should concentrate on for improvement. For example, the teachers in the first stage of teaching skills received guidance on the distribution of teaching time so that students can effectively construct and implement new knowledge. A case study was administered to the teachers in this group, in order to identify the problem and particularly to encourage them to discuss the importance of the '*opportunity to learn*' factor. In addition, material from the literature was provided regarding the management of the classroom as an efficient learning environment, in order to maximise engagement rates (Creemers & Reezigt, 1996; Wilks, 1996). Through discussion, it was explained to teachers that learning takes place in restricted time limits in which many important activities must be implemented. Extra-curricular administrative activities such as announcements, dealing with discipline problems and commenting on irrelevant issues could further reduce the time available for learning. Finally, the teachers concluded that they should allocate sufficient time to each learning activity.

The A&R Team also provided the teachers of this group with guidelines related with their improvement priorities, supplemented by research literature material. For instance, for the improvement area related to the '*provision of application activities*' the A&R Team first provided general principles such as: the teacher should provide the opportunity to students to practice the implementation of knowledge and skills involved in each lesson; feedback should be provided to students while they are working on application activities; and the teacher could raise questions to individual students while they are working on application activities to identify and deal with misunderstandings. Following this, examples for teaching specific material from the school curriculum were provided to teachers and they were asked to both reflect on these and provide their own examples of implementing the principles in the school curriculum.

Subsequently, under the guidance of the A&R Team each teacher developed their own action plan for improvement. This allowed teachers to adopt and customise the provided guidelines to the specific context of their school. The basic elements of a general plan of action were also discussed and it was agreed that action plans should include:

1   A revised statement of the general idea related to the purpose of improvement.
2   A statement of the factors and dimensions the teacher plans to improve.
3   Specific actions the teacher will undertake in this direction. For example, one teacher situated at Level 2 planned to modify the way she retrieves and relates prior knowledge to new knowledge by asking questions, assigning a relevant problem and asking students to interpret a map or tree-diagram which requires knowledge from previous lessons.
4   A statement of the resources required in order to undertake the proposed courses of action (e.g., materials, rooms, equipment).
5   Evaluation: Teachers were asked to use various techniques and methods for gathering evidence on the effectiveness of their action plans. For this reason, teachers were encouraged to keep a Reflective Diary. This Diary could contain personal accounts of observations, feelings, reactions, interpretations, reflections, hunches, hypotheses and explanations. Teachers could also ask their pupils to keep Diaries. As Brophy and Good (1986) argue, this enables teachers to compare their experiences of the situation with those of the

pupils'. Moreover, other teachers at the school could observe their teaching (e.g., acting as 'critical friends).

C) Establish formative evaluation mechanism

The next step of the teacher professional development programme, based on the grouping of factors of the dynamic model, comprises the establishment of formative evaluation procedures. This step is equivalent to step E of the DASI (see Chapter 3). Formative evaluation is the method of ongoing and concurrent evaluation which aims to improve the programme. The formative evaluation procedures developed for the teacher professional development programme were carried out once a month throughout the programme to provide information and feedback for improving: (a) the quality of teachers' learning, (b) the extent to which they implement the teaching skills in their classrooms and finally (c) the quality of the programme itself.

The formative evaluation procedures involved: the identification of the learning goals, intentions or outcomes, and criteria for achieving them; the provision of effective, timely feedback to enable teachers to advance their learning; the active involvement of teachers in their own learning, and lastly teachers responding to identified learning needs and priorities by improving their teaching skills. These procedures were completed by the A&R Team and participating teachers.

In particular, after the second session and development of teachers' initial action plans, one session was scheduled each month until the end of the school year. This provided the teachers with sufficient time to implement the activities included in their action plans into their teaching, and also to reflect on the effectiveness of these activities. Furthermore, the monthly sessions provided teachers in each stage with the opportunity to revise and develop their action plans further on a systematic basis, based on their own and others' experiences and also research on effectiveness factors which corresponds to their developmental stage. This was achieved with the assistance and guidance of the A&R Team.

Throughout formative evaluation in each monthly session, teachers had the opportunity to:

a) report teaching practices and comment on them
b) identify effective and non-effective teaching practices
c) understand the significance of the teacher factors which correspond to their developmental stage
d) understand how these factors could be linked with effective teaching and learning.

At the same time, the teachers received systematic feedback and suggestions from the A&R Team at each stage, in the form of materials related to the application of teaching skills to specific content. To achieve this, relevant case studies were used extensively (see Antoniou, 2009).

During this time, members of the A&R Team visited teachers at their schools to discuss emerging issues related to the implementation of their action plans into everyday teaching, providing support and feedback. Through close observation of teachers and the frequent collection of feedback on teachers' skills, the A&R Team could identify how teachers implemented their action plans and developed their teaching skills.

D) Establish summative evaluation mechanism

The final step of the proposed approach to the teacher professional development programme is concerned with the summative evaluation of the project. This step is equivalent to step F of DASI. The emphasis of the summative evaluation was not on comparing teachers with each other, but on identifying the overall impact of the programme on the development of teachers' skills and its indirect effect on student learning. The results of the summative evaluation assist in measuring the effectiveness of this approach and allow subsequent decisions to be made regarding the continuity of the programme.

At the end of the school year the teaching skills, teacher perceptions and students' outcomes were measured using the same procedures and instruments as in the initial evaluation of the programme. Thus the teaching skills of the participating teachers were again evaluated, by focusing on the eight factors of the dynamic model concerning teacher behaviour in the classroom. The teacher questionnaire was then administered to identify changes in teacher attitudes and perceptions. Finally, data on student achievement were collected by using external forms of written assessment, in order to measure the effectiveness of each experimental treatment in terms of student outcomes.

The next section provides a detailed description of the group randomization study conducted in order to compare the impact of the teacher professional development approach based on the dynamic model (DASI) with the Holistic (or Reflective) Approach. The purpose is not only to present the results of the summative evaluation of DASI, but also to provide readers with a detailed description of the study and facilitate their efforts to replicate or design their own research on teacher professional development based on DASI.

A group randomization study investigating the effectiveness of the teacher professional development programme based on DASI and the holistic (or reflective) approach

A group randomization study was conducted in order to compare the impact of the teacher professional development programme based on DASI and the Holistic approach in improving teachers' perceptions of teaching, teaching skills and student outcomes in mathematics.

A) Participants

A total of 130 primary teachers volunteered to participate in the professional development programme. Data were also collected for all students (n=2356) of the teacher-sample. Data were collected both at the beginning and end of the intervention. Students with missing prior attainment or background data comprised less than 7% of the original sample and were consequently excluded from each analysis. In the teacher sample, only seven teachers left the experimental study and were equally distributed in the two intervention groups and appropriate stage of development.

B) Phases of the study

The four phases of the experimental study are elaborated upon below.

Phase 1: Initial Evaluation

At the beginning of the school year 2008–2009, the teaching skills of the participants were evaluated by external observers. Data on student achievement were collected using external written forms of assessment designed to assess knowledge and skills in mathematics, which are identified in the Cyprus Curriculum (Ministry of Education, 1994). Teacher questionnaires were administered to collect data on teachers' background characteristics and measure their perceptions towards teaching. In addition, a student questionnaire was administered in order to collect information related to students' background characteristics. Observation data were then analysed using the same procedure as described by Kyriakides et al. (2009) in order to classify teachers into developmental stages according to their teaching skills. Using the Rasch and the Saltus models, it was found that teachers could be classified into the same five developmental stages which emerged from the previous study (see Table 7.1).

Phase 2: The formation of the two experimental groups

The teachers at each developmental stage were randomly allocated into two groups of equal size. The first group employed the dynamic approach presented in the previous section, while the second group used the Holistic approach. For example, the 32 teachers at Stage 1 were randomly allocated into the two experimental groups, each one consisting of 16 teachers.

Phase 3: The establishment of the training sessions

In the third phase of the study, the teachers of each experimental group began to work towards improving their teaching skills. This phase sought to initiate changes in educational practices, working with the teachers throughout the whole curriculum. It was also concerned with whether, and to what extent, teachers can develop their teaching skills and integrate them into a more self-consciously articulated model of classroom pedagogy. In doing so, action research procedures were initiated for teachers of both experimental groups. According to Somekh (1995), action research is designed 'to bridge the gap between research and practice, thereby striving to overcome the perceived failure of research to impact on and improve practice' (p. 340). The interventions for experimental groups A and B are described below respectively.

Experimental Group A: Intervention based on the DASI Approach

Teachers participating in the experimental group A (employing DASI) were engaged with activities which corresponded solely to skills appropriate to their developmental stage. The teachers in both groups were required to attend eight sessions. The content and purpose of each session is described below.

First Session   The first session could be perceived as equivalent to the first step of the DASI, since it aims to build consensus in relation to the main aims of the improvement initiative. Particularly, in the first session the rationale of the professional development programme, as well as the main characteristics and value assumptions of the action research approach, were analysed. The main aims of the programme were illustrated (i.e. the improvement of teaching practices and student outcomes) as well as the programme procedures and other administrative issues. The importance of evaluating the impact of the programme on teacher behaviour and student outcomes was emphasised, and the relevant procedures for the classroom observations, questionnaires and test administrations at both time points were explained. It was also made clear to the participants that provisions had been taken to ensure the anonymity and confidentiality of the results of the evaluation.

Second Session   In the second session, the teachers employing the Dynamic Integrated Approach were assigned to four groups according to their own development stage, based on the results of their teaching skills evaluation. Following this the research team provided supporting literature to the teachers of each group, which was related to teaching skills appropriate to their developmental stage, and identified specific areas for improvement (see Appendix 7.1).

Third – Seventh Sessions   After the second session and the development of teachers' initial action plans, one session was scheduled each month until the end of the school year. This provided the teachers with sufficient time to implement the activities in their action plans into their teaching, whilst reflecting on the effectiveness of these activities. The monthly sessions also provided teachers with the opportunity to revise and further develop their action plans on a systematic basis with the assistance of the A&R Team. This was based upon their own and others' experiences, as well as on research concerning the effectiveness factors of their developmental stage (see Antoniou, 2009). In each monthly session, teachers' training was based on 'active teaching' and was not restricted solely to lecturing. Thus, the participating teachers had the opportunity to report teaching practices and comment on them, to identify effective and non-effective teaching practices, to understand the significance of the teacher level factors in their stage of the dynamic model, and to comprehend how these factors could be linked to effective teaching and learning.

At the same time, the teachers received systematic feedback and suggestions from the A&R Team with additional reading materials and tasks concerning how teaching skills could be used for teaching specific content. To achieve this, guidelines were developed and distributed to teachers. According to Desimone et al. (2002), professional development is more effective in changing teachers' classroom practices when it has the collective participation of teachers sharing the same priorities. Finally, members of the A&R Team visited teachers at their schools to discuss issues regarding the implementation of their action plans into their everyday teaching, and also to provide support and feedback.

Experimental Group B: Intervention based on the Holistic Approach

Teachers who participated in the experimental group employing the Holistic approach were engaged in activities involving the whole spectrum of teaching elements, attitudes and perceptions; these were not specific to their initial competences or development stage. As defined by Schon (1987), this intervention was based on reflection. It involves thoughtfully considering one's own experiences and beliefs in applying knowledge to practice, while being coached by professionals in the discipline. This intervention was based on the argument that professional development programmes need not always focus on specific teaching methods and strategies; they can also focus on teacher attitudes which affect practice. As Wilhelm et al. (1996) report, the curriculum of this professional development programme was based on providing teacher interns with an opportunity to explore attitudes and reflect on the ethical implications of practice in classrooms whilst also focusing on their previous experiences. Given its nature, this method of professional development causes teachers to step back and critically reflect not only on how they teach, but also on why they teach in a particular way. Teachers participating in the Holistic Approach were required to attend eight sessions, in the same way as the teachers employing DASI in group A. The content of the first session was the same for both groups (see first session on the section concerned with DASI).

Second Session   In the second session, the teachers employing the Holistic Approach (Experimental Group B) were assigned to groups based on their own preferences. The elements of an action plan were described to teachers in all four groups, who then created their own action plan under the supervision of the A&R Team. Through discussion the teachers identified problems they considered important, which led to the formulation of action plans to tackle them.

Third – Seventh Sessions   After this second session, one session was scheduled each month until the end of the school year. The primary aim of reflective practice was for teachers to gain a deeper understanding of their own teaching style. Specifically, teachers were encouraged to make use of journals, observation notes, transcribed conversations, and self-reports. The aim was to enable individuals to critically evaluate their own beliefs and practice and help them to transform their experiences from a past event into an ongoing learning process. Moreover, the intervention was designed to engage participating teachers in writing narrative stories of experiences, and participate in guided reflective questioning as a process of teacher inquiry and professional development.

The monthly sessions also provided the teachers of each stage with the opportunity to revise and further develop their action plans. The participating teachers could report and comment on their own teaching practices, and identify both effective and non-effective teaching practices, attitudes and beliefs. For example, the teachers were asked to reflect on what they perceived to be successes and failures in terms of effective teaching and learning. They were then encouraged to focus on and write down their story of one critical incident, whether positive or negative, which occurred in their classrooms. They were asked to describe the incident in detail (e.g. situation, people involved, feelings, reasoning), what they had learned about teaching as a result, how their perspectives changed and the resulting changes in how they taught. In each monthly meeting the A&R Team encouraged teachers within the same group to co-operate and share both ideas and teaching materials, to exchange and discuss their experiences and generally to share the results of their exploration. Finally, as with the teachers of experimental group A, the A&R Team visited teachers at their schools during this period to discuss emerging issues related to the implementation of their action plans into their everyday teaching. They provided consistent support and feedback to all teachers.

Phase 4: Final evaluation and 8th Session: Measurement of teaching skills, teacher perceptions towards teaching and student outcomes

This is the last phase of the teacher professional development programme, which corresponds to the last step of DASI. By the end of the school year, the teaching skills, teacher perceptions and student achievement in mathematics were measured using the same procedures and instruments as in Phase 1.

Following the data analyses, a common final meeting was held with participating teachers in the two experimental groups. During this meeting, the teachers were first invited to express their views and comments about the developmental programme in which they participated. This enabled the collection of data concerning the formative evaluation of the project. The overall results of the summative evaluation were then presented to the teachers, and they were asked to reflect on these results.

Results

The results of the analysis evidenced the impact of the two approaches to teacher professional development on the improvement of teaching skills, teacher perceptions, and student academic outcomes. These are presented in this section. Additional technical information emerged from analysing the results of the study, and this is also presented below for information. A summary of the main findings is also provided at the end of this section.

A) Impact on teaching skills

The observational data of each time period were analysed separately following the procedure described by Kyriakides et al. (2009). Specifically, the Rasch model was used in order to identify the extent to which the five dimensions of the eight teacher factors (i.e. the 44 first order factor scores) could be reduced to a common unidimensional scale. The Rasch model not only tests for the unidimensionality of the scale, but is also able to ascertain whether the tasks can be ordered according to their degree of difficulty. Furthermore, it assesses whether the people completing these tasks can be ordered according to their performance in the specific construct under investigation.

The Rasch model was applied to the data of the baseline measure (i.e. the teaching skills of teachers participating in the study). It was found that all of the teaching skills included in the dynamic model were appropriately targeted against the person measures (i.e., the skills of teachers, participating in the study) since Rasch person estimates ranged from -3.06 to 3.12 logits and the estimates of the difficulties of teaching skills ranged from -2.93 to 3.16 logits. Moreover, the reliability of each scale (teachers and teaching skills) was higher than 0.93 and thus deemed satisfactory. Having established the reliability of the scale, it was investigated whether teaching skills could be grouped into the five stages described in the previous section. The procedure for detecting pattern clustering, developed by Marcoulides and Drezner (1999), was used. This procedure segments the observed measurements into constituent groups (or clusters) so that the members of any one group are similar to each other, according to selected criterion that stands for difficulty. Applying this method to segment the teaching skills on the basis of their difficulties that emerged from the Rasch model showed that they are optimally clustered into the five clusters proposed by previous research findings (see Kyriakides et al., 2009).

Pattern clustering was also applied to data which emerged from the final measurement of teaching skills. The Rasch model revealed that all participants fitted the model and all teaching skills were well matched to measures of the teachers, since the latter scores range from -2.99 to 3.24 logits. It was also found that the difficulties of the teaching skills could be considered invariant across the two measurement periods within the measurement error (i.e. 0.10 logits). Applying the aforementioned clustering method, it was found that teaching skills could once again be optimally clustered into five clusters (see Antoniou, 2009).

Considering the results of the analyses of initial and final data related to teaching skills, we can conclude that on both occasions the results validated the five developmental stages of teaching skills proposed by previous research findings (Kyriakides et al., 2009; Antoniou, 2009; Antoniou, Creemers, & Kyriakides, 2009). Since the teachers were grouped into the same five stages of teaching competencies, a decision was made to compare the initial and final stages of each teacher. This could identify the extent to which some teachers improved their teaching skills and progressed to the next stage of teaching skills. By comparing the classification of teachers into stages at the beginning and end of the intervention, the analysis found that none of the teachers of the group employing the Holistic Approach (HA) moved from one stage to another. On the other hand, 21 out of 65 teachers employing DASI progressed to the next stage.

In order to measure the impact of the two professional development programmes upon teaching skills, the Rasch person estimates were also compared. This comparison revealed that the final scores of teachers employing the DASI (Mean=0.36, SD=1.05) were higher than initial scores (Mean=-0.28, SD=1.01) and this difference was statistically significant (t=4.14, df=64, p<.001). On the other hand, the final scores of teachers employing the HA (Mean=-0.25, SD=1.04) were not higher than their initial scores (Mean=-0.26, SD=1.05) and paired samples t-test did not reveal any statistically significant differences in progress (t=0.87, df=64, p=0.38).

B) Impact on teacher perceptions and attitudes

In the first stage of the analysis two independent samples t-tests were employed to identify any statistically significant differences between the teachers of the two experimental groups, at the beginning and end of the interventions. No statistically significant differences were identified between the teachers of the two experimental groups at the beginning or the end of the interventions. Finally, a paired samples t-test revealed no statistically significant changes in perceptions, either for the teachers who employed the DASI or for those who employed the HA.

C) Impact on student achievement

The results of the multilevel analysis to measure the impact of each of the two approaches to teacher professional development on student achievement are presented in this section. In particular, this analysis aimed to identify the extent to which student achievement gains were significantly different for teachers participating in the DASI as compared to those employing the HA. It is also important to note that other explanatory variables, such as teacher qualification and student SES, were taken into consideration in the multilevel analysis. Although the teachers were randomly assigned to the experimental groups, this procedure was still conducted to identify the net impact of each approach on students' academic progress.

In the data analysis presented below, the variables related to the interventions were added at the last stage of the multilevel modelling analysis. This procedure enabled the authors to supplement the analysis with data for teachers' personal characteristics and perceptions, in order to investigate for possible variation both within groups and between groups. The models presented in Table 7.2 were estimated solely using variables which had a statistically significant effect (p<.05).

In model 1 of Table 7.2, the variables related to the student context were added into the empty model (model 0). This model explained 23.4% of the variance, most of which was situated at the student level. All of the student context variables (i.e. *prior achievement in maths, gender, SES, Cultural capital*) had statistically significant effects upon student achievement. Nevertheless, *prior knowledge* was the strongest predictor of student achievement at the end of the school year. In addition, *prior achievement* was the only contextual variable which had a consistent effect upon achievement when aggregated either at the classroom or the school level.

In model 2 the explanatory variables of the student level, related to the opportunity to learn, were added to the previous model. The amount of time students spent doing their homework showed a statistically significant effect on student achievement. In the third model, all variables related to teachers' background factors, perceptions and attitudes were added to model 2. The *years of teaching experience* had a statistically significant effect on student achievement.

In model 4 the variable related to the quality of teaching was added to model 3. Quality of teaching was measured through classroom observations, with teachers then assigned to one of four developmental stages according to their teaching skills. In order to measure the effect of each developmental stage on student outcomes, teachers at stage 3 were treated as the reference group (i.e. stage 3 = 0) and three dummy variables were entered into model 4. The results revealed that the developmental stage in which a teacher is situated had a reasonably large and significant effect on student achievement. In particular, we can observe that the students of teachers at stage 1 showed the lowest achievement, whereas students of teachers at stage 4 had higher achievement levels than students within the first three stages. This finding provides support for the

Table 7.2 Parameter Estimates and (Standard Errors) for the analysis of student achievement in mathematics (Students within classes, within schools)

Factors	Model 0	Model 1	Model 2	Model 3	Model 4	Model 5	Model 6
Fixed part (Intercept)	5.19 (0.80)	4.10 (0.78)	3.80 (0.80)	3.70 (0.90)	2.90 (0.80)	2.10 (0.80)	1.90 (0.70)
Student level							
Context							
Prior achievement in maths		0.80 (.12)	0.79 (.12)	0.81 (.12)	0.80 (.11)	0.80 (.12)	0.80 (.11)
Grade 3		-1.20 (.40)	-1.09 (.40)	-1.08 (.40)	-1.10 (.40)	-1.07 (.40)	-1.07 (.40)
Grade 4		-0.72 (.30)	-0.66 (.30)	-0.62 (.30)	-0.63 (.30)	-0.62 (.30)	-0.62 (.29)
Grade 6		0.65 (.30)	0.64 (.30)	0.64 (.30)	0.65 (.30)	0.66 (.30)	0.64 (.30)
Sex (0=Girls, 1=Boys)		0.10 (.04)	0.10 (.04)	0.11 (.04)	0.10 (.04)	0.09 (.04)	0.10 (.04)
SES		0.40 (.14)	0.41 (.14)	0.40 (.14)	0.41 (.14)	0.40 (.14)	0.40 (.13)
Cultural capital		0.19 (.08)	0.19 (.09)	0.20 (.08)	0.18 (.08)	0.18 (.08)	0.18 (.08)
Opportunity to learn							
Homework			0.12 (.04)	0.12 (.04)	0.12 (.04)	0.12 (.04)	0.12 (.04)
Private tuition (0 =no, 1=yes)			N.S.S.	N.S.S.	N.S.S.	N.S.S.	N.S.S.
Classroom level							
Context							
Average achievement in maths		0.40 (.10)	0.40 (.10)	0.40 (.10)	0.40 (.10)	0.40 (.10)	0.40 (.10)
Average SES		N.S.S.	N.S.S.	N.S.S.	N.S.S.	N.S.S.	N.S.S.
Average cultural capital		N.S.S.	N.S.S.	N.S.S.	N.S.S.	N.S.S.	N.S.S.
Percentage of girls		N.S.S.	N.S.S.	N.S.S.	N.S.S.	N.S.S.	N.S.S.
Teacher background							
Gender (0=male, 1=female)				N.S.S.	N.S.S.	N.S.S.	N.S.S.
Years of experience				0.08 (.03)	N.S.S.	N.S.S.	N.S.S.
Position				N.S.S.	N.S.S.	N.S.S.	N.S.S.

Factors	Model 0	Model 1	Model 2	Model 3	Model 4	Model 5	Model 6
Teacher expectations							
Plans for postgraduate degree				N.S.S.	N.S.S.	N.S.S.	N.S.S.
Plans for promotion to head				N.S.S.	N.S.S.	N.S.S.	N.S.S.
Attitudes towards teaching as a profession				N.S.S.	N.S.S.	N.S.S.	N.S.S.
Perceptions towards characteristics of effective teachers							
A) Importance of knowledge				N.S.S.	N.S.S.	N.S.S.	N.S.S.
B) Classroom management				N.S.S.	N.S.S.	N.S.S.	N.S.S.
C) Personal traits				N.S.S.	N.S.S.	N.S.S.	N.S.S.
D) Communication skills				N.S.S.	N.S.S.	N.S.S.	N.S.S.
Attitudes towards tasks that teachers have to undertake							
A) Lesson preparation				N.S.S.	N.S.S.	N.S.S.	N.S.S.
B) Teaching				N.S.S.	N.S.S.	N.S.S.	N.S.S.
C) Assessment				N.S.S.	N.S.S.	N.S.S.	N.S.S.
D) Homework assignment				N.S.S.	N.S.S.	N.S.S.	N.S.S.
E) Record keeping and reporting to parents				N.S.S.	N.S.S.	N.S.S.	N.S.S.
F) Administrative work				-0.06 (.02)	-0.05 (.02)	-0.06 (.02)	-0.06 (.02)
Attitudes towards professional development							
Quality of teaching				N.S.S.	N.S.S.	N.S.S.	N.S.S.
Level 1					-0.52 (.09)	-0.51 (.09)	-0.52 (.09)
Level 2					-0.24 (.09)	-0.25 (.09)	-0.25 (.09)
Level 4					0.32 (.10)	0.32 (.10)	0.31 (.10)
Experimental group (0=only reflection, 1=competence based)						0.24 (.08)	0.23 (.08)

Factors	Model 0	Model 1	Model 2	Model 3	Model 4	Model 5	Model 6
Teachers who managed to move to the next stage (0=no movement was observed, 1=move to the next)							0.09 (.03)
School Level							
Context							
Average achievement in maths		0.09 (.04)	0.10 (.04)	0.08 (.04)	0.10 (.04)	0.09 (.04)	.09 (.03)
Average SES		N.S.S.	N.S.S.	N.S.S.	N.S.S.	N.S.S.	N.S.S.
Average cultural capital		N.S.S.	N.S.S.	N.S.S.	N.S.S.	N.S.S.	N.S.S.
Percentage of girls		N.S.S.	N.S.S.	N.S.S.	N.S.S.	N.S.S.	N.S.S.
Variance components							
School	10.2%	10.0%	9.8%	9.5%	9.1%	8.5%	8.4%
Class	18.5%	17.6%	17.2%	16.0%	11.0%	9.0%	8.6%
Student	72.3%	49.0%	45.0%	44.3%	44.1%	44.0%	44.0%
Explained		23.4%	28.0%	30.2%	35.8%	38.5%	39.0%
Significance test							
X^2	1213.4	687.3	650.1	590.1	520.0	480.5	460.1
Reduction		526.1	37.2	60.0	70.1	39.5	20.4
Degrees of freedom		9	1	2	2	1	1
p-value		.001	.001	.001	.001	.001	.001

N.S.S. = No statistically significant effect at level .05.

developmental nature of the four stages, since students of teachers situated at higher stages performed better than students of teachers at lower stages. It is important to note that similar results were found at the start of the intervention and also in previous research (e.g. Kyriakides et al., 2009). Finally, we can observe that model 4 explained 35.8% of the variance, while the X^2 test revealed a significant change between model 3 and model 4 (p<0.001). This suggests that a teacher's developmental stage is an important predictor of student outcomes.

In model 5, the effect of each approach to teacher professional development was investigated. A dummy variable representing the approach (0 = HA) was entered into the analysis. The DASI showed a statistically significant effect on student achievement, compared to the HA which did not have a significant effect. The effect of this DASI variable was 0.24 (0.08), indicating that the students of teachers employing this approach had better results than those whose teachers employed the HA.

Finally, in model 6 the effect of teachers moving to the next developmental stage was investigated. As aforementioned in the analysis of observational data related to teaching quality, all teachers employing the DASI improved in their teaching skills. Moreover, 21 out of 65 teachers made progress to such an extent that they advanced to the next developmental stage of teaching skills. It was therefore necessary to investigate the impact of this 'movement' to the next developmental stage on student academic outcomes. A dummy variable indicating whether teachers progressed to the next developmental stage was entered into the analysis (0 = no movement observed, 1= moving to the next stage of teaching competences). The results indicated that moving to the next developmental stage had a statistically significant effect upon student achievement (see Table 7.2).

Discussion

This section provides a brief review of the research findings and discusses the relevant implications for policy and practice. Finally, suggestions for future research in the field are provided.

A) Summary of results

Firstly, the results of the analysis of both the initial and final data related to teaching skills suggest that the five stages of teaching skills were formulated in a consistent manner. This provides support for the generalisability of the five developmental stages of teaching skills proposed by previous research findings (Antoniou et al., 2009). In addition, it was found that teachers demonstrating higher-level competencies were more effective than those situated at the lower stages, in terms of student outcomes. Secondly, the results indicated that the DASI is more effective than the Holistic approach in improving teaching skills, for all teachers. By comparing the two experimental groups it was found that, overall, teachers employing the Holistic approach neither made statistically significant progress nor moved from one stage to another. On the other hand, statistically significant progress in teaching skills was found for the teachers employing the approach based on the grouping of teaching skills in the dynamic model. Thirdly, it was found that employing the DASI approach had a reasonable and statistically significant effect on student achievement, compared with employing the holistic approach. Finally, the findings revealed that teachers' perceptions and attitudes towards teaching did not change, regardless of the approach they employed. Teachers' perceptions of teaching were also not found to be related to student achievement gains in mathematics. This finding supports that the DASI can develop improvement programmes focused on enhancing teaching skills, rather than perceptions towards teaching.

B) Implication of research findings

The above findings support that teachers can improve and ultimately progress to the next developmental stage of teaching skills, by undertaking appropriate interventions and participating in effective professional development programmes. As this study demonstrated, teachers employing the DASI improved their teaching skills, whereas those employing the HA did not. In addition, the use of the DASI had a significant impact upon student achievement gains in mathematics. A similar argument was made by King and Kitchener (1994). They argued that stage growth was most apparent for teachers who continued their informal education and participated in effective professional development programmes. This is an important reminder that teacher improvement and stage growth do not unilaterally unfold, but also require a stimulating and supportive environment.

The issue concerning the content of teacher professional development programmes has been addressed in this study, by drawing from a validated theoretical model of EER. In particular the dynamic model of educational effectiveness emphasises not only the importance of specific factors, but also the grouping of factors, when addressing the complex nature of effectiveness. This implies that improvement of teacher effectiveness cannot be focused solely on the acquisition of isolated skills or competencies (Gilberts & Lignugaris-Kraft, 1997), nor on reflection across the whole teaching process to help teachers get 'greater fulfilment as a practitioner of the art' (of teaching) (Clarke & Hollingsworth, 2002, p. 948).

At the same time, the results of this study indicate that reflection is more effective when teachers' priorities for improvement are taken into account, and when they are encouraged to develop action plans which address their professional needs; these were identified through a relevant empirical investigation. Although both interventions encouraged and utilised teachers' critical reflections of their teaching practices, teachers employing the DASI were asked to reflect on those aspects which related to their priorities for improvement based on their developmental stage. These stages were defined by taking into account the knowledge base of EER, especially teacher factors found to be associated with student achievement. On the other hand, teachers employing the Holistic Approach adopted a less focused reflection strategy, which allowed them to reflect on any aspect of their teaching practice irrespective of the stage on which they were situated. For example, some teachers at stage 1 employing the HA developed action plans aiming to differentiate their instruction; yet their attempts to incorporate this into their teaching were not successful. This may be attributed to the fact that they did not possess basic skills corresponding to their stage, such as classroom management and structuring, which could be considered pre-requisites for the differentiation of teaching. Therefore the Holistic Approach does not take into account research evidence supporting the grouping of teacher factors and their dimensions, grouped into stages, structured in a developmental order and associated with student outcomes. It must be emphasised that the importance of thinking and critical analysis are important, and thus those aspects of the HA were utilised in the development of DASI. However, complimenting reflection with the knowledge base of EER, which addresses the needs of specific groups of teachers, could help us to establish more effective approaches to teacher professional development.

Moreover, the findings of this study revealed that teachers' perceptions towards teaching did not change, either for the teachers employing the DASI or the HA. This finding is in line with many studies which support that changing teacher perceptions is difficult to achieve (Sharon, 1987; Joyce & Showers, 1980; Goodrum, Cousins, & Kinnear, 1992). For example, research was conducted in the USA in a district offering 'a myriad of choices of professional development from workshops on particular strategies to development of small learning communities' (Alger, 2009, p. 8). Yet it was surprising that only one teacher out of 110 indicated that professional development was responsible for a shift in their perceptions towards teaching. As research has shown, teachers' beliefs about teaching and learning are resistant to change because they are at the core of a student-teacher's world view (Pajares, 1992; Phelan & McLaughlin, 1995). An alternative explanation may be that teacher perceptions are mitigated by other less tangible context variables in individual schools, such as school size and school climate (Grossman & Stodolsky, 1995). In addition, this might be attributed to the fact that the study only took place during one year. Longitudinal studies are needed to further explore the potential and characteristics of professional development programmes capable of improving teachers' perceptions towards teaching. Yet although teachers' perceptions towards teaching did not change in this study, those teachers employing the DASI did improve in their teaching skills and their students' outcomes. This might imply that improving teachers' perceptions and attitudes towards teaching should not necessarily be considered as a prerequisite for improving teacher effectiveness.

Finally, suggestions for further research are provided. Longitudinal studies may assist in measuring both the short and long term effects of the DASI. Further studies are also required in order to test the generalisability of the findings of this study, and to expand the proposed theoretical framework (see Chapter 8). These studies may reveal that, when helping teachers to improve their skills, other factors such as school policy towards teaching or the school culture should be considered. Such results may not only contribute to further development of the framework concerning the use of the dynamic model for improvement purposes, but may also help us to establish a theory-driven and evidence-based approach to improving the quality of education.

Chapter 8

Development of DASI

Studies on teacher effectiveness in different educational settings

Introduction

This chapter is concerned with the use of DASI for improvement purposes at the teacher level. The previous chapter described an experimental study investigating the impact of DASI on the improvement of teacher effectiveness. It was demonstrated that teachers employing DASI improved in their teaching skills more than teachers using the Holistic approach (HA). The use of DASI also had an impact on student achievement gains in mathematics, since teachers employing DASI improved their skills and consequently helped their students to achieve their learning outcomes. Therefore empirical support for this approach has been provided.

In this chapter, three projects on the use of DASI for the improvement of teacher effectiveness are reported. These projects have been conducted in different countries, and each explores ways to expand the DASI approach by taking into account areas of concern addressed by teacher professional development research. Specifically, two main strands of research in teacher education can be discerned. The first is concerned with the focus of teacher education on the development of specific competencies (Berliner, 1994), and the other with the provision of a more holistic approach. The latter addresses not only specific knowledge and skills, but also a reflection on experiences and beliefs (Calderhead & Shorrock, 1997). The other strand is related to the question of where teacher in-service training should take place and its impact on the school learning environment (Ponte et al., 1994). Two of the projects described in this chapter attempt to expand DASI by providing answers to questions emerging from these strands of teacher education. They also investigate the importance of using DASI to offer courses internally (school based in-service training) or externally, and the relative impact of DASI compared to either the Holistic approach (HA) or the Competence-based approach (CBA).

The cross-cultural validity of the dynamic model of educational effectiveness at teacher level: A canadian study

A) The theoretical background of the project

The main aim of this project was to further test the validity of the dynamic model at the teacher level, by investigating the extent to which the teaching skills of teachers in Canada could be grouped into the same stages as those reported by the study conducted in Cyprus (Kyriakides, Creemers, & Antoniou, 2009). Based on the key findings of teacher effectiveness research, the dynamic model refers to factors which describe teachers' instructional roles and are associated with student outcomes. These factors refer to observable, instructional behaviours of teachers in the classroom, rather than to factors which may explain such behaviours. The eight factors included in the model are: *orientation, structuring, questioning, teaching-modelling, application, management of time, teachers' role in making classroom a learning environment, and classroom assessment.* These eight factors were presented in Chapter 2, in which it was shown that they do not refer solely to one approach of teaching such as structured or direct teaching (Joyce, Weil, & Calhoun, 2000), nor to approaches associated with constructivism (Schoenfeld, 1998). In the first part of the book, it was also shown that each factor was operationalised through five dimensions: *frequency, focus, stage, quality,* and *differentiation.* These dimensions assist more in describing the functioning of each factor. Moreover, the dynamic model is based on the assumption that factors operating at the same level are inter-related. This approach to modelling educational effectiveness reveals grouping of factors which make teachers and schools effective.

Support for the validity of the dynamic model has also been provided (see Chapter 2). Three longitudinal studies revealed that classroom and school factors can be defined by reference to the five dimensions of the dynamic model. The additional value of using these dimensions of classroom level factors to explain variation in student achievement, in both cognitive and affective outcomes, was also demonstrated. The validity of the dynamic model at the teacher level was supported by the results of a meta-analysis of 88 studies exploring the impact of teacher factors on student achievement (see Kyriakides & Christoforou, 2011). Chapter 7 includes a study which investigated the possible grouping of teacher factors. It was shown that teaching skills in the dynamic model could be grouped into five distinct levels, which are discerned in a distinctive way and progress gradually from skills associated with direct teaching to skills concerned with new learning. It was also demonstrated that students of teachers situated at higher levels showed better outcomes in three different subjects. The study reported in the following section aimed to ascertain whether similar stages of effective teaching could be identified in different educational contexts.

B) *The design of the first phase of the study*

In the first phase of the study the eight teacher factors and their dimensions were measured, by administering a questionnaire to students. Students were asked to indicate the extent to which their teacher behaved in a certain way in their classroom; a Likert scale was used to collect these data. This questionnaire has been used to collect data from Cypriot students of grades 5 and 6, and a Generalisability study (Creemers & Kyriakides, 2008a) on the use of students' ratings revealed that data from almost all the questionnaire items could be used for measuring teaching quality. Support for the construct validity of the questionnaire has also been demonstrated (see Kyriakides & Creemers, 2008). For the development of the French version of the questionnaire, the process of double translation was used and thus both the face and content validity of the instrument were examined. Consequently, 78 items were kept in the final version of the questionnaire.

The sample was taken from seven primary schools in the suburb area of Montreal (Canada), who agreed to participate in the study. All grade 3, 4, 5, and 6 students (n=959) from each class (n=42) of the school sample were asked to complete the questionnaire. The response rate was 73%.

C) *Main results of the first phase of the study*

The Generalisability study (G-study) revealed that the data from 63 out of 65 questionnaire items could be used for measuring the teaching quality of each teacher separately for each subject. The following two items were not found to be generalisable at the teacher level:

- I find very easy the activities my mathematics teacher assigns me.
- I have to think a lot in order to be able to answer a question posed by our teacher.

It is important to note here that the student questionnaire was administered to far younger students than those participating in the Cyprus study. However, age effects on the results of the G-study were not identified. This implies that, at least in Canada, younger students could also generate reliable data on their teachers' classroom behaviours, in relation to the eight factors of the model and their five dimensions. Since the data were found to be generalisable at the teacher level, the research team calculated a score for each teacher in each of the 63 questionnaire items deemed generalisable. Specifically, for each teacher a score for each item was created by calculating the mean score from the responses of the students of their class. Following this, the Rasch model was applied to the whole sample of teachers and all 62 measures concerning their teaching skills, using the computer program Quest (Adams & Khoo, 1996). Five items did not fit the model. By analysing the data on the other 58 items, a scale with appropriate psychometric properties was established (see Janosz, Archambault, & Kyriakides, 2011). The results of the various approaches used to test the fit of the Rasch model to the data revealed a good fit when teachers' performance in other teaching skills were analysed. Specifically, all teaching skills were found to have item infit with the range of 0.83 up to 1.20, and item outfit with the range of 0.71 up to 1.42. In addition, all the values of infit for both individuals and teaching skills were greater than -2.00 and smaller than 2.00. The procedure proposed by Yen (1993) was used to test for local independence. It found that local independence was generally not violated. However, if a correct response was given to the teaching skill concerned with differentiation of application, the difficulty parameter of the teaching skill concerned with assessment quality decreased by 0.32. Nonetheless, this model violation did not result in substantial bias estimates of teaching skills parameters. Finally, the fit of the Rasch model to the existing data was also tested against alternative item response theory models, but the improvement of fit by the Two-Parameter Logistic (2PL) over the Rasch model was not statistically significant.

Subsequently, the procedure for detecting pattern clustering in measurement designs, developed by Marcoulides and Drezner (1999), was used to establish whether teaching skills were grouped into levels of difficulty corresponding to easier or more difficult types of teacher behaviours. This method of clustering teaching skills, on the basis of their difficulties from the Rasch model, showed that they are optimally clustered into four types of teacher behaviour (stages of teaching) described in detail below.

Type 1 of teacher behaviour: Basic elements of direct teaching

Teaching skills included in this stage refer to quantitative characteristics of factors associated with the direct teaching approach. For example, the frequency dimension of the management of time, questioning, structuring, and application were found to be situated at this stage. By looking at the teaching skills included in this stage, it can be suggested that teachers mastering this stage are able to effectively use daily routines in their teaching.

Type 2: Putting aspects of quality into direct teaching, and touching on active teaching

Skills concerned with the qualitative aspects of three factors in the direct teaching approach (i.e. structuring, application and questioning) were found to be situated at this stage. In addition, this level refers to the frequency and stage dimensions of the factor involving the teacher's role in establishing interactions among students. Although this factor is not exclusively associated with direct teaching, only the frequency and stage dimensions of this factor are included at this level. This implies that teachers of this level are not only able to put aspects of quality into the factors of the direct teaching approach, but can also encourage interactions among students which may then facilitate active involvement in learning.

Type 3: Acquiring quality in active teaching and reaching out

Teaching skills situated at this level generally refer to qualitative characteristics of active teaching. For example, the focus and quality dimensions of assessment, structuring and questioning were found at this level of effective teaching. It was also found that teachers at this level could create a learning environment in their classroom since all the dimensions of this overarching factor, but differentiation, are part of this type of teacher behaviour. A new element at this level is concerned with the frequency dimension of two factors, teaching modelling and orientation, which are associated with the new teaching approach. This implies that these teachers are not only able to effectively incorporate strategies related to direct and active teaching, but also use techniques in their instruction which are associated with constructivism. The fact that teachers at this level make use of both active teaching and constructivist approaches provides further support for the integrated approach of effective teaching adopted by the dynamic model.

*Type 4: Achieving quality and differentiation in teaching using
different approaches*

All the remaining teaching skills included in the dynamic model were found to be situated at this final level. More specifically, teaching skills at this level are concerned with the qualitative characteristics of factors related to the new teaching approach, and to the establishment of the classroom learning environment.

D) Implications of findings

This study provides some support to the assumption of the dynamic model that teacher level factors are interrelated, and thus should not be treated as isolated. Moreover, the use of specific ways to describe both quantitative and qualitative characteristics of these factors assists in classifying these skills into types of teacher behaviours, which range from relatively easy to the more advanced. The four types of behaviour which emerged from this study are similar to the five levels identified by the study conducted in Cyprus. However, skills associated with the differentiation of teaching were not found to belong to a single level. The results of this study also provide support to the dynamic model's attempt to describe effective teaching using an integrated approach. Specifically, skills associated with both direct teaching and the new teaching approaches were found to belong to the same levels. Moreover, the types of teacher behaviour identified support the idea of combining teaching skills within each type of behaviour, rather than treating each skill or factor in an isolated way. These findings appear to provide support for the use of DASI for teacher improvement purposes (see Chapter 7). However, further research is needed to ascertain whether teachers in Canada who use more advanced types of behaviour are more effective than those demonstrating the easier types; this question was taken into account when designing the second phase of this project. Nevertheless, its first phase can be seen as a step towards the development of a comparative research programme, searching for stages of teaching skills by using the dynamic model as a theoretical framework. Furthermore, the results of this first phase support that the impact of using DASI for teacher improvement purposes should be explored in Canada as well as in other educational settings, since some support for the cross-cultural validity of the dynamic model has been provided here.

The added value of using DASI to offer inset courses on a school basis: a group randomisation study

A) The theoretical background of the study

This second project is funded by the European Science Foundation (ESF/0308/01) and attempts to further expand the DASI to investigate the extent to which INSET courses should be offered on a school-basis. The main aim of this study is related to the various debates on teacher professional development which occur in different countries. In most countries, there is discussion about teacher quality, which research has shown to be one of the most important factors for influencing learning and learning outcomes (Teddlie & Reynolds, 2000; Townsend, 2007). Alongside questions regarding the selection of teachers and their working conditions, there is also a debate on how to improve teacher education, especially teacher professional development (Dall'Alba & Sandberg, 2006). Two main strands of research in teacher education can be identified, which are related to this issue. One is concerned with the focus of teacher education on the development of specific competencies (Berliner, 1994) and the other with the provision of a more holistic approach addressing not only specific knowledge and skills, but also reflection on experiences and beliefs (Calderhead & Shorrock, 1997). The other strand is related to the question of where teacher in-service training should take place and its impact on the school learning environment (Ponte et al., 1994).

This project addresses teacher professional development by integrating findings of research on teacher education with the dynamic model and its use for teacher improvement purposes (see Chapter 7). The dynamic model is used as a theoretical framework to deal with policy and practice in teacher education because it emphasises the quality of teaching. It also utilises an integrated approach in defining effective teaching, by focusing on factors found to be associated with student outcomes. The results of a longitudinal study conducted in Cyprus revealed that teacher factors and their dimensions could be grouped into five distinctive types of teacher behaviour, which move gradually from factors associated with direct teaching to more advanced skills in new teaching approaches and the differentiation of teaching (Kyriakides et al., 2009). It was also found that students of teachers employing more advanced types of behaviour showed better cognitive and affective student outcomes. This study provides empirical support for the grouping of teacher factors and highlights the need to help teachers progress gradually to more complicated types of teacher behaviour, which encompass specific teacher competencies. In addition, the experimental study reported in Chapter 7 showed that teachers employing DASI improved their teaching skills and progressed to a higher level of teaching, whereas those employing the Holistic approach (HA) did not improve their teaching skills. DASI also had a significant impact upon student learning.

However, the two experimental groups were offered external in-service training. This project investigates the added value of using DASI for offering in-service training on an internal school-basis instead, rather than externally. This is an important aim, because the dynamic model emphasises the relationship between school level factors (i.e. policy on teaching and the school learning environment) and teacher professional development (see Chapter 2). Therefore it is not only important to identify how the dynamic model can be used for teacher improvement, but also to investigate the functioning of school factors and their impact on teaching quality. Emphasis is given to the functioning of the *provision of opportunities for teacher professional development* aspect of the school learning environment factor in the dynamic model. For this reason, the project reported in this section attempts to identify the extent to which changes in the functioning of this factor influence other school factors, the quality of teaching or student outcomes and thereby illustrate the dynamic perspective of educational effectiveness.

B) Research design and methods

A sample of 60 primary schools was selected. At the beginning of the school year 2010–2011, data on student background variables and achievement in mathematics and science were collected. The schools were then randomly assigned into four programmes of professional development and a group randomisation study was conducted. Two of the programmes were in line with the dynamic model, in terms of grouping teacher skills into less complicated or more difficult types of teacher behaviour. Therefore these two programmes were concerned on addressing the specific needs of teachers to progress from one level to the next. For example, teachers situated in level 1 who could only use the basic elements of direct teaching were trained to progress to level 2; the latter includes aspects of quality in direct teaching and encouragement of student interactions. The structure of the programme was similar to the INSET course offered to teachers participating in group A of the study reported in Chapter 7. However, the difference between these first two programmes is that one was carried out externally, by asking teachers to attend courses offered by the A&R Team at the University of Cyprus. On the other hand, the second was offered internally; the A&R Team helped each school to develop its own strategies for teacher professional development by using DASI.

The other two programmes followed the Holistic approach to teacher professional development. The A&R Team encouraged reflection and understanding of experiences and beliefs, without taking into account the different development levels of teachers' behaviours; this is explained further in Chapter 7 with the treatment offered to teachers participating in the second 'Holistic' group of the study. Once again, one of them was offered externally and the other internally.

In order to compare the impact of these programmes on teacher behaviour, changes in the behaviours of all grade 4–6 teachers of the school sample were measured. For this purpose, data regarding teacher behaviour both at the beginning and end of the programmes (i.e. the school year 2010–2011) were collected, using the three observation instruments which refer to the teacher factors of the dynamic model (see Kyriakides & Creemers, 2008). Data were also collected on year 4 students' achievement at the beginning and end of the school year. The analysis of the data is currently being conducted and its results will be available on the project's website (http://www.ucy.ac.cy/goto/esf/en-US/GeneralInformation. aspx). This analysis will assist in identifying the impact of these four programmes on learning outcomes. In this way, it might identify the added value of using DASI to develop school-based INSET courses. Finally, it is important to note that data on school level factors using teacher questionnaires were also collected. This will enable the investigation of whether variation in student achievement within each of the four school groups can be attributed to school level factors. For this reason, multilevel structural equation modelling approaches will be used to examine effects of these four programmes on the functioning of the school level factors. The added value of school based INSET courses may therefore be due to its impact on both the improvement of teaching skills and of the school learning environment. Thus, the implications of the findings of this project may be to establish better links between educational effectiveness research and research on teacher professional development.

Searching for stages of teacher skills in assessment: Implications for research on teacher professional development

A) The theoretical background of the study

Teacher assessment is considered an integral part of teaching (Broadfoot & Black, 2004; Delandshere, 2002; Gipps, 1994; Harlen & James, 1997; Linn, 1993). It is defined as the systematic process of gathering information about student learning (Shepard, 2000). It involves making our expectations explicit and public; setting appropriate criteria and high standards for learning quality; systematically gathering, analysing, and interpreting evidence to determine how well performance matches those expectations and standards; and using the resulting information to document, explain, and improve performance (Angelo, 1995).

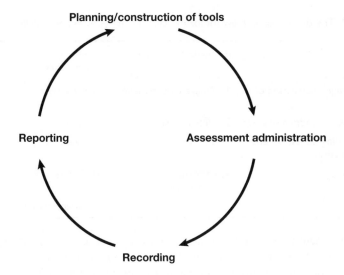

Planning/construction of tools

Reporting

Assessment administration

Recording

Figure 8.1 The assessment cycle illustrating the four phases of assessment.

Teacher assessment's impact on learning has been widely documented in the literature (Boud, 1995; Butler & Winnie, 1995; Crooks, 1988; Nicol & Macfarlane-Dick, 2006; Sadler, 1989). Consequently, the dynamic model refers to teacher assessment as an important teacher factor. It is also stressed that assessment should serve a formative purpose, and research evidence shows that teachers and schools which make use of assessment data for formative reasons are more effective (Brookhart, 2004; Delandshere, 2002; Krasne et al., 2006; Kyriakides, 2005a). Although the formative purpose of assessment has been widely promoted by the educational community (Gipps, 1994; Stiggins, 1999; Shepard, 2000; Stobart, 2004; Popham, 2006), assessment research literature has failed to impact upon teachers' everyday assessment practices, which still appear to be outcome-oriented (Earl & Katz, 2000; Lock & Munby, 2000). Furthermore, there is little research investigating teachers' assessment skills either for formative or summative purposes (Mok, 2010; Wiliam, Lee, Harrison, & Black, 2004). This project not only attempts to find out whether teacher assessment skills can be grouped into different developmental levels, but also whether teachers mastering higher level skills are more effective than others. This project moves a step further to investigate the extent to which DASI can be used to help teachers develop their assessment skills.

Using the dynamic model to measure teachers' assessment skills

In order to measure teachers' assessment skills, the project addresses the four distinct phases of the assessment cycle (see Figure 8.1), which show that teachers should ensure that:

Table 8.1 The theoretical framework for measuring teacher assessment skills

Assessment phases	Assessment techniques	Measuring dimensions of the dynamic model
1) Planning/construction of tools	1) Written assessment	1) Frequency
2) Assessment administration	2) Oral assessment	2) Focus
3) Recording of assessment information	3) Observation	3) Stage
4) Reporting	4) Performance assessment	4) Quality
		5) Differentiation

a) appropriate assessment instruments are used to collect valid and reliable data
b) appropriate procedures in administering these instruments are followed
c) the data emerging from assessment are recorded efficiently and without losing important information
d) the results are reported to parents and students, to assist them in decisions on how to provide support to students to increase their learning and learning outcomes.

The dynamic model was also utilised in order to measure teacher assessment skills. Specifically, the five dimensions used to measure the functioning of each classroom factor were taken into account. For example, the stage dimension addresses the period in which assessment is used, and teachers are expected to use assessment at different periods to inform students about their progress and their learning needs, and not solely at the end of the school year or semester. Similarly, the differentiation dimension investigates the extent to which teachers use different approaches for reporting results to parents or students. Finally, the techniques used by teachers are taken into account when measuring their skills. The importance of using various techniques is supported in the literature, and also relates to the dynamic model's measurement of this teacher factor through the frequency dimension. Table 8.1 shows the theoretical framework that was used in measuring teacher assessment skills. The research design of the project is described in the next section.

B) Research design and results of the first phase of the study

By taking into account the theoretical framework and its dimensions, a teacher questionnaire was developed and administered to a representative sample of 10% of primary Cypriot teachers at the beginning of the school year 2010–2011. Of the 240 teachers approached 178 responded, a response rate of 74.2%. The questionnaire was concerned with their skills in assessment of mathematics in grades 3–6 of primary school. In order to examine the internal validity of the questionnaire data, semi-structured interviews with eight teachers were also conducted. These qualitative data were analysed using the constant comparative method. Comparing the results from each interviewee with their responses to the questionnaire provided support for the internal validity of the study (see Christoforides & Kyriakides, 2011).

The Rasch model was used to analyse data from teachers' responses to the questionnaire; the scales which were created showed satisfactory psychometric properties (see Kyriakides & Christoforides, 2011). It was also found that assessment skills could be grouped into four distinct types of assessment behaviour, which range from skills associated with everyday assessment routines to more advanced skills concerned with differentiation in assessment. The stages are described below:

Stage 1: Basic skills in assessment

Teachers using assessment skills in this stage typically use assessment in order to improve students' learning. They are able to effectively use assessment routines such as:

- Enrichment or alteration of ready-made written tests
- Using different types of written questions to assess students' performance
- Assessing group work based on more than just the overall result
- Being consistent in checking homework
- Keeping records for written assessment
- Reporting assessment results in a summative way.

Stage 2: Using assessment for improvement purposes

The assessment skills included in this stage reveal that teachers using these behaviours are able to use assessment for formative purposes. The skills included in this stage are:

- Developing a specification table in order to construct written tests
- Using test items which not only ask for the final product of a task, but also the process used to reach this outcome
- Using oral assessment and observation
- Offering clarification comments during the administration of written tests
- Marking homework for formative reasons
- Keeping records using descriptive comments
- Reporting assessment results to parents.

Stage 3: Using assessment techniques to measure the three main learning domains (cognitive, affective and psychomotor) and reporting data covering these domains

Teachers using the assessment skills included in this stage are not only able to measure knowledge in mathematics, but also measure skills and abilities of students working together. Skills included in this stage are:

- Evaluating skills by developing relevant observation tools
- Assessing group work
- Reporting results derived from all assessment techniques to both parents and students
- Keeping records for the performance of students in each exercise/goal included in the specification table of the assessment instrument.

Stage 4: Differentiation in Assessment

Teachers demonstrating the assessment skills in this stage are able to differentiate assessment procedures and tools based on their students' needs. This differentiation refers to:

- Construction and administration of written assessments
- Construction and administration of oral assessments
- Reporting to parents and students.

C) The second phase of the project

Due to four developmental stages of teacher assessment skills being identified, a decision was taken to investigate the extent to which DASI can be used for improving teachers' skills in assessment. In order to achieve this, an experimental study was conducted using a similar approach to the study reported in Chapter 7. Specifically, this second phase of the study aims to compare the impact of a teacher professional development programme in mathematics assessment, based on DASI, with the impact of a programme using the Competence-based approach. For this reason, teachers who participated in the first phase of the study and were situated in a certain developmental stage were randomly assigned to one of the two programmes. For example, the 30 teachers situated at Stage 1 were randomly allocated into the two experimental groups, each one then consisting of 15 teachers. Data on student achievement in mathematics were also collected both at the beginning and end of the intervention (i.e. school year 2010–2011). In addition, the teacher questionnaire was administered to the teachers participating in the experimental study at the end of the school year. In this way, the A&R Team will compare the impact of each programme on both improving the assessment skills of teachers and also on student achievement gains in mathematics. The results of this project will be available on the project website (http://www.ucy.ac.cy/goto/esf/en-US/GeneralInformation.aspx). Finally it is important to note that, by comparing the results of this project with those reported in Chapter 7, it will be possible to identify the added-value of using DASI to develop teacher professional development programmes on the development of teachers' skills and effectiveness status (as measured through the achievement of their students). This can be compared to using either the HA or the CBA for this purpose.

Main conclusions emerging from the second part of the book

The main arguments emerging from the second part of the book are presented in the final section of this chapter. In order to demonstrate the development and use of this approach in educational practice, this part is concerned with results of projects showing the conditions and methods with which the DASI approach can be used for school and teacher improvement. The projects presented address important challenges which many schools in different countries face, such as bullying prevention and promoting teacher professional development. It was shown in these studies that the DASI approach helped participating schools to develop their own strategies and actions for improvement, in relation to specific challenges they faced, and also assisted in the improvement of their effectiveness status. In Chapter 4, it was demonstrated that DASI can be used to help schools develop school self-evaluation mechanisms, and design strategies and action plans for improving their effectiveness. The experimental study showed that the A&R Team have an important role in supporting schools, to address school factors related to school effectiveness and also design strategies and action plans in line with the literature. Schools which made use of the dynamic model to identify their priorities for improvement, with the design and implementation of strategies and action plans, improved their effectiveness status.

In Chapter 5, it was also shown that DASI can be used for schools which are facing important challenges that affect their school learning environment. Specifically, it was shown that by integrating research on bullying with literature on educational effectiveness, the A&R Team are able to provide support to schools to identify their improvement priorities and reduce bullying. The fact that DASI was applied in different educational settings suggests that the theoretical framework of this approach is sufficiently flexible to be used in different school contexts. In addition, the dynamic model provides possibilities to integrate research in specific areas, such as the aforementioned bullying research, with the knowledge base of educational effectiveness and improvement. At the same time, the projects presented in Chapters 4 and 5 can be seen as starting points for schools to develop strategies and actions for other challenges they might face in the future, such as the reduction of drop-out rates or providing equal opportunities to various groups of students.

In Chapter 6, the two case studies of schools using DASI for school improvement reveal the important role that both the A&R Team and school stakeholders have, in using the steps of DASI to design and implement a school improvement project. In schools where the commitment and involvement of school stakeholders can be encouraged by the A&R Team, it is more likely that DASI will be used in an effective way and thus improve both learning and learning outcomes.

The last two chapters of this part of the book are concerned with projects on teacher professional development. Chapter 7 suggests that DASI can be used to design teacher professional development courses, which can help teachers improve their teaching skills and effectiveness. It is also shown that, rather than disputing the use of approaches either too focused on isolated teaching skills or too broad to address teacher's specific needs, DASI can help us develop a dynamic integrated approach to teacher professional development; it is more effective than traditional approaches to teacher education (Antoniou & Kyriakides, in press). In Chapter 8, three projects conducted in different educational settings are reported, which raise important issues on teacher education. These projects are evidence for the need to expand the DASI approach, so that schools and other educational institutions can offer courses on both an internal school-basis and also externally, aiming to improve teaching quality and assessment practice.

Furthermore, the projects presented in this part represent different types of research design ranging from experimental studies to case studies. In addition, they were conducted in different educational systems and contexts, and help readers to see that DASI can be applied in various situations by different stakeholders of education. These stakeholders include all teachers, school advisors, policy-makers, and researchers who accept the value assumptions of the theoretical framework of this approach.

The third part of the book will draw implications from the results of this project for practice and research on school improvement, and facilitate further use of the model. One method of achieving this is to provide guidelines to schools on how they can use DASI, and establish school self-evaluation mechanisms which aim to improve the functioning of the schools in order to improve learning outcomes.

Part C

Translating the approach into action

Guidelines and instruments

Using DASI to establish mechanisms for school self-evaluation for improvement purposes

Introduction

The results of the projects presented in the second part of the book reveal that schools in different educational settings can improve their effectiveness status by making use of DASI. For this reason, the third part of the book provides some more practical suggestions to help school stakeholders make use of DASI and design strategies and action plans for school improvement. Specifically, in this part, we provide guidelines to schools on how they can use the proposed improvement approach and build school self-evaluation mechanisms which will help them take decisions on their priorities for improvement and on how to design relevant action plans. A collection of instruments for measuring quality of teaching and the functioning of school level factors is also offered to school stakeholders. In this way, in the first two parts of the book, we explain the proposed approach and its value assumptions, provide examples on how school stakeholders can apply this approach for specific areas of improvement, and generate empirical evidence for the impact of this approach on educational effectiveness. Thus, in the third part we move a step forward and provide practical support to school stakeholders who may like to follow this approach.

In the first chapter of this part of the book, we begin by drawing information from the first two parts of the book to explain the importance of school self-evaluation and its place in the proposed school improvement approach. Then, we present the steps that schools could follow to establish their own school self-evaluation mechanisms. These steps are presented in a practical way and illustrated by examples of schools that already used this approach. We also explain how data on the functioning of school and classroom factors can be collected and analysed. Finally, we give guidelines to schools on how to make use of the results of school self-evaluation in order to prioritise their improvement needs. Examples of schools using the data to prioritise their improvement needs are provided.

Why School self evaluation (SSE) is an essential part of DASI?

Barber (1996) argues that the essence of a successful organization in the post-modern world is the search for improvement and that effective self-evaluation is the key to it. He describes self-evaluation as restless in its quest for evidence in a school's transparent sense of purpose, behaviour, relationships and classroom performance. Devos (1998) argues that School Self Evaluation (SSE) should be seen as 'a process mainly initiated by the school to collect systematic information about the school functioning, to analyze and judge this information regarding the quality of the school's education and to make decisions that provide recommendations' (p. 1–2). In this book, it also is argued that the overarching goals for SSE are twofold: to improve the quality of the organization and to improve teaching and learning. For this reason, SSE is conducted for formative reasons and can be treated as an essential part of the DASI. In practice, it implies that schools which conduct SSE are not simply expected to collect data and announce results on what works and what does not work in a school. This is usually the task of external school evaluation, and studies investigating the consequential validity of external evaluation reveal that it very rarely has an impact on introducing school improvement strategies that affect learning and learning outcomes (e.g., Kane, 2001; Kifer, 2001; Kyriakides, 2004).

The end product of SSE is not only the identification of priorities for improvement, as may be the case in external school evaluations (Kyriakides & Campbell, 2004). In addition to identifying areas of improvement, action plans for improvement are also expected to be implemented in order to improve the functioning of school and increase student learning outcomes. As a consequence, SSE is not simply considered as the starting point of school improvement but for schools to remain among the most effective they need data from SSE to take decisions on how to improve teaching practice and the learning environment of the school. This argument is supported by research evidence and was taken into account in establishing the dynamic model of educational effectiveness (see Creemers & Kyriakides, 2006). For example, two of the overarching school factors included in the dynamic model refer to school evaluation which is seen as essential for school stakeholders in their attempt to improve the functioning of the other two overarching school factors (school policy on teaching and school policy on the school learning environment). This view about the role of SSE is reflected in Figure 3.1 (presenting DASI) which shows that improvement process cannot be treated as linear but should be viewed instead as dynamic in character. This implies that schools should always attempt to improve their functioning and no golden standards should be able to be achieved for schools to remain stable in quality.

The essential difference of the DASI to other approaches on school improvement is that our approach to school improvement is based on the assumption that SSE should be concerned with specific school factors that are found to be associated with student achievement. These two major factors are school policy on teaching and the school policy on the School Learning Environment (SLE). This is due to the fact that these two overarching factors are related with learning and learning outcomes. Since practicality is a property that needs to be taken into account for any evaluation, DASI promotes the idea that SSE should be about the two most important overarching school factors and not to cover anything that may happen in a school. In order to elaborate this point to a group of 25 school managers, we invited them to define their own criteria for evaluating their schools. Each of them was asked to put down the first five criteria that come to his/her mind as a brainstorming activity. As a result of this task, we managed to develop a questionnaire with 115 criteria of school evaluation, some of which were not related either with teaching or with the school learning environment. The school leaders were then asked to reflect on this list of criteria. It was agreed that the list was too large to be able to collect data on all of the factors. So the list was reduced by only using factors which were found to be associated with student achievement. In Chapter 4, the approach described above was used by schools participating in experimental group A. Some of these schools ended up identifying a priority of improvement which was not associated with any school factor. It is demonstrated that these schools did not manage to improve learning. On the other hand, those schools addressing school factors included in the dynamic model managed to improve their effectiveness status.

Another important element of SSE that is taken into account in designing improvement strategies has to do with its participatory character. SSE promotes the idea that all school stakeholders should be involved in the evaluation of their school. Thereby, as soon as the schools attempt to design an improvement project, stakeholders should be brought together and each given a role to play in the project. The readers are reminded that the dynamic model refers to partnership as a school factor. Effective schools are expected to improve this important aspect of the school learning environment. For this reason, DASI refers to the importance of conducting SSE rather than any other form of internal evaluation that might be the initiative of a specific group of school stakeholders only (e.g., school evaluation conducted by the school management team).

The DASI also supports that the A&R Team has a very crucial role to play in helping schools to design SSE, analyze data emerged from SSE, identify priorities for improvement and develop their strategies and action plans for school improvement. They are therefore expected to take an active role in providing their knowledge and expertise to school stakeholders at all stages of DASI. For example, school stakeholders may like to develop their policy on teaching and especially its aspect concerned with the provision of learning opportunities by organizing activities that promote creativity. In such cases, members of the A&R Team are expected not only to provide suggestions based on research evidence on creativity but may also have to help schools either develop their own instruments to measure creativity or help the stakeholders to use relevant tests that have good psychometric properties and were used in several studies (e.g., Clapham, 1998;

Kim, 2006). However, in some countries, schools are expected to carry out SSE but no emphasis is placed on establishing close relations between the A&R Team and school stakeholders. For example, schools may simply invite an external research team or a research centre to conduct school evaluation and this team may visit the school in order to collect and analyse data and give a report to schools without working closely with them. Studies on the use of SSE in countries such as Scotland and the Netherlands show that in many schools this approach is followed (Visscher & Coe, 2002). In such schools, teachers, students and parents may not be even aware that a SSE took place. As a consequence, no impact of establishing SSE on student learning is reported (Coe, 2009; Hofman, Dijkstra, & Hofman, 2009). DASI takes a different position on the contribution of A&R Team and school stakeholders in conducting SSE and using it for improvement purposes. It is expected that A&R Team and school stakeholders should actively be involved and work together at all stages of SSE. In this way, we can establish closer links of research with improvement of practice and draw on experiences of both researchers and practitioners in identifying priorities for improvement and designing improvement strategies and action plans. Although the A&R Team may have technical expertise and may have to conduct the analysis of evaluation data, school stakeholders should have a say for this process too. For example, the A&R Team may analyse the results and produce a report to school stakeholders (that should be written in a way that even young students can understand). In addition, anyone may ask from members of A&R Team to run extra analysis and give them answers to questions that may be of interest to them. In schools participating at the experimental study reported in Chapter 4, members of A&R Team produced a report and presented the results in a meeting with representatives of parents, students and teachers. In some cases, some interesting questions were raised by various school stakeholders and the researcher had access to data and run the relevant analysis immediately to answer these questions (see Demetriou, 2009).

It is finally important to note that one of the major assumptions of SSE is that 'human beings can learn from their experiences' (see Kyriakides & Campbell, 2004). This implies that SSE encourages school stakeholders to reflect on their practice and identify their weaknesses. In this way, targets can be set up in order to contribute to student learning. DASI takes into account this value assumption of SSE but it also moves a step forward and reminds that reflection is important but not enough to take improvement initiatives. School stakeholders need support from A&R Team to reflect on their practice and identify ways to improve their functioning in the school. For example, in Chapter 5, school stakeholders in schools which made use of DASI to deal with bullying did not have simply to reflect on their experiences and develop their strategies and action plans. Without the support of A&R Team, it is likely that they may not have seen any problem with their functioning in the school in the first place. It was in fact the SSE conducted by the A&R Team that revealed that bullying incidents occurred during school breaks. In addition, some schools did not have any policy on how to deal with bystanders, and unless the A&R Team raise this issue, school stakeholders may not have to pay attention to it. In this context, the involvement of school stakeholders in SSE is not only expected to encourage them to reflect about their practice but to reflect by having in mind the literature which refers to best practices to deal with bullying or any other challenge that their school is facing. At this point, school stakeholders are expected to make use of the dynamic model and the A&R Team to reflect on the functioning of their school factors that promote learning and learning outcomes.

What steps do schools have to follow in using the DASI to improve their effectiveness?

The first step of the DASI presented in Chapter 3 concerns the establishment of consensus regarding the main aim of the school improvement project. The fact that people may have different perceptions about change is taken into account and the importance of establishing consensus is explained. For this reason, it is acknowledged that establishing consensus about school improvement aims is not an easy task. However the stand point of DASI is that school stakeholders have to understand that learning is the main function of school and for this reason the ultimate aim of any school improvement project should be to promote learning and learning outcomes. It is vital that the A&R Team and the management team of the school share this basic assumption of the DASI and discuss it with the various school stakeholders (teachers, parents, students). They may find groups of school stakeholders that may not consider learning as the main task of school. If so, it is the task of school leaders and the A&R Team to emphasise the important contribution that schools have on student learning.

At this point, it is important not to expect all stakeholders to agree or to spend time and energy in implementing the school improvement project. What is most important is to clarify the aims of the school improvement project to all stakeholders and to ensure that everybody feels welcome in joining the project. In this way, the schools can make use of teachers/parents/students who agree to the assumption that learning is important and would like to be involved in the project. Although we do not expect that everybody will be involved in the project, at the same time we hope to gradually persuade those who may be more sceptical to become more involved. This is especially true with schools that attempt to improve the school policy of partnership as not as many parents tend to share this value assumption but this is not an indication that it is not worthy to take actions and improve partnership policy. Obviously, schools should not expect a rush of parents to be interested in the project from the beginning. However they should expect a reasonable increase in the number of parents as the project progresses.

The second step to improving educational effectiveness regards the presentation of the theoretical framework of DASI. The framework is expected to help school stakeholders understand that school improvement initiatives should be concerned with school factors included in the dynamic model. The A&R Team has to present the framework of the DASI to those involved in the school improvement process in a simple way. Included in this presentation would be the value assumptions and basic elements of the dynamic model. For example, the importance of the assumption of maximising the use of teaching time can easily be understood by everybody (students, parents and teachers). However, sometimes we forget the importance of this very obvious factor which affects learning and may reduce available teaching time. For example, some parents and students may not give sufficient attention to the importance of coming to school on time and may disturb the teaching process by coming late and interrupting the lesson. Similarly, some school managers may interrupt teaching to make announcements. By explaining these simple examples, the A&R Team may help school stakeholders understand why the policy of maximising teaching time should be in place and why actions should be taken in order to explain to everyone what is expected from him/her to do.

At this point, we would like to give an example of how a school has dealt with those who did not respect the policy of time management. In a primary school that was situated in a remote area that takes students from different small villages, the headteacher found out that one of the bus drivers was always late in the morning. She explained to the bus driver why it is important to be on time to school. The bus driver told her that one of the students was coming to the bus stop late and he had to wait for this student. The headteacher asked the bus driver not to wait for the student and to come on time to school every day. The next day the mother of the student came to the school complaining that the bus driver had left her son. The head teacher explained to her that because teaching time should be guaranteed, she asked the bus driver to be more punctual. It was also explained to her that unless her son arrived at the bus stop on time every day, she would have to find an alternate method of transportation for her son. In another school, the teacher had to argue with a mother to bring her daughter on time to school and not half hour late. The mother refused to do it and had the impression that her daughter could catch up easily and there was no reason to bring her on time. The headteacher had also to talk with the mother but with no result. In this case, you can see that some stakeholders may not understand the importance of even the most obvious factors that affect learning such as the quantity of teaching time. Although the school did not manage to persuade the mother to respect the school policy, in a year's time her daughter's results in the subject taught in the first period went down, so the teacher showed the mother the test results in order to persuade her to pay more attention to coming to school on time. These two examples show us that not all school stakeholders may understand the importance of school factors for various reasons. In the first case, the bus driver and the mother were not aware of the importance of the factor of maximizing the use of teaching time. Consequently, the head teacher helped them understand what was expected from them. In the second case, the mother underestimated the importance of teaching time and had the impression that when students are clever they don't need teachers and time for learning. Given that school stakeholders may have different views (which may not be valid) about the factors affecting learning, the DASI puts emphasis on the use of a valid theoretical framework in defining the content of SSE. The importance of communicating this framework to all stakeholders is also stressed and it is expected that teachers, parents and students understand why it is important for the school to improve the functioning of these factors.

Step 3 is concerned with the administration of instruments in order to measure the factors of the dynamic model and with the analysis of data in order to identify priorities for improvement. At this step, it is first of all important that the school management team and the A&R Team inform stakeholders about the instruments that are used and explain that the analysis of data is concerned with the identification of general trends that exist in the school and not with exposing individuals who may perform less well than others. They should also make sure that anonymity and confidentiality of the data they are handling is guaranteed. It is for this reason that stakeholders should give special attention to the process that is used for the administration of the instruments. For example, administering teacher questionnaires in order to measure school factors (see Chapter 10) implies that each teacher should give his/her answers individually and not in cooperation with other teachers. In addition, the members of A&R Team should not collect the questionnaires from each teacher individually but give them the chance to complete the questionnaire in their own time and return the completed questionnaire to a box so nobody can have access to their responses. It is also very important that the school management team and A&R Team explain to school stakeholders participating in the initial evaluation, to express themselves in a clear and honest way. Moreover, they should be aware that the results of school self evaluation should reveal some priorities for improvement but this does not mean that school stakeholders responsible for these areas should consider themselves as less competent than others since SSE is expected to support the improvement of the school rather than to blame individuals.

Related to the anonymity issue, it is important that school stakeholders and the A&R Team be careful with raising questions on background characteristics of teachers and other stakeholders which may help someone to identify who answered the questionnaire. Although questions on background characteristics are useful for testing the generalizability of the data and for identifying differences in the responses of different groups of stakeholders, the school management team and the A&R Team should be extremely careful in including them in groups which are relatively small.

Another issue that has to be discussed concerns the assumption of the 'commitment to gathering evidence' (see Kyriakides & Campbell, 2004). School stakeholders are expected to express commitment to objectivity and a readiness to alter their practice in the light of evidence (Fitz-Gibbon, Tymms, & Hazlewood, 1990; Visscher & Coe, 2002). It is important to acknowledge that each member of the school may have his/her own views on what the priorities for improvement are. However, after the results of the SSE have identified a priority area for improvement all stakeholders are expected to show a willingness to work on this area. In some schools which make use of SSE to identify improvement efforts, the A&R Team may find members of the school that are opposing the results of SSE because they still believe that another area needs to be treated as priority for school improvement rather than those areas identified through analysing the results of the SSE. To avoid this kind of problem, at the very first stage of DASI an agreement that everybody has to respect the results of evaluation should be reached.

Since at step A it was agreed that the ultimate aim of DASI is the improvement of learning and learning outcomes, at this point school stakeholders should take a decision on the learning outcomes that will be measured. In choosing the type of learning outcomes that the school will measure, several considerations can be taken into account. Schools may take into account practicality issues such as the availability of a battery of tests that can be administered to different age groups of students and/or the time that is needed for collecting and marking the tests. Moreover, the decision may have to do with the interests of school stakeholders in finding out student performance in specific areas, such as social cognition and creativity. At this point, the A&R Team may encourage stakeholders to measure more than one learning outcome. In this way, the results of summative evaluation will help school stakeholders see that the DASI had an impact on more that one learning outcome. In addition, it might help schools to give answers to those that are afraid that focusing on one learning outcome may negatively affect other outcomes. For example, some parents may be under the impression that if achievement in social science is measured then student achievement in another subject (e.g., mathematics) may be negatively affected due to the fact that teachers will not pay enough attention to this outcome. In such cases, measuring more than one type of learning outcomes can help school stakeholders to understand that the DASI is about the improvement of school factors that affect all types of learning outcomes.

Finally, rules for the use of data should be established to ensure confidentiality of the data. Much of the data collected through SSE is personal information. For example, it may relate to individual teacher performance or to parental support. For this reason, it is essential for the A&R Team to establish procedures to control the use of data and to agree with the stakeholders on the purpose for which data are being collected (Fitz-Gibbon & Tymms, 2002). For instance, school stakeholders and the A&R Team may inform parents that collecting data on quality of teaching (see Chapter 10) does not serve checking upon or supervising teachers' work. At the same time, the A&R Team will ensure teachers that SSE aims at outlining general tendencies in the school and is not directed at measuring the effectiveness of individual teachers. Thus, the main focus of SSE is to help the improvement of the organization rather than identifying the performance of individuals. This implies that the data collected should be focused on how to influence decision-making about the priorities of school improvement and on how to develop strategies and action plans for school improvement.

The establishment of rules on using data has important implications on how data will be analysed. Since the main aim of the DASI is to identify priorities for improvement, the analysis of data should help us rank order the functioning of factors and identify those that need more attention. In some cases, a network of schools using the DASI for improvement purposes may be established (see Chapter 5). In this case, a risk of using the data for summative rather than formative reasons may arise. However, if analysis of data refers to mean ranks of school factors, then no comparison among schools can be achieved. For example, policy on partnership may be the first priority for improvement in school A, whereas policy on teacher collaboration may be the priority of school B. However, if the report presenting the results refers to mean ranks then there is no way to claim that school A is doing better than School B on teacher collaboration and the school B is doing better than school A on partnership. This example demonstrates the advantage of conducting SSE: avoiding comparing results between schools, and instead focusing on how to identify priorities for school improvement and take actions to improve schools.

Another problem that may arise in analyzing data has to do with the initial measure of student achievement in different learning outcomes. Some stakeholders may be interested to find out how students of different classrooms within their school managed to perform in the tests. To avoid this problem, the A&R Team should make clear that for the purposes of school improvement, such questions damage the formative function of SSE and concentrate on a completely different approach to school improvement which supports that improvement can come through accountability mechanisms.

Beyond collecting and analysing the data, the A&R Team should present the results of the analysis of data with school stakeholders in a meeting showing the list of areas that could be addressed. In this meeting, stakeholders are encouraged to express their views about this list. Initially, school stakeholders may indicate whether they found these results what they expected to be. By asking school stakeholders to share their expectations with the A&R Team may also help schools to investigate the external validity of the initial evaluation. In addition, school stakeholders may express their first ideas of how they could contribute to improving the functioning of the school factors. For example, in a school where the policy on assessment was identified as an important priority area for improvement, teachers may first try to search for reasons that parents do not visit schools. This may shed light on children's performances and what the stakeholders can do in order to report more effective results in the assessment. For example, they could ask themselves how easy it is for parents who are working to come and visit schools at the time allocated in the program for parents visit and what kind of changes are needed in order to facilitate the communication with parents. Similarly, parents may have to ask themselves how to establish better communication with teachers in order to learn from teachers how to support their children's learning rather than to simply negotiate their children's grades. In this way, a focused reflection is encouraged and some initial thoughts about the action plans are exchanged. It is finally very important at this stage to reach consensus among school stakeholders on the area(s) that need to be addressed. At this point, the readers are reminded that the dynamic model assumes that factors operating at the same time are often related to each other. It is therefore possible for school stakeholders to combine areas for improvement from the list presented to them. In addition, at this stage, teachers are also expected to share the results of the assessment with students and their parents. During this discussion, the aim is to work together in order to make plans on how the student can achieve specific learning objectives with the support of his/her parents and teacher.

Since not every stakeholder will be able to participate at the meeting where the results of evaluation are presented, it is the responsibility of the school management team (with support from the A&R Team) to inform all stakeholders that were not present at the meeting of the results of the evaluation and the decision taken at the meeting. In addition, the stakeholders that were not present at the meeting are also requested to express their views about the results in a written form. In this way, the school has the chance to define the area(s) of the school improvement project more precisely and to announce the final decision in a formal way (e.g. by sending a letter to all stakeholders).

At step D of the DASI schools are expected to develop their action plans. The A&R Team should first of all help school stakeholders to understand the elements that need to be included in an action plan. In developing the action plans, all schools must specify which tasks need to be undertaken, who is going to be responsible for implementing each task, when each task is expected to be implemented, and what resources should be provided to the stakeholders in order to implement these tasks. The A&R Team should also give specific suggestions on the type of actions that the schools can take in order to improve the functioning of factors associated with the improvement area(s) of the school. In Chapter 5, schools making use of the DASI for reducing bullying were offered a handbook from the A&R Team including specific suggestions (from the literature) on how each factor can be improved (see also Appendix 5.1). Although it is the responsibility of the A&R Team to provide suggestions on the content of the action plans, the final decisions regarding the action plans should be taken by the school stakeholders who are more aware of the special context of their school in relation to the priority area(s). For example, the A&R Team presented to school stakeholders different types of partnership programs that could be undertaken (see Epstein, 1992) and also results of a meta-analysis indicating the impact of each type on student achievement (see Fan & Chen, 2001). In one school, teachers were keen to develop an improvement project encouraging active parental involvement. At this stage the A&R Team had its reservations for moving towards such a rapid change. Although they expressed their reservations, school stakeholders insisted on developing this program, and managed to develop relevant action plans and improvement strategies. They had the chance to implement the improvement project and it turned out to be very successful due to the fact that teachers of this school were very keen, and committed to making it a success, and had no problem in inviting parents to come to their classrooms and work with them (see Kyriakides, 2005b). However, such a project might not be successful in a school where effort has to be taken to improve policy partnership, and teachers are more sceptical on active parental involvement and its impact on achievement.

Beyond developing action plans, formative evaluation mechanisms should also be established. The results of formative evaluation will help schools to redefine their action plans on time and provide the support that some stakeholders many need in order to implement these action plans. For example, the coordinator of the improvement project and/or other stakeholders involved in implementing specific action plans may be encouraged to keep a reflective diary which will inform the A&R Team and school stakeholders about the implementation of the action plans and the problems that may arise. Obviously, it is not necessary for the coordinator to put down their every day progress. However they should mention the events that were very crucial to the success of the project (e.g., problems that turn up, difficulties, achievements, remarks, hesitations). Co-ordinators can share these events with the A&R Team who is expected to help school stakeholders in their attempts to redefine their strategies and actions to make them more relevant to their context as the improvement process progresses. This is a very useful strategy in implementing projects that last for a long period and/or that are addressing more complicated/sensitive priority areas and challenges that schools are facing such as dealing with bullying incidents (see Chapter 5).

Though the A&R Team will be monitoring the implementation of the improvement project, it is very likely that school stakeholders will identify practical difficulties and weaknesses in their action plans. It is essential that *immediate actions are taken to improve and redefine* the action plans in order to achieve their goals. Schools may discover that, in some cases, they may have to make changes in their plans many times during a school year. This does not necessarily imply that the original action plans were insufficient, but merely that they were not fit for long time-periods. On the contrary, the A&R Team should be surprised if the initial action plan can remain the same over a long period of time. If this is the case, it might be an indication that the monitoring system is not providing valid data. For example, the monitoring team may be trying to please the school management team by indicating that all the actions are implemented sufficiently and major progress is being made.

In this Chapter the main steps that schools have to follow in order to implement the DASI are described. Some issues that need to be taken into account by the school stakeholders and the A&R Team in their attempt to undertake specific activities associated with each step are raised. In the next two chapters, we analyse two very crucial elements of DASI in more detail. In Chapter 10, suggestions on how school and classroom factors can be measured are provided and relevant instruments are presented. Suggestions on analysing data emerged from these instruments are also given. In the final chapter of this part, the design of improvement strategies and action plans are referred to and specific suggestions on tasks that need to be undertaken in order to improve the functioning of each school factor are given.

Chapter 10

Instruments for measuring quality of teaching and school level factors

Introduction

In this chapter, we present instruments which have been developed for measuring the quality of teaching and the school level factors. These instruments have been used in different studies testing the dynamic model (for a detailed review see Chapter 2) and in improvement projects presented in the second part of the book. Beyond presenting the instruments and their properties, guidelines on how to use them for collecting data are also provided. Moreover, different ways for analysing the data in the context of an improvement project (single or multiple cases) are illustrated. We also give examples of analysing data collected through these instruments and interpreting the results of the analysis for school improvement purposes. Obviously, schools have to adopt these instruments to their context and make use of the expertise of the Advisory and Research Team (A&R Team) in developing their own instruments to measure classroom and school factors. For example, in the project on using DASI to face and reduce bullying (Kyriakides, Charalambous, Kaloyirou, & Creemers, 2011) the teacher questionnaire had to be adopted in the context of the five participating countries. A typical example is the fact that in some countries (e.g., Cyprus and Greece) bullying incidents occurred during the visit of students to the school canteen. Relevant items were therefore included in the teacher questionnaire. However, in other countries (e.g., Belgium/Flanders and the Netherlands), small primary schools do not have a school canteen. Therefore these items were not included in the teacher questionnaire of these countries.

Instruments for measuring teacher level factors

This section is concerned with measuring teacher level factors. In Chapters 7 and 8, projects which made use of DASI to facilitate teacher professional development courses were presented. It is shown that it is possible for a school or other institutions to use DASI in order to organise a teacher professional development course, and improve the quality of teaching practice. The readers are also reminded that one of the case study schools (reported in Chapter 6) explicitly choose to concentrate on improving quality of teaching as a result of data emerged from school self-evaluation (SSE). In such cases, school stakeholders and the A&R Team have to collect initial data on the skills of teachers across the eight factors included in the dynamic model. In this way, priorities for teacher improvement can be identified. This will help schools and other institutions to design courses to meet these needs. In addition, for the purposes of a summative evaluation, final measures of the teaching skills of participating teachers were recorded. In this way, the impact of DASI on improving teaching skills can be identified. In order to measure teacher behaviour in the classroom, observations can be conducted (Schaffer, Nesselrodt, & Stringfield, 1994) and/or students may be asked to anonymously complete a questionnaire exploring the behaviour of their teachers (Gastel, 1991). In the literature the advantages and disadvantages of each method are discussed (Ellet, 1997; Stronge & Ostrander, 1997) and the importance of using multiple sources of data is advocated (e.g., Cheng & Marsh, 2010; Fresko & Nasser, 2001; de Jong & Westerhof, 2001; Marsh & Roche, 1997).

The instruments used to measure the eight factors in various studies testing the validity of the model (Creemers & Kyriakides, 2010a; Kyriakides & Creemers, 2008, 2009) are presented below. Obviously, school stakeholders may decide to use some of them due to practicality issues. The first project presented in Chapter 8 shows that valid data were collected through using student questionnaires only (Janosz, Archambault, & Kyriakides, 2011). Therefore some schools may choose to do the same. Those schools that are planning to conduct observations should make sure that appropriate training to external observers is provided. It is envisioned that the training should have the following elements: getting to know the theoretical background of the dynamic model, getting to know the instruments, using the instruments, and calculating/reporting inter-rater reliability. The Dynamic Model of Educational Effectiveness should be introduced, and the goals of the different instruments explained. Chapter 2 and the book on Dynamic Model (*The Dynamics of Educational Effectiveness: A contribution to Policy, Practice and Theory in Contemporary Schools* by Creemers and Kyriakides, 2008) can provide useful background reading in this respect.

In order for the instruments to be used effectively, it will be necessary to train observers in their use. Some suggestions on the issues that could be covered during the training are provided below:

i.   Explanation of the eight factors included in the dynamic model and their measurement dimensions: The background reading for the dynamic model could be given to the observers. Observers may also refer to teaching activities for which they are not sure whether they are associated with one or another factor or whether they are not sure how to code them by using a specific measurement dimension.

ii.   Presentation of each instrument separately and explanation of how it can be used: Trainees should be allowed to raise questions and discuss any worries that may have. Each item on the instruments should be discussed and emphasis should be placed on the specific meanings of the each individual item.

iii. Use of instruments: The practice part of the training should consist of observations conducted by the trainee observers using the instruments. For this purpose, video-taped lessons could be used to illustrate how each instrument can be used. When observers feel confident with the use of an instrument, the A&R Team may use video-taped lessons and all the members of the group can be asked to collect data about each lesson by completing the relevant instruments.

iv. Calculate the inter-rater reliability, present the results that emerged, and discuss the differences that are observed.

v. Repetition of steps iii and iv, as many times as possible, should be pursued until inter-rater reliability of around 0.70 is reached.

It is also important to note that during the training, the observers should be offered the opportunity to watch video taped lessons and use the instruments to rate these. By discussing how each observer has interpreted the recorded behaviour a better understanding of the instruments can be achieved. By the end of the training, observers should be able to reach adequate levels of inter-rater reliability as specified above.

Finally, the following should also be noted: sampling decisions should be made in conjunction with the A&R Team. It is also essential to conduct at least two observations per teacher.

Observations Instruments

Taking into account the way the five dimensions of each effectiveness factor are defined, one high-inference and two low-inference observation instruments were developed in order to test the validity the model (see Kyriakides & Creemers, 2008). The observation instruments and the guidelines on using the low-inference observation instruments are presented in Appendix 10.1. The first low-inference observation instrument (LIO1) is based on Flanders' system of interaction analysis (Flanders, 1970). However, we developed a classification system of teacher behaviour which is based on the way each factor of the dynamic model is measured. For example, in order to measure the quality dimension of teacher behaviour in dealing with disorder which is an element of the classroom as a learning environment factor, the observers are asked to identify any of the following types of teacher behaviour in the classroom:

a) The teacher is not using any strategy at all to deal with a disorder problem (code: 6a)

b) The teacher is using a strategy that has a long-lasting effect (code: 6b)

c) The teacher is using a strategy, but the problem is only temporarily solved (code: 6c).

The distinction between temporarily (i.e., category c) and long-lasting effect (i.e., category b) is based on observations of what is happening during the lesson and after the action of the teacher.

Similarly, in order to measure the focus dimension of the way the teacher deals with the negative aspects of competition, the following two types of teacher behaviour were given specific codes:

a) The teacher puts the problem in a more general perspective in order to help students see the positive aspects of competition and avoid the negative ones (code: 5a)

b) The teacher is dealing only with the specific problem that arises and which is associated with the negative effects of competition (code: 5b).

We also developed a classification system of student behaviour. In this system the observer is not only expected to classify student behaviour when it appears but also to identify the students who are involved in each type of behaviour. Thus, the use of this instrument enables data about teacher–student and student–student interaction to be generated. For example, the focus dimension of teacher–student interactions is measured by classifying each observed teacher–student interaction according to the purpose(s) that it was expected to serve (i.e., managerial reasons, social encounter, learning etc.). However, the quality dimension of this factor is measured by investigating the immediate impact that each teacher initiative has on establishing relevant interactions. In particular whether the teacher was able to establish on task behaviour through the interactions she/he promoted is explored. The measurement of the impact of teacher activity is based on observations of students' reactions and not on interpretation of the quality of teacher activity. As far as the measurement of the stage is concerned, the instrument generated data which takes into account at which phase of the lesson each interaction took place.

The second low-inference observation instrument (LIO2) refers to five factors of the model:

a) orientation
b) structuring
c) teaching modelling
d) questioning
e) application.

This instrument was designed in a way that enables the collection of more information in relation to the quality dimension of these five factors. For each factor the quality and focus dimensions are defined in a specific way (see Appendix 10.1). For example, in regard to the measurement of the quality of an application task, observers have to indicate whether the teacher is:

a) asking students to practice in using a specific process/algorithm to solve a number of similar exercises

b) expecting students to activate certain cognitive processes in order to find the solution of more complex tasks and/or algorithms.

The following two examples illustrate the difference between the two types of application task. First, after discovering the formula that gives the area of rectangles, students are given the dimensions (width and length) of 10 rectangles and are asked to find the area of each rectangle. Second, students are asked to find how much money they will need to paint the ceiling of their classroom if each bucket of paint covers $2m^2$ and costs £10. As far as the measurement of the focus dimension of structuring is concerned, the following three types of activities are discerned. First, a structuring task may refer to the structure of the day's lesson activities only without establishing any links with other lessons. Second, the teacher might relate that days lesson activities with the previous lessons. Finally, the teacher might not only show the relation of the day's lesson with the previous lessons but may also explain how the lesson is related to lessons in the future.

In regard to the other three dimensions, similar measurement ways are used irrespective of whether an activity belongs to one factor or another. Specifically, observers are asked to state the order of each activity observed. For example, if at the beginning of the lesson the teacher asks students to practice the content of the lesson that was taught the day before and then she/he comments on the structure of the lesson of the day. The first observed task is an application and the second a structuring task. By providing the order of the activities, a score for measuring the stage dimension of each factor can be established. Moreover, the observers are asked to report the time (in minutes) that was used for each activity. Therefore, the quantity dimension of each factor is measured by identifying not only how many activities associated with a factor were observed, but also by calculating the total time that was used for all the activities associated with this factor. In regard to the measurement of the differentiation dimension, observers are asked to indicate whether there is any type of differentiation in the observed task. For example, in the case of an orientation activity, a teacher may clarify further the aims of the lesson to a certain group of students (e.g., 'the less able ones'). Similarly, in the case of an application task, the teacher may assign to the less able students more application exercises or give them more time to solve them.

The high-inference observation instrument (see Appendix 10.1) covers the five dimensions of all eight factors of the model. The instrument also indicates how often each teacher-behaviour was observed. For example, an item concerned with the frequency dimension of orientation is asking observers to indicate how often the teacher explained the aims of the teaching activities (item 2). In order to measure the quality dimension of this factor, one of the items of the high-inference observation instrument is asking observers to indicate the extent to which the orientation activities that were organised during the lesson helped students understand the new content (item 1). Similarly, the quality dimension of the application factor is measured through items asking the observers to identify the extent to which the observed tasks were:

a)   A replication of the activities that were organised during the presentation of the new content
b)   The application tasks were used by the teacher as starting points for teaching new concepts (item 13).

Student questionnaire (Appendix 10.1)

The eight factors and their dimensions were also measured by administering a questionnaire to students. Specifically, students were asked to indicate the extent to which their teacher behaves in a certain way in their classroom. Take the example of an item concerned with the stage dimension of the structuring factor. This asks students to indicate whether at the beginning of the lesson the teacher explains how the new lesson is related to previous ones (see item 3). Similarly, another item asks whether at the end of each lesson they spend some time in reviewing the main ideas of the lesson (see item 48). The following item was used to measure the differentiation dimension of the application factor. This item asks whether the Mathematics teacher gives some students different exercises to do than the ones he gives to the rest (see item 22).

A Generalisability Study (Cronbach, Gleser, Nanda, & Rajaratnam, 1972; Shavelson, Webb, & Rowley, 1989) on the use of students' ratings was conducted. It was found that the data which emerged from almost all the questionnaire items could be used for measuring the quality of teaching of each teacher in each subject separately (see Creemers & Kyriakides, 2008a). For the purposes of a teacher improvement project using DASI, school stakeholders and the A&R Team could perform a one-way ANOVA. This would allow the exploration of search for statistical significant differences. This would identify if there is homogeneity in the responses of students who are in the same classroom. Thus, the score for each teacher participating in the project in each of the questionnaire item will be the mean score emerged from the responses of the students of his/her class. As previously mentioned (see Chapter 9), the A&R Team will ensure that the data are not used for comparing teachers according to their performance in each item. The emphasis should be on how to rank order the scores that each teacher has in each factor. Through this, his/her improvement needs can be identified. For example, the Kendall Coefficient of Concordance test can be used to calculate mean rank scores for the eight teacher factors and their dimensions. Based on these scores, a list with the improvement needs of each teacher could emerge.

The following information/guidelines could be given to the individual(s) responsible to administer the student questionnaire measuring teacher behaviour in teaching a specific subject.

Actions taken prior to administration

Before giving the general instructions to students about how to fill in the questionnaire additional information should be collected. A member of the A&R Team or a school stakeholder who may be responsible for administering the questionnaire should collect this information in order to define who are taking the questionnaire. Based on school records or information given by the teacher, only students who have *sufficient information about classroom instruction* should take part. Special attention should be given not to include students who just arrived in the classroom or don't understand the language (e.g., immigrants who recently arrived and don't speak the language of instruction) or do not regularly attend the classroom instructions (e.g., students with special needs taken out of the classroom). Researchers should also take into consideration the following points in organising the data collection process:

1) Time duration   In order for the instrument to be used effectively the individual(s) should first make sure that the students would have enough available time (40 minutes) to fill in the questionnaires.

2) Confidentiality   Through the questionnaire students are asked to comment on their teacher which may cause unease if they fear that their teacher has access to their answers. In advance the person administrating the questionnaires should make clear to the students that the data they will provide through their answers are confidential and that the teacher will have no access to them. Also students will be informed not to write anywhere on the sheets their name or anything that would reveal their identity so they remain anonymous.

3) Incentives to students   Students should be encouraged to read the statements and carefully choose their answer. It is important that students understand how filling in the questionnaire can aid improving schooling. Incentives such as the one who finishes completing the questionnaire first should be avoided. It is also useful to have an alternative assignment for each student who finishes early. This will stop students who have finished from disturbing the rest of the class who are still working on the questionnaires.

During the administration of the questionnaire

During the time the students are filling in their questionnaires the person responsible for administering the questionnaire should be available to answer any question that may come up. Also the classroom teacher should be available to resolve any disorder that may be caused during the administration of the questionnaires. Therefore, the students are free of any disruption to focus on the task.

Finally, it is important to note that the actions taken by the school stakeholders and the A&R Team to encourage students to complete the questionnaire will have an important impact in improving the quality of the data which will emerge. In addition, using this approach, a climate of openness and trust may gradually be developed in the school. A commitment to gathering evidence among school stakeholders and especially students may also be developed. Finally, students will be given the opportunity to contribute significantly in the design of the improvement strategies and action plans of their school.

Instruments for measuring SCHOOL level factors

Three different approaches can be used for measuring school level factors. School level factors refer to both the school policy on teaching and the school learning environment. Therefore, first a documentary analysis of the school policy documents can be conducted. Guidelines are seen as one of the main indications of school policy and this is reflected in the way each school level factor is defined (see Creemers & Kyriakides, 2010b). In using the term guidelines we refer to a range of documents, such as staff meeting minutes, announcements, and action plans. These make the policy of the school more concrete to the teachers and other stakeholders. By analysing these documents, scores for each aspect of the main overarching school factors and their dimensions can be generated. For example, the analysis of these documents can help us find out how many actions were taken to minimise student absenteeism or teacher absenteeism (which is an aspect of the policy on quantity of teaching) and at what period(s) these actions took place. In this way, an indicator of the frequency and the stage dimension of this factor may emerge. In addition, documentary analysis can help us find out whether not only actions to minimise student absenteeism are taken and also the schools attempt to find ways to regain the lost teaching time. In this way, an indicator of the quality of this factor may emerge. Finally, documentary analysis may show that school stakeholders are not only encouraged to keep data on student absenteeism but also to analyse them in order to take decisions on how to reduce this phenomenon. Thus, this analysis will help us generate a score on the quality dimension of the school evaluation factor concerned with the policy for teaching.

In conducting the documentary analysis of school policy and interpreting the data, school stakeholders and the A&R Team should be aware that the overarching factors concerned with policy on teaching and policy on the school learning environment do not simply imply that each school should develop formal documents to install the policy. The factors concerned with the school policy on teaching and on the school learning environment mainly refer to the actions taken by the school to help teachers and other stakeholders have a clear understanding of what is expected from them to do. Support offered to teachers and other stakeholders to implement the school policy is also an aspect of these two factors. For this reason, a teacher questionnaire has been developed to measure the school level factors aiming to find out how clear for teachers the school policy is. This instrument was used on a series of studies that tested the validity of the dynamic model at the school level. Its construct validity has been demonstrated (see Creemers & Kyriakides, 2010a, 2010b). The teacher questionnaire is given in Appendix 10.2. Below are some suggestions on how to analyse the data. This will help produce a list with the factors that seem to perform less well than others and identify priority area(s) for their school improvement project.

The A&R Team and the school coordinator are expected to look carefully at the items of this questionnaire and see if all items are relevant to the context of their school. They can also consider the possibility of administering items of the questionnaire to other stakeholders. For example, items dealing with the partnership policy or the policy on homework could be included in the parents' questionnaire. In regard to the analysis of data, it is first of all recommended to conduct a generalisability study to find out which of the items are generalisable. The extent to which the generalisability of data is influenced by the responses of specific stakeholders should also be considered. Then, the internal reliability of each scale should be investigated and items that are found to be problematic should be removed. At the third step of the analysis, factor scores should be calculated. By using the Kendall coefficient of concordance test, the school stakeholders and the A&R Team will be in a position to find out whether school stakeholders agree among themselves about the relative quality of the factors in their school. In this way, mean ranks for each school factor will be calculated, and the list of factors found to perform not as well as other factors can be produced. The A&R Team can produce a report providing descriptive statistical results as well as the results emerged from the Kendall coefficient of concordance test to be used in the meeting that will take place for identifying priorities for school improvement (see Chapter 9 for further explanation).

Another approach that can also be used for identifying the priority area(s) for school improvement is described below. This approach can be seen as complementary to the previous one and is concerned with the actions of teachers on aspects associated with the school factors of the dynamic model. The teacher questionnaire presented in Appendix 10.2 is only concerned with the five dimensions of the school policy about teaching and about the school learning environment. It does not measure the actions that different stakeholders may actually take (irrespective of whether there is school policy about a specific factor). For example, a school may not have a policy on student absenteeism but an individual teacher may decide to take actions in order to replace the lost time (e.g., visiting a child in a hospital to support him/her).

A questionnaire which was developed by following this approach is available on the web (http://www.ucy.ac.cy/goto/esf/en-US/GeneralInformation.aspx).

By using both approaches, the school will collect data not only about the policy at the school level but also about the actions of teachers in regard to their school policy. In order to collect data on policy in action, school stakeholders and the A&R Team may take into account the suggestions provided in Chapter 11 on the type of actions that teachers and other stakeholders could take in order to improve the functioning of school factors. Specifically, school stakeholders and the A&R Team can look at these actions and identify which of them are relevant to the context of their school and produce a list of these actions. Then, school stakeholders could be invited to express their views on whether these actions are actually taken in the school. If further attention should be given to them in order to improve their impact on the functioning of the school factor (with which each activity is associated with) should also be considered. In analysing the data, school stakeholders and the A&R Team may identify those factors for which not only policy is relatively weak (according to the results of the teacher questionnaire), but also relevant actions are not taken by school stakeholders.

The results which will emerge from this approach can also help schools to further develop their school evaluation mechanisms. In Chapter 2, it is argued that effective schools are those which evaluate their policy on teaching and their school learning environment. In the example given above, schools are expected to keep records on use of teaching time (including student and teacher absenteeism). If school stakeholders and the A&R Team find out that school policy on this factor is relatively weak and stakeholders do not take any actions (based on the results emerged from the list of actions that teachers usually take), a school can also look at the data of the school evaluation mechanisms to see how often (and when) the phenomenon (e.g., student absenteeism) is observed. In this way, they will find out how important it is to take actions to improve this factor. The reader is also reminded that in Chapter 2 it was explained that school factors included in the dynamic model have situational effects, implying that their effects depend on the situation of the school, and thereby schools should be aware of their situation (e.g., how often and when student absenteeism happens) before they take actions to improve a factor (e.g., policy on student absenteeism). In the above example, if school records show that student absenteeism rarely happens then dealing with this factor may not be the best decision. This is especially if the school is performing less well in other areas that may be more relevant to the problems they are facing and may also be related with the same factor (e.g., interruption of lessons for announcements).

To conclude, in this section we recommend three approaches to measure school level factors which are complementary to each other. The first approach was concerned with the analysis of policy documents and implies that schools need to make clear what the policy is and this needs to be done in a systematic way. Second, a teacher questionnaire measuring the perceptions of teachers about the functioning of school factors (and their dimensions) was presented. It was argued that this questionnaire is focused on measuring the school policy (as it is perceived by the school stakeholders). This implies that schools should not only make their policy explicit but this policy should be clear to the stakeholders. Support should also be provided to them in order to implement it. These two very important aspects of the school factors are measured by the teacher questionnaire. The third approach is focused on the actions that stakeholders take. In this chapter, it is suggested that both the school policy and the actions of teachers measured in order to find out the actual impact that policy has on the actions that stakeholders finally take. A recent study investigated the impact of school policy in action and demonstrates that schools with high performance on the policy in action factors are among the most effective schools (see Kyriakides & Demetriou, 2010). Finally, it is recommended that schools need to draw information from the school evaluation data that they keep in order to find out how often problems associated with each school factor occur in the schools. In this way, school stakeholders and the A&R Team will identify those factors that need to be addressed since it was supported that the school is facing relevant problems and the school policy in regard to this aspect is weak (either in terms of announcing the policy to the stakeholders or in terms of how stakeholders understand the policy) and thereby appropriate actions are not carried out. These factors can be considered in identifying the priority area(s) for school improvement.

In the next chapter, some practical suggestions on how to develop strategies and action plans associated with each school factor are provided. These are useful for identifying their priority area(s) for school improvement, whereas suggestions provided in Chapter 11 could be found helpful in developing their action plans.

The design of actions and strategies for improvement, their implementation and evaluation

Introduction

In the final chapter of part C, we refer to the actions that school stakeholders and the A&R Team can take, in order to design their improvement strategies and action plans. The implementation process is also outlined and special emphasis is given to the role of formative evaluation. Schools are expected to establish such mechanisms, which through the use of DASI will be flexible enough to adopt their improvement strategies and actions, to meet their intermediate targets and ultimately improve their effectiveness status. The authors would also like to stress that when developing their school policy and action plans, stakeholders should bear in mind how and why each aspect of the overarching school factor addressed (i.e. the policy on teaching, the policy on the learning environment, and school evaluation) is related to the learning and learning outcomes. The policy should also outline the *roles, responsibilities and procedures* for staff and other adults, including parents and community volunteers who will be involved in DASI and the specific school improvement project. When developing school policy and designing action plans and strategies, it is also very useful for school stakeholders and the A&R Team to take into account the following:

a) The term 'school policy' does not refer only to the various formal documents or letters sent to different school stakeholders which explain the policy of the school, but also to the various actions that the school management team (teachers, deputy heads, and administrator) undertake, to improve the quality of teaching and the school learning environment. It is further important for the format of the policy to be clear, especially in the messages that are delivered to the teachers and other stakeholders. This is because they provide specific direction for the role that each individual involved has to undertake, in regard to the implementation of the various aspects of school policy.

b) During the designing of action plans, it is advised that school stakeholders and the A&R Team take into account the abilities and skills of teachers, students and parents in implementing the intervention policy. For example, encouraging teachers to visit each other's classrooms to observe specific teaching skills, may not be an appropriate decision to make if a climate of openness among teachers has not yet been established at the school. On the other hand more approachable actions and strategies, such as staff meeting presentations of the successful approaches teachers may use, could have a positive impact on the effectiveness of the intervention. Equally they should ensure that the stakeholders are willing to be involved in implementing the policy, and that the school is further able to provide them with the support (not only financial) needed to implement the policy.

In this chapter, readers can find suggestions for specific actions and strategies that they could include in their own school policy design, both for teaching and the school learning environment. The strategies and action plans that are provided can be modified according to the reader's specific needs, yet they should remain in line with the skills of the various stakeholders of the school. The authors trust that the recommendations presented will assist readers to make decisions for the effective development of a school improvement project.

Overarching factor 1: School policy for teaching

In this section, suggestions regarding the three aspects of the first overarching factor can be found, which are concerned with school policy on teaching and the actions taken to improve teaching (see Chapter 2). The three aspects of this domain concern:

a)   quantity of teaching
b)   provision of learning opportunities
c)   quality of teaching.

Quantity of teaching

This factor refers to the ability of the school to face problems that may reduce teaching time. Two types of reactions are presented: the first regarding methods of persuading school stakeholders to avoid reducing teaching time (i.e. kind of disciplinary actions) and the second identifying techniques for regaining lost teaching time (or in part), by offering extra time for learning.

1) Absenteeism of Students

Student absenteeism is an aspect of this factor that has direct and negative consequences to the quantity of teaching offered to students. Some actions for reducing this phenomenon and for replacing the lost time are given below.

ACTIONS FOR REDUCING THE PHENOMENON

Firstly, teachers should keep record of student absenteeism on a daily basis and if possible, selected school stakeholders could be responsible for analysing this, by searching for general trends of which students are missing lessons and when this is occurring. Although schools usually keep record of student absenteeism, this is typically only for managerial purposes. Schools may also choose to present the results and send a short report to parents, which may display when the phenomenon is occurring, or on which days the students are usually absent. This report could also be publicised on the notice board. The analysis of data can also help school stakeholders to set targets that will be announced to all stakeholders, in order to reduce the phenomenon. Moreover, if the figures show that a greater number of students were absent on specific day(s), the school management team may investigate the reasoning for this by discussing such findings with the absent students. For example, if mass absenteeism occurs on the same day as an organised school trip, the reasoning for the students' lack of attendance could simply be that they did not want to participate in the event. Similarly, if a relatively high percentage of students are recurrently missing on a Friday, it may be due to particular families purposefully extending their weekends. In such cases, there would be a need to contact these parents to request that teaching time is respected.

Secondly, schools should announce their policy on student absenteeism to parents and students, clarifying that there should be a serious explanation for students that are not attending school (Ma, 1999). In addition, it can be reiterated to students and parents who missed lessons or a school day for an acceptable reason (e.g. illness, participating in competitions, representing the school in events), that they should provide supporting documents detailing the reason for their absence. These documents should be given promptly to the school staff members responsible for dealing with absenteeism and checked if necessary. On the other hand, those students who missed lessons or school days without acceptable reasoning should be addressed individually and measures should be taken to avoid absenteeism in the future.

REGAINING THE LOST TEACHING TIME

In some schools, each student is expected to nominate or have classmates whose responsibility it is to inform her/him of what happened during the day and of any homework that was assigned whilst she/he was absent. In this way, the student will have the opportunity to work on the topic at home and the parents (or other members of the family) may help her/him to catch up with the lost time. In other schools, it may be the teachers that are expected to find extra time to inform and assist students in catching up with the part of the curriculum they have missed. This can be either when the student returns to the school or even during the period that they are missing the lesson for, at a place outside of the school (e.g. visit students at hospital to inform them about the lessons that they missed).

2) Teacher Absenteeism

Teacher absenteeism is another important aspect of this factor that may have negative consequences to the quantity of teaching offered to students. Some actions for reducing this phenomenon and for replacing the lost time are given below.

ACTIONS FOR REDUCING THE PHENOMENON

The school management team usually keeps records for teacher absenteeism and may also analyse the data following a similar approach to the one described in the section concerned with student absenteeism. In some schools, the management team may also present the results of the teachers' attendance focussing on general trends that may exist (e.g. specific days or time periods that more teachers are absent), yet without exposing individuals who are absent for longer periods. The analysis of data should help the team to set targets (together with the teachers) on how to reduce the phenomenon. Secondly, the management team should announce the school policy to teachers, clarifying that serious reasoning is required for absenteeism. Similar to the procedure for students, teachers who missed lessons or other school tasks for an acceptable reason (e.g. illness, asked by the school to participate in an in-service training course provided externally) should provide evidence to whoever is responsible for dealing with absenteeism. This is expected promptly and will be checked if necessary. Teachers missing lessons or school days who fail to provide an acceptable reason should be addressed individually and appropriate measures taken to avoid further absenteeism (e.g. warnings, negative evaluation, no salary raise). In extreme cases, teachers may be suspended or fired for this reason.

REGAINING THE LOST TEACHING TIME

Teachers who know in advance that they will be absent (e.g. have to attend a course offered externally) are required to prepare teaching materials which can be used during their absence by replacement teachers. In cases when absenteeism cannot be predicted (i.e. teacher illness), other available teachers may be asked to cover the lessons affected and the management team should find a way to compensate those that are providing extra lessons. In those cases that there is no teacher available to run the lesson(s), students may be given the opportunity to undertake extra-curricular activities (e.g. going to the library and studying under the supervision of the librarian, playing educational games, developing a project by using the internet). If no action is taken, then students may lose the teaching time and could even cause problems for other classrooms as well, as misbehaviour is likely to occur especially if without supervision.

3) Management of teaching time

School policy on the management of teaching time is also an aspect of the factor concerned with quantity of teaching. In defining this policy, the dynamic model refers to several aspects of the management of teaching time, such as ensuring that:

a)   lessons start on time and finish on time
b)   there are no interruptions of lessons for staff meetings, announcements, or preparation of school events.

Resultantly, school stakeholders ensure that the time allocated for teaching is used to achieve the aims of the official curriculum.

ACTIONS FOR REDUCING THE PHENOMENON

Schools can take several actions to reduce the interruption of lessons and guarantee that they start and finish on time. For example, schools may have an official policy (which will be announced to all school stakeholders) that lessons will not be interrupted by anyone (e.g. other teachers, deputy heads or heads) or for any managerial reason (e.g. for making an announcement or collecting money for school trips/charity reasons etc). The starting and finishing times of the lessons can also be announced to the teachers, students and parents which the school management team should enforce, by ensuring that students and teachers go to class on time after each school break.

Schools can also consider the possibility of keeping record of students who are not on time to attend the lesson. In some schools these results are announced to various stakeholders and are also communicated with parents (for disciplinary reasons). If students arrive late in the morning, teachers can request that their parents bring them to school on time. Certain schools may enforce punishment for those arriving late in the morning, for example by not allowing them to enter the class, yet stakeholders should be aware that this approach can create more problems, as further teaching time is lost. Similarly, teachers who regularly start lessons late or not finish on time should be addressed individually by the head teacher and appropriate measures should be taken to avoid this phenomenon (e.g. warnings, negative evaluation) in the future.

REGAINING THE LOST TEACHING TIME

Students who are late can be asked to spend extra time in school or to do extra homework to compensate for the lost time. Therefore, not only is the lost teaching time regained, but students are also discouraged from arriving late to school. Some schools require late students to stay during their break time to discuss with their teacher how to compensate for the learning tasks they have missed.

4) Policy on Homework

Schools are expected to have a policy on homework and the policy should be announced not only to teachers but also to the parents and students. Policy on homework should cover the following aspects:

a)   amount of homework given to students;
b)   type of homework that should be given (i.e. giving application tasks and tasks that students are able to undertake without additional support by any adult)
c)   the role of parents in supervising homework (i.e. parents are only expected to check that their children spent time doing the homework and not teach them or solve the problems/tasks that their children are supposed to do)
d)   teacher evaluation of homework and feedback given to students on the homework assignments.

Some schools could organise special events which explain to parents how they can supervise and support their children. Schools may also encourage the parents to have regular communication with teachers and provide feedback of how their children behave whilst doing homework and the kind of problems their children face with it. It is finally important to note that teachers should keep record of those children who neglect their homework, as students with no acceptable reason for doing so can be addressed individually and appropriate measures can be taken to reduce this problem (e.g. warnings, communication with parents). Equally, the importance that teachers place on homework should be conveyed to the students and parents alike.

Provision of learning opportunities

School policy on provision of learning opportunities is measured by focusing on the extent to which the school has a mission concerning the provision of learning opportunities which is reflected in its policy on curriculum. School policy on long-term and short-term planning and on providing support to students with special needs is also examined. Furthermore, the extent to which the school attempts to make good use of school trips and other extra-curricular activities for teaching/learning purposes is investigated.

1) Making good use of school trips and other extra-curricular activities for learning purposes

Regarding this aspect of school policy, it is important to note that some schools may adhere to the notion that school trips are only for fun and not for educational purposes, presenting the impression that learning and fun cannot go together. However, school policy on provision of learning opportunities consists of ensuring that numerous learning opportunities are offered to children both inside and outside of the classroom. For this reason, schools should consider school trips a very good opportunity to show children that what is learnt in school has significant relevance to everyday life. For example, a school trip to another city could include a visit to a local museum, which would offer the children additional learning opportunities and could provide an integrated approach to teaching history, geography and art.

School stakeholders can therefore be informed that the various events and extra curricular activities that students are involved with are chosen on the basis that they can offer learning opportunities to students without negatively affecting the time that is offered for teaching a specific subject. This implies that the school management team should select their students' activities through specific criteria, which are used whenever a suggestion for a trip or involvement in a project is made. This further suggests that schools will have to offer different extra curricular activities to different groups of students (e.g. Year 1 students are likely to visit a different place than Year 5 students) by taking into account their learning needs. Evaluation of the impact that these activities have on student learning could also be undertaken.

Finally, school stakeholders may realise that the involvement of students in activities that do not provide any learning opportunities has a negative impact on student learning, because teaching time is simultaneously reduced. It is for this reason that the school management team should place a great deal of emphasis on the selection of activities offering learning opportunities to students that cannot be offered through the formal curriculum.

2) School policy on long-term and short-term planning

Some schools expect teachers to provide their short-term plans to head teachers or other school staff members (e.g. deputy heads, subject co-ordinator). Whilst this can be viewed as a method of ensuring that teachers are accountable for covering the curriculum in the time frame required, there is some scope for improvement. A more efficient technique of short-term planning would be for the head teacher or mentor to provide feedback and support to the teachers. Use of the latter approach will provide teachers with support to organise their time in a more efficient way and ultimately improve the quality of their teaching. Particular schools may also ask groups of teachers to cooperate and prepare their long-term planning together. For example, teachers of a specific subject (in secondary schools) or of a specific age group of students (in primary schools) may be asked to develop their planning for the year at the beginning of the school year, which should be adapted at the end of each term.

Schools may also consider announcement of the long-term planning to students and/or parents. In this way, the parents are aware of what takes place in the school and may also be encouraged to find ways to support the implementation of the planning both inside (e.g. by providing resources to teachers) and outside of the school (e.g. by monitoring the homework or offering relevant opportunities in the trips or other events that they are organising as a family).

In some schools, the long-term planning does not only cover the curricular activities, it also refers to the extra-curricular activities which are expected to contribute to the achievement of specific aims of the curriculum. In this way, the long-term planning takes into account that some teaching time may be spent on extra-curricular activities and is thereby an accurate portrayal of what will eventually happen during the school year.

3) School policy on providing support to students with special needs

In some schools, additional time outside of school hours is allocated to children with special needs, including gifted or talented children, to support their learning in different domains (e.g. Art, Music, Physical Education, Mathematics, Language, Science). Schools may also ensure that teachers are available during the school hours to provide support to children with special needs, in order to facilitate and promote their learning in the regular classrooms. Other schools provide relevant support outside of the classroom, yet within school hours (e.g. during school breaks).

Announcement to students and/or parents of the school policy on providing support to students with special needs is essential. Various methods can be employed to announce such policy (e.g. documents including the official policy can be sent to parents, the policy can be made available on the web page of the school). In this way, parents of children with special needs are informed of the opportunities offered to their children, whilst other parents can encourage the positive attitudes of their own children towards their classmates who have special needs.

Quality of teaching

Policy on quality of teaching mainly refers to the eight teacher factors included in the dynamic model (see Chapter 2). When developing school policy to improve teaching, one should pay close attention to each of these eight factors, because they have been found to be associated with student achievement gains. For example, if a teacher has not developed their time management skills or does not handle misbehaviour and disorder effectively, then she/he will face disciplinary problems in the classroom and teaching time will resultantly be reduced. In contrast, if the teacher creates a businesslike and supportive environment for learning, misbehaviour may become a rare occurrence and teaching aims are more likely to be achieved. Therefore, effective schools are those which develop clear, specific and concrete policy on the quality of teaching, whilst encouraging teachers to create the appropriate positive conditions for learning and instruction in the classroom. Below our suggestions are outlined for developing school policy on the quality of teaching, in regard to the eight teacher factors included in the dynamic model.

The school management team should encourage teachers to undertake activities which promote quality in their teaching and therefore improve their teaching practice. Initially, teachers could be informed during staff meetings of the importance of the eight factors and their five dimensions. Subsequently an exchange of teachers' ideas and views could take place, concerning the creation of a classroom climate which is supportive for learning and stimulates positive child behaviour. It could further be determined that certain staff meetings will not only deal with administrative issues, but will also establish policy on the quality of teaching. In such meetings, issues concerned with the quality of teaching should be discussed, including classroom strategies for improving teaching practice, as well as methods of dealing with misbehaviour problems effectively. Further suggestions are provided below for practices that can be used to create a safe learning environment in the classroom.

Firstly, we recommend that teachers avoid the negative aspects of competition among the students in the classroom, because the losing children may develop a sense of uselessness and a loss of self-esteem, which could extend across a range of valued classroom activities. Such feelings are likely to cause frustration and negative attitudes towards learning.

The head teacher should engage teachers in positive student-student and student-teacher interactions and mobilise them to promote those interactions actively in the classroom. Teachers should assign students cooperative activities where they can work together in small groups to achieve mutual learning goals. Such strategies can contribute to the common good, potentially through the inclusion of migrants, minority students, newcomers and different socio-ethnic groups of children. If teachers need to strengthen the interactions between their students, they should attempt to create cooperative experiences in the classroom. Such experiences can encourage the students' commitment to: contributing to the well being of other students, accepting responsibility to add to their partners' work, displaying respect for the efforts of others, and behaving with integrity, compassion and an appreciation for diversity. Teachers should also manage their classroom by focusing on promoting mutual goals that require self-regulation and productive interactions.

Another aspect that the school management team should seriously consider is the lack of direct teaching skills some teachers possess. Such teachers are considered insufficient when observed to lack skills of the direct teaching approach, such as: classroom management skills, application, management of time, structuring of the lesson, monitoring students behaviour, organisation of activities (e.g. preparation, distribution of materials) and discipline. Therefore, the school management team should identify teaching needs for professional development and support them in order to upgrade their skills.

Some schools may also offer common non-teaching time to a group of teachers (e.g. teachers of the same subject or teachers of the same age group of students) and expect each group of teachers to visit other classrooms and provide feedback to help each other to improve his/ her teaching skills.

It is finally important that school policy for the quality of teaching is announced to the teachers (either described in documents or placed on notice boards). The policy may refer to factors related to generic teaching skills, and support should also be provided to ensure that each teacher can improve their skills. In Chapters 7 and 8, projects were presented that used DASI to provide teacher professional development programmes offered both internally and externally. The A&R Team and school stakeholders can make use of the material and approaches used in order to design their action plans for how to improve the teaching practice.

School policy for creating a School Learning Environment (SLE) and actions taken to improve the SLE

In this section, suggestions are provided on the four aspects of the overarching factor included in the theoretical framework of DASI, namely school policy on the school learning environment and actions taken to improve the SLE:

a)   student behaviour outside the classroom
b)   collaboration and interaction between teachers
c)   partnership policy
d)   provision of learning resources.

Student behaviour outside of the classroom

With the development of a clear policy on student behaviour outside of the classroom, valuable information about student-student interactions that may promote or hinder learning can be collected and used for the development of action plans. For example, bullying incidents are likely to occur when children are outside of the classroom and if there is no school policy on this factor and no monitoring system in place, then the occurrence of bullying incidents may increase which will have a negative impact on student learning (see Kyriakides, Creemers, & Charalambous, 2008). On the other hand, student-student interaction during break times may promote learning. For example, students may use this time for working on a project or for exchanging experiences and ideas in order to solve a problem that was assigned to them.

Regarding student behaviour outside of the classroom, all school personnel (not only teachers, but also bus drivers, coaches, and after-school programme supervisors) have to be informed about the school policy and should be trained to implement those aspects that are relevant to their roles. For example, bus drivers should be aware of how to deal with misbehaviour and how to motivate and reinforce positive interactions among students. For incidences of mis-behaviour, they should also be informed of the appropriate staff members' contact details, or even those of the parents of misbehaving students. Similarly, after-school programme supervisors may encourage students to make good use of the time that they stay at school, such as spending it on homework. In addition, some students may provide support to others who are facing difficulties with their homework, although supervisors will monitor this support to avoid homework being completed for others or copying to take place without any understanding involved.

For this reason, provided below are some specific suggestions on the content of the policy, which take into account that different activities can be undertaken in the different time periods that students are outside of the classroom (i.e. student behaviour in break time, student behaviour before the lesson starts, student behaviour after school hours/after lessons finish). Also, specific suggestions are provided for the behaviour code that the school should develop, in order to avoid negative and encourage positive interactions among students.

Schools should develop a policy concerning the *effective supervision* of their students during the break sessions. *Increased monitoring* of student behaviour during break times and also before the start of the lessons can help to identify and intervene when bullying occurs. A carefully organised supervision plan can help to reduce the bulling phenomenon, especially when focused in the areas of the school where the majority of bullying incidents have been observed.

Although a list of the teachers responsible for supervision is usually determined in most schools, the role of each person involved and the areas each teacher is expected to supervise must also be stated. In regard to the role of teachers, the school management team may recommend that whilst supervising, the teachers should try to encourage students to interact with each other. They can also conduct informal interviews with students in which questions are open-ended and asked in a neutral way. This should create conditions under which students feel free to openly express their feelings about schooling. In this way, interactions between teachers and students are encouraged and teachers may use the opportunity to provide direct support to learning difficulties that students may face.

Teachers should also be visible and vigilant in such common areas as hallways, stairwells, the canteen, gym and other hot spots where student misbehaviour may occur. Additional supervision may also be required in school bathrooms, as vandalism, disorder and mess are likely to occur. This can be dealt with by addressing students with specific directions (e.g. throw away any rubbish properly and keep the place tidy). Such tasks can aid students in developing positive attitudes towards the school and encourage desirable behaviour that can be characterised as respectful, reliable and responsible.

Teachers should also be encouraged to look out for any *isolated students* at break times. For example, an isolated student sitting in front of the teachers' office at break time may be attempting to convey a message, which can be interpreted by the supervising teacher if they not only see, but observe and interpret the situation. A possible explanation could be that other students are bullying her/him and in order to obtain some kind of protection, she/he chooses a very visible place considered to be safe and secure, due to the increased teacher supervision there.

The next step for the teacher should be to discuss with the isolated child and provide support, yet any conclusions drawn should not be arbitrary, rather they should relate to the discussion and reception of appropriate information. For example, the child in the previous case may merely be sitting outside the office, because she/he resting from a game or prefers to enjoy their meal in silence.

During break time, *playground activities such as playing in cooperative groups* can be organised. These activities may promote learning, for example *table games* can be organised to keep students occupied and entertained during the break time. These games may also demonstrate how the lessons taught at school can be applied to real life situations. Specific directions usually have to be given to students (e.g. include others in the game, follow the rules and return equipment when done). Another example would be the organisation of a *science fair*, which provides an opportunity for students to see and take part in experiments, being educated of science whilst doing so.

Rewarding good behaviour not only in the classroom but also outside of it (during break time, and also before and after the lessons start) can be very beneficial. Schools can develop a *motivation system* for the improvement of the social environment of the school, by taking actions to emphasise the maintenance of the behaviour code and the promotion of appropriate and positive behaviours outside the classroom.

Behaviour code determined by the school (with cooperation of students, teachers and parents) concerning student behaviour outside the classroom

Rules should be brief and clear, stating the immediate consequences for aggressive behaviour and the immediate rewards for inclusive behaviour. The behaviour code should reinforce the values of *empathy, care, respect, fairness, and personal responsibility*, and must *clearly define unacceptable behaviour, expected behaviour and values, and consequences for violations*. In addition, the code should:

a)   apply to adults and students
b)   use age-appropriate language
c)   be prominently placed throughout the school.

In order to ensure that positive behaviour will be sustainable, *weekly meetings* to communicate with students may be arranged. Through these meetings, teachers can motivate their students to follow the rules of the behaviour code.

Another aspect of the behaviour code to be determined is the nature of *students' arrival and exit from the school* (e.g. using self control, walking and not running when entering and leaving the school, reporting any problems to the teacher). Special attention must be given to the behaviour of students that travel to and from school by bus. Specific expectations concerning the students' behaviour code in the bus must be announced to all students:

a)   be ready when the bus arrives
b)   be polite to the bus driver and other students
c)   follow the driver's rules and instructions
d)   remain seated
e)   speak in a quiet voice
f)   carry all personal belongings onto the bus
g)   be prepared to share seating in the bus.

Last but not least, the desired behaviour during *school assemblies* has to be defined. This firstly comprises that students follow their line into assembly, with the younger students taking their places first. The time of the school assembly should also be foresighted and arranged to take place in morning hours when the students are not likely to be tired or upset. Also, the school has to limit the time of assemblies and make their content as brief as possible. If the assembly is expected to take more than 15 minutes, then arrangements should be made for students to be seated: otherwise students are likely to misbehave. Beyond each class's teacher, a general supervisor (not class teacher) must be appointed for each assembly. The following expectations for school assemblies should be announced to students:

a)   follow directions
b)   control temper
c)   have self control
d)   walk quietly in line after the end of the assembly.

If misbehaviour occurs, the following consequences could be announced to the students:

a)   apologise
b)   discuss the incident with the teacher, head teacher, and/or parents
c)   spend time in the office or in another classroom
d)   forfeit break times or other privileges.

Collaboration and interaction between teachers

Collaboration and interaction between the teachers is particularly important because it can contribute to improving teachers' teaching skills and their every day practice. It therefore has a positive effect on learning outcomes (cognitive and affective). In effective schools, teachers interact on issues associated with learning and teaching, in order to create a business-like environment which can promote students' learning and knowledge. This can subsequently lead to the achievement of cognitive and affective outcomes in education (Creemers & Kyriakides, 2008a).

Some schools are characterised by teacher collaboration only on the level of personal and social interaction, without also involving cooperation on the tasks that are expected to be undertaken. For those schools, it is considered important that teachers have good relations but they do not necessarily expect to interact on issues associated with their teaching practice. Nevertheless, interaction and collaboration among teachers can only be beneficial if focused on the tasks teachers undertake, which could boost quality in the school learning environment. This active interaction on issues associated with teaching is also needed for teacher professional development purposes.

In order to encourage teacher collaboration, in the development of the timetable, attention is given to provide to groups of teachers common non-contact time that provides opportunities for such interactions. The collaboration may refer to short or long term planning, the use of specific teaching aids/handouts/materials for delivering an aspect of the curriculum or the design of a common assessment instrument.

Teachers may also be encouraged to exchange visits to each others' classrooms. During such visits, the observation of teaching by specific observation instruments, in line with the policy on quality of teaching, could be promoted (see Chapter 10). The results from observing their colleagues can be discussed and help teachers learn from each other.

In addition, some activities such as supervising students during break time can be appointed to not just one teacher but to *pairs of teachers*. By working collaboratively, teachers can discuss what they observe, exchange opinions and workout solutions, presenting to the whole faculty the efforts that they found as more effective. In this way, teachers have access to appropriate *professional development* opportunities that develop and refresh their skills, enabling them to promote learning both inside and outside the classroom.

A very useful strategy in this domain is the development of a *system of mentors* (more experienced teachers). More experienced teachers and/or the head teachers can provide support to younger teachers on how to improve their teaching skills. For example, teachers with less than five years of experience are found to be over-represented in stage 1 concerned with the use of teaching routines (see Chapter 7). More experienced teachers can help them to manage more effectively their teaching time and provide appropriate structuring and application tasks.

Partnership policy (i.e. the relations of schools with community, parents, and advisors)

Involvement of the wider community in school improvement projects is promoted by DASI (see Chapter 3) and can be achieved by establishing a committee that involves the school head teacher, representatives from parent councils, teachers, other school staff, and students. By including staff, students, and parents in the creation and implementation of the improvement project, the school management team receive valuable input from all those that are able to influence learning. Research evidence shows that this factor is one of the most important factors strongly associated with the effectiveness status of the school (Fan & Chen,

2001; Kyriakides, Creemers, Antoniou, & Demetriou, 2010; Waterman & Walker, 2009). By establishing good relations with the parents and the school community and encouraging them to be actively involved in the implementation of school policy, we make use of all available human and other learning resources to not only achieve learning aims (cognitive and affective) but also to deal with various challenges that the school will have to face such as the bullying incidents (see Kyriakides, 2005b).

At the beginning of the school year, it is important for the school to *announce* to parents the school policy on teaching and on the SLE, to analyse it and to ask them to provide feedback and suggestions. At the initial stages of these efforts, the school has to raise parents' awareness and provide all the information for the action plan. The school community has to *convince* parents that the programme is going to work and that they are able to make a difference. During the implementation of the improvement project, *specific positive feedback* to parents about raising standards helps the school continue its efforts to implement the policy on teaching. Parents also need to be given accurate information on how they can help their children achieve their learning aims (e.g. on how to monitor homework), along with encouragement to contact the school if they are not sure how to support their children.

Usually schools offer some lectures/sessions to parents. In some schools the topics that are covered are not related to the role that parents play in supporting the learning of their children. The school management team must be careful to select appropriate topics and invite lecturers who are aware as to how to give practical suggestions and present their messages in a clear way, appreciating that some parents may have a low educational background.

The school should help parents find roles within the framework of the school's intervention and give credit where due. Parents can also be invited to suggest improvements to the intervention ('What would you like us to do next time?') rather than potential defensive reaction to criticism of the strategies that have already been designed.

The school can develop its policy in order to explain to parents *when they can meet* the teachers and be informed about the progress and the behaviour of their children. Where there are regular issues between parents and the school, meeting with parents regularly (not just when there is a crisis) can strengthen working relationships. The school has to assure parents that they can share all of their concerns with their child's teachers. If they do not want to involve the teacher for any reason, they can ask for the *school counsellor* to become involved *or the coordinator.*

Because there is always difficulty in accommodating parents' schedules, a *procedure with details for contacting the appropriate staff members must be developed.* This procedure should refer to convenient ways of contacting the teachers, the school management team or the school coordinator, in order to be informed of the progress that their children make. For example, parents who have set working hours and cannot leave their job and be present at school before the time teachers leave, should be notified that they can contact the school by phone or by email.

The school may also invite parents (and especially those whose child is not making enough progress) to *visit the classrooms of their children* or the school more often and observe teaching in order to find out how to support their children. Meetings at the classroom level help build connections among parents and teachers. In this way, the parents can learn how to support the efforts of the school and what is expected from them so that they may effectively help their child. The teachers may also invite parents to take an *active role*. For example, some schools may invite parents and/or other members of the school community to help teachers organise the teaching of a specific unit for which they have special expertise. For example, a coach of the volleyball team in the school community may be invited to help the PE teacher to teach volleyball to his/her students.

Some schools may invite advisors to provide guidelines for helping them to deal with specific problems (e.g. bullying) or to help them design/implement a research action plan. Advisors may also be asked to offer school based INSET courses on issues associated with the tasks that teachers are undertaking in the school (see Chapter 8).

Finally, financial support may also be provided to schools. This support can be used for buying teaching materials and other learning resources. This topic is also related with the last aspect of the SLE, concerned with the use of resources and for which some further suggestions are provided.

Provision of sufficient learning resources to students and teachers

The availability and especially the good use of learning resources in schools have an effect on student learning (cognitive and affective outcomes) (Hanushek, 1989). For example, a computer with access to the Internet as an educational tool in teaching a specific unit may be useful for all students in achieving particular aims. However, if there is only one such computer and there are twenty or more students, fighting may occur. This implies that teachers should organise their classroom learning environment and offer tasks that can be achieved by students using the available resources without any practical difficulties. The above example shows that the provision of learning resources and the good use of resources by the teachers prevent misbehaviour in the classroom and on similar occasions in school when whole school projects or extra-curricular activities are undertaken. Below, some general recommendations on the establishment of a policy on the proper use of learning resources are provided.

In order to improve students' learning, schools must develop a policy for the use of visual material and technological equipment in teaching. Teachers should also be strongly encouraged by the school management team to use the available recourses in an appropriate way, by taking into account how these resources help students successfully undertake tasks and achieve specific learning aims. A plan must be designed for the fair allocation of the resources between the teachers (and in some cases among students of different age groups). To avoid complaints, it is very important for the teachers to remember that the distribution of resources to students should be just. The use of the school library should also be promoted. Records on the use of library and other resources can be kept by the school management team. Analysing the data on the use of resources can also help teachers to set targets for how to maximise the appropriate use of resources for promoting learning.

Schools should also develop a policy on how to identify appropriate teaching aids such as computer software that can be bought by the school to help improve the teaching of specific subjects. Parents and the whole school community can also contribute to the enrichment of teaching aids.

A point to remember in the development of policy on the provision of learning resources is that educational resources include the use of human resources. Some schools may decide to appoint extra personnel for supporting their needs and helping them (e.g. appoint an expert to help teachers dealing with children who have learning difficulties) or encourage parents to visit schools and work with the teacher (see the section on partnership policy).

School evaluation

School evaluation is seen as one of the most important factor for improving the effectiveness of schools (Kyriakides et al., 2010; Scheerens, Seidel, Witziers, Hendriks, & Doornekamp, 2005). More specifically, effective schools have to develop continuous evaluation mechanisms that measure the effects of their strategies and actions on student learning and use these results (for formative rather than summative reasons) to further improve their actions and strategies on teaching and the school learning environment. In fact, the development of formative evaluation mechanisms at the school level will also help school stakeholders identify priorities for improvement (see Chapter 3).

Effective schools are also expected to review the impact of their strategies and actions and identify any errors that occur (see step E of DASI). In this way, they can define new actions and strategies, as well as modify and redesign their action plans for improvement. The main aim of the school evaluation process is to identify general trends associated with the strengths and weaknesses of the school policy for the learning environment and teaching. In order to collect valid and reliable data on the impact of school policy on improving teaching and the SLE, more than one source of evaluation data is needed. This is because one cannot simply 'trust' a single source of data, or rely only on the stakeholders' opinions. The use of systematic observations should also be considered, since using different sources of data enables one to test the internal validity of the school evaluation data (see Chapter 10).

School stakeholders should also decide how many times during the school year they need to collect evaluation data concerning their policy for teaching, the SLE and the actions taken for improving teaching and the SLE. The need to establish continuous formative evaluation mechanisms should be taken into account. These mechanisms are expected to help the school modify its strategies and actions according to the circumstances and specific needs of different groups of the school population.

In addition, the quality of the instruments used to collect data should be evaluated (questionnaires, observation instruments). Special attention should be given to investigating the validity (the extent to which a measurement instrument or test accurately measures what it is supposed to measure) of these instruments. Obviously, schools are not expected to use advanced statistical techniques to test the construct validity of their instruments, but the use of triangulation (i.e. searching for the extent to which different instruments provide similar data) is recommended.

In addition, the purposes for which the evaluation data are collected should be explained to all stakeholders. The stakeholders should also be aware that the school evaluation is done for formative and not summative reasons. This implies that evaluation is a natural part of the improvement efforts that the school tries to develop (see Chapter 3). The school management team should guarantee that the school will make use of the information gathered from evaluation, in order to meet their students' and teachers' needs and thereby give more emphasis to the formative purpose of evaluation.

Moreover, all participants involved (schools, parents, children) should be informed that confidentiality will be maintained throughout the procedure. To achieve this, the teachers responsible for the school evaluation must use specific software with restricted access, so as to prevent unwanted entry to the data files. Code numbers will also be assigned to students, teachers and schools to ensure confidentiality. Repeated efforts should be made to convince all stakeholders of the confidentiality of the evaluation process and the anonymity of the answers. At the same time, the school management team should make explicit to all stakeholders that in addition to openly criticising the current policy, they should also give suggestions on how school policy can be redefined. In this way, a climate of openness is gradually developed in the school, while each stakeholder is encouraged to be actively involved in the design of strategies and action plans for school improvement.

Main conclusions emerging from the third part of the book

Since the results of the projects presented in the second part of the book (Chapters 4-8) reveal that schools in different educational settings can make use of DASI to improve their effectiveness status, more practical suggestions on the design of such improvement strategies and actions are offered to school stakeholders and the A&R Team in the third part of the book (see Chapters 9-11). In Chapter 9, we describe the steps that schools have to follow in order to use DASI as well as design strategies and action plans for improvement. The importance of conducting

SSE to identify the priorities for school improvement is illustrated. It is also argued that SSE should be concerned with the functioning of school factors, as these factors were found to be associated with student learning. This argument is further supported by the results of the experimental study presented in Chapter 4. In the next two chapters, we analyse two very crucial elements of DASI in greater detail. In Chapter 10, we provide suggestions on how school and classroom factors can be measured and present relevant instruments. The importance of using different sources of data (i.e. observations and student questionnaires) to measure quality of teaching is explained. We also provide suggestions for training the observers to measure teaching skills in relation to the eight teacher factors and their dimensions. In addition, we refer to three different approaches that need to be used in order to measure the school policy for teaching. The SLE and the impact it has on actions taken by school stakeholders to improve teaching is also discussed. Suggestions on analysing data that emerged from these instruments are provided and the role of A&R Team in sharing the results of the analysis with school stakeholders is emphasised.

In Chapter 11, we refer to the design of improvement strategies and action plans, and provide suggestions for tasks that could be undertaken by schools, in order to improve the functioning of each factor included in the theoretical framework of DASI. In this way, this part of the book offers a basis for establishing networks in different countries of academics, researchers, policy makers and professionals in schools interested in implementing DASI for school improvement purposes. Practical tools for conducting SSE, identification of priorities for improvement and guidance for the design of strategies and action plans are also provided. In the final chapter of the book, we draw conclusions about the strengths and weaknesses of DASI and the extent to which this approach can be used by school stakeholders and the A&R Team in order to improve the quality of education.

Further developments of the dynamic approach to school improvement

Part D

Further developments of the dynamic approach to school improvement

Chapter 12

Reflections on the viability of the approach

Introduction

In the preface of this book, we promised to look at the extent to which the dynamic model can be used for establishing an evidence-based and theory-driven approach to school improvement. This was one of the main aims for which a dynamic model was developed and presented in our first book (see Creemers & Kyriakides, 2008a). During the last seven years, studies testing the validity of the model were conducted (e.g., Creemers & Kyriakides, 2010a, 2010b; Heck & Moriyama, 2010; Kyriakides & Creemers, 2008, 2009; van der Werf, Opdenakker, & Kuyper, 2008). These studies provide empirical support to the main assumptions and the factors included in the dynamic model (see Chapter 2). We also tried to promote further research on using the model for improvement purposes (Antoniou, 2009; Demetriou, 2009). In addition, in a book concerned with the methodological advances in educational effectiveness research, we provide suggestions for conducting studies which aim to further establish the knowledge base of educational effectiveness research and investigate its use for improvement purposes (see Creemers, Kyriakides, & Sammons, 2010). In this book, we have developed a dynamic and integrated approach to school improvement and illustrate how it can be used for designing strategies and action plans to improve the quality of education at the classroom and school level. Projects investigating the impact of using the DASI for improvement purposes were also conducted (Antoniou & Kyriakides, in press; Kyriakides, Charalambous, Kaloyirou, & Creemers, 2011). These studies are presented in the second part of this book and revealed that it is possible to use the dynamic model for improvement purposes in different educational settings. School stakeholders in different educational settings made use of this approach and designed teacher and school improvement projects. These projects were found to have significant impact on student learning and learning outcomes. In Part C, we show how school stakeholders and the Advisory and Research Team (A&R Team) can work together in order to use DASI and improve educational practice.

In this final chapter of this book, we identify the essential characteristics of DASI and examine the extent to which this approach is different from other approaches to school improvement which were presented in the first part of the book. We also refer to the conditions under which DASI can be applied in schools and contribute to the improvement of the quality of education. Implications for policy, practice and research on school improvement are also discussed. Although the DASI mainly refers to designing school improvement projects, it was also found to be relevant for designing teacher improvement projects. Thus, in this chapter, we examine the extent to which this approach can be used for designing system level interventions. Finally, we provide suggestions for further research that could help us examine the conditions under which DASI can be used for improving quality in education in a more systematic way.

The value assumptions of DASI

In the first part of the book, the background of the proposed improvement approach and the major steps of the DASI are provided. In the second part, the main results of projects investigating the impact of using the DASI on improving learning and learning outcomes are presented. These two parts of the book help us to see that the DASI is based on specific assumptions that need to be shared by school stakeholders and the A&R Team.

The first assumption is that the DASI supports that student learning is the main function of schools and thereby the ultimate aim of any improvement project. Although many researchers, policy makers, and practitioners may agree that schools should provide learning opportunities to students, they may not accept the implications that this statement has on the improvement process. Promotion of student learning should not only be the ultimate aim of any improvement project, it should also be treated as the main criterion for evaluating any school improvement project. It is for this reason that the DASI does not only refer to the importance of conducting formative evaluation of school improvement projects. The DASI also refers to the summative evaluation of the improvement project (see step F) by investigating its impact on student achievement gains in different learning outcomes. This value assumption also has implications for applying DASI in schools. Since promotion of student learning is seen as the ultimate aim of any improvement project, the approach refers to the importance of addressing factors associated with learning (see step B). Thus, the proposed approach is more focused in terms of the areas that improvement projects are expected to address. In other school improvement approaches, school stakeholders may be encouraged to design their own intervention programs which could address any area they may like to deal with, assuming that these could be beneficial for education. And sometimes these other intervention approaches may not have the appropriate impact on student learning outcomes (Sammons, 2008).

In the first part of the book, the theoretical framework of DASI is also presented and it is argued that specific factors found to be associated with student learning outcomes need to be addressed. In this way, a more focused approach to school improvement is promoted since school stakeholders and the A&R Team are expected to design strategies and action plans addressing some factor(s) included in the dynamic model in order to promote student learning and learning outcomes. Thus, the second value assumption upon which DASI is based has to do with the importance of using an evidence-based and theory-driven approach. This implies that improvement projects are concerned with factors that are related to student learning and learning outcomes. This is another assumption that is not necessarily shared by other school improvement approaches, especially those that are based on the assumption that school stakeholders should be given the opportunity to define their priorities for improvement by themselves, without considering the knowledge base that is available (see Chapter 1).

Third, this book shows that SSE has an important role to play in helping schools define their improvement areas. This is attributed to the fact that DASI is based on the assumption that stakeholders and the A&R Team should demonstrate in practice their commitment to gathering evidence. Although many educators, school stakeholders and researchers agree with the importance of gathering evidence, it is not always easy for them to accept the results of an evaluation especially when these are not in line with their own expectations. However, DASI is based on the assumption that school stakeholders and the A&R Team should respect the results of their SSE and take them into account in identifying their priority area(s) for improvement (see steps C and D). In addition, the DASI promotes the idea that school stakeholders should not only design action plans for improvement but also formative evaluation mechanisms in order to monitor the implementation of the school improvement project and find out whether there is a need to redefine their action plans during the process of the project. This implies that school stakeholders and the A&R Team do not expect to develop perfect action plans and have the willingness to evaluate their own action plans and to redefine them, if needed. Again this step implies that they take the evaluation data seriously into account and learn by their mistakes in order to further develop their strategies and action plans. In this way, not only a climate of openness and trust is promoted, but also a data-driven approach to school improvement is followed.

Finally, DASI is based on the assumption that effective school improvement projects can be established through a close collaboration between the A&R Team and school stakeholders. In this book, we describe the different roles that each partner is expected to have and it is stressed that in all steps both of them need to be involved. This implies that school improvement projects can only be implemented when not only the experiences of school stakeholders are taken into account but also when the expertise of the A&R Team is available to support school stakeholders in making project implementation decisions.

The main value assumptions of DASI can only be implemented when specific conditions exist. These conditions are discussed below and it is shown that the DASI can be applied in different educational settings and not only to projects aiming to develop the DASI further and test its impact for academic factors. This approach could be used not only by individual schools aiming to improve their effectiveness but also in national projects aiming to improve education at system level.

Conditions for effective use of DASI

In this section, it is a given that the DASI cannot be applied in any school unless school stakeholders consider themselves as agents of change in their school setting and share the assumptions of the DASI. Thus, the main conditions for effective use of the DASI are discussed. First of all, it is stressed that the DASI can be applied in schools where stakeholders do not believe that their school is among the most effective schools. Although you can very rarely identify a school manager or a school stakeholder to admit that she/he believes that her/his school is among the most effective, there are many cases where school managers and other stakeholders have difficulties to admit that there is a need to improve any of the factors operating at the school level. Second, the DASI can only be used by school stakeholders who consider themselves as responsible for improving the effectiveness status of their schools. In centralised educational systems, it is likely to find school managers and teachers who believe that it is not their responsibility to change their school and expect policy makers to introduce changes at the macro level and change the quality of education in their schools (Kyriakides & Campbell, 2004). In schools where teachers and school managers do not see themselves as responsible for improving the quality of education, neither the DASI nor any other school improvement approach can be used.

In identifying some other conditions of effective use of the DASI, we also take into account its assumptions (presented in the previous section) and the main results of the projects which were concerned with the impact of using the DASI for school improvement purposes (presented in the second part of the book). These projects helped us to see that the DASI can be applied only when school stakeholders share its assumptions, especially the claim that promotion of student learning should be the ultimate aim of any improvement project. In the previous section, it is argued that this assumption has important implications for selecting the priority area(s) of school improvement and designing strategies and action plans to improve school effectiveness. This section also refers to implications of the assumptions of the DASI in conducting summative evaluation of the school improvement project.

However, it has to be acknowledged that not all school stakeholders must share the main assumptions of DASI. Based on the findings of the projects presented in Part B, it can be argued that in order to apply this approach, you need to establish a critical mass of school stakeholders who share the value assumptions of DASI (Creemers & Kyriakides, 2010c). The first two steps of DASI are actually concerned with making the assumptions of the DASI and the theoretical framework of the DASI clear and establishing this critical mass of school stakeholders who are keen to be involved in their improvement projects (see Chapters 4 and 5). The projects presented in the second part of the book also reveal that although students, parents and teachers have to be actively involved in school improvement projects, the role of teachers is very critical (Antoniou & Kyriakides, in press). This was made clear to schools participating in the project on reducing bullying (see Chapter 5). These projects also show that the school management team should not only be aware of the DASI and share its assumptions, but should also be ready to share responsibilities with other teachers and school stakeholders in designing their school improvement projects. This is another critical condition that needs to exist in schools which use DASI for improvement purposes and for this reason school managers should be encouraged to share their power with others and to help their schools become more effective (Firestone & Fisler, 2002).

In the projects reported in Part B, we demonstrate the importance of having school stakeholders that share the assumptions of the DASI. However, another important factor that needs to be considered is the role of the A&R Team and the extent to which they share the assumptions of the DASI. The members of the A&R Team in the projects presented in Part B share the assumptions of the DASI and this might be one of the reasons that these projects were successful. However, it is not clear what the impact of these projects could have been in cases that members of the A&R Team did not share the value assumptions of the DASI. Nor is it clear what the impact of these projects would have been if the members of the A&R Team considered themselves as responsible for introducing DASI and evaluating its impact but not as responsible for participating in the development of action plans and in the monitoring of the implementation of school improvement (steps D and E). However, the national variation in the impact of DASI on reducing bullying reported in Chapter 5 could partly be attributed in variations in the involvement of A&R Team in the projects run in different countries. This implies that school stakeholders should select the A&R Team with which they will work with carefully.

Members of the A&R Team should share the value assumptions of DASI and believe that they have a significant role to play at each step of DASI. This implies that they do not follow either a strict experimental design approach in introducing an intervention to improve their effectiveness (e.g., Rowan, Correnti, Miller, & Camburn, 2009; Shadish, Cook, & Campbell, 2002; Slavin, Lake, & Groff, 2009) or the action research project paradigm (McTaggert, 1997; MacBeath, 1999) in the improvement projects that they are involved with. Those that follow the strict experimental design approach see themselves as the owners of the school improvement projects and as the experts which ask from school stakeholders to follow their interventions. The members of this research team are also responsible for conducting summative evaluation and reporting the results of the interventions to the research community. This approach has been used in the past and was not found to be successful for several reasons including the fact that the intervention does not take into account the special needs of each school (see Chapter 1). On the other hand, those using the action research approach usually see themselves as responsible for establishing the appropriate climate for introducing change rather than supporting the school with their expertise in defining their priorities and designing their action plans and very rarely conduct any summative evaluation to measure the impact of the improvement project on student achievement gains (Demetriou, 2009; Hopkins, 2001; MacBeath, 2006). As a consequence, school stakeholders should search for an A&R Team which has expertise in designing SSE mechanisms and organising both the formative and summative evaluations of school improvements. The A&R Team should also be able to offer advice to schools on how to use the available knowledge-base for establishing strategies and action plans for improvement. Thus, members of the A&R Team should have expertise in using different research methods to collect data on teacher and school factors (see Creemers, Kyriakides & Sammons, 2010) as well as expert knowledge of the main findings of educational effectiveness research which supports the theoretical framework of DASI (see Chapters 2 and 11). At the same time, in Chapter 3, it was made explicit that school stakeholders should be those who make the final decisions about the content of the school improvement project. This implies that members of A&R Team should be aware of the limits of their role and of the fact that the school stakeholders are ultimately in charge of the school improvement project. In cases where the A&R Team and stakeholders have conflicting views, the A&R Team are expected to explain their views, but not to insist that schools should follow their advice (Kyriakides & Campbell, 2004).

In this book, it is also demonstrated that the DASI can be used for teacher improvement purposes (see Chapters 6 and 7). Although the DASI is concerned with projects for school improvement, the main steps of this approach can be used for designing an evidence-based and theory-driven approach to teacher's development. The dynamic integrated approach to teacher development was found to be more effective than using the traditional approaches to teacher development (see Chapters 7 and 8). It is also important to acknowledge here that when the DASI is used for teacher improvement projects, only the teachers participating in the courses and those offering the courses should share the assumptions of the DASI. Thus, the DASI can be applied in a much easier way for teacher, rather than school, improvement purposes. However, one limitation of using the DASI for teacher improvement projects is that this intervention is likely to influence only the teachers participating in the intervention (directly) and their students (indirectly) but not the school learning environment, especially when the course is offered externally.

Finally, the DASI could be criticised on the basis that it is usually concerned with improvement projects undertaken by specific schools only and may thereby have a limited effect on improving quality in education (Datnow, Hubbard, & Mehan, 2002). Although it is acknowledged that the DASI can be implemented only in schools where a critical mass of stakeholders (and especially the school management team) share its assumptions and are committed to take responsibilities for school improvement, in the second part of the book, it was shown that the dynamic approach had an impact on promoting learning in a relatively large groups of schools (e.g., the networks established for the project on bullying in Chapter 5). This implies that the DASI can be applied in practice and for this reason in the third part of the book we provide suggestions to school stakeholders and the A&R Team on how to put this approach into practice.

One of the aims of this book is actually to promote the use of the DASI by encouraging readers (school stakeholders, researchers and policy makers) who may share its assumptions to use the DASI for designing school improvement projects. Obviously, further research is also needed to find out how we can convince school stakeholders who do not share the assumptions of the DASI to adopt them and to encourage them to be involved in school improvement projects which make use of DASI. One approach could be through illustrating to them that the approach can be used effectively in other schools and help them identify the impact this approach has had on promoting learning and learning outcomes. Obviously, further research is needed in order to identify how to establish conditions that enable schools to make use of the DASI for improvement purposes. In the next section we move a step forward and provide suggestions on how to expand the DASI and propose its use for improving the quality of education at different levels, especially at the system level.

To what extent DASI can be used for system improvement purposes?

This book refers to an approach, the DASI, that is expected to be used by school stakeholders to improve the quality of education at the classroom and school level. Past projects conducted on the use of the DASI for improvement purposes were concerned with applying the DASI in school improvement and teacher improvement projects (see Part B of this book). However, the theoretical framework of this approach explores factors of the DASI which operate at different levels: student, classroom, school and system (see Chapter 2). A question that seems to arise, regarding research on the DASI, has to do with the extent to which this approach can be used for system improvement purposes. Adopting DASI for system improvement purposes implies that policy makers and other stakeholders should first of all accept the main value assumption of DASI that promotion of student learning should be the ultimate aim of any improvement project (see step A of DASI). It also implies that system improvement projects should address the functioning of system level factors which are expected to be related with student achievement (see step B). However, there is not much evidence supporting the importance of system level factors included in the dynamic model (Creemers & Kyriakides, 2010d). This is partly due to the fact that effectiveness studies have not been conducted in a varied amount of countries (Reynolds, 2006) and it is therefore not possible to find which system level factors can explain variation in student achievement gains worldwide. Comparative studies in educational effectiveness from varied countries in order to develop the model at the system level are greatly needed (Reynolds, 2006). What also needs to be established is an evidence-based and theory-driven approach to improve the quality of education at system level (Kyriakides, 2006).

Nevertheless, several national reform policies have been introduced in different countries and it is, therefore, important to draw implications of using the strategies promoted in DASI for the development of national reform policies. More specifically, the third step of DASI reveals the important role of evaluation in introducing national reform policies. It implies that the introduction of specific reform policies should be based on the results of systematic evaluations investigating the quality of the national policy and of the actions taken by the system in order to improve teaching and the school learning environment (see Chapter 2). However, research on the impact of various national reform policies reveals that this approach is rarely used and for this reason, schools are not receiving enough support to improve their teaching and their school learning environment (e.g., Bickman, 1985; Kyriakides, Charalambous, Philippou, & Campbell, 2006; Sammons, Mujtaba, Earl, & Gu, 2007). This phenomenon can be observed both in more and less centralised educational systems (Hofman, Hofman, & Gray, 2008, 2010; Maslowski, Scheerens, & Luyten, 2007).

Another element of the DASI that needs to be considered by the policy makers has to do with the establishment of formative evaluation mechanisms of reform policies which will help policy makers to further develop their reform policies and find out how to respond to the needs of different school stakeholders in their attempt to implement the reform. However, policy makers introducing several reforms are usually under the pressure to ensure that the policy is applied in a large number of schools and to demonstrate the positive impact of the reform policy on improving education. As a consequence, they are looking for the immediate impact of the reform policies and ignore the importance of collecting data for redefining the reform policy and adapting it to the needs of different schools (Stringfield, 2000).

Although further research is needed to find out how the DASI can be used for system improvement purposes, policy makers can still design reform policies using the DASI framework and evaluate them for formative reasons. We acknowledge that it is too soon to suggest that the DASI can be used for system improvement purposes, but by conducting projects using DASI for teacher and school improvement projects, a pressure may also be created to use a similar approach in introducing national reform policies.

Although we have also discussed the success of the DASI, there are also areas in which it can be expanded. The first area has to do with the use of instruments to measure the functioning of school and teacher factors. An important step that reveals one of the essential differences of DASI with other approaches to school improvement has to do with its suggestion that schools should use specific instruments to measure teacher and school level factors in order to identify priority area(s) for school improvement. In Chapter 10, instruments that can be used by school stakeholders and the A&R Team are presented. In regard to the measurement of the teacher factors included in the dynamic model, three observation instruments and a student questionnaire have been developed. As far as the measurement of the school factors is concerned, we also refer to the use of three complementary approaches (see Chapter 10).

The instruments proposed for measuring factors in the DASI have been used in various studies and evidence supporting their validity is available (see Creemers & Kyriakides, 2010b; Kyriakides & Creemers, 2008). However, school stakeholders and the A&R Team should still spend time to use the instruments to collect and analyse data. Doing this will help them identify the priority area(s) of their schools. By applying DASI in different educational settings we may find out whether a more *practical and efficient approach* can be established to collect valid and reliable data on the functioning of teacher and school factors. For example, we could examine the extent to which schools can generate data on teacher factors by administering a student questionnaire. Such an examination has taken place in Canada (see Chapter 8) and the results of this project revealed that most teacher factors and their dimensions were measured through the current version of the student questionnaire. By conducting further studies, we may test the generalisability of the study conducted in Canada and develop a more practical and efficient way to measure teacher factors. Finally, we may discover that the schools can collect valid data about school factors by using only some of the techniques proposed in Chapter 10. In this way, more school stakeholders and A&R Teams may be encouraged to use DASI for establishing school improvement projects.

Another issue that could emerge from projects using the DASI to improve the quality of education has to do with the extent to which these projects will not only have an effect on the quality but also on the equity dimension of measuring school effectiveness. In the case of quality, student achievement gains in cognitive and other domains are examined. On the other hand, the equity is measured by looking at the extent to which schools and teachers manage to reduce unjustifiable differences in outcomes of schooling (Sammons, 2010; Strand, 2010; Thomas, 2001). Thus, projects using the DASI to develop school improvement projects may not only look at the extent to which this type of intervention had an impact on promoting student learning, but also on the extent to which initial differences in achievement of students of different groups are reduced. Moreover, projects concerned with the use of the DASI on providing equal educational opportunities should be implemented especially in schools where the unjustifiable differences in initial achievement are much higher than in other schools.

Finally, the long lasting effect of using the DASI in school improvement projects can be identified by collecting data from schools where this approach was implemented for many years. These projects will not only reveal the impact of this approach on student achievement gains but also help us to identify conditions for effective use of the DASI for a long period of time. In addition, we need to find out how the roles of school stakeholders and A&R Teams may change over time. Given that the DASI depends on the collaboration between the school stakeholders and the A&R Team, it is important to find out whether the stakeholders in schools which have used this approach for a long period are now able to run their projects with minimal or even without the need of substantial assistance from the A&R Team. Evaluations of schools using the DASI may suggest that by using the DASI, a culture which is in favour of using data and research evidence for improvement purposes can be created. In this way, the functioning of their school factors will continuously be improved and thereby they will remain among the most effective schools. This is the main target that we hope that this book may help schools to achieve. By presenting the theoretical framework of the DASI, illustrating its impact in different educational settings, and providing guidelines to school stakeholders and the A&R Team on how to use this approach, we hope that DASI will promote the improvement of the quality and equity in education because that is, ultimately, the aim we all share.

References

Adams, R.J., & Khoo, S. (1996). *Quest: The interactive test analysis system, Version 2.1.* Melbourne: ACER.

Alger, C. (2009). Secondary teachers' conceptual metaphors of teaching and learning: Changes over the career span. *Teaching and Teacher Education, 25*(5), 743–751.

Allport, G. (1937). *Personality: A psychological interpretation.* New York: Holt.

Alsaker, F., & Brunner, A. (1999). Switzerland. In P. K. Smith, Y. Morita, J. Junger-Tas, D. Olweus, R. Catalano, & P. Slee (Eds.), *The nature of school bullying: a cross national perspective,* (pp. 250–263). London: Routledge.

Anderson, L.W. (1995). Time allocated and instructional, In L.W. Anderson (Ed.), *International Encyclopaedia of Teaching and Teacher Education,* (pp 204–207). Oxford: Elsevier.

Angelo, T.A. (1995). Reassessing and defining assessment. AAHE Bulletin (Nov.), 7–9.

Antoniou, P. (2009). *Using the Dynamic Model of Educational Effectiveness to Improve Teaching Practice: Building an Evaluation Model to Test the Impact of Teacher Professional Development Programs.* Unpublished Doctoral Dissertation, University of Cyprus, Cyprus.

Antoniou, P., Creemers, B.P.M., & Kyriakides, L. (2009). (Eds.). Integrating Research on Teacher Education and Educational Effectiveness: Using the Dynamic Model for Teacher Professional Development. In M.S. Khine, & I.M. Saleh, *Transformative Leadership and Educational Excellence: Learning Organizations in the Information Age.* Sense Publishers: Rotterdam, the Netherlands.

Antoniou, P., & Kyriakides, L. (in press). The impact of a dynamic approach to professional development on teacher instruction and student learning: results from an experimental study. *School Effectiveness and School Improvement.*

Baldry, A.C., & Farrington, D.P. (2007). Effectiveness of programs to prevent school bullying. *Victims and Offenders, 2,* 183–204.

Ball, S.J. (1987). *The micro-politics of the school: Towards a theory of school organization.* London: Methuen/Routledge & Kegan Paul.

Bamburg, J.D. (1994). *Raising Expectations to Improve Student Learning. Urban Monograph Series,* CS: North Central Regional Educational Lab., Oak Brook, IL.

Bandura, A. (1996). Regulation of cognitive processes through perceived self-efficacy. *Developmental Psychology, 25*(5), 729–735.

Bandura, A. (1997). *Self-Efficacy: The Exercise of Control.* New York, W.H. Freeman and Company.

Barber, M. (1996). *The learning game: Arguments for an Education Revolution.* London: Victor Gollanz.

Baumert, J., & Demmrich, A. (2001). Test motivation in the assessment of student skills: The effects of incentives on motivation and performance. *European Journal of Psychology of Education, 16*(3), 441–462.

Beaton, A.E., Mullis, I.V.S., Martin, M.O., Gonzalez, E.J., Kelly, D.L., & Smith, T.A. (1996). *Mathematics Achievement in the Middle School Years. IEA's Third International Mathematics and Science Study.* Chestnut Hill, MA: Boston College, TIMSS International Study Center.

Beerens, D.R. (2000). *Evaluating teaching for professional growth.* Thousands Oaks, California: Corwin Press, Inc. Sage.

Berliner, D. (1988). *The Development of Expertise in Pedagogy.* Charles W. Hunt Memorial Lecture for the American Association of Colleges in Teacher Education, New Orleans, LA.

Berliner, D. (1992). Expertise in teaching. In F. Oser, J. -L. Patry, & A. Dick (Eds.), *Effective and responsible teaching,* (pp. 227–249). San Francisco: Jossey-Bass.

Berliner, D. (1994). Expertise: The wonder of exemplary performances. In J. Mangieri & C. Block (Eds.), *Creating powerful thinking in teachers and students: Diverse perspectives,* (pp. 161–186). Fort Worth, TX: Harcourt Brace College.

Berman, P. (1978). The study of macro- and micro-implementation. *Public Policy, 26*(2), 157–184.

Besag, V. (1989). *Bullies and victims in schools.* Milton Keynes, UK: Open University Press.

Bickman, L. (1985). Improving established statewide programs – a component theory of evaluation. *Evaluation Review, 9*(2), 189–208.

Black, P., & Wiliam, D. (1998). *Inside the Black Box: Raising Standards through Classroom Assessment.* London: King's College London School of Education.

Borich, G.D. (1992) (2nd Ed) *Effective teaching methods.* New York: Macmillan Publishing Company.

Borman, G.D., Hewes, G.M., Overman, L.T., & Brown, S. (2003). Comprehensive School Reform and Achievement: A Meta-Analysis. *Review of Educational Research, 73(2),* 125–230.

Boud, D. (1995). Assessment and learning: contradictory or complementary? In P. Knight (Ed.) *Assessment for Learning in Higher Education.* London: Kogan Page.

Brejc, M., Jurič, A., Persson, M., Pol, M., Scheerens, J., Stronach, I., Širok, K., & Townsend, T. (2008). *Študija nacionalnih in mednarodnih pristopov h kakovosti v vzgoji in izobraževanju [Study of national and international approaches to quality in education].* Ljubljana: Šola za ravnatelje [National School of Leadership in Education].

Bridges, E.M., & Groves, B.R. (1999). The macro- and micro-politics of personnel evaluation: A Framework. *Journal of Personnel Evaluation in Education, 13*(4), 321–337.

Broadfoot, P., & Black, P. (2004). Redefining assessment? The first ten years of Assessment *in Education. Assessment in Education, 11*(1), 7–27.

Brookhart, S.M. (1997). Effects of the classroom assessment environment on mathematics and science achievement. *Journal of Educational Research, 90*(6), 323–330.

Brookhart, S.M. (2004). Classroom assessment: Tensions and intersections in theory and practice. *Teachers College Record, 106*(3), 429–458.

Brookover, W.B., Beady, C., Flood, P., Schweitzer, J., & Wisenbaker, J. (1979). *School systems and student achievement: schools make a difference.* New York: Praeger.

Brooks, G., Burton, M., Cole, P., Miles, J., Torgerson, C., & Torgerson, D. (2008). Randomised controlled trial of incentives to improve attendance at adult literacy classes. *Oxford Review of Education, 34*(5), 493–504.

Brophy, J., & Good, T.L. (1986). Teacher behavior and student achievement. In M.C. Wittrock (Ed.), *Handbook of research on teaching* (3rd ed, pp. 328–375). New York: MacMillan.

Busato, V., Prins, F., Elshout, J., & Hamaker, C. (1999). The relationship between learning styles, the Big Five personality traits and achievement motivation in higher education. *Personality and Individual Differences, 26,* 129–140.

Butler, D.L., & Winne, P.H. (1995). Feedback and self-regulated learning: A theoretical synthesis. *Review of Educational Research, 65,* 245–281.

Byrne, B. (1992). *Bullies and victims in a school setting with reference to some Dublin schools.* Dublin: University College.

Calderhead, J., & Shorrock, S.B. (1997). *Understanding teacher education.* London: Falmer Press.

Caldwell, B., & Spinks, J. (1988). *The Self Managing School*. Lewes: Falmer Press

Campbell, R.J. (1985). *Developing the Primary School Curriculum*. London: Cassell.

Campbell, R.J. (2010). Conservative Curriculum and Partial Pedagogy: a critique of proposals in the Cambridge Primary Review. *Forum, 52*(1), 25–36.

Campbell, D.T., & Fiske, D.W. (1959). Convergent and discriminant validation by the multitrait-multimethod matrix. *Psychological Bulletin, 56*, 81–105.

Campbell, R.J., & Kyriakides, L. (2000). The National Curriculum and Standards in Primary Schools: a comparative perspective. *Comparative Education, 36*(4), 383–395.

Campbell, R.J., Kyriakides, L., Muijs, R.D., & Robinson, W. (2003). Differential Teacher Effectiveness: Towards A Model For Research And Teacher Appraisal. *Oxford Review of Education, 29*(3), 347–362.

Campbell, R.J., Kyriakides, L., Muijs, R.D., & Robinson, W. (2004). *Assessing Teacher Effectiveness: A Differentiated Model*. London: Routledge/Falmer.

Cankar, G. (2009). Varianca dosežkov slovenskih učencev med šolami in znotraj šol na lestvicah dosežkov iz matematike, branja in naravoslovja raziskave PISA 2006 [Within and between school variance among Slovenian students' achievement in science, reading and mathematics on PISA 2006]. *Šolsko polje [School field], 20*(1/2), 41–53.

Cankar, G. (2010a). Prehajanje na višje ravni izobraževanja in razlike v strukturi glede na spol v luči dosežkov na zunanjih preizkusih znanja [Transition between levels of education and changes in gender structure in view of achievement on external examinations]. *Sodobna pedagogika [Contemporary Pedagogy], 61*(2), 98–116.

Cankar, G. (2010b). Allowing Examinee Choice in Educational testing. *Metodološki zvezki [Advances in Methodology and Statistics], 7*(2), 151–166.

Carver, F.D., & Sergiovanni, T.J. (1969). *Organizations and human behavior: focus on schools*. New York: McGraw-Hill.

Chapman, C., & Hadfield, M. (2010). Realising the potential of school-based networks. *Educational Research, 52*(3), 309–323.

Chapman, C., & Harris, A. (2004). Improving schools in difficult and challenging contexts: strategies for improvement. *Educational Research, 46*(3), 219–228.

Charach, A., Pepler, D., & Ziegler, S. (1995). Bullying at school: A Canadian perspective. *Education Canada, 35*, 12–18.

Charlot, B., & Emin, J.C. (Eds.). (1997). *La violence à l'école: état des savoirs*. Paris: A. Colin.

Cheng, J.H.S., & Marsh, H.W. (2010). National student survey: are differences between universities and courses reliable and meaningful? *Oxford Review of Education, 36*(6), 693–712.

Cheng, Y.C. (1993). Profiles of Organizational Culture and Effective Schools. *School Effectiveness and School Improvement, 4*(2), 85–110.

Cheng, Y.C. (1996). *School effectiveness and school-bases management: A mechanism for development*. London: The Falmer Press.

Cheng, Y.C., & Mok, M. (2008). What effective classroom? Towards a paradigm shift. *School Effectiveness and School Improvement, 19*(4), 365–385.

Christoforides, M., & Kyriakides, L. (2011). Using the dynamic model to identify stages of teachers' skills in assessment. *Paper presented at the 24th International Congress for School Effectiveness and Improvement (ICSEI) 2011*. Limassol, Cyprus, January 2011.

Clapham, M.M. (1998). Structure of figural forms A and B of the Torrance tests of creative thinking. *Educational and Psychological Measurement, 58*(2), 275–283.

Clark, R.E., & Salomon, G. (1986). Media in teaching. In M. Wittrock (Ed.), *Handbook of Research on Teaching*, 3rd Edition (pp. 464–478). New York: Macmillan.

Clarke, D., & Hollingsworth, H. (2002). Elaborating a model of teacher professional growth. *Teaching and Teacher Education, 18*(8), 947–967.

Coe, R. (2009). School Improvement: Reality and Illusion. *British Journal of Educational Studies 57*(4), 363–379.

Coleman, P. (1998). *Parent, Student and Teacher Collaboration: The Power of Three.* Thousand Oaks, CA: Corwin Press.

Coleman, J.S., Campbell, E.Q., Hobson, C.F., McPartland, J., Mood, A.M., Weinfeld, F.D., & York, R.L. (1966). *Equality of Educational Opportunity.* Washington, DC: US Government Printing Office.

Combs, A.W., Blume, R.A., Newman, A.J., & Wass, H.L. (1974). *The professional education of teachers: A humanistic approach to teacher preparation.* Boston: Allyn & Bacon.

Conley, S., Schmidle, T., & Shedd, J.B. (1988). Teacher participation in the management of school systems. *Teachers College Record, 90,* 259–280.

Conway, J.A. (1984). The myth, mystery, and mastery of participative decision making in education. *Educational Administration Quarterly, 20*(3), 11–40.

Cook, T.D., Murphy, R.F., & Hunt, H.D. (2000). Comer's School Development Program in Chicago: A Theory-Based Evaluation. *American Educational Research Journal, 37*(2), 535–597.

Cousins J.B., & Earl L.M. (1992). The case for participatory evaluation. *Educational Evaluation and Policy Analysis, 14*(4), 397–418.

Creemers, B. (1994). *The Effective Classroom.* London: Cassell.

Creemers, B.P.M. (1997). *Effective schools and effective teachers: An International perspective.* Warwick, UK: University of Warwick Centre for Research in Elementary and Primary Education.

Creemers, B.P.M. (2002). From school effectiveness and school improvement to Effective School Improvement: background, theoretical analysis, and outline of the empirical study. *Educational Research and Evaluation, 8*(4), 343–362.

Creemers, B.P.M. (2006). The importance and perspectives of international studies in educational effectiveness. *Educational Research and Evaluation, 12*(6), 499–511.

Creemers, B.P.M., & Kyriakides, L. (2006). Critical analysis of the current approaches to modelling educational effectiveness: The importance of establishing a dynamic model. *School Effectiveness and School Improvement, 17*(3), 347–366.

Creemers, B.P.M., & Kyriakides, L. (2008a). *The dynamics of educational effectiveness: A contribution to policy, practice and theory in contemporary schools.* London: Routledge.

Creemers, B.P.M., & Kyriakides, L. (2008b). A theoretical based approach to educational improvement: Establishing links between educational effectiveness research and school improvement. In Bos, W.; Holtappels, H.G.; Pfeiffer, H., & Rolf, H. (Eds.). *Yearbook on School Improvement* (pp. 41–61). Germany: Juventa Verlag Weinhem und Munchen.

Creemers, B.P.M., & Kyriakides, L. (2009). Situational effects of the school factors included in the dynamic model of educational effectiveness. *South African Journal of Education, 29*(3), 293–315.

Creemers, B.P.M., & Kyriakides, L. (2010a). Explaining stability and changes in school effectiveness by looking at changes in the functioning of school factors. *School Effectiveness and School Improvement, 21* (4), 409–427.

Creemers, B.P.M., & Kyriakides, L. (2010b). School factors explaining achievement on cognitive and affective outcomes: establishing a dynamic model of educational effectiveness. *Scandinavian Journal of Educational Research, 54*(3), 263–294.

Creemers, B.P.M., & Kyriakides, L. (2010c). Using the dynamic model to develop an evidence-based and theory-driven approach to school improvement. *Irish Educational Studies, 29,* 5–23.

Creemers, B.P.M., & Kyriakides, L. (2010d). Validity of educational indicators. In P. Peterson, E. Baker, & B. McGaw, (Editors), *International Encyclopedia of Education.* Oxford: Elsevier.

Creemers, B.P.M., Kyriakides, L., & Sammons, P. (2010). *Methodological Advances in Educational Effectiveness Research.* London and New York: Taylor & Francis.

Creemers, B.P.M., & Reezigt, G.J. (1996). School level conditions affecting the effectiveness of instruction. *School Effectiveness and School Improvement, 7*(3), 197–228.

Creemers, B.P.M., & Reezigt, G. J. (1997). School effectiveness and school improvement: Sustaining links. *School Effectiveness and School Improvement, 8*(4), 396–429.

Creemers, B.P.M., & Reezigt, G.J. (2005). Linking school effectiveness and school improvement: The background and outline of the project. *School Effectiveness and School Improvement, 16*(4), 359–371.

Creemers, B.P.M., Stoll, L., & Reezigt, G. (2007). Effective School Improvement Ingredients for Success: The results of an International Comparative Study of Best Practice Case Studies. In T. Townsend (Ed.), *International Handbook of School Effectiveness and Improvement*, pp. 825–838. Dordrecht: Springer.

Cronbach, L.J. (3rd Ed) (1990). *Essentials of Psychological Testing*. New York: Harper & Row.

Cronbach, L.J., Gleser, G.C., Nanda, H., & Rajaratnam, N. (1972). *The Dependability of Behavioral Measurements: Theory of Generalizability Scores and Profiles*. New York: Wiley.

Crooks, T. J. (1988). The impact of classroom evaluation practices on students. *Review of Educational Research, 58*, 438–481.

Dall'Alba, G., & Sandberg, J. (2006). Unveiling professional development: a critical review of stage models. *Review of Educational Research, 76*, 383–412.

Danielson C., & McGreal, T.L (2000). *Teacher Evaluation to Enhance Professional Practice*. Alexandria, V.A.: Association for Supervision and Curriculum Development.

Darling-Hammond, L. (2000). Teacher quality and student achievement: a review of state policy evidence. *Education Policy Analysis Archives, 8*(1), http://epaa.asu.edu/epaa/v8n1/.

Datnow, A., Borman, G., & Stringfield, S. (2000). School Reform through a Highly Specified Curriculum: Implementation and Effects of the Core Knowledge Sequence. *The Elementary School Journal, 101*(2), 167–191.

Datnow, A., Borman, G., Stringfield, S., Overman, L.T., & Castellano, M. (2003). Comprehensive School Reform in Culturally and Linguistically Diverse Contexts: Implementation and Outcomes form a Four-Year Study. *Educational Evaluation and Policy Analysis, 25*(2), 143–170.

Datnow, A., Hubbard, L., & Mehan, H. (2002). *Extending Educational Reform: From one school to many*. New York: RoutledgeFalmer Press.

De Corte, E. (2000). Marrying theory building and the improvement of school practice: a permanent challenge for instructional psychology. *Learning and Instruction, 10*(3), 249–266.

De Jong, R., & Westerhof, J.K. (2001). The quality of student ratings of teacher behaviour. *Learning Environments Research, 4*, 51–85.

De Jong, R., Westerhof, K.J., & Kruiter, J.H., (2004). Empirical evidence of a comprehensive model of school effectiveness: A multilevel study in mathematics in the 1st year of junior general education in the Netherlands. *School Effectiveness and School Improvement, 15*(1), 3–31.

Debus, G., & Schroiff, H.W. (1986). The psychology of work and organization: Current trends and issues. *Selected and edited proceedings of the West European conference on the psychology of work and organization, North Holland, Amsterdam.*

Delandshere, G. (2002). Assessment as Inquiry. *Teachers College Record, 104*(7), 1461– 1484.

Demetriou, D. (2009). *Using the dynamic model to improve educational practice*. Unpublished doctoral dissertation, University of Cyprus.

Desimone, M.L., Porter, C.A., Garet, S.M., Yoon, S.K., & Birman, F.B. (2002). Effects of professional development on teachers' instruction: Results from a three-year longitudinal study. *Educational Evaluation and Policy Analysis, 24*(2), 81–112.

Den Brok, P., van Tartwijk, J., Wubbels, T., & Veldman, I. (2010). The differential effect of the teacher-student interpersonal relationship on student outcomes for students with different ethnic backgrounds. *British Journal of Educational Psychology, 80*(2), 199–221.

Denzin, N.K., & Lincoln, Y.S. (Eds.) (1998). *Collecting and interpreting qualitative materials*. Thousand Oaks, California: SAGE

Devos, G. (1998). Conditions and caveats for self-evaluation. The case of secondary schools. *Paper presented at the Annual Meeting of the American Educational Research Association*. San Diego, CA (ERIC Document Reproduction Service No. ED421493).

Donaldson, L. (2001). *The Contingency Theory of Organizations: Foundations for Organisational Science*. Thousands Oaks, CA: Sage.

Dowson, M., & McInerney, D.M. (2003). What do students say about motivational goals?: Towards a more complex and dynamic perspective on student motivation. *Contemporary Educational Psychology*, 28(1), 91–113.

Doyle, W. (1986). Classroom organization and management. In M.C. Wittrock (Ed.), *Handbook of Research on Teaching, Third Edition* (pp. 392–431). New York: Macmillan.

Dreyfus, H.L., & Dreyfus, S.E. (1986). *Mind over machine: The power of human intuition and expertise in the era of the computer*. New York: Free Press.

Driessen, G., & Sleegers, P. (2000). Consistency of Teaching Approach and Student Achievement: An Empirical Test. *School Effectiveness and School Improvement*, 11(1), 57–79.

Duke, D.L., Showers, B.K., & Imber, M. (1981). Studying shared decision making in schools. In S.B. Bacharach (Ed.), *Organizational behavior in schools and school districts* (pp. 313–351). New York: Praeger.

Earl, L., & Katz, S. (2000). Changing classroom assessment: Teachers' struggles. In N. Bascia & A. Hargreaves (Eds.), *The sharp edge of educational change* (pp. 97–111). London: Routledge.

Edmonds, R.R. (1979). Effective schools for the urban poor. *Educational Leadership*, 37(1), 15–27.

Elboj, C., & Niemelä, R. (2010). Sub-Communities of Mutual Learners in the Classroom: The case of Interactive Groups, *Revista de Psicodidáctica*, 15(2), 177–189.

Ellett, C.D. (1997). Classroom-based Assessments of Teaching and Learning. In J.H. Stronge (Ed.) *Evaluating Teaching: A guide to current thinking and best practice*, (pp 107–128). Thousand Oaks, California: SAGE.

Emmer, E.T., & Evertson, C.M. (1981). Synthesis of Research on Classroom Management. *Educational Leadership*, 38(4), 342–347.

Emmer E.T., & Stough, L.M. (2001). Classroom management: A critical part of educational psychology, with implications for teacher education. *Educational Psychologist*, 36(2), 103–112.

Epstein, J.L. (1992). School and Family Partnerships. In M. Akin (Ed.) *Encyclopaedia of educational research* (2nd ed.) (pp 1139–1151). New York: Macmillan.

Espalage, D.L., & Swearer, S.M. (2004). *Bullying in American schools: A social-ecological perspective on prevention and intervention*. Mahwah, N.J: Erlbaum.

Fairman, S.R., & Quinn, R.E. (1985). Effectiveness: The perspective from the organization theory. *Review of Higher Education*, 9, 83–100.

Fan, X., & Chen, M. (2001). Parent Involvement and students academic achievement: A meta-analysis. *Educational Psychology Review*, 13(1), 1–22.

Feiman-Nemser, S., & Remillard, J. (1996). Perspectives on learning to teach. In F.B. Murray (Ed.), *The teacher educator's handbook*, (pp. 63–91). San Francisco: Jossey-Bass.

Firestone, W.A., & Fisler, J.L. (2002). Politics, Community, and Leadership in a School University Partnership. *Educational Administration Quarterly*, 38(4), 449–493.

Fitz-Gibbon, C.T. (1996). *Monitoring Education: Indicators, Quality and Effectiveness*. London: Cassell-Continuum.

Fitz-Gibbon, C., & Tymms, P. (2002). Technical and Ethical Issues in Indicator Systems: Doing Things Right and Doing Wrong Things. *Education Policy Analysis Archives*, 10(6), http://epaa.asu.edu/ojs/article/download/285/411

Fitz-Gibbon, C.T., Tymms, P.B., & Hazlewood, R.D. (1990). Performance indicators and information systems. In Reynolds, D., Creemers, B.P.M., & Peters, D. (Eds.) *School Effectiveness and Improvement*. Groningen, RION.

Flanders, N. (1970). *Analyzing Teacher Behavior*. Reading, MA: Addison-Wesley.

Fraser, B.J. (1995). Students' perceptions of classrooms. In L.W. Anderson (Ed.), *International encyclopaedia of teaching and teacher education*, (pp. 416–419). Oxford: Elsevier.

Freiberg, H.J. (1999) (Ed.) *School Climate: Measuring Improving and Sustaining Healthy Learning Environments.* London: Falmer.

Fresko, B., & Nasser, F. (2001). Interpreting student ratings: Consultation, instructional modification, and attitudes towards course evaluation. *Studies in Educational Evaluation, 27*, 291–305.

Fullan, M. (2001). *The new meaning of educational change* (3rd ed.). New York: Teachers College.

Fullan, M., Bennett, B., & Rolheiser-Bennett, C. (1990). Linking Classroom and School Improvement. *Educational Leadership, 47*(8), 13–19.

Gaber, S., Klemenčič, S., Marjanovič-Umek, L., Koren, A., Logaj, V., Mali, D., Milekšič, V., Zupanc, D., & Kos-Kesojevič, Ž. (2011). Pregled stanja, primerjave z izbranimi državami in predlogi dogradite ugotavljanja in zagotavljanja kakovosti v Sloveniji [Overview of the situation, comparisons with selected countries and proposals for upgrading of quality assessment and assurance in Slovenia]. In Ž. Kos Kecojevič and S. Gaber (Eds.). *Kakovost v šolstvu v Sloveniji [Quality in Education in Slovenia]* (pp. 37–73). Ljubljana: Pedagoška fakulteta Univerze v Ljubljani [Faculty of Education of the University of Ljubljana] and Šola za ravnatelje [National School of Leadership in Education].

Gastel, B. (1991). A menu of approaches for evaluating your teaching. *BioScience, 41* (5), 342–345.

Gijbels, D., Van de Watering, G., Dochy, F., & Van den Bossche, P. (2006). New learning environments and constructivism: The students' perspective. *Instructional Science, 34*(3), 213–226.

Gilberts, G.H., & Lignugaris-Kraft, B. (1997). Classroom management and instruction competencies for preparing elementary and special education teachers. *Teaching and Teacher Education, 13*(6), 597–610.

Gipps, C. (1994). *Beyond Testing.* RoutledgeFalmer, London.

Good, T.L., Wiley, C.R.H., & Sabers, D. (2010). Accountability and educational reform: A critical analysis of four perspectives and considerations for enhancing reform efforts. *Educational Psychologist, 45*(2), 138–148.

Golby, M., & Viant, R., (2007). Means and ends in professional development. *Teacher Development, 11* (2), 237–243.

Goldstein, H. (2003) (3rd Edition). *Multilevel statistical models.* London: Edward Arnold.

Goodrum, D., Cousins, J., & Kinnear, P.J. (1992). The reluctant primary school teacher. *Research in Science Education, 22*(2), 163–169.

Gorard S., Rees G., & Salisbury J. (2001). Investigating the patterns of differential attainment of boys and girls at school. *British Educational Research Journal, 27*(2), 125–139.

Gray, J., Goldstein, H., & Jesson, D. (1996). Changes and improvements in schools' effectiveness: trends over five years. *Research Papers in Education, 11* (1), 35–51.

Gray, J., Goldstein, H., & Thomas, S. (2001). Predicting the future: the role of past performance in determining trends in institutional effectiveness at A-level. *British Educational Research Journal, 27*(4), 1–15.

Gray, J., Hopkins, D., Reynolds, D., Wilcox, B., Farrell, S., & Jesson, D. (1999). *Improving school: Performance and potential.* Buckingham: Open University Press.

Gray J., Peng, W.J., Steward S., & Thomas S. (2004). Towards a typology of gender-related school effects: some new perspectives on a familiar problem. *Oxford Review of Education, 30*(4), 529–550.

Grigorenko, E.L., & Sternberg, R.J. (1997). Styles of thinking, abilities, and academic performance. *Exceptional Children, 63*(3), 295–312.

Grossman, P.L., & Stodolsky, S.S. (1995). Content as contest: the role of school subjects in secondary school teaching. *Educational Researcher, 24*(8), 5–11.

Hallinger, P., & Heck, R.H. (2011a). Exploring the journey of school improvement: classifying and analyzing patterns of change in school improvement processes and learning outcomes. *School Effectiveness and School Improvement, 22*(1), 1–27.

Hallinger, P., & Heck, R.H. (2011b). Conceptual and methodological issues in studying school leadership effects as a reciprocal process. *School Effectiveness and School Improvement, 22*(2), 2011.

Hanushek, E.A. (1986). The economics of schooling: production and efficiency in public schools. *Journal of Economic Literature, 24,* 1141–1177.

Hanushek, E.A. (1989). The impact of differential expenditures on student performance. *Educational Research, 66*(3), 397–409.

Hargreaves, D.H. (1995). School culture, school effectiveness and school improvement. *School Effectiveness and School Improvement, 6,* 23–47.

Hargreaves, D.H., & Hopkins, D. (1991). *The Empowered School.* Cassell: London.

Harlen, W., & James, M. (1997). Assessment and Learning: Differences and relationships between formative and summative assessment. *Assessment in Education, 4*(3), 365–379.

Harris, A. (2001). Building the capacity for school improvement. *School Leadership and Management, 21*(3), 261–270.

Harskamp, E.G. (1988). *Een evaluatie van rekenmethoden* [An evaluation of arithmetic curricula] (Dissertation). Groningen, The Netherlands: RION.

Hauptman, A. (2010). Equating of grades at basic and higher level of mathematics achievement. *Metodološki zvezki [Advances in Methodology and Statistics], 7*(2), 167–181.

Hauptman, A., Zupanc, D., Bren, M., & Cankar, G. (2011). Building on school self-evaluation: using the dynamic model to improve educational practice. *Paper presented at the 24th International Congress for School Effectiveness and Improvement (ICSEI) 2011.* Limassol, Cyprus, January 2011.

Heck, R.H., & Moriyama, K. (2010). Examining relationships among elementary schools' contexts, leadership, instructional practices, and added-year outcomes: a regression discontinuity approach. *School Effectiveness and School Improvement, 21*(4), 377–408.

Hextall, I., & Mahony, P. (1998). *Effective Teachers Effective Schools.* London: Biddles Ltd.

Hoeben, W.Th.J.G. (1994) Curriculum evaluation and educational productivity. *Studies in Educational Evaluation, 20*(4), 477–502.

Hofman, R.H., Dijkstra, N.J., & Hofman, W.H.A. (2009). School self-evaluation and student achievement. *School Effectiveness and School Improvement, 20*(1), 47–68.

Hofman, R.H., Hofman, W.H., & Gray, J.M. (2008). Comparing key dimensions of schooling: towards a typology of European school systems. *Comparative Education, 44*(1), 93–110.

Hofman, R.H., Hofman, W.H., & Gray, J.M. (2010). Institutional contexts and international performances in schooling: Comparing patterns and trends over time in international surveys. *European Journal of Education, 45*(1), 153–173.

Hopkins, D. (1989). *Evaluating for School Development.* Milton Keynes: Open University Press.

Hopkins, D. (1995). Towards effective school improvement. *School Effectiveness and School Improvement, 6,* 265–274.

Hopkins, D. (1996). Towards a theory for school improvement. In J. Gray, D. Reynolds, C. Fitz-Gibbon, & D. Jesson (Eds.), *Merging traditions: The future of research on school effectiveness and school improvement,* pp. 30–51. London: Cassell.

Hopkins, D. (2001). *School Improvement for Real.* London: RoutledgeFalmer.

Hopkins, D., Ainscow, M., & West, M. (1994). *School Improvement in an Era of Change.* London: Cassell.

Houtveen, A.A.M., van de Grift, W.J.C.M., & Creemers, B.P.M. (2004). Effective School Improvement in Mathematics. *School Effectiveness and School Improvement, 15*(3), 337–376.

Hoyle, R.J., & Skrla, L. (1999). The politics of superintendent evaluation. *Journal of Personnel Evaluation in Education, 13*(4), 405–419.

Hu, L., & Bentler, P.M. (1999). Cut-off criteria for fit indexes in covariance structure analysis: Conventional criteria versus new alternatives. *Structural Equation Modeling, 6*, 1–55.

Isac, M.M., Maslowski, R., & van der Werf, G. (in press). Effective civic education: an educational effectiveness model for explaining students' civic knowledge. *School Effectiveness and School Improvement.*

ISCED, International Standard Classification of Education. (1997). Retrieved May 26, 2011, from http://www.unesco.org/education/information/nfsunesco/doc/isced_1997.htm

Janosz, M., Archambault, I., & Kyriakides, L. (2011). The cross-cultural validity of the dynamic model of educational effectiveness: A Canadian study. *Paper presented at the 24th International Congress for School Effectiveness and Improvement (ICSEI) 2011.* Limassol, Cyprus, January 2011.

Japelj-Pavešič, B. (2005). Celovito zagotavljanje kakovosti v raziskavah znanja: primer raziskave TIMSS 2003 [Integral provision of quality in research of knowledge: The case of TIMSS research 2003]. *Šolsko polje [School field], 16*(3/4), 5–18.

Japelj, P.B., & Cankar, G. (2010). Dosežki dijakov v raziskavi TIMSS za maturante in ocene pri matematiki na splošni maturi v Sloveniji [Mathematics achievement of students in TIMSS Advanced and Slovenian general matura]. *Sodobna pedagogika [Contemporary Pedagogy], 61*(2), 118–140.

Jencks, C., Smith, M., Acland, H., Bane, M.J., Cohen, D., Gintis, H., Heyns, B., & Michelson, S. (1972). *Inequality: a Reassessment of the Effects of Family and Schooling in America.* New York: Basic Books.

Jensen, A.R. (1969). How much can we boost IQ and scholastic achievement? *Harvard Educational Review, 39*(1), 1–123.

Johnson, B. (1997). An organizational analysis of multiple perspectives of effective teaching: Implications of teacher evaluation. *Journal of Personnel Evaluation in Education, 11*, 69–87.

Joyce, B.R., & Showers, B. (1980). Improving in-service training: The messages of research. *Educational Leadership, 37*(5), 379–385.

Joyce, B., Weil, M., & Calhoun, E. (2000). *Models of teaching.* Boston: Allyn & Bacon.

Kane, M.T. (2001). Current Concerns in Validity Theory. *Journal of Educational Measurement, 38*(4), 319–342.

Kifer, E. (2001). *Large-scale assessment: dimensions, dilemmas and policy.* Thousand Oaks, CA: Corwin Press Inc.

Killen, R. (2007). *Effective teaching strategies: Lessons from research and practice* (4th ed.). Thomson: Social Science Press.

Kim, K.H. (2006). Can we trust creativity tests? A review of the Torrance tests of Creative Thinking (TTCT). *Creativity Research Journal, 18*(1), 3–14.

King, P.M., & Kitchener, K.S. (1994). *Developing reflective judgment: Understanding and promoting intellectual growth and critical thinking in adolescents and adults.* San Francisco: Jossey-Bass.

Kington, A., Sammons, P., Day, C., & Regan, E. (2011). Stories and Statistics: Describing a Mixed Methods Study of Effective Classroom Practice. *Journal of mixed methods research, 5*(2), 103–125.

Kline, P., & Gale, A. (1977). Extraversion, neuroticism and performance in a psychology examination. *British Journal of Educational Psychology, 41*, 90–94.

Knuver, A.W.M., & Brandsma, H.P. (1993). Cognitive and affective outcomes in school effectiveness research. *School effectiveness and school improvement, 13*, 187–200.

Kochenderfer, B.J., & Ladd, G.W. (1996). Peer victimization: Manifestations and relations to school adjustment in kindergarten. *Journal of School Psychology, 34*(3), 267–283.

Koren, A. (2007). Centralisation and autonomy: a case study of 'constructed' views. *International Journal of Innovation and Learning, 4*(5), 487–500.

Koren, A., & Brejc, M. (2011). Vloga države, šol, učiteljev in učencev pri ugotavljanju in zagotavljanju kakovosti [The role of national level, schools, teachers and students in quality assessment and assurance]. In Ž. Kos Kecojevič and S. Gaber (Eds.). *Kakovost v šolstvu v Sloveniji [Quality in Education in Slovenia]* (pp. 316–346). Ljubljana: Pedagoška fakulteta Univerze v Ljubljani [Faculty of Education of the University of Ljubljana] and Šola za ravnatelje [National School of Leadership in Education].

Krasne, S., Wimmers, P.F., Relan, A., & Drake, T.A. (2006). Differential effects of two types of formative assessment in predicting performance of first-year medical students. *Advances in Health Sciences Education, 11*(2), 155–171.

Krek, J. (Ed.). (1995). *Bela knjiga o vzgoji in izobraževanju v Republiki Sloveniji [White Paper on Education in the Republic of Slovenia]*. Ljubljana: Ministrstvo za šolstvo in šport.

Kumar, D.D. (1991). A meta-analysis of the relationship between science instruction and student engagement *Educational Review, 43*(1), 49–61.

Kuyper, H., Dijkstra, P., Buunk, A.P., & Van der Werf, G.P.H. (2011). Social comparisons in the classroom: An investigation of the better than average effect among secondary school children. *Journal of School Psychology, 49*(1), 25–53.

Kyriakides, L. (1997). Primary teachers' perceptions of policy for curriculum reform in Mathematics. *Educational Research and Evaluation, 3*, 214–242.

Kyriakides, L. (1999). The management of curriculum improvement in Cyprus: a critique of a 'centre-periphery' model in a centralised system. In Townsend, T., Clarke, P., & Ainscow, M. (Eds.) (1999). *Third Millennium Schools. A World of Difference in School Effectiveness and School Improvement,* pp. 107–124. Lisse: Swets and Zeitlinger.

Kyriakides, L. (2004). Investigating Validity from Teachers' Perspective through their engagement in Large-Scale Assessment: the Emergent Literacy Baseline Assessment Project. *Assessment in Education: Principles, Policy and Practice, 11* (2), 143–165.

Kyriakides, L. (2005a). Extending the Comprehensive Model of Educational Effectiveness by an Empirical Investigation. *School Effectiveness and School Improvement, 16*(2), 103–152.

Kyriakides, L. (2005b). Evaluating school policy on parents working with their children in class. *The Journal of Educational Research, 98*(5), 281–298.

Kyriakides, L. (2006). Using international comparative studies to develop the theoretical framework of educational effectiveness research: A secondary analysis of TIMSS 1999 data, *Educational Research and Evaluation, 12*(6), 513–534.

Kyriakides, L. (2007). Generic and Differentiated Models of Educational Effectiveness: Implications for the Improvement of Educational Practice. In T. Townsend (Ed.) *International Handbook of School Effectiveness and Improvement (pp. 41–56)*. Dordrecht, the Netherlands: Springer.

Kyriakides, L. (2008). Testing the validity of the comprehensive model of educational effectiveness: a step towards the development of a dynamic model of effectiveness. *School Effectiveness and School Improvement, 19* (4), 429–446.

Kyriakides, L., & Campbell, R.J. (2004). School self-evaluation and school improvement: a critique of values and procedures. *Studies in educational evaluation, 30*(1), 23–36.

Kyriakides, L., Campbell, R.J., & Gagatsis, A. (2000). The Significance of the Classroom Effect in Primary Schools: An Application of Creemers' Comprehensive Model of Educational Effectiveness. *School Effectiveness and School Improvement, 11*(4), 501–529.

Kyriakides, L., Charalambous, A., Kaloyirou, C., & Creemers, B.P.M. (2011). Facing and preventing bullying through improving the school learning environment: The theoretical background of the project. *Paper presented at the 24th International Congress for School Effectiveness and Improvement (ICSEI) 2011.* Limassol, Cyprus, January 2011.

Kyriakides, L., & Charalambous, C. (2005). Using educational effectiveness research to design international comparative studies: turning limitations into new perspectives, *Research Papers in Education, 20*(4), 391–412.

Kyriakides, L., Charalambous, C., Philippou, G., & Campbell, R.J. (2006). Illuminating reform evaluation studies through incorporating teacher effectiveness research: a case study in Mathematics. *School Effectiveness and School Improvement, 17*(1), 3–32.

Kyriakides, L., & Christoforides, M. (2011). Searching for stages of teacher skills in assessment: Implications for research on teacher professional development. *Paper presented at the 37th International Association for Educational Assessment Annual Conference (IAEA) 2011.* Manila, Philippines, October 2011.

Kyriakides, L., & Christoforou, Ch. (2011). A Synthesis of Studies Searching for Teacher Factors: Implications for Educational Effectiveness Theory. *Paper presented at the American Educational Research Association (AERA) 2011 Conference.* New Orleans, April 2011.

Kyriakides, L., & Creemers, B.P.M. (2006). Using the dynamic model of educational effectiveness to introduce a policy promoting the provision of equal opportunities to students of different social groups. In McInerney, D.M., Van Etten, S., & Dowson, M. (Eds.) *Research on Sociocultural Influences on Motivation and learning, Vol. 6: Effective schooling.* Information Age Publishing, Greenwich CT.

Kyriakides, L., & Creemers, B.P.M. (2008). Using a multidimensional approach to measure the impact of classroom-level factors upon student achievement: a study testing the validity of the dynamic model. *School Effectiveness and School Improvement, 19*(2), 183–205.

Kyriakides, L., & Creemers, B.P.M. (2009). The effects of teacher factors on different outcomes: two studies testing the validity of the dynamic model. *Effective Education, 1*(1), 61–86.

Kyriakides, L., & Creemers, B.P.M. (2010). Can schools achieve both quality and equity? *Paper presented at the American Educational Research Association (AERA) 2010,* Denver, Colorado, May 2010.

Kyriakides, L., Creemers, B.P.M., & Antoniou, P. (2009). Teacher behaviour and student outcomes: Suggestions for research on teacher training and professional development. *Teaching and Teacher Education, 25*(1), 12–23.

Kyriakides, L., Creemers, B.P.M., Antoniou, P., & Demetriou, D. (2010). A synthesis of studies for school factors: Implications for theory and research. *British Educational Research Journal, 36*(5), 807–830.

Kyriakides, L., Creemers, B.P.M., & Charalambous, A. (2008). Effective schools in facing and preventing bullying. *Paper presented at the EARLI SIG 18 Conference.* Frankfurt Main, Germany.

Kyriakides, L., & Demetriou, D. (2006). Investigating the generalisability of models of educational effectiveness: a secondary analysis of PISA study. *Paper presented at the 87th Annual Meeting of the American Educational Research Association.* San Francisco, CA, USA.

Kyriakides, L., & Demetriou, D. (2007). Introducing a teacher evaluation system based on teacher effectiveness research: An investigation of stakeholders' perceptions. *Journal of Personnel Evaluation in Education, 19,* 43–64.

Kyriakides, L., & Demetriou, D. (2010). Investigating the impact of school policy in action upon student achievement: extending the dynamic model of educational effectiveness. *Paper presented at the second meeting of the EARLI SIG18 Educational Effectiveness,* Leuven, August 2010.

Kyriakides, L., & Tsangaridou, N. (2008). Towards the development of generic and differentiated models of educational effectiveness: a study on school and teacher Effectiveness in Physical Education. *British Educational Research Journal, 34*(6), 807–838.

Lamb, S. (1996). Gender Differences in Mathematics participation in Australian schools: some relationships with social class and school policy. *British Educational Research Journal, 22*(2), 223–240.

Lane, K.L., Kalberg, J.R., & Menzies, H.M. (2009). *Developing schoolwide programs to prevent and manage problem behaviours: A step-by-step approach.* New York, N.Y.: Guilford Press.

Lee, V.E., & Smith, J.B. (1999). Social support and achievement for young adolescents in Chicago: the role for young adolescents in Chicago: The role of the school academic press. *American Educational Research Journal, 36*(4), 907–945.

Leithwood, K., & Jantzi, D. (2006). Transformational school leadership for large-scale reform: Effects on students, teachers, and their classroom practices. *School Effectiveness and School Improvement, 17,* 201–227.

Levin, B. (2010). The challenge of large-scale literacy improvement. *School Effectiveness and School Improvement, 21*(4), 359–376.

Levine, D.U., & Lezotte, L.W. (1990). *Unusually effective schools: a review and analysis of research and practice.* Madison (USA): National Center for Effective Schools Research and Development.

Lezotte, L. (1989). School improvement based on the effective schools research. *International Journal of Educational Research, 13*(7), 815–825.

Linn, R.L. (1993). Educational assessment: Expanded expectations and challenges. *Educational Evaluation and Policy Analysis, 15,* 1–16.

Linnakyla, P., Malin, A., & Taube, K. (2004). Factors behind low reading literacy achievement. *Scandinavian Journal of Educational Research, 48*(3), 231–249.

Lock, C.L., & Munby, H. (2000). Changing assessment practices in the classroom: A study of one teacher's change. *The Alberta Journal of Educational Research, 46,* 267–279.

Louis, K.S. (1994). Beyond "managed change:" Rethinking how schools improve. *School Effectiveness and School Improvement, 5,* 2–24.

Lundberg, C. (1989). On organizational learning: Implications and opportunities for expanding organizational development. *Research in Organizational Change and Development, 3,* 61–82.

Ma, X. (1999). Dropping out of advanced mathematics: the effects of parental involvement. *Teachers College Record 101*(1), 60–81.

MacBeath, J. (1999). *Schools must speak for themselves: The case for SSE.* London: Routledge.

MacBeath, J. (2006). A story of change: growing leadership for learning. *Journal of Educational Change, 7*(1–2), 33–46.

MacBeath, J., & McGlynn, A. (2003). *Self evaluation: What's in it for schools?* London: Routledge.

MacBeath, J., & Mortimore, P. (2001). *Improving School Effectiveness.* Buckingham, UK: Open University Press.

MacBeath, J., Schratz, M., Meuret, D., & Lakobsen, L. (2000). *Self-evaluation in European schools.* London: RoutledgeFalmer.

Marcoulides, G.A., & Drezner, Z. (1999). A procedure for detecting pattern clustering in measurement designs. In M. Wilson, & G. Engelhard, Jr. (Eds.), *Objective measurement: Theory into practice* (Vol. 5). Ablex Publishing Corporation.

Marsh, H. (2008). Big-fish-little-pond-effect: Total long-term negative effects of school-average ability on diverse educational outcomes over 8 adolescent/early adult years. *International Journal of Psychology, 43*(3–4), 53–54.

Marsh, H.W., & Parker, J.W. (1984). Determinants of student self-concept: is it better to be a large fish in a small pond even if you don't learn to swim as well? *Journal of Personality and Social Psychology, 47*(1), 213–231.

Marsh, H.W., & Roche, L.A. (1997). Making students' evaluations of teaching effectiveness effective: the Critical Issues of Validity, Bias and Utility, *American Psychologist, 52*(11), 1187–1197.

Maslowski, R., Scheerens, J., & Luyten, H. (2007). The effect of school autonomy and school internal decentralization on students' reading literacy. *School Effectiveness and School Improvement, 18*(3), 303–334.

McCormack-Larkin, M. (1985). Ingredients of a successful school effectiveness project. *Educational Leadership, 42*(6), 31–37.

McTaggart, R. (1997). *Participatory Action Research.* New York: Albany.

Mellor, A. (1990). *Bullying in Scottish secondary schools.* Edinburgh, UK: Scottish Council for Research in Education.

Messick, S. (1996). Bridging cognition and personality in education: the role of style in performance and development. *European Journal of Personality, 10*, 353–376.

Meuret, D., & Morlaix, S. (2003). Conditions of Success of a School's Self-Evaluation: Some Lessons of a European Experience. *School Effectiveness and School Improvement, 14*(1), 53–71.

Mijs, D., Houtveen, T., Wubells, T., & Creemers, B.P.M. (January, 2005). Is there empirical evidence for School Improvement? *Paper presented at the ICSEI 2005 Conference*, Barcelona, Spain.

Miles, M. (1993). 40 years of change in schools: Some personal reflections. *Educational Administration Quarterly, 29*, 213–248.

Ministry of Education (1994). *The New Curriculum*. Nicosia: Ministry of Education.

Mintrop, H., & Trujillo, T. (2007). The practical relevance of accountability systems for school improvement: A descriptive analysis of California schools. *Educational Evaluation and Policy Analysis, 29*(4), 319–352.

Mintzberg, H. (1979). *The structuring of organizations*. Englewood Cliffs, NJ: Prentice-Hall.

Mok, M.M.C. (2010). *Self-directed Learning Oriented Assessment: Assessment that Informs Learning & Empowers The Learner*. Hong Kong: Pace Publications Ltd.

Monk, D.H. (1994). Subject matter preparation of secondary mathematics and science teachers and student achievement. *Economics of Education Review, 13*(2), 125–145.

Morgan, G. (1986). *Images of organizations*. Beverly Hills, CA: Sage.

Mortimore, P. (1991). School effectiveness research: which way at the crossroads? *School Effectiveness and School Improvement, 2*(3), 213–229.

Mortimore, P., Sammons, P., Stoll, L., Lewis, D., & Ecob, R. (1988). *School matters: The junior years*. Somerset, UK: Open Books.

Muijs, D., & Reynolds, D. (2000). School Effectiveness and Teacher Effectiveness in Mathematics: Some preliminary Findings from the Evaluation of the Mathematics Enhancement Programme (Primary). *School Effectiveness and School Improvement, 11*(3), 273–303.

Muijs, D., & Reynolds, D. (2001). *Effective Teaching: evidence and practice*. London: Sage.

Munro, J. (1999). Learning more about learning improves teacher effectiveness. *School Effectiveness and School Improvement, 10*(2), 151–171.

Murphy, J. (2009). Turning Around Failing Schools Policy Insights From the Corporate, Government, and Nonprofit Sectors. *Educational Policy, 23*(6), 796–830.

Murphy, J., & Beck, L. (1995). *School-based management as school reform: Taking stock*. Thousand Oaks, CA: Corwin.

Nakou, I. (2000). Elementary school teachers' representations regarding school problem behaviour: Problem children in talk. *Educational and Child Psychology, 17*, 91–106.

Nevo, D. (1995). *School-based evaluation: a dialogue for school improvement*. Oxford: Pergamon Press.

Nicol, D.J., & Macfarlane-Dick, D. (2006). Formative Assessment and self-regulated learning: a model and seven principles of good feedback practice. *Studies in Higher Education, 31*(2), 199–218.

Noble, T. (2004). Integrating the revised Bloom's taxonomy with multiple intelligence: a planning tool for curriculum differentiation. *Teachers College Records, 106*(1), 193–211.

Nuttall, D., Goldstein, H., Prosser, R., & Rasbach, J. (1989). Differential school effectiveness *International Journal of Educational Research, 13*, 769–776.

Olweus, D. (1978). *Aggression in the schools: Bullies and whipping boys*. Washington, DC: Hemisphere.

Olweus, D. (1993). *Bullying at school. What we know and what we can do?* Oxford: Blackwell.

Olweus, D. (1994). Annotation: Bullying at school: Basic facts and effects of a school based intervention program. *Journal of Child Psychology and Psychiatry, 35*, 1171–1190.

Olweus, D. (1996). *The revised Olweus Bully/Victim Questionnaire for Students*. Bergen, Norway: University of Bergen.

Opdenakker, M.C., & Van Damme, J. (2000). Effects of Schools, Teaching Staff and Classes on Achievement and well-being in secondary education: Similarities and Differences Between school Outcomes. *School Effectiveness and School Improvement, 11*(2), 65–196.

Opdenakker, M.C., & Van Damme, J. (2006). Differences between secondary schools: A study about school context, group composition, school practice, and school effects with special attention to public and Catholic schools and types of schools. *School Effectiveness and School Improvement, 17*(1), 87–117.

Pajares, M.F. (1992). Teachers' beliefs and educational research: cleaning up messy concept. *Review of Educational Research, 62*(3), 307–332.

Pajares, F. (1999). Current Directions in Self-Efficacy Research. In M. Maehr, & P.R. Pintrich (Eds.), *Advances in motivation and achievement.* (pp. 1–49). Greenwich, CT: JAI Press.

Pajares, F., & Schunk, D.H. (2001). Self-Beliefs and School Success: Self-Efficacy, Self-Concept, and School Achievement, In R. Riding and S. Rayner (Eds.), *Perception.* Ablex Publishing, London, pp. 239–266.

Paris S.G., & Paris, A.H. (2001). Classroom applications of research on self-regulated learning. *Educational Psychologist. 36*(2), 89–101.

Patton, M.Q. (1991). *Qualitative Evaluation and Research Methods.* London: SAGE.

Pellegrino, J.W. (2004). Complex learning environments: Connecting learning theory, Instructional design, and technology. In N.M. Seel & S. Dijkstra (Eds.), *Curriculum, plans, and processes in instructional design* (pp. 25–49). Mahwah, NJ: Lawrence Erlbaum Associates.

Perat, Z. (2005). Kaj bi se lahko naučili iz objave izsledkov raziskave TIMSS 2003? [What can we learn from publication of the TIMSS 2003 research results?] *Sodobna pedagogika [Contemporary Pedagogy], 56*(3), 128–141.

Phelan, A.M., & McLaughlin, H.J. (1995). Educational discourses, the nature of the child, and the practice of new teachers. *Journal of Teacher Education, 46*(3), 165–174.

Polettini, A.F.F. (2000). Mathematics teaching life histories in the study of teachers' perceptions of change. *Teaching and Teacher Education, 16,* 765–783.

Ponte, J.P., Matos J.F., Guimaraes, H.M., Leal, L.C., & Canavarro, A.P. (1994). Teachers' And Students' Views and Attitudes Towards a New Mathematics Curriculum: A Case Study. *Educational Studies in Mathematics, 26,* 347–365.

Popham, W.J. (2006). Phony formative assessments: Buyer beware! *Educational Leadership, 64*(3), 86–87.

Požar-Matijašič, N., & Gajgar, M. (2007). Self-evaluation in the system of quality assessment and assurance in Slovenia. In M. Brejc (Ed.), *Professional challenges for school effectiveness and improvement in the era of accountability: proceedings of the 20th Annual World ICSEI Congress.* (pp. 177–180). Ljubljana: National School for Leadership in Education and Koper: Faculty of Management. Retrieved April 27, 2011, from http://www.fm-kp.si/zalozba/ISBN/978-961-6573-65-8/177-180.pdf

Preskill, H., Zuckerman, B., & Matthews, B. (2003). An exploratory study of process use: Findings and implications for future research. *American Journal of Evaluation, 24*(4), 423–442.

Ramsay, P.D.K., Sneddon, D.G., Grenfell, J., & Ford, I. (1982). Successful versus unsuccessful schools: a South Auckland study. *Australia and New Zealand Journal of Sociology, 19*(1), 217–234.

Raudenbush, S.W., & Bryk, A.S. (1986). A hierarchical model for studying school effects. *Sociology of Education, 59,* 1–17.

Reezigt, G.J., & Creemers, B.P.M., (2005). A Comprehensive Framework for Effective School Improvement. *School Effectiveness and School Improvement, 16*(4), 407–424.

Reezigt, G.J., Guldemond, H., & Creemers, B.P.M. (1999). Empirical Validity for a Comprehensive Model on Educational Effectiveness. *School Effectiveness and School Improvement, 10*(2), 193–216.

Reid, K., Hopkins, D., & Holly, P. (1987). *Towards the Effective School,* Oxford. Blackwell.

Renihan, F.I., & Renihan, P.J. (1989). School improvement: Second generation issues and strategies. In B.P.M. Creemers, T.A. Peters & D. Reynolds (Eds.), *School effectiveness and school improvement,* pp. 365–377. Amsterdam/Lisse: Swets & Zeitlinger.

Reynolds, D. (1991). Changing Ineffective Schools. In M. Ainscow (Ed.), *Effective Schools for all,* pp. 92–105. London: David Fulton.

Reynolds, D. (1996). Turning around ineffective schools: some evidence and some speculations. In J. Gray, D. Reynolds, C. Fitz-Gibbon, & D. Jesson (Eds.), *Merging traditions: The future of research on school effectiveness and school improvement,* pp. 150–165. London: Cassell.

Reynolds, D. (2006). World Class Schools: Some methodological and substantive findings and implications of the International School Effectiveness Research Project (ISERP). *Educational Research and Evaluation, 12*(6), 535–560.

Reynolds, D., Creemers, B., Stringfield, S., Teddlie, C., & Schaffer, G. (Eds.) (2002). *World Class Schools: International Perspectives on School Effectiveness.* London: RoutledgeFalmer.

Reynolds, D., Hopkins, D., & Stoll, L. (1993). Linking School Effectiveness Knowledge and School Improvement Practice: Towards a Synergy. *School Effectiveness and School Improvement,* 4(1), 37–58.

Reynolds, D., & Stoll, L. (1996). Merging school effectiveness and school improvement: The knowledge base. In D. Reynolds, R. Bollen, B. Creemers, D. Hopkins, L. Stoll, & N. Lagerweij (Eds.), *Making good schools: Linking school effectiveness and school improvement,* pp. 94–112. London: Routledge.

Reynolds, D., Stringfield, S., & Schaffer, E. (2006) The High Reliability Schools Project: Some preliminary results and analyses In J. Chrispeels & A. Harris (Eds.), *Improving schools and educational systems,* pp. 56–76. London: Routledge.

Reynolds, D., Teddlie, C., Hopkins, D., & Stringfield, S. (2000). Linking school effectiveness and school improvement. In C. Teddlie & D. Reynolds (Eds.), *The international handbook of school effectiveness research* (pp. 206–231). London: Falmer Press.

Reynolds, A.J., & Walberg, H. J. (1990). *A Structural Model of Educational Productivity,* Illinois: Northern Illinois University.

Rigby, K., Smith, P.K., & Pepler, D. (2005). *Bullying in schools: How successful can interventions be?* Cambridge: Cambridge University Press.

Rosenshine, B., & Furst, N. (1973). The use of direct observation to study teaching. In R.M.W. Travers (Ed.) *Second Handbook of Research on Teaching.* Chicago: Rand McNally.

Rosenshine, B., & Stevens, R. (1986). Teaching Functions. In M.C. Wittrock (Ed.), *Handbook of Research on Teaching* (3rd ed., pp. 376–391). New York: Macmillan.

Rowan, B., Correnti, R., Miller, R.J., Camburn, E.M. (2009). School Improvement by Design: Lessons from a study of comprehensive school reform programs. In G. Sykes & B. Schneider (Eds.). *Handbook on Educational Policy Research* (pp 637–651). London: Routledge.

Rutter, M., Maughan, B., Mortimore, P., Ouston, J., & Smith, A. (1979). *Fifteen thousand hours: secondary schools and their effects on children.* Cambridge, MA: Harvard University Press.

Sackney, L. (1989). School effectiveness and improvement: the Canadian scene. In Reynolds, D., Creemers, B., & Peters, T. (Eds.), *School Effectiveness and Improvement.* Groningen: RION.

Sadler, D.R. (1989). Formative assessment and the design of instructional systems. *Instructional Science, 18,* 119–144.

Salomon, G. (1979). *Interaction of media, cognition and learning.* San Francisco: Jossey Bass.

Sammons, P. (2008). Zero Tolerance of Failure and New Labour Approaches to School Improvement in England. *Oxford Review of Education, 34*(6), 651–664.

Sammons, P. (2009). The dynamics of educational effectiveness: a contribution to policy, practice and theory in contemporary schools. *School Effectiveness and School Improvement.* 20(1), 123–129.

Sammons, P. (2010). Equity and Educational Effectiveness. In P. Peterson, E., Baker & B. McGaw (Editors). *International Encyclopedia of Education, Volume 5, Leadership and Management – Politics and Governance,* (pp 51–57). Oxford: Elsevier.

Sammons, P., Mujtaba, T., Earl, L., Gu, Q. (2007). Participation in Network Learning Community Programmes and Standards of Pupil Achievement: Does it make a difference? *School Leadership and Management, 27*(3), 213–238.

Saunders, L. (1999). Who or what is self-evaluation for? *School Effectiveness and School Improvement, 10*(4), 410–430.

Schaffer, E., Nesselrodt, P., & Stringfield, S. (1994). The contributions of classroom observations to school effectiveness research. In D. Reynolds, B.P.M. Creemers, P.S. Nesselrodt, E.C. Schaffer, S. Stringfield, & C. Teddlie (Eds.) *Advances in school effectiveness research and practice,* (pp. 133–152). London: Pergamon.

Scheerens, J. (1992). *Effective Schooling: Research, Theory and Practice.* London: Cassell.

Scheerens, J. (1993). Basic school effectiveness research: items for a research agenda. *School Effectiveness and School Improvement, 4*(1), 17–36.

Scheerens, J. (1994). The school level context of instructional effectiveness: A comparison between school effectiveness and restructuring models. *Tijdschrift voor Onderwijsresearch, 19,* 26–39.

Scheerens, J., & Bosker, R.J. (1997). *The foundations of educational effectiveness.* Oxford: Pergamon.

Scheerens, J., & Demeuse, M. (2005). The theoretical basis of the effective school improvement model (ESI). *School Effectiveness and School Improvement, 16*(4), 373–385.

Scheerens, J., Glas, C., & Thomas, S. (2003). *Educational evaluation, assessment and monitoring: a systemic approach.* Lisse: Swets & Zweitlinger Publishers.

Scheerens, J., Seidel, T., Witziers, B., Hendriks, M., & Doornekamp, G. (2005). *Positioning and validating the supervision framework.* Enschede/Kiel: University of Twente, Department of Educational Organisational and Management.

Schmidt, W., Jakwerth, P., & McKnight, C.C. (1998). Curriculum sensitive assessment: Content *does* make a difference. *International Journal of Educational Research, 29,* 503–527.

Schmidt, W., & Valverde, G.A. (1995). *National Policy and Cross-National Research: United States Participation in the Third International and Science Study.* East Lansing, MI: Michigan State University, Third International Mathematics and Science Study.

Schoenfeld, A.H. (1998). Toward a theory of teaching in context. *Issues in Education, 4*(1), 1–94.

Schon, D.A. (1971). *Beyond the Stable State.* Harmondsworth: Penguin.

Schon, D.A. (1987). *Educating the reflective practitioner: Toward a new design for teaching and learning in the professions.* San Francisco: Jossey-Bass.

Schunk, D.H. (1991). Self-Efficacy and academic motivation. *Educational Psychologist, 26*(3), 207–231.

Scriven, M. (1994). Duties of the teacher. *Journal of Personnel Evaluation in Education, 8,* 151–184.

Semen, E. (2010). Objektivnost meril za izbiro kandidatov pri omejitvi vpisa v programe srednješolskega izobraževanja [Objectivity of criteria for admission to upper secondary education]. *Sodobna Pedagogika [Contemporary Pedagogy], 61*(2), 164–179.

Senge, P. (1990). *The Fifth Discipline: The Art and Practice of the Learning Organization.* New York: DoubleDay.

Shadish, W.R., Cook, T.D., & Campbell, D.T. (2002) *Experimental and quasi-experimental designs for generalized causal inference.* Boston: Houghton-Mifflin.

Sharp, S., & Smith, P. (1994). *Tackling bullying in your school: A practical handbook for teachers.* London: Routledge.

Shaw, K.M., & Replogle, E. (1996). Challenges in evaluating school-linked services – toward a more comprehensive evaluation framework. *Evaluation Review, 20*(4), 424–469.

Sharon, D. (1987). The Renfrew Quality Education Project: Teachers' views after the first year. *Working Papers of the Planning and Development Research Branch*, TV Ontario, *87*(2).

Shavelson, R.J., Webb, N.M., & Rowley, G.L. (1989). Generalizability theory. *American Psychologist, 44*(6), 922–932.

Shepard, L.A. (2000). The role of assessment in a learning culture. *Educational researcher, 29*(7), 4–14.

Shipman, M.D. (1985). Ethnography and educational policy-making. In R.G. Burgess (Ed.), *Field methods in the study of education*. London: The Falmer Press.

Simons, H. (1990). Evaluation and the reform of schools. In *The evaluation of educational programmes: Methods, uses and benefits*. Report of the Education Research Workshop held in North Berwick (Scotland), 22–25 November 1998 (pp. 46–64). Amsterdam/Lisse, The Netherlands: Swets & Zeitlinger.

Sirin, S.R. (2005). Socioeconomic status and academic achievement: A meta-analytic review of research. *Review of Educational Research, 75*(3), 417–453.

Slater, R.O., & Teddlie, C. (1992). Toward a theory of school effectiveness and leadership. *School Effectiveness and School Improvement, 3*(4), 247–257.

Slavin, R.E. (1983). When does cooperative learning increase student-achievement? *Psychological Bulletin, 94*(3), 429–445.

Slavin R.E., & Cooper, R. (1999). Improving intergroup relations: Lessons learned from cooperative learning programs. *Journal Of Social Issues, 55*(4), 647–663.

Slavin, R.E., Lake, C., & Groff, C. (2009). Effective Programs in Middle and High School Mathematics: A Best-Evidence Synthesis. *Review of Educational Research, 79(2)*, 839–911.

Slee, P.T. (1994). Situational and interpersonal correlates of anxiety associated with peer victimization. *Child Psychiatry and Human Development, 25*, 97–107.

Smith, P., Morita, Y., Junger-Tas, J., Olweus, D., Catalano, R., & Slee, P. (Eds.). (1999). *The nature of school bullying: A cross-national perspective*. London: Routledge.

Smith, J.D., Schneider, B., Smith, P.K., & Ananiadou, K. (2004). The effectiveness of whole-school anti-bullying programs: A synthesis of evaluation research. *School Psychology Review, 33*, 548–561.

Smylie, M.A., Lazarus, V., & Brownlee-Conyers, J. (1996). Instructional Outcomes of School-Based Participative Decision Making. *Educational Evaluation and Policy Analysis, 18*(3), 181–198.

Snijders, T., & Bosker, R. (1999). *Multilevel Analysis: An Introduction to Basic and Advanced Multilevel Modeling*. London: Sage.

Snyder, J., Bolin, F., & Zumwalt, K. (1992). Curriculum implementation. In P. W. Jackson (Ed.), *Handbook of research on curriculum*, pp. 402–435. New York: Macmillan.

Soar, R.S., & Soar, R.M. (1979). Emotional climate and management. In P. Peterson & H. Walberg (Eds.), *Research on Teaching Concepts: Findings and Implications*. Berkeley, CA: McCutchan.

Somekh, B. (1995) The Contribution of Action Research in Social Endeavours: a position paper on action research methodology. *British Educational Research Journal, 21*(3), 339–355.

Spencer M.B., Noll E., & Cassidy E. (2000). Monetary incentives in support of academic achievement – Results of a randomized field trial involving high-achieving, low-resource, ethnically diverse urban adolescents. *Evaluation Review, 29*(3), 199–222.

Sternberg, R.J. (1988). Mental self-government: A theory of intellectual styles and their development. *Human Development, 31*, 197–224.

Sternberg, R.J. (1994). Allowing for thinking styles. *Educational Leadership, 52*(3), 36–39.

Sternberg, R.J., Forsythe, G.B., Hedlund, J., Hovath, A.J., Wagner, R.K., Williams, W.M., Snook, S.A., & Grigorenko, E.L. (2000). *Practical intelligence in everyday life*. New York: Cambridge University Press.

Stevenson, H.W., Chen, C., & Lee, S.Y. (1993). Mathematics Achievement of Chinese, Japanese and American Children: Ten Years Later. *Science, 259*, 53–58.

Stiggins, R.J. (1999). Evaluating classroom assessment training in teacher education programs. *Educational Measurement: Issues and Practice, 18*(1), 23–27.

Stobart, G. (2004). *The formative use of summative assessment: possibilities and limits.* Philadelphia: 30th Annual IAEA Conference.

Stoll, L., & Fink, D. (1989). An effective schools project: the Halton Approach. In Reynolds, D., Creemers, B., & Peters, T. (Eds.), *School Effectiveness and Improvement.* Groningen: RION.

Stoll, L., & Fink, D. (1992). Effecting school change: the Halton Approach. *School Effectiveness and School Improvement, 3*(1), 19–41.

Stoll, L., & Fink, D. (1994). School effectiveness and school improvement: Voices from the field. *School Effectiveness and School Improvement, 5,* 149–178.

Stoll, L., Reynolds, D., Creemers, B., & Hopkins, D. (1996). Merging school effectiveness and school improvement: Practical examples. In D. Reynolds, R. Bollen, B. Creemers, D. Hopkins, L. Stoll, & N. Lagerweij (Eds.), *Making good schools*, pp. 113–147. London/New York: Routledge.

Stoll, L., Wikeley, F., & Reezigt, G. (2002). Developing a Common Model? Comparing Effective School Improvement Across European Countries. *Educational Research and Evaluation, 8*(4), 455–475.

Strand, S. (2010). Do some schools narrow the gap? Differential school effectiveness by ethnicity, gender, poverty, and prior achievement. *School Effectiveness and School Improvement, 21*(3), 289–314.

Štraus, M. (2004). Mednarodne primerjave kot podlaga za oblikovanje strategije razvoja izobraževalnega sistema [International comparisons as the basis for forming the development strategy of the education system]. *Sodobna pedagogika [Contemporary Pedagogy], 55*(5), 12–27.

Stringfield, S. (1994). A model of elementary school effects. In D. Reynolds, B.P.M. Creemers, P.S. Nesselrodt, E.C. Schaffer, S. Stringfield, & C. Teddlie (Eds.), *Advances in School Effectiveness Research and Practice* (pp. 153–187). Oxford: Pergamon Press.

Stringfield, S. (1995). Attempting to enhance students' learning through innovative programs: the case for schools evolving into high reliability organisations. *School Effectiveness and School Improvement, 6*(1), 67–96.

Stringfield, S. (2000). A synthesis and critique of four recent reviews of whole-school reform in the United States. *School Effectiveness and School Improvement, 11,* 259–269.

Stringfield, S.C., & Slavin, R.E. (1992). A hierarchical longitudinal model for elementary school effects. In B.P.M. Creemers & G.J. Reezigt (Eds.), *Evaluation of Educational Effectiveness*, pp. 35–69. Groningen: ICO.

Stronge, J.H, & Ostrander, L.P., (1997). Client Surveys in Teacher Evaluation. In J. Stronge (Ed.), *Evaluating teaching: a guide to current thinking and best practice* (p. 129–161). Calif: Corwin Press.

Stronge, J.H., & Tucker, P.D. (2000). The politics of teacher evaluation: A case study of new system design and implementation. *Journal of Personnel Evaluation in Education, 13*(4), 339–359.

Stufflebeam, D.L., & Shinkfield, A.J. (1990). *Systematic Evaluation.* Lancaster: Kluwer-Nijhoff.

Swearer, S.M., Espelage, D.L., & Napolitano, S.A. (2009). *Bullying prevention and intervention: Realistic strategies for schools.* New York, NY: Guilford Press.

Sztajn, P. (2003). Adapting Reform Ideas in Different Mathematics Classrooms: Beliefs Beyond Mathematics. *Journal of Mathematics Teacher Education, 6,* 53–75.

Teddlie, C., & Reynolds, D. (2000). *The International Handbook of School Effectiveness Research.* London: Falmer Press.

Teddlie, C, & Roberts, S.P. (1993, April). *More clearly defining the field: A survey of subtopics in school effectiveness research.* Paper presented at the Annual Meeting of the American Educational Research Association, Atlanta.

Teddlie, C., & Stringfield, S. (1993). *Schools make a difference. Lessons learned from a 10-year study of school effects.* New York: Teachers College Press.

Thomas, S. (2001). Dimensions of secondary school effectiveness: Comparative analyses across regions. *School Effectiveness and School Improvement, 12*(3), 285–322.

Thomas, S., Peng, W.J., & Gray, J. (2007). Modelling patterns of improvement over time: value added trends in English secondary school performance across ten cohorts. *Oxford Review of Education, 33*(3), 261–295.

Torres, R.T., & Preskill, H. (2001). Evaluation and organizational learning: Past, present, and future. *American Journal of Evaluation, 22*(3), 387–395.

Townsend, T. (2007). *International Handbook of School Effectiveness and Improvement.* Dordrecht, the Netherlands: Springer.

Trautwein U., Koller O., Schmitz B., & Baumert J. (2002). Do homework assignments enhance achievement? A multilevel analysis in 7th-grade mathematics. *Contemporary Educational Psychology, 27*(1), 26–50.

Valverde G.A., & Schmidt, W.H. (2000). Greater expectations: learning from other nations in the quest for 'world-class standards' in US school mathematics and science. *Journal of Curriculum Studies, 32*(5), 651–687.

Van den Berg, R., Sleegers, P., Geijsel, F., & Vandenberghe, R. (2000). Implementation of an Innovation: Meeting the Concerns of Teachers. *Studies in Educational Evaluation, 26* 331–350.

Van der Schaaf, M.F., & Stokking, K.M. (2011). Construct Validation of Content Standards for Teaching. *Scandinavian Journal of Educational Research, 55*(3), 273–289.

Van der Werf, G., Opdenakker, M.C., & Kuyper, H. (2008). Testing a dynamic model of student and school effectiveness with a multivariate multilevel latent growth curve approach. *School Effectiveness and School Improvement, 19*(4), 447–462.

Visscher, A.J., & Coe, R. (2002). *School Improvement through Performance Feedback.* Rotterdam: Swets & Zeitlinger Publishers.

Walberg, H.J. (1984). Improving the productivity of America's schools. *Educational Leadership, 41*(8), 19–27.

Walberg, H.J. (1986). What works in a nation still at risk. *Educational Leadership, 44*(1), 7–10.

Waterman, J., & Walker, E. (2009). *Helping at-risk students. A group counselling approach for grades 6–9.* New York: The Guilford Press.

Wehrens, M.J.P.W., Kuyper, H., Dijkstra, P., Buunk, A.P., & Van der Werff, M.P.C. (2010). The long-term effect of social comparison on academic performance. *European Journal of Social Psychology. 40*(7), 1158–1171.

West, R., & Crighton, J. (1999). Examination Reform in Central and Eastern Europe: issues and trends. *Assessment in Education, 6*(2), 271–289.

Wiggins, G., & McTighe, J. (1998). *Understanding by design.* Alexandria, VA: ASCD.

Wilhelm, R.W., Coward, M.F., & Hume, L.M. (1996). The effects of a professional development institute on pre-service teachers' perceptions of their intercultural knowledge and diversity. *Teacher Educator, 32*(1), 48–61.

Wiliam, D., Lee, C., Harrison, C., & Black, P.J. (2004). Teachers developing assessment for learning: Impact on student achievement. *Assessment in Education: Principles, Policy & Practice, 11*(1), 49–65.

Wilks, R. (1996). Classroom management in primary schools: A review of the literature. *Behaviour Change, 13*(1), 20–32 1996.

Wilson, S.J., Lipsey, M.W., & Derzon, J.H. (2003). The effects of school-based intervention programs on aggressive behavior: A meta-analysis. *Journal of Consulting and Clinical Psychology, 71,* 136–149.

Witziers, B., Bosker, J.R., & Kruger, L.M. (2003). Educational Leadership and Student Achievement: The Elusive Search for an Association. *Educational Administration Quarterly, 39*(3), 398–425.

Worthen, B.R., Sanders, J.R., & Fitzpatrick, J.L. (1997). *Program Evaluation: Alternative Approaches and Practical Guidelines* (2nd ed.). USA: Longman Publishers.

Wright, S.P., Horn, S.P., & Sanders, W.L. (1997). Teacher and classroom context effects on student achievement: Implications for teacher evaluation. *Journal of Personnel Evaluation in Education, 11*(1), 57–67.

Yair, G. (1997). When classrooms matter: Implications of between-classroom variability for educational policy in Israel. *Assessment in Education, 4*(2), 225–248.

Yeh, S.S. (2009). The cost-effectiveness of raising teacher quality. *Educational Research review, 4*(3), 220–232.

Yen, W. (1993). Scaling and performance assessments: strategies for managing local item dependence. *Journal of Educational Measurement, 30*, 187–213.

Zhang, L.F. (2001). Do thinking styles contribute to academic achievement beyond self-rated abilities? *The Journal of Psychology, 135*, 621–638.

Zhang, L.F. (2002). Measuring thinking styles in addition to the measuring personality traits? *Personality and Individual Differences, 33*, 445–458.

Zhang, L.F. (2011). The developing field of intellectual styles: Four recent endeavours. *Learning and Individual Differences, 21*(3), 311–318.

Zhang L.F., & Sternberg, R.J. (1998). Thinking styles, abilities, and academic achievement among Hong Kong university students. *Educational Research Journal, 13*, 41–62.

ZOFVI – Zakon o organizaciji in financiranju vzgoje in izobraževanja [Law on organization and financing of education]. (2008, April). *Uradni list RS [Official Gazette of the Republic of Slovenia], XVIII (36)*, 3536– 3542.

Zupanc, D., & Bren, M. (2010). Inflacija pri internem ocenjevanju v Sloveniji [Grade inflation in Slovenia]. *Sodobna pedagogika [Contemporary Pedagogy], 61*(3), 208–228.

Zupanc, D., Urank, M., & Bren, M. (2009). Variability analysis for effectiveness and improvement in classrooms and schools in upper secondary education in Slovenia: assessment of/for learning analytic tool. *School Effectiveness and School Improvement, 20*(1), 89–122.

Appendix 4.1

Descriptive statistics of each group
and statistical figures of tests used to
compare their background
characteristics

Characteristics of sample	Control (n=1048)	Group 1 (n=1051)	Group 2 (n=1059)	Group 3 (n=1054)	Values of statistical tests
Percentage of girls	518 (49.4%)	533 (50.7%)	539 (50.9%)	542 (51.4%)	Chi-square test: (X^2=0.904, df=3, p=0.824)
Percentage of grade 4	510 (48.7%)	533 (50.7%)	527 (49.8%)	529 (50.2%)	Chi-square test: (X^2=0.954, df=3, p=0.812)
Educational background of father					
Graduate of a primary school	367 (35%)	378 (36%)	349 (33%)	358 (34%)	Kruskal-Wallis Analysis of
Graduate of secondary school	398 (38%)	410 (39%)	423 (40%)	411 (39%)	Variance (K-W=2.534, df=3,
Graduate of a college/ university	283 (27%)	263 (25%)	287 (27%)	285 (27%)	p=0.469)
Educational background of mother					
Graduate of a primary school	356 (34%)	336 (32%)	349 (33%)	379 (36%)	Kruskal-Wallis Analysis of
Graduate of secondary school	440 (42%)	462 (44%)	445 (42%)	432 (41%)	Variance (K-W=3.231, df=3,
Graduate of a college/ university	252 (24%)	253 (24%)	265 (25%)	243 (23%)	p=0.357)
Father occupation occupations held by working class	346 (33%)	336 (32%)	339 (32%)	358 (34%)	Kruskal-Wallis Analysis of
occupations held by middle class	388 (37%)	389 (37%)	381 (36%)	390 (37%)	Variance (K-W=2.397, df=3,
occupations held by upper-middle class	314 (30%)	326 (31%)	339 (32%)	306 (29%)	p=0.494)

Characteristics of sample	Control (n=1048)	Group 1 (n=1051)	Group 2 (n=1059)	Group 3 (n=1054)	Values of statistical tests
Mother occupation occupations held by working class	388 (37%)	368 (35%)	360 (34%)	390 (37%)	Kruskal-Wallis Analysis of
occupations held by middle class	388 (37%)	399 (38%)	381 (36%)	369 (35%)	Variance (K-W=4.138, df=3,
occupations held by upper-middle class	272 (26%)	284 (27%)	318 (30%)	295 (28%)	p=0.247)
Financial situation of the family	Mean=2.02 SD=1.12	Mean=2.04 SD=1.02	Mean=2.05 SD=1.08	Mean=1.99 SD=1.04	ANOVA (F=0.650, p=0.583)
Prior Knowledge in Mathematics	Mean=0.21 SD=0.95	Mean=0.19 SD=0.98	Mean=0.22 SD=0.94	Mean=0.20 SD=0.96	ANOVA (F=0.192, p=0.902)

Appendix 5.1

Excerpt from the handbook providing guidelines to schools on how to develop strategies and action plans on student behaviour outside the classroom

Policy and actions to improve the school learning environment

School policy concerning bullying should be announced to teachers (and, if possible, to all school stakeholders) at the beginning of the school year. There are many different ways to announce the school policy:

a) In staff meetings with the entire school staff
b) handout to the teachers of a document/statements containing the school policy
c) inform the deputy heads and ask them to present the policy to the rest of the teachers
d) appoint a co-ordinator to be responsible for the project, and also for the announcement of the policy.

After the announcement, suggestions and ideas from the faculty are expected. The teachers will present their expectations for the objectives and the entire policy, and feedback will be provided. Thus, after analysing the proposed ideas, the final version of the school policy can be established, and common expectations can be determined.

In this section you can find suggestions on the four aspects of the overarching factor included in our theoretical framework – namely, school policy on the school learning environment, and actions taken to improve the SLE:

a) student behaviour outside the classroom
b) collaboration and interaction between teachers
c) partnership policy
d) provision of learning resources.

Student behaviour outside the classroom

Student behaviour outside the classroom is a very important aspect of dealing with bullying because most of the incidents happen when students are outside (e.g., during the break time, or before and after school). With the development of a clear policy on student behaviour outside the classroom, valuable information about bullying incidents and targets (bullies, victims, bystanders, isolated students) can be collected.

Regarding student behaviour outside the classroom, all school personnel (not only teachers, but also bus drivers, coaches and after-school program supervisors) have to be trained to identify and respond to bullying, as well as to motivate and reinforce positive behaviour. They should be aware of the various symptoms of victimization (see Chapter 2), and be able to reach out to victims, and know the protocol for contacting the appropriate staff members or a student's parent. For this reason, we provide below some specific suggestions on the content of the policy, by taking into account that different activities can be undertaken in different time periods that students are outside the classroom (i.e., student behaviour in break time, student behaviour before the lesson starts, student behaviour after school hours/after lessons finish). Also, there are specific suggestions for the behaviour code that the school should develop in order to face effectively, and reduce, bullying which may happen outside the classroom.

Student behaviour in break time

Schools should develop a policy concerning *effective supervision* of their students during the break. *Increased monitoring* of student behaviour during breaks, and also before the start of the lessons, can help to identify and intervene when bullying occurs. A carefully organized supervision plan, especially in areas of the school where it has been observed that more bullying incidents happen, can help reduce the phenomenon.

Although a list of the teachers responsible for supervision is usually determined in most schools, this is not enough unless the role of each person, and the places where each teacher is expected to supervise, are also mentioned. With regard to the role of teachers, your school policy could recommend to them that, during this supervision, they should try to encourage students to seek help if they are being bullied. It is also suggested that teachers can observe student behaviour in order to detect any mental or physical health symptoms, or any systematic changes in their mood. They can also conduct informal interviews with students, where questions are open-ended and asked in a way to normalise the experiences and to create conditions in which students feel free to express their feelings openly.

Teachers should also be visible and vigilant in such common areas as hallways, stairwells, the canteen, the gym, and the crèche, and in other hot spots where bullying occurs consistently. Increased supervision is also needed in the toilets, where vandalism, disorder and mess usually occur. In toilets, specific directions must be given to students (e.g., throw away any rubbish properly, flush toilet, keep the place tidy, and keep water in the sink). Although this action seems not to be directly related to bullying, it has an impact on the development of positive and desired behaviour that can be characterized as respectful, reliable and responsible. As long as these characteristics (e.g., respect, responsibility) are found to associate negatively with bullies, you should try to develop them (see Lane, Kalberg, & Menzies, 2009).

Teachers should also be encouraged, during break time, to search for any *isolated students who may be victims of bullying*. For example, an isolated and sad-looking student sitting in front of the teachers' office, on their own, may be trying to communicate something. The message can be understood as long as the teacher who supervises not only sees her/him, but observes, thinks over what they have seen, and tries to interpret the situation. A possible explanation could be that some other students are bullying her/him, and in order to obtain some kind of protection, she/he chooses a very visible place that is considered to be safe and secure (bullies will not dare to bully a student in a place where teacher supervision is increased). The next step for the teacher should be to talk to the isolated child, and provide support.

After such contact and communication, low-profile students (who may experience bullying) may feel more confident in reporting incidents. On the other hand, conclusions should not be arbitrary, but should be drawn after discussion and receipt of sufficient and appropriate information. For example, the child in the previous case might be sitting there because she/he is tired and wants to rest from a game, or prefers to enjoy his or her meal in silence. The role of the supervisors could also be to support peer bystanders and encourage them to speak up in safe ways about bullying: to tell staff what they see and hear, and be friends with isolated peers. Teachers should also *thank and protect students who report aggressive behaviour* towards themselves or others. It is very important to keep in mind that *confidentiality* must be ensured, and a non-threatening way for students to report bullying of themselves or classmates must be established.

During break time, *playground activities such as playing in co-operative groups* can be preventative of bullying. In order to reduce student discipline problems, *table games* can be organized to keep students busy during the break time and also provide them with some fun. The plan for such tasks has to take into account participation from as many students as possible. Specific directions have to be given to students (include others in their game, be active, follow the rules, use equipment appropriately, return equipment when they are finished, line up when the bell rings, and respect other people's personal space). This contributes to building strength and resilience in children, and the ability to tolerate different perspectives on the same issue. In addition, a decision from the school board to offer *music during the break* can calm students' aggressive emotion as it can increase students' feelings of safety, happiness, and liking of school (see Swearer, Espelage, & Napolitano, 2009).

Efforts of the school to create a more *attractive natural environment (benches, tables)* can also be made. In such cases, financial support from parents or the school community or sponsors (where possible) may be provided in order to obtain the budget to make the school environment as attractive as possible. In fact, by creating a more beautiful natural environment, some isolated spots can be utilized, and therefore the school spaces will become safer and more secure for the students to play in, and spend their time happily, outside the classroom.

Rewarding good behaviour not only in the classroom, but outside (during break time, and also before lessons start and after they end) can be very beneficial. School can take decisions and set up a motivation system for the improvement of the social environment of the school, by taking actions to emphasise the maintenance of the behaviour code and the promotion of appropriate and positive behaviours outside the classroom. For example, students who interact and approach isolated students, show respect for peers and teachers, are responsible, and give their best efforts, can earn 'tickets'. For the students who manage to earn a significant number of 'tickets', the school may decide that praise should be verbal. In these cases, recognition can also be provided during assembly, in front of the classroom, or during the faculty meeting.

Using frequent descriptive praise for positive behaviour is important when an aggressive student starts to act responsibly and kindly, or even when aggression is less frequent or less intense over a period of time. Descriptive feedback ('I notice that you have been playing without fighting.') is more effective than trait-based praise ('You're so kind.') or I-messages ('I'm so happy you are acting better.'). Praise that names the result of the improved behaviour helps the student see the positive effects of their changed behaviour. Even more, a praise card can be sent home and the student can win extra computer or sport time. It is also up to the school to decide whether students can win desired items as well (e.g., a cd, sporting event invitation, sweets, school t-shirt, stickers, free pass for the theatre, or food coupon).

Student-made videos can be developed by the school's video team (consisting of higher-grade students and a teacher) to teach specific social skills, and can be used as a boost by showing positive attitudes and behaviour outside the classroom (e.g., on the bus, in the toilets, in the canteen, in the assembly, during a school visit). The staff and the students can submit ideas for the videos.

A peer-student to support, counsel, and empower a victim is also recommended. Social pressure brought by peer groups can have an important role in combating bullying. These students-counsellors can improve their skills with special training by *developing listening skills, communication skills, confidentiality, acceptance, and friendship skills.* During the break time, older students can mentor/tutor younger students. These students will be responsible for spotting isolated kids and keeping them company. In this way, a more inclusive environment in school will be created. It is stressed that peer counsellors will not handle situations alone in which there is a serious possibility of harm to the person seeking help. Peer counsellors should be supervised by teachers, and ask for immediate guidance by adults when the problem is serious.

Student behaviour before the lesson starts (early in the morning)

The school should find ways to be aware of students' behaviour *on buses, and on the way to and from school for students who walk or ride bikes.* A possible way could be by obtaining information with the co-operation of the additional staff (not educational). For example, the bus driver and the school traffic warden can provide information on bullying incidents. It can also be arranged for a teacher to be in the school's entrance every day, and welcome the students and their parents. In order to avoid discipline problems before the bell rings, the teachers can go to class as soon as they arrive at school. Another measure could be to make it clear to students that, as soon as they put their bag on their seats, they have to go outside the classroom. Supervision of the students should cover not only the playground and external areas, but also the classrooms area. In addition, a document should be sent home, stating to parents the exact time that all students should be at school in order to avoid discipline problems and misbehaviour after the bell rings. Moreover, it should be explained to parents that the school asks for punctuality in the students' arrival and departure, in order to eliminate the occurrence of misbehaviour and bullying incidents. A further reason that the school should request punctuality in the time of arrival is because when students present late to their classrooms, they miss precious learning time and therefore the quantity of teaching is affected negatively.

Special attention should be given to providing instructions to children about their arrival-entry to school. More specifically, the school can define specific expectations concerning students' arrival-entry to the school that are announced to all students:

a) walk and not run
b) enter the school quickly and quietly
c) minimize chatting
d) arrive at class on time
e) put your bag in the classroom and go to the playground
f) respect materials (e.g., posters in the hallways)
g) avoid interaction with persons that you do not know outside the school
h) do not bring valuable items into school.

Student behaviour after school hours/after lessons finish

It has to be made clear to the parents that they have to arrange to take their children from school as soon as lessons finish. For the children who are supervised in school after hours, a professional person (preferably a qualified teacher) registering the school's requirements should be appointed, and not an adult without basic qualifications in how to deal with children (e.g., a secretary or a parent with no suitable background). In some countries, it is expected and taken for granted that the school appoints a caretaker responsible for security after-hours. However, where that measure has not already been undertaken, and vandalism does occur in the afternoon, it is up to the school or the community to nominate a caretaker as soon as possible to supervise the school and its property.

Special attention should be given to providing instructions to children about their exit from the classroom and school. More specifically, the school can define specific expectations concerning exit from school that are announced to all students:

a) leave the school quickly and quietly
b) minimize chatting
c) remember to take all your belongings from class
d) when you are outside the school, waiting for your parents to take you, avoid interaction with persons that you do not know.

Behaviour code determined by the school (with co-operation of students, teachers and parents) concerning student behaviour outside the classroom

Rules should be brief and clear, stating immediate consequences for aggressive behaviour and immediate rewards for inclusive behaviour. The behaviour code should reinforce the values of *empathy, caring, respect, fairness, and personal responsibility*, and must *clearly define unacceptable behaviour, expected behaviour and values, and consequences for violations*. In addition, the code should *apply to adults and students*, reflect age-appropriate language, and should be prominently placed throughout the school.

CONTENT OF THE BEHAVIOUR CODE

For the development of the behaviour code, we consider it useful to give emphasis to specific aspects that need to be taken seriously and can reinforce positive, acceptable and respectful behaviour from students. Particular aspects that need to be addressed are as follows:

a) definition of bullying
b) statements-rules to be followed by all the students
c) significance of weekly meetings with the students
d) expectations from victims, and responsibilities of bystanders
e) queue in the canteen
f) students' arrival and exit from the school
g) school assembly.

Initially, *a clear and comprehensive definition of bullying* has to be determined with the co-operation of students, teachers and their parents. Ideas for *school rules* can be debated by all the parties in order to result in brief and clear rules to be included in the behaviour code. The following examples are rules, formulated as comprehensive and clear-cut statements, that could be included in the code:

1   We will not bully other students.
2   We will try to help students who are bullied.
3   We will include students who might be left out.
4   When we know someone is being bullied, we will tell an adult at school and an adult at home.

In order to ensure that positive behaviour will be sustainable, *weekly meetings* to communicate with students have to be arranged. Through these meetings, teachers can increase motivation of their students to follow the rules of the behaviour code.

In the behaviour code, *expectations from victims* (what victims of bullying should do) should be stated clearly:

a)   tell a teacher
b)   report to the head
c)   tell the parents
d)   not suffer in silence
e)   seek help
f)   act decisively with confidence
g)   draw, write or discuss your feelings
h)   associate with reliable peers.

Beyond expectations from victims, the *responsibilities of pupil bystanders/ expectations from bystanders* should also be stated in the behaviour code:

a)   report to an adult
b)   try to help students who are bullied
c)   include students who are easily left out – invite the victim to join you and your friends
d)   when you know that somebody is being bullied, tell an adult at school and an adult at home
e)   do not gossip about what happened.

Emphasis, when developing the behaviour code, should be given on the *queue in the canteen*. Specific, appropriate, positive behaviour for students to follow must be defined:

a) use a quiet voice
b) keep hands to themselves
c) good manners
d) make their choices quickly
e) stay in line and wait patiently
f) follow adults' requests
g) have money ready
h) clear away any rubbish.

Actions that can facilitate the process could be using different queues for younger and older students, a quick service by skilled persons, and different break times for younger and older students. For example, younger students could have their break 10 minutes before the older ones in order to be served in the canteen earlier, and avoid overcrowding.

Another aspect of determining the behaviour code is *students' arrival and exit from the school* (e.g., use self control, enter and leave the school walking and not running, report any problems to the teacher, keep hands and feet to self). Special attention must be given to the behaviour of students on the bus. Specific expectations concerning students' behaviour code on the bus must be announced to all students:

a) be ready when the bus arrives
b) speak politely to the bus driver and other students
c) follow the driver's rules
d) remain in your seat after you enter the bus
e) speak quietly
f) carry all personal belongings
g) share seating on the bus.

Last, but not least, desired behaviour during *school assembly* has to be defined. The students have to follow their line in assembly. Younger students should be told to take their place first. The time of the school assembly should be planned and arranged for the morning, when the students are not tired and fractious. Also, the school has to limit the time of assemblies and make their content as brief as possible. If the assembly will take more than 15 minutes, then arrangements for students to be seated must be made: otherwise, misbehaviour is likely to occur. Beyond each class's teacher, a general supervisor (not class teacher) for each assembly must be appointed. The following expectations for school assemblies should be announced to students:

a) follow directions
b) control your temper
c) self control
d) walk quietly in line after the end of the assembly.

Misbehaviour should have specific consequences:

a) apologize
b) discuss the incident with the teacher, principal and/or parents
c) spend time in the office or another classroom
d) forfeit break or other privileges.

However, punishment as a means to make bullies realise their limits has to be used with caution, as they may experience it as another form of frustration which they cannot tolerate. The administration of physical punishment is found to be strongly related to negative relationships and may increase bullies' aggressiveness (Olweus, 1993). In order for punishment of bullies to be effective, teachers have to take into consideration the following:

a) Bullies must be clear about the ground rules regarding bullying behaviour in their school, and the sanctions of possible digressions.
b) There must be an agreed and consistent way in the use of punishment by all teachers and by the bullies' parents, so that the bully gets a common message from all their caretakers regarding their behaviour (thus, they cannot initiate manipulation).
c) Punishment should be administered within a framework of a personal relationship between teachers and children so that it will have a personal meaning for the bullies. A serious talk with the bully before the punishment should aim to help them understand why they are being punished, that they are responsible for the consequences of their behaviour, and that they are able and expected to change their reactions.
d) In no case should bullies experience punishment as a kind of revenge or rejection on behalf of the adults, and believe that being punished means resolving their relationship. This perception would enhance their emotional anxiety and insecurity, reinforcing their anger and leading to a vicious cycle regarding the expression of bullying behaviour. Bullies should be clear that what we reject is their behaviour and not them, as individuals.

Appendix 6.1

The educational system of Slovenia: an overview

West and Crighton (1999) noticed that the majority of countries in Central and Eastern Europe, including Slovenia, had uniform national or regional educational systems with controlled input. All the inputs for all subjects in schools were centrally planned and carried out in every classroom in a consistent manner. Curricula, timetables, learning content and methods were prescribed. A single textbook was approved for any individual subject and outcomes were rarely externally assessed. Furthermore, no data on students' achievement were gathered and the outputs were seldom systematically evaluated.

Prior to the legislative reform of the educational system, a comprehensive conceptual study called the *White Paper* was published on the education in the Republic of Slovenia (Krek, 1995). Its theoretical foundation *inter alia* states that 'the system of education is based on autonomy' (Krek, 1995, p.15). This implies more open curricula, school autonomy, professional autonomy of teachers and an individual approach to teaching and learning. The *White Paper* (Krek, 1995) also indicated a link between school autonomy and the inspection of the quality of work in schools. The autonomy 'goes hand in hand' with responsibility for the quality of work in schools (Koren, 2007). The 'demands for reaching internationally comparable standards of knowledge of developed countries' (*ibid*, p.16) are also important. In its desire to reach internationally adequate standards of knowledge of developed countries (Krek, 1995), Slovenia participated in the main international comparative studies (i.e. Third International Mathematics and Science Study – TIMSS, Programme for International Student Assessment – PISA and Progress in International Reading Literacy Study – PIRLS). In the last fifteen years the Ministry of Education and Sport in Slovenia has launched numerous projects. The aim of these is to attain a high quality educational process, through building a system of quality assessment and assurance with emphasis on self-evaluation (Požar-Matijašič & Gajgar, 2007).

The Slovene *Organization and financing of education act* (ZOFVI, 2008, p. 3536–3542) states that head teachers have an obligation to 'assess quality through self-evaluation and preparation of the annual report on self-evaluation'. The content of the report, however, is not prescribed.

In 2006, another law formally obliged schools to provide quality assurance according to the TQM principles, in the area of vocational education and training; this also takes into account the European Quality Assurance Reference Framework in VET (Brejc *et al.*, 2008). In practice, however, many schools do not carry out self-evaluation or write reports. The National Inspectorate for Education and Sport's task is to oversee the implementation of legislation, other regulations and acts governing the organisation and targeted use of public finances. The Inspectorate has negligible responsibilities in the areas of student achievement, quality of teaching, learning and quality assurance. In 2008, the Ministry of Education and Sport started two projects '*Designing and implementation of a system of quality assessment and assurance in educational organisations*' and '*Training for implementation of a system of quality assessment and assurance in educational organisations*' (Koren & Brejc, 2011, p.316). The aim was to gradually introduce the system of quality assessment and assurance, to lead to comprehensive and focused self-evaluations and external evaluations in schools. Within this project, the Expert Group proposed to upgrade the system of quality assessment and assurance with the key role of SSE (Gaber et al., 2011).

In Slovenia, during the last dozen years, a new 9-year (previously 8-year) primary education has been introduced. Pupils now begin schooling at the age of six (a year earlier than before) and attend primary school for one year longer. In TIMSS 2003, Year 3 students were offered the old curriculum while Year 4 students were offered the new programme. Results in Mathematics revealed that the achievement of pupils with one extra year of schooling was equal or lower than the achievement of Year 3 pupils taught with the old programme (Perat, 2005). The Educational Research Institute (ERI) in Slovenia is involved in permanent networks of international educational research (TIMSS, PISA, PIRLS) and also in strategically important domestic studies. Secondary analyses of this data (Cankar, 2009; Japelj-Pavešić, 2005; Japelj-Pavešić & Cankar, 2010; Štraus, 2004) emphasise the meaning of achievement studies, the quality of reporting on their findings and the importance of the validity of inferences from comparisons. Furthermore, the interpretations of conclusions about the status of the education system, and the improvement based on the results of the data analyses, were also found to be important. Moreover, a group of experts within the National Examinations Centre (NEC) was formed. They held several years of experiences in national and international measurements of achievement and, due to their expertise in the research methods, they were critical of negative trends in knowledge. They recognised the inadequate educational policy and the introduction of novel changes which were not an improvement. Furthermore, they saw the viewpoints of other groups of experts who, in spite of disagreeable facts and negative trends, refused to reformulate their concepts in depth. In the endeavour to achieve quality in the Slovene education policy, one can recognise a multitude of different approaches (Gaber et al., 2011). For instance, there is a lack of a systematic and uniform approach, as well as a lack of theoretically based framework, with clearly defined and measurable objectives and pathways to improvement. The group of experts within the NEC often contrasted typical questionnaire based educational research in Slovenia through emphasising outcomes, usually cognitive in nature from national assessment and public examinations. Following this stance, this group has repeatedly contributed research papers providing data-driven insights into specific and problematic issues of the Slovene educational system. These include equity, fairness (Cankar, 2010a; Cankar 2010b; Hauptman, 2010; Semen, 2010) and the inflation of awarded grades (Zupanc & Bren, 2010). The group of experts advocate the relevant international findings in Slovenia, and emphasise the significance of nationally determined objectives and outcomes; these include more than just cognitive outcomes. In addition to this, the group aims to link the areas of effectiveness and improvement research; they attempt to find agreement in Slovenia among the experts and practitioners who advocate outcomes, and others who favour the processes. In this context, the National Examinations Centre in Slovenia developed a software solution called the Assessment of/for Learning Analytic Tool (ALAT). Teachers, head teachers and other professionals in Slovenia are able to access the examination database, analyse both assessment results and teachers' grades, interpret the achievement of their students and analyse the efficiency of teaching and learning in classrooms and schools (Zupanc, Urank, & Bren, 2009). Further development in the Slovene educational system now needs to be linked with contemporary world trends; it must be based upon the theoretical framework of EER, such as on the dynamic model of educational effectiveness (Creemers & Kyriakides, 2008a).

Appendix 7.1

Description of the content of the Teacher Professional Development Programme based on DASI

This appendix presents the content of the teacher professional development programme based on DASI. The teachers employing the Dynamic Integrated Approach were assigned to the four groups according to the developmental stage in which they were found to be situated, based on the results of their teaching skills evaluation. The members of the research advisory team provided the teachers of each group with supporting literature and research findings, which were solely related to the teaching skills which corresponded to their developmental stage. They also made it clear which area each group should concentrate their efforts on for improvement. Therefore this appendix refers to the area on which each group targeted their efforts for improvement.

First Group (Stage 1): Basic elements of direct teaching

The area of interest in this stage was the distribution of teaching time, so that students were able to construct and implement new knowledge effectively. The opportunity to learn is related to student engagement and time spent on task, and engagement has been used as a criterion variable in classroom management studies (Emmer & Evertson, 1981). Therefore effective teachers are expected to organise and manage the classroom as an efficient learning environment and thus maximise engagement rates (Creemers & Reezigt, 1996). It was explained to the teachers that learning takes place in restricted time limits, in which many important activities have to be implemented. Extra-curricular administrative activities such as announcements, dealing with discipline problems and commenting on irrelevant issues could further reduce the time available for learning. Finally, the teachers should allocate sufficient time to each important activity for learning. The areas of activities were related to:

a) *Lesson Structuring:* Issues discussed concerned the extent to which: each lesson is connected with previous ones; the structure of the lesson is explained to students when appropriate; the activities taking place in the lesson are linked with previous ones; the lesson is developed based on ideas proposed by the students, and the main points and important elements of each lesson are both identified and emphasised.

b) *Use of application activities/exercises:* Issues discussed were related to: the teacher provides the opportunity for students to practice the implementation of knowledge and skills in each lesson; feedback should be provided to students while they are working on application activities, and the teacher could raise questions to individual students while they work on application activities in order to identify and tackle misunderstandings.

c) *Questioning and providing feedback:* Issues discussed concerned the extent to which effective teachers ask many questions and involve students in class discussion, and also whether students are given sufficient time to think about their answers after a question is raised.

Second Group (Stage 2): Incorporating aspects of quality and touching on active teaching

The area of interest in this stage was the distribution of learning activities throughout the lesson or unit (Stage Dimension), focusing on when an activity takes place. The areas of activities were related to:

a) *Stage of the application tasks:* When should they be assigned and what should the content include? Issues discussed concerned: the application tasks should take place at different time points during each lesson and not necessarily at the end of the lesson; the application activities should be part of every lesson; application activities could involve knowledge and skills taught during the lesson which the student might also need to apply to new contexts, and application tasks could also involve learning targets and knowledge from previous lessons or units.

b) *Quality of the lesson structuring:* Issues discussed were related to: structuring should take place at different time points during a lesson; the lesson or activity should be linked with previous ones; the main points and important elements of each lesson should be identified and stressed, and regular revisions should take place (e.g. through questioning).

Third Group (Stage 3): Acquiring quality in direct teaching and reaching out

The area of interest here was the development of the classroom learning environment, with particular emphasis on the active involvement of students in the construction of new knowledge. The areas of activities were related to:

a) *Orientation of the students to the learning goals and objectives of the lesson activities:* Issues discussed were related to: involvement of students in identifying the objectives and learning goals of the lesson; the teacher should explain the purposes and objectives of the lesson or activity when appropriate; the teacher may also ask students to think and explain why certain activities take place during the lesson, and the need to 'sum up' at the end of each lesson with a review of the initial learning goals.

b)   *Development of the classroom as a learning environment:* Issues discussed were concerned with the extent to which: interactions between the teacher and students, as well as between students, take place regularly and at different time intervals; the purpose of the interactions is for learning; the teacher encourages the students to express different and opposing views and opinions; the teacher challenges the students to defend their arguments from opposing standpoints; students are encouraged to find different ways of solving problems, and students are encouraged to interact in order to discover knowledge (e.g. finding a solution to a given mathematic problem by drawing their own diagram).

Fourth Group (Stage 4): Differentiation of teaching and putting aspects of quality into new teaching

The area of interest for this group was the differentiation of teaching in relation to the application tasks, questioning, lesson structuring and orientation of the students to the lesson's learning objectives. The areas of activities were related to:

a)   *Differentiation of teaching:* The teachers should shape their teaching by taking into account all factors associated with students' attainment, personal characteristics and background variables, in order to maximise each student's learning potential. These factors include students' readiness, pre-existing knowledge, interests, learning profile, self-esteem and socio-economic level. Issues discussed were related with the extent to which: differentiation in the type and difficulty level of teacher questioning; certain questions might be directed to specific students and not to the whole class; the teacher should think of the type of questions they raise to certain groups of students (convergent/divergent thinking); the teacher should be aware of the feedback they provide to certain groups of students; differentiation in the application tasks: the teacher might not assign the same application tasks to all students in their classroom, and the teacher should organise anchor activities to manage students who often finish their application tasks first.

b)   *Orientation of the students to the learning goals and objectives of the lesson activities:* Issues discussed were related with the extent to which: groups of students could be asked to identify different lesson objectives and learning goals of different activities, and the teacher may also ask different students to consider and explain why certain activities take place in the lesson. Following this, each teacher developed his or her own action plan under the supervision and guidance of the research team.

Appendix 10.1

Instruments for measuring teacher factors and guidelines on using the instruments to observe teaching

Observation instruments for measuring the quality of teaching:

–   The first low-inference observation instrument (LIO1)
–   The second low-inference observation instrument (LIO2)
–   The high-inference observation instrument
–   The student questionnaire.

The two low-inference observation instruments (LIO1 and LIO2) generate data for all eight factors of the dynamic model and their five dimensions. Specifically, the first low-inference observation instrument enables us to generate data about teacher-student and student-student interaction (i.e., the classroom as a learning environment factor) and the time-management factor. The second low-inference observation instrument refers to five factors of the model:

a)   orientation
b)   structuring
c)   teaching modelling
d)   questioning
e)   application.

The LIO2 instrument was designed in a way that enables the collection of more information in relation to the quality dimension of these five factors. The high-inference observation instrument covers the five dimensions of all eight factors of the model. Observers are expected to complete a Likert scale to indicate how often each teacher-behaviour was observed.

The eight factors and their dimensions are also measured by administering a questionnaire to students. In this questionnaire, students are asked to indicate the extent to which their teacher behaves in a certain way in their classroom.

FIRST LOW-INFERENCE OBSERVATION INSTRUMENT (LIO1)

Observer: .... Teacher: ....

School: .... Date: .... Time: .... Class: ....   Number of students: ....

Lesson: .... Subject: ....

				Type of interaction/Student			
Teacher initiated behaviour	Minute	Comments					
1. Lectures or presents her/his opinion: Teacher presents the content of the lesson and gives information, either verbally or by using audio-visual means. She/he poses her/his opinion regarding the content of the lesson. She/he makes rhetorical questions.	1						
	Student						
2. Gives instructions: Teacher gives instructions or directions for procedures or teaching tasks that are related to the lesson and which students are asked to undertake.	2						
	Student						
3. Makes comments on students' answers or builds on students' ideas in order to cover the topic she/he intended to teach: She/he listens, restates and makes comments on students' answers without presenting her/his opinion. Teacher clarifies or builds on students' ideas.	3						
	Student						
4. Presents problematic situations or poses questions: She/he asks students to answer a question or to deal with a problem without presenting her/his opinion. She/he encourages students to make up a decision concerning open-ended problems or questions. She/he poses questions concerning the content or the procedures of the lesson in order to encourage students to answer.	4						
	Student						
5. Awards/encourages collaboration among his/her students: (a) She/he encourages fair competition and collaboration among students. (b) She/he discourages the negative aspects of competition (e.g. students hiding their work).	5						
	Student						
6. Deals with disorder: (a) She/he ignores disorder deliberately. (b) She/he resolves the disorder. (c) She/he does not solve the disorder.	6						
	Student						
7. Spends time to organise a teaching activity (e.g., dealing with classroom organisation/preparation, finding or distributing lesson materials.) (a) Teacher manages to interact with students while organizing classroom/materials. (b)Teacher does not manage to interact with any student while organizing classroom/materials.	7						
	Student						
8. When students are working, the teacher: (a) Does other activities without checking students' tasks/work/exercises. (b) Examines students' work but without providing any feedback. (c) Examines students' work and gives feedback. (d) Examines students' work differentiating the type of feedback.	8						
	Student						
9. Teacher interacts with student(s) for establishing to create better social relations.	9						
	Student						
Student-initiated behaviour	10						
10. Behaves improperly/causes disorder: (a) Verbal harassment (e.g., talking, singing, or making ironic comments) (b) Serious verbal harassment (e.g., verbally assaulting) (c) Bodily harassment, without placing others in danger. (d) Bodily harassment, placing her/his classmates in danger.	Student						
	11						
11. Gives answers: Student gives a response to teacher question.	Student						
12. Asks questions or ask teacher to help him/her with a task: Student asks questions: (a) Concerning the content of the lesson or issues related to the lesson. (b) On issues not concerning the lesson.	12						
	Student						
13. Takes initiatives: a) Spontaneous speech from student to the teacher and his/her classmates concerning the lesson. b) She/he gives suggestions to a group of students on how to deal with a task they are expected to undertake. c) Spontaneous speech from student aiming to social interaction.	13						
	Student						
14. Collaboration: Students collaborate (a) Without being prompted by the teacher. (b) After being prompted by the teacher.	14						
	Student						
15. Works on her/his own: Each student works on her/his own on a project assigned by the teacher. In case that some students are not on task write the numbers of students who are on task in the column entitled 'comments'. Do not write the code number of each student who works on her/his own.	15						
	Student						
	16						
	Student						
	17						
Behaviour that is initiated neither from the teacher nor from the student	Student						
16. Lesson interruption due to external factors (e.g., a visitor comes to the classroom to make an announcement for the next school trip).	18						
	Student						
17. Silence: Pauses, small periods of silence and periods of confusion in which the behaviour of students and/or the teacher cannot be clustered in any of the categories listed above. The reason(s) of silence should be recorded in the column entitled 'comments'.	19						
	Student						
	20						
	Student						
	NOTES:						

Teacher initiated behaviour

1. Lectures or presents her/his opinion: Teacher presents the content of the lesson and gives information, either verbally or by using audio-visual means. She/he poses her/his opinion regarding the content of the lesson. She/he makes rhetorical questions.

2. Gives instructions: Teacher gives instructions or directions for procedures or teaching tasks that are related to the lesson and which students are asked to undertake.

3. Makes comments on students' answers or builds on students' ideas in order to cover the topic she/he intended to teach: She/he listens, restates and makes comments on students' answers without presenting her/his opinion. Teacher clarifies or builds on students' ideas.

4. Presents problematic situations or poses questions: She/he asks students to answer a question or to deal with a problem without presenting her/his opinion. She/he encourages students to make up a decision concerning open-ended problems or questions. She/he poses questions concerning the content or the procedures of the lesson in order to encourage students to answer.

5. Awards/encourages collaboration among his/her students:
(a) She/he encourages fair competition and collaboration among students.
(b) She/he discourages the negative aspects of competition (e.g. students hiding their work).

6. Deals with disorder:
(a) She/he ignores disorder deliberately.
(b) She/he resolves the disorder.
(c) She/he does not solve the disorder.

7. Spends time to organise a teaching activity (e.g., dealing with classroom organisation/preparation, finding or distributing lesson materials.)
(a) Teacher manages to interact with students while organizing classroom/materials.
(b)Teacher does not manage to interact with any student while organizing classroom/materials.

8. When students are working, the teacher:
(a) Does other activities without checking students' tasks/work/exercises.
(b) Examines students' work but without providing any feedback.
(c) Examines students' work and gives feedback.
(d) Examines students' work differentiating the type of feedback.

9. Teacher interacts with student(s) for establishing to create better social relations.

Student-initiated behaviour

10. Behaves improperly/causes disorder:
(a) Verbal harassment (e.g., talking, singing, or making ironic comments)
(b) Serious verbal harassment (e.g., verbally assaulting)
(c) Bodily harassment, without placing others in danger.
(d) Bodily harassment, placing her/his classmates in danger.

11. Gives answers: Student gives a response to teacher question.

12. Asks questions or ask teacher to help him/her with a task: Student asks questions:
(a) Concerning the content of the lesson or issues related to the lesson.
(b) On issues not concerning the lesson.

13. Takes initiatives:
a) Spontaneous speech from student to the teacher and his/her classmates concerning the lesson.
b) She/he gives suggestions to a group of students on how to deal with a task they are expected to undertake.
c) Spontaneous speech from student aiming to social interaction.

14. Collaboration: Students collaborate
(a) Without being prompted by the teacher.
(b) After being prompted by the teacher.

15. Works on her/his own: Each student works on her/his own on a project assigned by the teacher. In case that some students are not on task write the numbers of students who are on task in the column entitled 'comments'. Do not write the code number of each student who works on her/his own.

Behaviour that is initiated neither from the teacher nor from the student

16. Lesson interruption due to external factors (e.g., a visitor comes to the classroom to make an announcement for the next school trip).

17. Silence: Pauses, small periods of silence and periods of confusion in which the behaviour of students and/or the teacher cannot be clustered in any of the categories listed above. The reason(s) of silence should be recorded in the column entitled 'comments'.

Minute	Comments	Type of interaction/Student			
21					
Student					
22					
Student					
23					
Student					
24					
Student					
25					
Student					
26					
Student					
27					
Student					
28					
Student					
29					
Student					
30					
Student					
31					
Student					
32					
Student					
33					
Student					
34					
Student					
35					
Student					
36					
Student					
37					
Student					
38					
Student					
39					
Student					
40					
Student					
NOTES:					

Guidelines for using the first low-inference observation instrument (LIOI)

THE FIRST LOW-INFERENCE OBSERVATION INSTRUMENT (LIO1) attempts to measure the type of teacher-student and student-student interactions that are observed during the teaching of a specific lesson. The instrument is exclusively concerned with 17 types of interactions that may be observed in a lesson. It also addresses time management and classroom learning environment factor scores, as well as their dimensions included in the dynamic model. Using the 17 codes for teacher and student behaviour that are given on the left of the instrument page, record in specific time intervals (e.g., every 10 seconds) the type of teacher-student interactions in the classroom. This procedure demands a very good knowledge of the observation-point codes, good observational skills and speed. You should, also, ensure in advance that you have learned the observation points well, and are able to connect each of the 17 codes with relevant examples of teacher and student behaviours.

Starting the observation:

Preparation

1. In the first page of the observation form you have to fill in some descriptive data for the lesson in the space shown below.

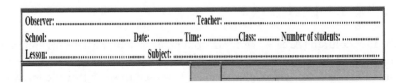

Observer: .... Teacher: ....

School: .... Date: .... Time: ....Class: .... Number of students: ....

Lesson: .... Subject: ....

2. Before starting the observation, draw a classroom diagram to show how the students are sitting, and give a code-number to each student which is going to be used for explaining who is involved, or initiating, specific activities. Since, in most classrooms, teachers keep records and have a list of their students, you could use this list to give a code number to each student. For example, if the student with the name Marc Andrew is number 4 on the students' name list, then you should write number 4 on the diagram to show the place where this student sits. Each student's seating-place should be clearly shown on the diagram, as well any other working groups are in the class. You may use the space below the diagram on the fourth page of the observation form to write any other comments you think are useful in explaining changes in seating arrangements that may occur. For example, some working groups may not be formed from the beginning of the lesson, so you could put down when these groups were formed. You can also put down any other information that you may have received from the teacher about the way the classroom is organised. For example, if ability-grouping was used by the teacher for some specific parts of the lesson, you could put down that students were split into groups according to their ability.

Recordings of observations:

As previously mentioned, observation notes are kept every 10 seconds. The space for writing down your observation codes is divided into 2 columns and 3 rows for each minute as shown below:

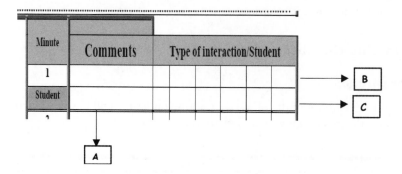

In the **first column (Area A)** write any comments or additional details important for understanding an observed behaviour. For example, the observer may use this column to explain that although the code '1' is used to show that the teacher is giving information to students, what actually happens is that the teacher is demonstrating how a computer software can be used for solving specific problems. In this column, the exact time the lesson started, as well as the time it finished, is also noted. Other comments concerning specific students (or groups of students) that the observer considers to be important could be written, e.g., 'students 1 and 6 are working on the computer'.

In the next six columns, observers should record the type of behaviour that is being observed every 10 seconds, as well as which students are either involved in, or initiate, this behaviour. Specifically, in the **first line (Area B)**, the type of interaction has to be recorded every 10 seconds. If, for example, the teacher is making some comments on the students' answers, then code '3' has to be noted down. In cases where more than two behaviours are being observed during the time interval of 10 seconds, i.e., the teacher is giving directions and at the same time a student makes ironic comments to another student in her/his class, then recode as following:

Minute	Comments	Typ
1		2/8a
Student		

In the **second line (Area C)**, the observer has to put down a code to show which student(s) is (are) involved in a specific activity (e.g., the code number of the student who is making ironic comments) or which students are addressed by the teacher (e.g., the teacher calls the name of a student to answer a question). You do not need to put down any student code in cases where the specific activity involves the <u>whole class or more than four students</u>. For example, when the teacher encourages the collaboration among all the students of her/his classroom and does not refer to a specific group, the activity should not be recoded for any specific student: this area should remain empty. Finally, in the example given in the previous paragraph, where the teacher gives direction, and at the same time a student (student 14 on the class diagram below) is making ironic comments to another student (student 20 on the class diagram), then the following recording has to be made:

Minute	Comments	Type of in
1		2/8a
Student		/14-20
2		

The above is an example of a complete recording during the first 10 seconds. For this reason, the codes are put down in the first two rows of the instrument, which refer to behaviours observed during the first minute of the lesson (see number 1 in the first column). For the second minute of the lesson, the next two rows should be used. Coding for each minute should continue in a similar way to the method described above. Further information about the meaning of each code is provided below, to help observers connect the tasks they will observe with the relevant codes of the observation instrument.

Information for the observation points

A) Teacher-initiated behaviour

Observation point I. Lectures or presents her/his opinion:

The teacher presents the content of the lesson and gives information, either verbally or by using audio-visual means. She/he poses her/his opinion regarding the content of the lesson. She/he asks rhetorical questions. This point is expected to make up a large proportion of the information that will be recorded.

Examples for observation point 1:

- Verbal teaching of the lesson's content.
- Use of audio-visual means (only the duration of use should be noted, not preparation time; this is included in another category).
- The teacher expresses her/his opinion on an issue that came up during the lesson.

Observation point 2. Gives instructions:

The teacher gives instructions or directions for procedures or teaching tasks that are <u>related to the lesson,</u> and which students are asked to undertake.

Attention should be drawn on this point in order to be able to distinguish it from point '7' (see below).

Examples for observation point 2:

- After assigning some group work to students, the teacher explains how to use the materials they have available.
- The teacher assigns students' homework and gives directions on how to complete it.

Observation point 3. Makes comments on students' answers or builds on students' ideas in order to cover the topic she/he intended to teach:

The teacher listens, restates and makes comments on students' answers without presenting her/his opinion. The teacher clarifies or builds on students' ideas. If the teacher stops making comments on a specific answer or opinion expressed by a single student or group of students, and presents her/his own opinion, then note down observation point '1'.

Observation point 4. Presents problematic situations or poses questions:

The teacher asks students to answer a question or to deal with a problem without presenting her/his opinion. She/he encourages students to make a decision concerning open-ended problems or questions. She/he poses questions concerning <u>the content or the procedures of the lesson</u> in order to encourage students to answer.

Observation point 5. Awards/encourages collaboration among his/her students:

a) The teacher encourages fair competition and collaboration among students. This can be recorded as verbal praise/encouragement of students/groups to co-operate, or/and when the teacher seems to have a class evaluation system for co-operation between students or groups (e.g. team scores on the board). With this point, even cases where the teacher gives praise to actions that do not necessarily refer to collaboration between students or groups, but show respect to other groups or students – as well as actions of polite rivalry – can be included (e.g. a student from one group is trying to help a 'rival' group).

b) The teacher discourages the negative aspects of competition. This can be recorded mainly when the teacher censures comments connected with disputes caused by competition between groups/students.

Observation point 6. Deals with disorder:

a) She/he ignores disorder deliberately. The teacher notices disorder but ignores it deliberately, either because she/he thinks it is not important or because it does not seem to distract students from the lesson.

b) She/he resolves the disorder. The teacher's reaction to disorder (i.e., remark, look, gesture) seems to resolve the problem and the observer can see that no misbehaviour is observed.

c) She/he does not resolve the disorder. Despite the teacher's reaction(s) (i.e., remark, look, gesture) the disorder is not resolved.

Observation point 7. Spends time to organise a teaching activity (e.g., dealing with classroom organisation/ preparation, finding or distributing lesson materials):

a) Teacher manages to interact with students while organising classroom/ materials

b) Teacher does not manage to interact with any student while organising classroom/materials.

Observation point 8. When students are working, the teacher:

a) Carries out other activities without checking students' tasks/work/exercises

b) Examines students' work but without providing any feedback

c) Examines students' work and gives feedback

d) Examines students' work, differentiating the type of feedback.

Observation point 9. Teacher interacts with student(s) to create better social relations:

The teacher interacts with a student in order to create better social relations with her/his students (e.g., establish a friendly classroom environment) but the interaction does not promote the achievement of a specific learning objective. For example, the mathematics teacher may ask his/her students about the results of a song competition that they were involved with.

B) Student-initiated behaviour

Observation point 10. The student behaves improperly/ causing disorder:

a)   Verbal harassment (e.g., talking, singing, or making ironic comments)
b)   Serious verbal harassment (e.g., verbally assaulting)
c)   Bodily harassment, without placing others in danger
d)   Bodily harassment, placing her/his classmates in danger.

Observation point 11. The student gives answers:

The student gives a response to teacher question. Observers are not expected to put down whether a correct or a wrong answer was given.

Observation point 12. The student takes the initiative to ask a question, or asks the teacher to help her/him with a task:

a)   The student asks questions concerning the content of the lesson or issues related to the lesson, or asks for help in order to complete a task (e.g., she/ he asks the teacher to give her/him suggestions in order to solve a problem).
b)   The student asks questions on issues that are not related to the observed lesson, but may have to do with the management of a school activity (e.g. the student asks the teacher what she/he is allowed to take on the school trip) or with a local event /outdoor activity (e.g., the student asks the science teacher to give her/his opinion about the results of a football match involving the local team).

Observation point 13. Takes initiatives:

a)   Spontaneous speech from student to the teacher and her/his classmates concerning the lesson

b) She/he gives suggestions to a group of students on how to deal with a task they are expected to undertake
c) Spontaneous speech from student aiming to social interaction.

Observation point 14. Collaboration:

Students collaborate:

a) Without being prompted by the teacher
b) After being prompted by the teacher.

Observation point 15. Works on her/his own:

Each student works on her/his own on a project assigned by the teacher. In cases where some students are not on-task, write the numbers of students who *are* on-task in the column entitled 'comments'. Do not write the code number of each student who works on her/his own, unless fewer than five students are working on their own. In cases where the majority of students are doing individual work, do not write the code number of each student, but write it down in the comments column.

C) Behaviour that is neither initiated by the teacher or the student

Observation point 16. Lesson interruption due to external factors:

For example, the head teacher/school secretary/chair of parents' association interrupts the lesson and makes an announcement about the next school trip or the school festival. The announcement has nothing to do with the lesson observed.

Observation point 17. Silence:

Pauses, small periods of silence and periods of confusion in which the behaviour of students and/or the teacher cannot be clustered in any of the categories listed above. The reason(s) for silence could be recorded in the column entitled 'comments'.

SECOND LOW-INFERENCE OBSERVATION INSTRUMENT (LIO2)

Observer: .... Teacher:...

School: .... Date:...................... Time: ....Class: .... Number of students:.........

Subject: .... Lesson: ....

(1) ORIENTATION

DIMENSIONS	Instructions for coding																							
Sequence of the activity	Ordinal number of the activity as observed during the lesson.																							
Duration	Duration in minutes.																							
Focus	*Relation with:* 1. an aim of the lesson 2. the day lesson 3. the unit/number of lessons.																							
Quality	1. typical 2. related to learning 3. students specify the aim(s).																							
Differentiation	Put down the sign √ for any type of differentiation you observe.																							

(2) STRUCTURING

DIMENSIONS	Instructions for coding																							
Sequence of the activity	Ordinal number of the activity as observed during the lesson.																							
Duration	Duration in minutes.																							
Focus	*Relation with:* 1. previous lessons 2. structure of the day lesson 3. the unit/number of lessons.																							
Quality: clarity	1. clear for the students 2. not clear for the students																							
Differentiation	Put down the sign √ for any type of differentiation you observe.																							

(3) APPLICATION

DIMENSIONS	Instructions for coding																							
Sequence of the activity	Ordinal number of the activity as observed during the lesson.																							
Duration	Duration in minutes.																							
Focus	*Relation with:* 1. only a part of the lesson 2. the whole lesson 3. the unit/a number of lessons.																							
Quality	1. use of the same activity to find a specific result, 2. activation of certain cognitive processes for the solution of more complex activities-algorithms.																							
Differentiation	Put down the sign √ for any type of differentiation you observe.																							

(4) NEW LEARNING-MODELLING

DIMENSIONS	Instructions for coding																							
Sequence of the activity	Ordinal number of the activity as observed during the lesson.																							
Duration	Duration in minutes.																							
Focus	1. can be used in the lesson only 2. can be used in the unit 3. can be used across units.																							
Quality: teacher's role	1. given by the teacher 2. guided discovery 3. discovery																							
Quality: appropriateness of the model	1. successful. 2. not successful.																							
Differentiation	Put down the sign √ for any type of differentiation you observe.																							

(5) QUESTIONING TECHNIQUES																							
DIMENSIONS	**Instructions for coding**																						
Sequence of the activity	Ordinal number of the activity as observed during the lesson.																						
Waiting time	Time given before answering																						
Focus	*Relation with*: 1. only a specific task 2. the whole lesson 3. the unit/a number of lessons.																						
Quality: type	1. product 2. process.																						
Quality: reaction if no answer from pupils (in case there is an answer put an X).	1. restate (easier words) 2. pose an easier question 3. move to another question or answers the question him/herself.																						
Quality: feedback-reaction to student	1. negative comment to incorrect and partly correct answers. 2. positive comment to correct answer only. 3. positive comment to correct answer and constructive comments to incorrect and to partly correct answers. 4. no comments.																						
Quality: feedback – reaction about the answer	1. teacher ignores the answer. 2. teacher indicates that the answer is correct or partly correct or incorrect. 3. students are invited to give comments on the answer.																						
Differentiation:	Put down the sign √ for any type of differentiation you observe.																						

Guidelines for using the second low-inference observation instrument (LIO2)

(A) General guidelines for using the instrument:

It is important that all parameters are carefully studied in order to make the necessary distinctions between the different categories and factors of the dynamic model, thus making the observer's task much easier. At first, the observer is asked to find out the kind of activity she/he is observing in the classroom, and afterwards to decide which one of the categories it belongs to. Further discussion of the categories follows. It is also important to note that the observer must wait each time for the activity to be completed, then record it. Before presenting the five categories, the following clarifications should be considered:

(a) How to use the differentiation box

Use the differentiation box to state whether there were any indications of any type of differentiation (use the sign √ in case that there is differentiation). For example:

–   In the case of the orientation activities, the teacher clarifies the aim(s) of the lesson to a specific group of students (e.g., the 'less able' students).
–   In the case of the application activities, the teacher gives to a specific group of students (e.g., the 'less able' students) more activities to complete, or more time for completing their activities.

(b) What is an 'activity'?

In the case of the questioning techniques, each question represents a single activity – therefore, you have to use a column for each activity. For the other categories, an activity can be a set of teacher actions/statements that have a certain goal. For instance, in the case of orientation, a teacher may undertake a series of activities (which may last for 2–3 minutes) in order to help students understand the importance of the aims of their lesson. However, this represents only one activity. It is noted that in the case of the teacher posing a question **which is not included in one of the first four categories,** then the observer fills in the table for the fifth category, which is the questioning techniques.

(c) How to use the duration

Specify the time (in minutes) that was used for each 'activity'. As mentioned before, in the case of the questioning techniques, you have to specify the waiting time (time elapsed after a question was posed and before requesting a student to answer the question).

(d) How to use the sequence of the activity

Consider the following example. First, the teacher asks students to practice the content of the lesson that was taught the day before. Then, she/he comments on the structure of the lesson of the current day, and then she/he presents a model for solving a specific type of problem. In this case, three activities are conducted. The first is an application task, the second is a structuring task, and the last corresponds to a new-learning activity. Therefore, using the first column of each category, we should write down the sequence of the activities observed. In this case, in the first column of the application, the number 1 is recorded in the 'sequence of the activity' row and the column under this box used to provide further information. The second activity would also be recorded in the first column of the structuring category and the number 2 written in the 'sequence of the activity' row. Again, any further information about the second activity should be noted in the other boxes in this column. Finally, the number 3 should be recorded in the first column of the new modelling behaviour category (row 'sequence of the activity') and further comments noted in the corresponding column.

(B) Clarification of the categories used in the instrument:

1. Orientation

1.1. Orientation refers to activities that are linked to the teacher's attempts to explain directly or indirectly why each activity or series of activities is organised, and how it serves to fulfil the aims of the lesson.

1.2. Orientation activities may appear in different forms that are described under the sub-category **'focus'**:

i.   They may be related to the task (i.e., teacher explains how the activity serves to meet the goals of a certain task. For example, she/he mentions: 'after measuring angles, we are going to learn how to classify them into three categories: acute angles, obtuse angles and right angles').

ii.   They may be linked to the day's lesson (i.e., teacher explains how an activity or a number of activities are related to the lesson. For example she/he says, 'Today we have to find out the paint we are going to need to paint the ceiling of our classroom. To achieve that, we have to find out the area of the ceiling, which has a rectangular shape. Therefore, we are going to discover the formula that gives the area of a rectangle').

iii. They may be linked to a unit or to a number of lessons (i.e., teacher explains how the activities of the lesson are related to previous or subsequent lessons. For example, she/he says, 'In previous lessons we discovered a formula that gives as the area of a rectangle. Today, we are going to find the areas of different shapes by using the formula that gives us the area of a triangle. In the two subsequent lessons, you will be requested to find the area of different shapes. Therefore, at the end of the week, I expect all of you to be able to find the area of any given shape').

1.3. Orientation activities may also take different forms in terms of their **quality**. For instance:

i.   They may be typical: the ultimate goal of organising such activities is not to help pupils understand how and why the lesson is delivered in such a way. The teacher may only carry out such activities because she/he has been prompted or urged to do so. For instance, the teacher writes on the board or tells pupils, 'Today we are going to find the area of rectangles', without explaining to them why it is important to achieve this aim.

ii.   They may be related to learning: the teacher tries to help pupils understand the reason for organising specific activities during the lesson. In the above-mentioned example, the teacher not only refers to finding the area of rectangles, but tries to specify what the area is and how the formula that gives the area of a rectangle can help in solving the problem.

iii.   Students may specify the aims of the lesson: moving a step forward, the teacher, in this case, directs pupils to find the aims of the lesson. For instance, she/he may ask them to refer to reasons related to the usefulness of finding the formula for the area of a rectangle.

2. Structuring

2.1. Structuring refers to the activities that are linked with the teacher's attempts to explain the structure of the lesson.

2.2. Structuring activities may appear in different forms that are described under the sub-category '**focus**':

i.   They may be related to previous lessons. In this case, the teacher refers to the content of previous lessons, to link them with the lesson of the current day. For instance she/he mentions: 'During the previous lessons we dealt with finding the perimeter of a rectangle. Today, we are going to find a formula that gives us the area of a rectangle'. Note that the teacher, contrary to what was mentioned in the orientation activities, did not refer to the reasons for finding the area of a rectangle.

ii. They may be related to the current day's lesson. In this case, the teacher refers to the lesson structure, without helping students realise how the activities of this lesson are related to the activities of other lessons. For instance, the teacher states: 'Today, you are first going to deal with measuring squares of $1 cm^2$ that are contained in different rectangles. Then I'll ask you to find out the formula that gives us the area of the rectangle. Once you have done that, you are then going to solve problems by using this formula'.

iii. They may be related to a unit or a series of lessons (i.e., the teacher specifies how the activities of the day's lesson are related to a series of lessons, or a lesson unit. For instance, the teacher says, 'Let me remind you of the activities of this lesson as well as the activities of the previous lessons; those that are going to be organised in the two subsequent lessons are related to finding the areas of different shapes').

2.3. In terms of **quality,** structuring activities may be clear to the students, or may not help them to understand the structure of the lesson. Indications that suggest structuring activities were clear to the students could be that the majority of students

i.   are able to specify the structure of the lesson
ii. are able to specify what preceded and what follows

iii.   do not seem puzzled or concerned about what they are going to do. On the contrary, students asking what they have to do, and ignoring what comes next, reveals that the structure of the lesson has not been made clear to them.

3. Application

3.1. Application activities refer to those activities intended to help students understand what has been taught during the day's lesson.

3.2. Application activities may be linked to:

i.   Certain parts of the lesson: e.g., the teacher asks students to measure how many squares of 1 cm^2 each of the three given rectangles consists of. *Note that this activity is not related to the whole lesson, but only to a part of it.*
ii.   The whole lesson: e.g., after students have discovered the formula that gives the area of rectangles, the teacher asks them to apply this formula to find the area of three rectangles.
iii.   The unit/a number of lessons: e.g., after students have discovered the formula that gives the area of rectangles, the teacher asks them to find the area of different shapes, which had been taught during previous lessons.

3.3. In terms of **quality**, application activities may be:

i.   Product-oriented: students are repeatedly carrying out the same application activity. For instance, after discovering the formula that gives the area of rectangles, they are given the dimensions (width and length) of 10 rectangles, and requested to find their area.
ii.   Process-oriented: students are requested to apply their new knowledge in order to find something more complex. For instance, students are required to find out how much money they will need to paint the ceiling of their classroom, if one bucket of paint covers 2m^2 and costs \$10.

4. New learning

4.1. New learning modelling refers to the activities that help students acquire learning strategies and procedures, or adopt a solution plan for solving problematic situations.

4.2. New learning modelling activities may appear in different forms that are described under the sub-category '**focus**':

i.   They may be used in the day's lesson: for example, the teacher helps students learn how to solve a specific problem, but insists on using the method only in the specific lesson.

ii. They may be used in the unit: for example, the teacher presents the way to use schema theory for solving change problems. This model is not only used for solving the problems of a specific lesson, but it is expected that the students will use it to solve change problems that appear in other lessons, too.

iii. They may be used across the units: for instance, the teacher presents a generic approach in dealing with problems that can be applied across the lessons (not only in the lessons of a specific unit). For example, after solving a problem, the teacher mentions: 'As soon as you arrive at an answer, try to verify it. Is it logical? Does it fit the data?' Students are expected to use this approach in solving any problem that is assigned to them in various lessons.

4.3.1. In terms of the **teacher's role**, new learning activities may take different forms:

i. They may be given by the teacher: For instance, the teacher explains how she/he would behave when given a problem (note point III mentioned above).

ii. Students are guided to discover a strategy (e.g., using the guided discovery method of teaching): in the example mentioned above, the teacher poses guiding questions to help students propose a strategy. For instance, she/he asks, 'What do we have to do, after being given a problem?' Students express their opinion and the teacher tries to help them find the best approach. To continue this example, the discussion proceeds as follows: 'Well, as you mentioned first, we have to read the problem carefully and try to understand it. How are we going to be sure that we have really understood the problem?'

iii. Students may be directed to discover a strategy to solve a problem: for example, students are requested to suggest a strategy for solving problems. Students suggest different methods, and the teacher encourages them to identify the advantages and disadvantages of each proposed strategy. The teacher does not expect students to use a specific strategy.

4.3.2. In terms of the **appropriateness of the modelled-behaviour strategy**, it can either be successful or unsuccessful.

i. *Successful* – if students are able to apply it, and if it leads to the desired goal, then the model is considered successful (e.g., in the example mentioned above, a number of students successfully apply the verification procedure and decide that their answer is not reasonable).

ii. *Unsuccessful* – the model should be categorised as not appropriate in two cases. First, students find difficulties in applying this model and solving the problem; and second, students use the approach but fail to reach the desired behaviour (e.g., solve a problem).

4.3.3. The **quality** of the modelling is determined in the terms of the **stage of the lesson** during which the model behaviour is be observed:

i.   *The model behaviour is observed after facing a problematic situation.* Students face a problem and then a model for confronting this situation is presented either by the teacher or the student.

ii. *The model behaviour is observed before a problematic situation.* The teacher mentions that students will be required to solve a certain problematic situation during the lesson. In order to be able to achieve it successfully, a particular approach will be presented.

5. Questioning techniques

> **IMPORTANT:** Please note that you cannot use this category if the teacher asks a question **but** this activity belongs to any of the four categories mentioned above.

5.1. Waiting time: refers to the time that elapses after a question is posed by the teacher, and before the teacher asks a student to answer this question. Write 0 seconds, in cases where the teacher waits for less than 15 seconds.

5.2. In terms of the **focus**, questions may be:

i.   Related only to a specific task: for instance, during a lesson that is concerned with the use of length-measurement units, students are required to mention the units they have been taught.

ii. Related to the whole lesson: in the above case, students are required to mention the units they have been taught and how each measurement unit is used (e.g., the metre is used for long distances, such as measuring the length of a table; kilometres are used for measuring much longer distances, such as measuring the distance between two towns, etc).

iii. Related to a number of lessons or a unit: in the above case, the teacher not only asks students to specify the units that are used for measuring the length of a segment, but also to refer to units that can be used for measuring capacity or time.

5.3. In terms of **quality**, there are:

i.   Product questions: these questions require students to recall facts, concepts or procedures mentioned by the teacher to the students (e.g., 'What do we call the "inside" of a shape?' (area) or 'What is the perimeter of a shape?'

ii. Process questions: these questions require students to specify a procedure for solving a problematic situation. For example, students may be asked what they can do in order to find out which of two glasses has more capacity than the other.

> **Important:** Please note that asking students to specify a procedure for solving a task or a problematic situation should be classified as a product and not as a process question. If the teacher had already presented this procedure before (e.g., the teacher says, I want somebody to remind me how are we going to solve a routine problem by using schema theory?)

5.4. How the teacher reacts to pupils' answers, after posing a question:

i.   In cases where there is an answer put an X in the box.
ii. If a student fails to give an answer, the teacher may react in the following ways:
   a) She/he may restate the question by using simpler words. In this case, teacher only substitutes difficult words with easier ones. For example, the initial question may be: 'Specify a solution plan for solving problems', and the second question may be: 'Specify a set of steps that can be taken in order to solve a problem'.
   b) She/he may pose an easier question. For example, the initial question may be: 'Find the least common multiplier of 18 and 46', and the second question may be: 'Well, I see that you face difficulties in finding the least common multiplier of these two numbers. Therefore, find the least common multiplier of 8 and 12'.
   c) She/he may move to another question or answer the question by herself or himself.

5.5. How the teacher reacts to students' answers:
We can discern the following categories:

i.   The teacher makes no comments: she/he listens to the answer, but she/he avoids commenting on it. She/he may even continue the lesson by raising another question.
ii. She/he makes negative comments to incorrect or partially-correct answers (e.g., 'Wrong', 'I don't agree with you', 'Can somebody else provide a better answer?' etc).
iii. She/he comments only on correct answers and avoids commenting on wrong ones (e.g., teacher ignores incorrect or partially-correct answers, and comments on the correct part of the answer).
iv. She/he makes positive comments about the correct answer, but at the same time comments constructively on incorrect or partially-correct answer(s) (e.g., George's attempt could have been more informative by explicitly stating the steps for solving routine problems. Nevertheless, George's answer reminded us that there is not just one solution plan that can be applied to solve all the problems we encounter in mathematics).

5.6. Feedback:

When the teacher gives feedback about an answer that a student has given, his/
her reaction may belong to one of the three following categories:

i.   She/he ignores the answer, irrespective of whether the answer is correct or
     not.

ii. She/he indicates that the answer is correct or partially-correct, or incorrect. In
     this case, the teacher explains to the students whether the answer is correct or
     not, without inviting other students to make any comment about the answer
     given.

iii. She/he invites students to comment on the answer, or expects them to find out
     whether the answer was correct or not (e.g. 'George suggested that when solving
     a problem, we first have to find the question. What is your opinion on that
     answer?').

High-inference observation instrument

Observer's Name: ....

Teacher's Name: ....

School: .... Date:..................... Time: ....

Class: .... Number of Students:......... Subject: ....

Lesson:...

DIRECTIONS: Use the scale to note the extent to which you agree with the following statements.
(*Scale:* 1:*Minimum point* ..... 4: *Maximum point*).

	STATEMENT	MINIMUM POINT				MAXIMUM POINT
1.	The orientation activities that were organized during the lesson helped students understand the new content.	1	2	3	4	5
2.	The teacher explained how each activity served in fulfilling the aims of the lesson.	1	2	3	4	5
3.	The teacher explained the structure of the lesson in a way that was clear for the pupils.	1	2	3	4	5
4.	The teacher explained how the lesson of the day was linked to previous or to subsequent lessons of a unit.	1	2	3	4	5
5.	The teacher asked pupils to discover the purpose of doing specific activities.	1	2	3	4	5
6.	The teacher explained how the different activities were linked to each other.	1	2	3	4	5
7.	The teacher posed questions to link the lesson of the day with previous or subsequent lessons.	1	2	3	4	5
8.	The teacher posed revision questions to examine what pupils had understood from the lesson of the day.	1	2	3	4	5
9.	The lesson transited from easier to more complex activities.	1	2	3	4	5

10.	The observed application activities referred (were linked) to whole lesson.	1	2	3	4	5
11.	The observed application activities referred (were linked) to certain parts of the lesson.	1	2	3	4	5
12.	The observed application activities referred (were linked) to previous lessons as well.	1	2	3	4	5
13.	The application activities were nothing else but a replication of the activities that were organized during the presentation of the new content.	1	2	3	4	5
14.	The teacher asked pupils to deal with application exercises that were more demanding than those used for teaching the new concept.	1	2	3	4	5
15.	The teacher organised application activities that resulted in something that could be exploited for new learning.	1	2	3	4	5
16.	The teacher used to differentiate the application exercises that she/he gave to the pupils, according to their abilities	1	2	3	4	5
17.	The teacher spent the teaching time on learning activities.	1	2	3	4	5
18.	The teacher challenged pupils to express their opinions on certain issues.	1	2	3	4	5
19.	During the lesson, the teacher gave only to some pupils the opportunity to participate in the lesson.	1	2	3	4	5
20.	The teacher encouraged pupils to co-operate with each other.	1	2	3	4	5
21.	During the lesson, pupils co-operated on their own initiative.	1	2	3	4	5
22.	Each pupil was engaged in individual work assigned to him/her by the teacher.	1	2	3	4	5
23.	The teacher encouraged competition between pupils.	1	2	3	4	5
24.	The teacher was interacting with pupils for the whole of the lesson.	1	2	3	4	5
25.	During the lesson, some pupils were co-operating with each other while others did not.	1	2	3	4	5
26.	Pupils interacted with each other during the whole of the lesson.	1	2	3	4	5
27.	Interaction between pupils contributed in achieving the lessons goals.	1	2	3	4	5
28.	The teacher discouraged the negative aspects of competition.	1	2	3	4	5
29.	There was pupil misbehaviour in the form of verbal harassment during the lesson.	1	2	3	4	5

30.	There was pupil misbehaviour in the form of serious verbal harassment during the lesson.	1	2	3	4	5
31.	There was pupil misbehaviour in the form of bodily harassment without putting others in danger during the lesson.	1	2	3	4	5
32.	There was pupil misbehaviour in the form of bodily harassment putting others in danger during the lesson.	1	2	3	4	5
33.	The lesson was interrupted by the misbehaviour of some pupils.	1	2	3	4	5
34.	The teacher was forced to make remarks to some students because they were talking to each other.	1	2	3	4	5
35.	In the case of misbehaviour in the classroom, the teacher ignored it deliberately.	1	2	3	4	5
36.	In the case of misbehaviour in the classroom, the teacher reacted and temporarily solved the problem.	1	2	3	4	5
37.	In the case of misbehaviour in the classroom, the teacher reacted and managed to solve the problem.	1	2	3	4	5
38.	In the case of misbehaviour in the classroom, the teacher reacted but did not manage to solve the problem.	1	2	3	4	5
39.	The lesson was interrupted by external factors.	1	2	3	4	5
40.	The aims that the teacher had set before the lesson were met during the 40-minute period of the lesson.	1	2	3	4	5
41.	The activities that were organised during the lesson helped each pupil to advance conceptually, according to her/his abilities.	1	2	3	4	5
42.	The majority of pupils were engaged in activities that were provided by their teacher.	1	2	3	4	5
43.	During the lesson the majority of the pupils were on task.	1	2	3	4	5
44.	Less able pupils considered the lesson activities as very difficult.	1	2	3	4	5
45.	More able pupils considered the lesson activities as very easy.	1	2	3	4	5
46.	The teacher used to pose questions that were clear for the pupils in terms of their content.	1	2	3	4	5
47.	The teacher used to correct pupils' misconceptions using their wrong answers.	1	2	3	4	5
48.	When teacher posed a question that was not clear for the pupils, she/he used to rephrased (restate) it.	1	2	3	4	5

49.	When teacher posed a question that was not clear for the pupils, she/he used to pose a simpler question to help pupils find the answer.	1	2	3	4	5
50.	Pupils were puzzled by the procedures or strategies that the teacher presented to them for overcoming problematic situations.	1	2	3	4	5
51.	When pupils faced certain learning obstacles or were confronted with a problematic situation, the teacher used to provide them with useful procedures or strategies for overcoming them.	1	2	3	4	5
52.	The procedures or strategies that teacher presented to the pupils to help them overcome the problematic situations they faced can be used in other lessons as well.	1	2	3	4	5
53.	The teacher used to explain the procedures and strategies to the pupils and then she/he requested using them.	1	2	3	4	5
54.	Pupils understood the procedures and strategies that were presented by the teacher.	1	2	3	4	5
55.	Pupils used on their own initiative, ways or strategies presented by the teacher, to solve similar problems.	1	2	3	4	5

If you have any further comments, please use the space provided below:

....
....
....
....
....
....
....
....
....

Thank you for your assistance

Student questionnaire

Dear Student,

We would like to know your opinion about the teaching of **Mathematics** in your classroom.

The answers you give will not be shown to your teachers, anyone else in your school or your parents.

Please answer **all** of the questions. To answer the questions, please circle a number on each line.

Please ask the interviewer if you do not understand what to do.

Part A

After each statement, there are five numbers. Think carefully and put a circle around the number that most fits your opinion:

1   this **never** happens in your class
2   this **rarely** happens in your class
3   this **sometimes** happens in your class
4   this **often** happens in your class
5   this **almost always** happens in your class

		Never	Rarely	Sometimes	Often	Almost Always
Q1.	In Mathematics, we start the lesson with things that are easy to understand. As the lesson goes on, what we cover is more difficult.	1	2	3	4	5
Q2.	The teacher gives us exercises at the beginning of the lesson to check what we have learnt from the previous lesson.	1	2	3	4	5
Q3.	At the beginning of the lesson, the teacher starts with what we covered in the previous lessons.	1	2	3	4	5
Q4.	My teacher helps us to understand how different activities (such as exercises, subject matter) during a lesson are related to each other.	1	2	3	4	5
Q5.	A few days before the test, my teacher gives us similar exercises to those that will be in the test.	1	2	3	4	5
Q6.	My teacher tells my parents how good I am compared to my classmates when they visit her/him (or in my school report).	1	2	3	4	5
Q7.	When the teacher is teaching, I always know what part of the lesson (beginning, middle, end) we are in.	1	2	3	4	5
Q8.	When doing an activity in Mathematics I know why I am doing it.	1	2	3	4	5
Q9.	When we go over our homework, our teacher finds what we had problems with and helps us to overcome these difficulties.	1	2	3	4	5
Q10.	Our teacher has good ways of explaining how the new things we are learning are related to things we already know.	1	2	3	4	5
Q11.	At the end of each lesson, the teacher gives us exercises on what we have just been taught.	1	2	3	4	5

Q12.	During the lesson our teacher often covers the same things that we have already been taught or done exercises in.	1	2	3	4	5
Q13.	The teacher immediately comes to help me when I have problems doing an activity.	1	2	3	4	5
Q14.	The teacher gives more exercises to some pupils than the rest of the class.	1	2	3	4	5
Q15.	The teacher gives some pupils different exercises to do than the rest of the class.	1	2	3	4	5
Q16.	The teacher gives all pupils the chance to take part in the lesson.	1	2	3	4	5
Q17.	Our teacher encourages us to work together with our classmates during Mathematics lessons.	1	2	3	4	5
Q18.	Some pupils in my classroom work together when our teacher asks us, but some pupils do not.	1	2	3	4	5
Q19.	Our teacher makes us feel that we can ask her/him for help or advice if we need it.	1	2	3	4	5
Q20.	Our teacher encourages us to ask questions if there is something that we do not understand during the lesson.	1	2	3	4	5
Q21.	During the lesson, our teacher encourages and tells us that we are doing good work (i.e. she/he says to us 'well done').	1	2	3	4	5
Q22.	When we are working in teams, our teacher encourages competition between teams. (If you do not work in teams, please circle the number 1).	1	2	3	4	5
Q23.	In Mathematics lessons, some of my classmates hide their work and answers so that none of the other pupils can see it.	1	2	3	4	5
Q24.	When a pupil gives a wrong answer the teacher helps her/him to understand her/his mistake and find the correct answer.	1	2	3	4	5
Q25.	When the teacher asks us a question about the lesson she/he asks us for the answer but does not ask us to explain how we worked out the answer.	1	2	3	4	5
Q26.	When one of the pupils in the class is having difficulties with the lesson, our teacher goes to help her/him straight away.	1	2	3	4	5

Q27.	There are some pupils in the classroom that tease some of their classmates during Mathematics lessons.	1	2	3	4	5
Q28.	I know that if I break a class rule I will be punished.	1	2	3	4	5
Q29.	The teacher has to stop teaching the class because one of the pupils is being naughty	1	2	3	4	5
Q30.	When a pupil gives a wrong answer in Mathematics class some of the other children in the class make fun of her/him.	1	2	3	4	5
Q31.	Our teacher keeps on teaching us even though it is break-time or the lesson is supposed to be over.	1	2	3	4	5
Q32.	When I finish a task before my classmates my teacher immediately gives me something else to do.	1	2	3	4	5
Q33.	When the teacher talks to a pupil after they have been naughty, sometimes after a while, that pupil will be naughty again.	1	2	3	4	5
Q34.	We spend time at the end of the lesson to go over what we have just been taught.	1	2	3	4	5
Q35.	There are times we do not have the necessary materials for the lesson to take place (e.g., dienes, unifix, test tubes, thermometers, calculators, rulers)	1	2	3	4	5
Q36.	There are times when I do not have anything to do during a lesson.	1	2	3	4	5
Q37.	During a Mathematics lesson, our teacher asks us to give our own opinion on a certain issue.	1	2	3	4	5
Q38.	Our teacher asks us questions at the beginning of the lesson to help us remember what we did in the previous lesson.	1	2	3	4	5
Q39.	Our teacher uses words that are hard to understand when she/he asks us a question.	1	2	3	4	5
Q40.	When we do not understand a question, our teacher says it in a different way so we can understand it.	1	2	3	4	5
Q41.	When a pupil gives a wrong answer our teacher gets another pupil to answer the question.	1	2	3	4	5
Q42.	When I give a wrong answer to a question the teacher helps me to understand my mistake and find the correct answer.	1	2	3	4	5

Q43.	Our teacher praises all pupils the same when we answer a question correctly.	1	2	3	4	5
Q44.	When we have problem solving exercises and tasks in Mathematics lessons, our teacher helps us by showing us easy ways or tricks to solve the exercises or tasks.	1	2	3	4	5
Q45.	Our teacher lets us use our own easy ways or tricks to solve the exercises or tasks we have in Mathematics.	1	2	3	4	5
Q46.	In Mathematics lessons, our teacher teaches us ways or tricks that can be used in different lessons.	1	2	3	4	5
Q47.	Our teacher encourages us to find ways or tricks to solve the exercises or work she/he gives us.	1	2	3	4	5
Q48.	I am there when my teacher talks to my parents for my progress.	1	2	3	4	5
Q49.	When we are having a test, I finish up within the time given to us.	1	2	3	4	5

Part B

In this part there are some statements. For each statement, circle the answer that shows what usually happens in your class during Mathematics lessons.

We have tests

A.   Every week

B.   Every two weeks

C.   Every month

D.   Every term

E.   Never

The teacher gives corrected tests back to us

A.   Within a week

B.   Within two weeks

C.   Within three weeks

D.   In a month or even longer

E.   She/he never returns them.

The teacher explains to us what she/he expects us to learn from the Mathematics lessons. This happens:

A.   In every lesson

B.   In most of the lessons

C.   Only sometimes

D.   Very rarely

E.   Never.

When no student raises her/his hand to answer a question, the teacher usually (please choose one answer)

A,   Answers the question and moves to something else

B.   Repeats the question using the same words

C.   Restates the question using simpler words

D.   Asks an easier question

E.   Gives us hints or clues to help us answer the question.

In addition, write below any comments you wish to make about the questionnaire and about the teaching of Mathematics in your classroom.

....
....
....
....
....
....
....
....
....
....
....
....
....
....
....
....
....
....

Thank you for your co-operation

Appendix 10.2

Teacher questionnaire for measuring school factors

This instrument (see below) is only concerned with the five dimensions of the school policy about teaching and about the school learning environment and does not measure the actions that different stakeholders may actually take (irrespective of whether there is school policy about a specific factor).

Teacher questionnaire

Dear Teacher,

This questionnaire aims to investigate teachers' opinions on their school's policy. The questionnaire items mainly examine the policy developed by your school with respect to the following aspects of teaching:

A. Making good use of teaching time

As far as the use of teaching time is concerned, issues related to management of time, student absenteeism, teacher absenteeism, homework assignment, school timetable scheduling and teaching time spent on extra-curriculum activities (e.g., practice time for school events) are examined.

B. Provision of learning opportunities:

The school policy is examined in relation to the achievement of specific goals set by the school, use of visual material and technological equipment in teaching, when dealing with students that have educational needs (e.g., gifted children, children with learning difficulties) as well as the long-term planning of teaching by the teachers.

C. Quality of teaching:

The school policy is examined in relation to the following factors concerned with the teacher behaviour in the classroom: Student evaluation, structuring, orientation of students in achieving specific goals, application exercises, posing and using questions in teaching, use of learning strategies, time management, and classroom as a learning environment.

Your views about the policy on the broader learning environment of your school are also examined. Four aspects of the **School Learning Environment (SLE)** are taken into account:

- Policy on student behavior outside the classroom
- Teacher collaboration
- Relations with parents and the wider school community
- Use of educational resources

Thank you very much for your help

PART A: ABOUT YOU

Put an ✓ in the appropriate box or fill where necessary:

Q1.   Are you male or female?

Male ❑   Female ❑

Q2.   What is your teaching position in this school?

Teacher ❑   Deputy Head Teacher/Principal ❑

Q3.   How many years have you been teaching at primary school level? (Please count this school year and exclude career breaks)

a) in this school...................._____years

b) in other primary schools......_____years

c) Total.............................._____years

PART B: THE FORMATION OF SCHOOL POLICY AND THE LEARNING ENVIRONMENT OF THE SCHOOL

Part B refers to statements concerned with practices that may occur in your school. Please circle a number from 1–4 on each line to show the extent to which you agree with the statements describing what happens in your school. After reading carefully each statement circle the number:

1: If you **strongly disagree** with the statement
2: If you **disagree** with the statement
3: If you **agree** with the statement
4: If you **strongly agree** with the statement

		Strongly Disagree	Disagree	Agree	Strongly Agree
Q4.	At staff meetings in our school we discuss and take decisions on issues concerned with:				
	a. Making good use of teaching time	1	2	3	4
	b. Provision of extra learning opportunities in addition to those offered by the formal curriculum (e.g., extra-curricular activities, festivals, fairs, school trips, clubs)	1	2	3	4
	c. Methods to effectively teach students (e.g., structuring lessons, questioning, application, student assessment etc.)	1	2	3	4
	d. Teacher's role during break time	1	2	3	4
	e. Developing trust between teachers and children	1	2	3	4
Q5.	My school keeps systematic records concerned with:				
	a. Student absenteeism	1	2	3	4
	b. Teacher absenteeism	1	2	3	4
	c. Special educational needs of students	1	2	3	4
	d. Long-term planning by teachers	1	2	3	4
	e. Organization of trips, visits and other extra-curricular activities not included in the formal curriculum	1	2	3	4
	f. Problems that arise among students during break time	1	2	3	4

	g. The use of educational tools for teaching supplied by the school (e.g., maps, software etc.)	1	2	3	4
Q6.	My school participates in programmes (e.g., Comenius, action research projects, collaboration with other schools, pilot initiatives) that aim at:				
	a. Making good use of teaching time	1	2	3	4
	b. Providing learning opportunities beyond the ones offered by the formal curriculum	1	2	3	4
	c. Improving the quality of teaching	1	2	3	4
Q7.	When designing the school-timetable we take into account that enough time should be provided for students and/or teachers to move between classrooms	1	2	3	4
Q8.	I feel that I am positively influenced by the staff meetings in relation to the following:				
	a. Management of teaching time	1	2	3	4
	b. Dealing with student absenteeism	1	2	3	4
	c. Homework	1	2	3	4
	d. Making good use of teaching time that is spent on activities not included in the formal curriculum (e.g. rehearsals)	1	2	3	4
	e. Use of visual aids and technological equipment in teaching (e.g. overhead projector, computer)	1	2	3	4
	f. Dealing with students that have special educational needs (e.g., gifted children, children with learning disabilities, children with special interests)	1	2	3	4
	g. Long-term planning of teaching	1	2	3	4
	h. Interaction with students during break time	1	2	3	4
	i. Student evaluation	1	2	3	4
	j. Structuring of lessons	1	2	3	4

	k. Student orientation (i.e., helping students to understand why a unit is taught)	1	2	3	4
	l. Using exercises to help students apply their learning (i.e., giving them tasks which apply the concepts taught to a situation in everyday life)	1	2	3	4
	m. Asking questions and making good use of them	1	2	3	4
	n. Strategies for learning	1	2	3	4
	o. The learning environment of the classroom (e.g., promoting interaction among students)	1	2	3	4
Q9.	My school takes into consideration the professional needs of each teacher and does not expect each teacher to implement the school policy for teaching in the same way	1	2	3	4
Q10.	We take into account research findings (e.g., recently published articles in scientific journals, results of research studies) in developing the school policy on teaching	1	2	3	4
Q11.	We take into account research findings when we form a school policy concerned with:				
	a. parental involvement	1	2	3	4
	b. teacher collaboration	1	2	3	4
	c. use of resources for teaching provided by the school	1	2	3	4
Q12.	Incentives are provided and/or support is given to teachers to implement the school policy on teaching (e.g., reward teachers who spend extra time with students who were absent from school in order to explain to them the concepts taught during their absenteeism)	1	2	3	4
Q13.	My school encourages teachers to co-operate with the parents of children who struggle academically	1	2	3	4
Q14.	The teachers in my school co-operate with each other by exchanging ideas and material when teaching specific units or series of lessons.	1	2	3	4
Q15.	Discussions at staff meetings help me to improve my practice in:				

	a. Making good use of teaching time	1	2	3	4
	b. Providing learning opportunities to students beyond the ones offered by the formal curriculum	1	2	3	4
	c. My teaching behaviour in the classroom	1	2	3	4
	d. My role during break time	1	2	3	4
	e. Using different educational tools for teaching provided by the school	1	2	3	4
	f. Involving parents in the learning process	1	2	3	4
Q16.	In my school, teachers observe each other teaching as a way to discuss and share opinions on effective teaching	1	2	3	4
Q17.	The teachers in my school participate in educational school-based seminars (e.g., workshops) which deal with **specific** issues that the school faces	1	2	3	4
Q18.	My school has formed a **specific** policy for student behaviour during break time	1	2	3	4
Q19.	In my school we share the opinion that break time is an opportunity for teachers to approach and interact with children that face problems which may affect their learning	1	2	3	4
Q20.	In my school, we have taken the decision to organise fun activities during break time that may help students to achieve specific learning goals (e.g., games, dance, sports)	1	2	3	4
Q21.	In parent-teacher meetings organised by the school, the way in which parents can help in dealing with the following issues are discussed:	1	2	3	4
	a. Student absenteeism	1	2	3	4
	b. Homework	1	2	3	4
	c. Addressing children's educational needs (e.g., gifted children, children with learning difficulties, children with special interests)	1	2	3	4

	d. Parents providing learning opportunities in the school through activities organised on their own initiative (e.g., educational visits, educational games)	1	2	3	4
Q22.	There is material on noticeboards in the school relevant to:				
	a. Good use of teaching time	1	2	3	4
	b. Provision of learning opportunities beyond the ones provided by the formal curriculum	1	2	3	4
	c. Characteristics of effective teaching	1	2	3	4
	d. The use of different educational tools for teaching provided by the school	1	2	3	4
Q23.	At staff meetings, we usually make decisions on the ways in which parents can be involved in the learning process	1	2	3	4
Q24.	During break time, the teachers spend more time with students who face learning difficulties than with other students	1	2	3	4
Q25.	Parents are often invited to our school to observe teaching so that they are aware of the policy the classroom teacher adopts	1	2	3	4
Q26.	My school has a **clear** policy for parental involvement in the learning process	1	2	3	4
Q27.	In my school, there is an opportunity for different groups/ people outside the school to become involved with and co-operate in the **learning process** of (for example, a basketball player of a local team together with teachers teaches different basketball techniques)	1	2	3	4
Q28.	Discussions at staff meetings lead to an improvement in the way in which the school offers teachers opportunities for professional development and training	1	2	3	4
Q29.	My school invites specialists in to conduct in-service training for teachers (e.g., an expert that works on developing students' creativity or other types of in-service)	1	2	3	4

		Strongly Disagree	Disagree	Agree	Strongly Agree
Q30.	The management team (principal and deputy heads) organises in-service seminars for a specific group of teachers when they think it is needed (e.g., newly appointed teachers)	1	2	3	4

PART C: EVALUATION OF SCHOOL POLICY

This section is concerned with the evaluation of school policy. To answer questions in Part C, please circle a number from 1–4 on each line to show the extent to which you agree with each statement describing what happens in your school. After reading carefully each statement circle the number:

1: If you **strongly disagree** with the statement
2: If you **disagree** with the statement
3: If you **agree** with the statement
4: If you **strongly agree** with the statement

		Strongly Disagree	Disagree	Agree	Strongly Agree
Q31.	The principal and/or other members of the school staff observe the way the teaching policy is put into practice and presents the results of their observations to staff	1	2	3	4
Q32.	To evaluate the implementation of the school policy on teaching, we collect information from:				
	a. Teachers	1	2	3	4
	b. Students	1	2	3	4
	c. Parents	1	2	3	4
Q33.	Teachers' **capacity** to implement the school policy on teaching (e.g. quantity of education, quality of education, provision of learning opportunities for students)is evaluated within the school	1	2	3	4
Q34.	Information collected during evaluation of the school policy on teaching is used for re-designing the policy or for taking new decisions	1	2	3	4

Q35.	The results of the evaluation of the school policy on teaching are used by the school **principal** for the summative evaluation of teachers (e.g. career development purposes)	1	2	3	4
Q36.	We evaluate the extent to which student discipline problems during break time **are reduced** as a result of the school policy	1	2	3	4
Q37.	Aspects of my school's policy on teaching which are considered problematic are evaluated **further** and/or **in more detail**	1	2	3	4
Q38.	The principal and/or school staff observe the implementation of the learning environment policy and present the results of their observations to staff	1	2	3	4
Q39.	Aspects of my school's policy concerned with the broader learning environment which are considered problematic are evaluated **further** and/or **in more detail**	1	2	3	4
Q40.	Our school identifies the professional development/further education needs of its teachers	1	2	3	4
Q41.	The evaluation of the school policy on the broader learning environment (e.g. students' behaviour outside the classroom, the co-operation and interaction between teachers) is carried out in a way that refers to **a single aspect** of the policy each time (i.e., evaluation focuses on student behaviour, relations with parents etc. separately)	1	2	3	4
Q42.	Information collected during the evaluation of the policy on the broader learning environment is used for re-designing the policy or for taking new decisions	1	2	3	4
Q43.	Evaluation results are useful to pinpoint areas in teaching for which we need support and/or further training	1	2	3	4

In the space provided below, please put down anything you consider important for the development and the evaluation of a school policy concerned with teaching and the learning environment of your school.

_____
_____
_____
_____
_____
_____
_____
_____
_____
_____
_____
_____
_____
_____
_____
_____

Thank you very much for your co-operation

Index